DEFENDING

RUMBA

IN HAVANA

DEFENDING RUMBA IN HAVANA

THE SACRED AND THE BLACK CORPOREAL UNDERCOMMONS

MAYA J. BERRY

Duke University Press   *Durham and London*   2025

Project Editor: Liz Smith
Designed by Matthew Tauch
Typeset in Alegreya and Retail by Westchester Publishing Services

Library of Congress Cataloging-in-Publication Data
Names: Berry, Maya J., [date] author.
Title: Defending rumba in Havana : the sacred and the black corporeal
undercommons / Maya J. Berry.
Description: Durham : Duke University Press, 2025. | Includes
bibliographical references and index.
Identifiers: LCCN 2024023860 (print)
LCCN 2024023861 (ebook)
ISBN 9781478031338 (paperback)
ISBN 9781478028147 (hardcover)
ISBN 9781478060352 (ebook)
Subjects: LCSH: Rumba (Dance)—Cuba—History. | Dance—Cuba—History. |
Folk dancing, Cuban—Political aspects. | Dance—Anthropological
aspects—Cuba. | Dance—Social aspects—Cuba. | Dance and race— Cuba.
| Black people—Race identity—Cuba. | Feminist anthropology.
Classification: LCC GV1796.R8 B47 2025 (print) | LCC GV1796.R8 (ebook) |
DDC 793.3/197291—dc23/eng/20240903
LC record available at https://lccn.loc.gov/2024023860
LC ebook record available at https://lccn.loc.gov/2024023861

Cover art: Rumba Morena performing at El Callejón de Hamel,
Havana, Cuba. Kike Calvo / Alamy Stock Photo.

Publication of this book is supported by Duke University Press's
Scholars of Color First Book Fund.

Para mi Ía,
Celia Llerena Ayala

CONTENTS

PREFACE

Jennyselt "Jenny" Galata was never one to answer my questions directly. In the ten years I knew her, she refused the format of a sit-down interview. To her, I was, first and foremost, her dance student. To remain her student over the roughly ten years she trained me in what I call the dances of the *Black corporeal undercommons*, otherwise known as *Cuban folkloric dance*, I had to abide by her rules. She required that I take meticulous notes after each class to retain her detailed corrections. She also insisted that I seek out informal opportunities to learn outside of our time together, to put my body in different situations where people were dancing, and to take notes on what I observed there just as carefully. These were the skills that she told me she herself developed to know what she knew now. My future graduate training in anthropology would lead me to associate these activities with that discipline's signature ethnographic method: participant observation. Yet contrary to the conceit of anthropology to gather "emic" or insider knowledge, originally established by European conquest, she was critical of the entitlement of outsiders who expected to be handed explanations for what they did not understand. Embodied inquiry required a different sense of accountability, and vulnerability. My dance training under Jenny involved learning what not to ask and other ways of knowing.

Jenny dictated that I would grow to understand the intricacies of the bodily techniques she imparted through the process of literal and figurative self-reflection. I once asked permission to videotape her demonstrating a step so I could study it in between our sessions. Recording dance demonstrations by teachers was a common practice for tourists who traveled to Cuba. But she refused. She alone dictated who would be doing the looking, and how, during our time together. Instead, she offered to record *me* doing the steps she had just taught. For her, my ability to see for myself how I was falling short was a more accurate measure of the extent to which I was paying attention and could reasonably claim that I learned anything at all. In effect, she forced me to turn what Zora Neale Hurston called the "spy-glass of Anthropology" on myself ([1935] 2008, 1).

In the dozens of video recordings from this archive, I see myself from her vantage. The sight of my image is mostly an unflattering one to me. But then comes the sense of gratification from a mentor witnessing the fruit of one's dedication. I hope that at least, for Jenny, the recordings evince a student making mistakes but trying her best, over and over again, to adjust and do better. In these numerous video clips, the soundscape of the music and the noisy street is sprinkled with the tiny clicks of her freshly manicured nail extensions hitting the metal of the camera, and her shouts directing me, often harshly, toward an ideal. Also registered are my grunts of frustration at my inability to perform to her standard. Her validation largely went unmarked, heard only in the moments of silence rather than explicit praise. It is both embarrassing and humbling to watch. D. Soyini Madison reminds us, "That tension [between feeling foolish and feeling inspired] must always remain unresolved because it is that very tension that keeps us circumspect about our intrusions and concerned that our voyeurism is not gratuitous" (2010, 37). Although it wasn't what I had in mind to attain, I have a record of myself growing in empathy for what it feels like to be observed, with or without a camera lens mediating the encounter. More than any graduate seminar, those dance classes imprinted on me a critical awareness about the process of constructing knowledge about others through looking.

One day Jenny abruptly stopped the music in exasperation after I missed the drum's cue to change steps once again. Sweat pooled at my lower back as I returned to a resting straight posture and waited for her correction. "Do you know why it's important to me that you learn this? Because we are both Black women. And as Black women, we have to give ourselves value! Because no one else gives us value." Her scolding, prompted by a technical error in my physical musicality, affirmed a racialized and gendered consciousness undergirding how she knew her body in relation to others, including myself. Although she did not exactly ascribe to the label of "Black feminist," Jenny underscored the specificity of her experience as a Black woman. This distinctly intersectional analysis infused and informed the way she understood her dancing, the conditions under which she danced, and why and how she taught others to do the same. It also signaled the political stakes that converge in Black popular dance at the critical intersection of racialized class and gender oppression in Cuba. This Black feminist consciousness emerged historically in relation to enslaved women's everyday negotiations with violence, and it persists vis-à-vis the forms of racial and gender marginalization that their descendants have continued to experience after emancipation, and after socialist revolution.

Jenny's pedagogical approach and critical lens demanded a kind of intellectual rigor as her student that I later located within a genealogy of Black feminist inquiry; it advocates self-reflexivity grounded in relationality with others and understanding how one's body is located within intersecting axes of power. Inherent to this praxis was a sense of worth, "value," as she put it, that Black women needed to give ourselves. Thus, she challenged me to engender what the larger society deprived Black women of, what socialism alone did not distribute, what no state would, or anyone else could, offer.

Approaching fieldwork as a fundamentally intersubjective practice of embodied entanglement thus shifts the project away from one of extraction, or secret-gleaning via assumed access, to one of participatory engagement in which I too was implicated and had a stake. *Defending Rumba in Havana: The Sacred and the Black Corporeal Undercommons* dutifully follows these movements already rehearsed by Black feminist ethnographers (both those who self-identify as such and those, like Jenny, who may not) while motioning toward future critical feminist embodied inquiry. That is to say, it contributes to and centers Black feminist genealogies of knowledge production.

While Jenny was not my first formal teacher of Cuban folkloric dance—after returning from an initial dance study abroad program in Cuba 2004, then offered by NYU's Tisch School of the Arts, I apprenticed under Neri Torres and her Ife-Ile Afro-Cuban dance company in Miami in 2005, and then continued my education under Xiomara Rodriguez at the Museo del Barrio in Harlem, NYC, until 2010—my decision to apply to anthropology graduate programs two years into my training under Jenny may have been facilitated, ironically, by her teaching philosophy. Around the same time, while finishing a master's degree in performance studies at NYU, I came across the work of Yvonne Daniel, a Black US American dance anthropologist who conducted fieldwork in Cuba from 1985 to 1990, a time when very few US Americans were permitted to conduct research there, just before the infamous Special Period changed the socioeconomic landscape, and so much more. Daniel was trained in anthropology at the University of California, Berkeley. Like others of her generation, she sought to orient anthropological research in service of liberation struggles waged in the so-called Third World (Anderson 2019).

In her landmark dance ethnography, *Rumba: Dance and Social Change in Contemporary Cuba* (1995), Daniel decidedly positions her research endeavors in solidarity with the Cuban revolutionary project, identifying dance as a performative act directly imbricated with the monumental changes to the social fabric of the island. Similar to an important segment of scholarship about Cuba in the wake of the 1959 Revolution, Daniel investigated Black and poor people's "upliftment" or integration into the rebel nation's political project. Specifically, her study chronicled what was entailed in the shift from rumba being a spontaneous, community-based event that included a vast repertoire of dances performed in neighborhoods where poor Black people lived, to a genre of staged, discrete, public performances sponsored by state institutions. In that process, rumba became a symbol of revolutionary Cuban identity. Her research stood out at the time for its attentiveness to changing race, gender, *and* class dynamics. There has not been a book-length anthropological study of rumba dance since. However, her analytical attention to the arts, and the performance and performativity of racial and gender identity as a medium for the mediation of revolutionary contradictions, opened the door for the ethnographies of Cuba that came after in the early 2000s (e.g., S. Fernandes 2006; Allen 2011; Roland 2011).

Jenny did not seem surprised when, in the summer of 2011, I returned to Havana and told her that I had entered a graduate program where observant participation was a core research method, and my body, being there, was my primary entryway to understanding. The African Diaspora Program in the Anthropology Department at University of Texas at Austin, also born from the "decolonizing generation," where I eventually received doctoral training, shared the kind of political commitments to leftist revolutionary movements that Daniel expressed through her work. "The Austin School" stipulated the articulation of scholarship and activism, seeking social transformation through both (Gordon 2007). This articulation was compelled by both one's positionality and one's political identification. In my case, the interaction of the two, as I came to understand them through dialogue with others, indelibly shaped and shifted the way I thought about the politics of my research over time.

During graduate fieldwork on the streets of Havana, I was often mistaken for Cuban-born. For many, my Blackness and the fact of my Cuban ancestry, as a third-generation Cuban American, satisfied this misrecognition. Yet, I do not boast unmediated access to "the truth" as something pure and readily available, existing inside the subject or outside of historically situated and politically laden social relations of power. The constraints of difference between me and the community of practice I learned from were also openings for positioned paths of further examination; or as Marc Perry (also a student of the Austin School who researched in Cuba) has said, they were "standpoint[s] from which to initiate conversations . . . not to elide power" (2016, 22). Although Jenny and I both identified as women with overlapping racial and ethnic affiliations, those identities were not social equalizers by any means. And even if I could, she wouldn't let me forget it.

Moreover, my interpretation of the sacred poetics of rumba rests on my level of initiation into the Lucumí practice at the time, warranting that certain explanations remained closed to me and, by extension, the reader. This study necessarily thinks through the social fact of the researcher's own positionality, investments, and sense of responsibility to the living and the more-than-human. Out of respect for those ties and boundaries of belonging, I take care to discern when certain explanations I was given should or should not be shared in writing. I hope that what is not published, or what questions are left unanswered, honors a politics of opacity, respect, and care that my godparents and the people represented in these pages hold dear. While this may be at odds with the logics of academic interrogation, it also has much to teach us about the dynamics of representation and political maneuver that this ethnography brings attention to. It is a delicate dance.

I found my footing thanks to Yvonne Daniel, who traveled before me. While firmly sympathetic to the revolutionary project, Daniel's dance ethnography deftly shows how rumba performance after 1959 performed the contradictions between socialist ideology and social equality in the flesh. Rather than evidencing the full realization of racial and gender equality in the Revolution, she argued that rumba might just as well be regarded as a microcosm of the revolutionary principles yet to be fully embodied in practice. Daniel identifies the important role of rumba in the Cuban revolutionary project and subtly gestures toward the constrictive bounds of rumba's legibility within those contours. She urges that *rumberos* must be released from any possessor's grasp lest the very meanings that fuel their artistic creativity be stifled: "Cuban artists, particularly *rumberos*, need and deserve such a loose hold" (1995, 142).[1] While acknowledging the merits of state patronage for rumba since 1959, her plea alludes to the need to go beyond a statist, paternalistic, self-congratulatory narrative of "lifting up" these humble artists to national stature in symbolically overdetermined ways. Her writing about the earlier revolutionary period is so skillful in its nuance and graceful in its delivery, just like her dancing (something she demonstrated when performing as an honorary member of the Conjunto Folklórico Nacional de Cuba). It had to be in order to navigate such contentious geopolitical waters.

Echoing Daniel, I call for a loosened attachment to rumberos' symbolic use-value for the state and go a step further to ascertain the myriad ways practitioners meaningfully deploy rumba in their everyday lives beyond its grasp. To honor Daniel's foundational intellectual labor, without which my work would not have been possible, each chapter begins with an epigraph from her work that I consider a harbinger for an avenue of inquiry I took up in a very different historical period (post–Special Period and post-Fidel) and in my own way.

As is the case with other Black feminist ethnographers who incorporated arts-based methodologies, Hurston and Dunham being fundamental examples, Daniel has been largely marginalized if not ignored in the intellectual genealogy of anthropology. Accordingly, she has been written out of its "decolonizing generation" (Harrison 1991; Allen and Jobson 2016), perhaps because, unlike others of her generation, she did not take as frontal a stance against the discipline; instead, she endeavored to reclaim it.[2] Perhaps she still felt the need to prove her "aesthetic project"—as she refers to it in her book's preface—as worthy of study, multiply marginalized, and illegible in its own way. I hope that my work can facilitate conversations with Daniel and other Black feminist artist-scholars among a wider cast of politically engaged anthropologists of the African Diaspora that have not been had before.

Despite all the decolonial turning in the discipline, mainstream anthropology seems to have maintained a loyalty to the mind-body Cartesian split in the academy that prevents it from taking Black dance seriously as a source of critical theory. While on the one hand, the disregard for dance is an acknowledgment of the limits of cultural representation as a field of political maneuver, on the other, it functions as its own form of respectability politics, if not a deep-seated misogynoir. And yet, or rightfully so, it is Black women who have been at the forefront of innovations at the intersection of the arts, anthropology, and critical theory. As Gina Ulysse exclaims in her performance "Untapped Fierceness / My Giant Leaps," "Why do they think so many Black women in anthropology keep turning to the arts!?" Performance frames of analysis and, specifically, Black performance theory do the nimble labor of attending to the generative forces that constitute Black performance (cultural staging), performativity (stylized norms that mark identity), and the performative (which "does something," makes a material difference) (Madison 2014). Daniel has written about Caribbean and Atlantic Diaspora dance more broadly: "In the moments of dance, feelings of belonging are generated and solidarity is affirmed, even if temporarily; in the moments of dance, feelings of fierce self-worth, strength, and rebellion are also activated" (2011, 193). Maybe this is what Katherine Dunham gave up trying to talk to anthropology about when the discipline largely abandoned her intellectual legacy to be taken up by what would become the vibrant field of Black dance studies.

Defending Rumba in Havana contends that more concerted attention to how and why Black people move their bodies the way they do can uniquely contribute new dimensions to our understanding of Black political thought, praxis, and fugitive planning. Insofar as "movement might narrate texts that are not always legible" (Cox 2015, 28), through rumba, I attend to narratives otherwise invisible to the study of Black political thought in Cuba. Then again, Jenny's irreverence toward the academy, and her critique of the consuming gaze's entitlement to understand her at all, should remind me to temper any desire for a particular kind of disciplinary recognition. Nevertheless, this book offers a space for anthropology, Cuban studies, feminist studies, Black studies, and performance studies to join in conversation.

This book is indebted to the teachings and example of Jenny, the Austin School, Yvonne Daniel (and the scholarship of the foremothers that made hers possible), and the energies and spirits, both seen and unseen, that rule my head. I am honored to be guided by their creative maneuvers within structures of power and webs of relations in which I, too, am entangled and move. These movements are shaped by systemic conditions, political commitments, affective investments, and ancestral responsibilities. Iterative self-reflection on my role in co-producing the understandings I offer holds the study accountable for the situated place from which I observe, relate to others, understand explanations, and draw conclusions. I have endeavored to make this explicit in my work whenever possible, with the caveat that some things may never be put into writing for the sake of those same conditions, commitments, investments, and responsibilities. The reader may find that I have fallen short, but I have tried my best.

The people who take center stage in this ethnography remind us that Black popular dance is inextricable from the imperative praxis of the formerly enslaved to survive modern national development at all costs. In doing so, *Defending Rumba in Havana* demonstrates what a concerted analysis of people in collective motion can offer for sensing and sustaining fugitivity.

ACKNOWLEDGMENTS

An ethnography is only as credible as one's relationships are strong with people who share what they know to be true of their experience. I am forever indebted to the community of rumberas and rumberos who ushered me through their Havana. I pay homage to those practitioners who cleared a path for me to find my way, whose generosity of time and spirit shaped my thinking, whose connections expanded my outlook, and who are now ancestors: Geovani del Pino, Valentín Márquez Quiñones, Vladimir Silvio Quevedo Armenteras, Yerilú Lugo Valespino, *Ibae baye tonu* . . . Among the living are Jennyselt, Chan, Zulema, Lekiam, Didier, Ronald, El Gordo, Guillermo, Regla, Yamilé, Derlis, Morcilla, Silvia, Tailyn, Tito, and Lázaro. Tremendous thanks are also owed to Ned Sublette and Cary Diez for their long-standing work of rumba promotion from which this book has benefited indirectly and directly.

Intensive dance training became the pretext for me to travel to the Caribbean island that my maternal grandmother's family had migrated from. A study abroad trip to Cuba in 2004, the fruit of a collaboration between Catherine Coray at New York University's Tisch School of the Arts and Fernando Sáez at the Fundación Ludwig in Havana, opened a portal to this book's beginning. At that time, I was completing an undergraduate interdisciplinary liberal arts degree at NYU so I'd have "something to fall back on" if my professional dance career in NYC was cut short due to injury or financial unsustainability. During the classes with Danza Contemporanea in Havana and Conjunto Folklórico del Oriente in Santiago de Cuba, I fell into a new understanding of what dance could be. The endorsement and guidance of Fernando Sáez (who would later cofound Malpaso Dance Company) would make it possible for me to return to Cuba and continue training long after the completion of the program. Subsequent study under Alfredo O'Farrill (*ibae*), and Johannes Garcia's Compañia JJ with Siria Maria Robles-Rojas, and, eventually, another summer intensive with the Conjunto Folklórico

Nacional de Cuba solidified my commitment to learning the encyclopedic dance repertoire I continue to marvel at. These pages teem with gratitude for everyone involved in those early trips who opened the possibilities for my relationships to specific dancing communities in Cuba that would deepen thereafter.

At NYU, the Gallatin School allowed me to craft an individualized program of undergraduate study that instilled the rigor of and supported the unique challenge of interdisciplinarity. In that, Asale Angel-Ajani was an inspiration. I thank José Munoz (*ibae*) for making critical theory feel accessible and for making the master's program in Performance Studies at NYU feel welcoming. There I was deeply impacted by the teachings of Andre T. Lepecki, Randy Martin (*ibae*), Karen Shimakawa, and Barbara Browning. Jill Lane and Diana Taylor at the Hemispheric Institute of Performance and Politics opened my eyes to a more expansive understanding of the power and polemics of artistic expression in the region's past and present.

I found political community in the "Austin School" that once occupied the Anthropology Department at University of Texas at Austin. As a doctoral student on the Diaspora Track, I found camaraderie and peer mentorship in Courtney Desiree Morris, Traci-Ann Wint, Luciane Rocha, Melissa Burch, Maria Andrea dos Santos Soares, Sade Anderson, Monique Ribeiro, Nedra Lee, Mohan Ambikaipaker, Lynn Selby, Ayana Omilade Flewellen, and, in the last leg, the brilliant and blazing sojourners of the Department of African and African Diaspora Studies (AADS), Gustavo Melo Cerqueria, Agatha Oliveira, Pablo José López Oro, Natassja Gunasena, Caitlin O'Neill, and Dora Silva. No amount of words can do justice to the innumerous office hours, detailed comments on countless drafts, steadfast advocacy, and earnest care that my doctoral advisor, Edmund T. Gordon, put into making the Austin School what it was for me. Charles R. Hale was another mentor who supported me and helped me process the contradictions I encountered in "the field" and in the academy without relinquishing the potential of both as sites of mutually reinforcing collective struggle. Christen Smith, Robin D. Moore, Omi Osun Joni Jones, and Frank Guridy made profound impressions on my scholarship and how I imagined I could one day inhabit the academic profession. Heartfelt thanks go to Deborah Paredez, who unofficially adopted me into UT's Performance as Public Practice program (PPP) and believed that a book about dance could hold everything I wanted to say. Abundant gratitude goes to Julie Skurski for sharing essential connections in Havana and for continuing to be my most meticulous and challenging reader.

Creative collaborations with Czarina Aggabao Thelen, Maria Andrea, and later the Performing Research Lab hosted by AADS held me accountable to a creative practice alongside my scholarship. Ninoska Escobar, Nicole Martin, and Cassidy Browning made PPP an institutional home away from home. The Black brilliance of Chelsi West Ohueri and drea brown got the dissertation written. I found my voice as a feminist thanks to the "Gang of Five": Shanya Cordis, Sarah Ihmoud, Elizabeth Velásquez Estrada, and Claudia Chávez Argüelles. Our collective work serendipitously brought me to Dána-Ain Davis, who has exemplified the kind of mentorship I didn't know I needed. In the broader Austin community, I grew as a teacher of the dance forms I write about thanks to the faith, trust, and support given by Odaymar and Oli (Krudxs Cubensi), Rebekah Fowler, Tonya Lyles, Tonya Pennie and the Austin Dance Africa Fest, Carla Nickerson at the African American Cultural and Heritage Facility, the folks at the Orun Center for the Performing Arts, and too many others to name.

My research would not have been possible without the institutional support of the Instituto Juan Marinello under the auspices of the Cuban Ministry of Culture. At the Marinello, my professional debt to Henry Heredia, as head of international relations, cannot be understated. Rodrigo Espina (ibae), an avid research supervisor, was a blessing. Elena Socarrás de la Fuente and Marcia Peñalver Armenteros also played important roles from their institutional locations.

This book is equally a product of both informal and formal graduate-level education in the historical legacy and lived experience of anti-racist struggle within the Cuban revolutionary project. A network of Cuban activists, working through artistic, academic, social, and religious institutions, and grassroots neighborhood organizing (often hand in hand) have been edifying for my understanding of the social debates circulating during the period the book chronicles. During this time, my accompaniment of the formation of the Articulación Regional Afrodescendiente de América Latina y el Caribe, Capítulo Cuba (ARAAC Cuba), was illuminating. ARAAC Cuba's executive board included Tomás Fernández Robaina (ibae), Roberto Zurbano, Gisela Arandia, Norma Guillard, and Lidia Turner, and was coordinated by Giselita Morales. The experiences of ARAAC Cuba's Eje de Cultura (Cutural working group), coordinated by Magia López, were particularly salient. However, many more people than can be named here contributed tirelessly to this civic initiative. Also notable and timely was my 2012 enrollment in what was, up until that point, the first graduate course to be taught on racialidad (race, as a social construct) at the University of Havana

(School of Biology). The multidisciplinary course was co-taught by Antonio Martínez Fuentes (*ibae*), Esteban Morales Domínguez (*ibae*), and Jesús Guanche. Many scholars from the broader activist network imparted guest lectures. Listening closely to and keeping up with this vibrant and diverse network during fieldwork taught me lasting and sobering lessons that infuse my analysis of the strategies taken and forestalled to address enduring racism in Cuba, and thus many are cited in this book's pages. The list of names keeps growing, but those not already mentioned who became ancestors along the way warrant special recognition. They include Inés "La Lita" María Martiatu, Serafín "Tato" Quiñones, Rogelio Martínez Furé, and Robaina Garmillo, *ibae baye tonu*.

And then there are the friends in Cuba who, over many years, have grown into family: Dashiel, mi "tocaya" Ana Mayda, and mis "primas" Juana and Tamara, watched me grow up, kept me out of harm's way, lent me a helping hand, and made me feel safe and cared for when I was the most vulnerable. Linda Rodriguez (*ibae*), Hope Bastian, Ruthie Meadows, Alexander Sotelo Eastman, and Amandla Shabaka Haynes provided dear friendship and fellowship during fieldwork. And last but foremost, Bárbara Danzie León, who, in addition to all of the above, gave me a home away from home and has even become a beloved *abuela* to my daughter.

A beloved community of Cuban artists based in the United States taught me what it means to belong in Blackness across fraught geopolitical borders. Whether in Havana, NYC, Miami, or Austin, collaborations, conversations, and many dances with Yesenia Selier (*ibae*), Neri Torres, Xiomara Rodriguez, Carlos Mateu, Abraham Salazar, Ariel Fernandez, Chino Pons, Pedrito Martínez, Román Díaz, Odaymar Pasa Kruda, Beatrice Capote, Melvis Santa, and Jadele McPherson kept me grounded and in good company.

Writing this book has required time and space to think, often out loud, with others. Some of the most influential thinking has come as result of feedback received at workshops or from speaking invitations. While finishing my dissertation, I benefited from participation at the Mark Claster Mamolen Dissertation Workshop at the Afro-Latin American Research Institute, hosted by the Hutchins Center for African and African American Research at Harvard University. After completing my doctoral degree, I was fortunate to accept a postdoctoral fellowship at the Institute of Sacred Music at Yale University. Sally Promey and the Sensory Cultures of Religion Research Group, the Anthropology Department, Josef Sorett, Rehanna Kheshgi, Soo Ryon Yoon, Albert Laguna, and Anne Eller, among others, made my time at Yale particularly meaningful and memorable. Subsequent gatherings as a multiyear fellow of the Center for the Study of Material and Visual Cultures of Religion (MAVCOR)'s "Material Economies of Religion in the Americas" Project helped me to see my work within new constellations of disciplinary relation outside my prior orbit. Special thanks to Sally Promey for this opportunity and to Paul Christopher Johnson, Kathryn Lofton, Pamela Klassen, Alexandra Kaloyanides, Kati Curtis, and Emily C. Floyd for supporting the circulation of my work in different ways. At the Mellon Seminar for Emergent Scholars in Dance Studies, organized by Jasmine E. Johnson, I received insightful feedback from Sarah Wilbur and Aimee Meredith Cox. Special thanks to Rosemarie Roberts, Judith Hamera, Melissa Blanco Borelli, and Lester Tomé for their confidence in and encouragement of my work's development and contribution to Dance Studies.

I mark the moment when this manuscript truly became a book to a workshop cofacilitated by Kia Caldwell and Florence Babb during my Woodrow Wilson Foundation (now Institute for Citizens and Scholars) Career Enhancement Fellowship term, which coincided with the first year of pandemic life on Zoom. Jafari Allen gave more than a close read but a soulful recognition of, and advocacy for, the Black feminist spirit that moved the words to the page. Thomas DeFrantz had the most elegant and poignant way of shining new light on my work and calling me into curiosity about the stance from which I theorize, and the politics of the underlying premises entailed. I benefited greatly from Alejandro de la Fuente's meticulous feedback driven by his insatiable curiosity about Afro-Latin America, and relentless defense of the complexity brought to bear by marginalized voices within Cuban humanities and social sciences. Jossianna Arroyo urged me in generative ways to put a finer point on the diasporic scope of the book, naming its nodes across the Caribbean and in the United States, and to honor its kinship to *afro-caribeña* feminist practice, which she so generously models in the academy.

During a fellowship at the Institute for the Arts and Humanities at the University of North Carolina at Chapel Hill, I received detailed feedback and accompaniment from Timm Marr, Florence Babb, Oswaldo Estrada, Serenella Iovino, Priscilla Layne, Townsend Middleton, Katherine Turk, Courtney Rivard, and Claudia Yaghoobi. Other deeply influential readers of parts of the manuscript have included Devyn Spence Benson and Elizabeth Schwall. I am forever indebted to Julie Skurski and Berta Jottar for many scrupulous suggestions in the last stretch that have made a big difference. Invitations to speak about different parts of this project at Florida International University, Williams College, UC Boulder, UC at Irvine, and Washington University in St. Louis helped me crystallize and enhance the work's resonances with conversations in Cuban Studies, Black Studies, Anthropology, and Gender and Feminist Studies.

Many thanks are owed to the co-conveners of the Afro-Feminist Performance Routes project—Dasha Chapman, Mario LaMothe, Thomas DeFrantz, Andrea Woods Valdés, and Ava LaVonne Vinesett—for bringing me into the fold. These artist residencies at Duke University, in conjunction with the Collegium for African Diasporic Dance, held me accountable to not just talking the talk about my work, but also dancing it. I have been nourished by these embodied dialogues with Yanique Hume, Jade Power-Sotomayor, Rujeko Dumbutshena, Léna Blou, Halifu Osumare, Luciane Ramos-Silva, and Sephora Germain.

Many people and programs have sustained my writing process since my arrival to the African, African American and Diaspora Studies Department at the University of North Carolina at Chapel Hill. Kia L. Caldwell (and her TEAM ADVANCE) and Eunice Sahle have played vital roles as consummate mentors and models. There aren't enough ways to thank Petal Samuel for carrying me through all the ups and downs of the day-to-day. In the Anthropology Department, Florence Babb has been another exemplary mentor and advocate, and thanks to Angela Stuesse and the rest of the Race, Difference, and Power Concentration, I have found intellectual community away from my Austin School home. Rudi Colloredo-Mansfeld, Karla Slocum, Pat Parker, and Louis Pérez stood up for my research when it mattered most. My fellow co-conveners of the UNC-CH Global Dance Studies Working Group, sponsored by the Center for Global Initiatives, gave me a lovely introduction to the potential for cross-campus collaboration. The dangerous playground writing group, including Sara Smith, Lilly Nguyen, Andrew Curley, Annette Rodríguez, Jessica Namakkal, Banu Görkarıksel, and Danielle Purifoy, was the kind and constructive readership I needed to jumpstart getting words on the page. I am continually restored by the company of people across campus who've welcomed me into little assemblages of care that extend far, far beyond the walls of the institution. Among those not mentioned already are Sharon Holland, Meta DuEwa Jones, Lyneise Williams, Rebecka Futledge Fisher, Antonia Randolph, and Caela O'Connell. I am continuously grateful for how these villages activate, grow, and form new nodes (often out of shared outrage), and always when I need them the most. There are too many names to mention them all here and I feel fortunate that the list keeps growing.

Additional funding for the research and writing that would become this book came from the Tisch School of the Arts, the Warfield Center for African and African-American Studies at the University of Texas at Austin, the Ford Foundation, the Institute for Citizens and Scholars (formerly the Woodrow Wilson Foundation), UNC Center for Global Initiatives, the UNC College of Arts and Science, the UNC Institute for the Study of the Americas, and the UNC Office of the Provost.

The National Center for Faculty Development and Diversity's (NCFDD) Faculty Success Program (FSP) and its FSP Alumni Program gave me invaluable tools, skills, and accountability for establishing and maintaining a daily writing practice along the way. Shanya Cordis and Melissa Burch kept me motivated me to get it done, every Monday (and sometimes on Tuesday mornings, and Fridays too . . .) one pomodoro at a time. Other people who have talked me out of stuck-ness, shaped my thinking, shown me a way forward when I couldn't see it for myself, or helped me feel less alone along the way include Danielle Roper, Hope Bastian, Meredith Coleman-Tobias, Courtney Desiree Morris, Akissi Britton, Orisanmi Burton, Damien Sojoyner, Bianca C. Williams, and the formidable Mary McKinney. To all the members of the EthnoCuba Facebook group, and its supreme founder and administrator Ariana Hernández-Reguant, thank you for providing innumerous resources, tips, insights, and leads that have made the maze-like challenges of Cubanist research considerably easier and convivial.

Warm thanks to Gisela Fosado at Duke University Press for believing in the project early on, to Elizabeth Ault for taking it on with care, and to Ben Kossak and Liz Smith for attending to all the devilish details. I still struggle to find the words to express my gratitude for the generous and robust comments given by the anonymous reviewers culled by the press. (They later revealed themselves to be none other than the praiseworthy Deborah Thomas and Jafari Allen.) It would not be an exaggeration to say that only through passing through their hands did I come to realize what this book was (and wasn't) about. I am grateful to David Garten, Michael Eastman, and Dashiel Rodriguez Alfonso for giving me permission to reprint their photographs. If the writing in this book has any clarity and flow, it is certainly owed to the superlative editorial eye of Anitra Grisales. Rebecca Bodenheimer provided specialized research assistance for chapter 1 at a critical juncture. Additional research assistance was imparted by Alejandro Escalante. Katie Pace helped me with the daunting work of shedding and sifting through the word weeds. Biridiana brought her valuable expertise to bear on the index.

This book would not exist if not for the seeds of pride in being Cuban planted in my consciousness from birth by my maternal grandmother, Celia—in her words, a proud Afro-Cuban woman—who we lovingly called Ía.

That pride became a curiosity to more fully understand who we were, and who we might have been, from those still living on the island. That curiosity led me to a path of inquiry that has propelled this research and persisted into print. However, I would never have been able to follow the calling if not for the faith and unequivocal support of my parents, Karen and Philip Berry, and my brother, Kiel ("Atlas"). Thanks to my family, together with the sister of my heart, Tina, I have been able to lean on unconditional faith in my ability to see this through, even if they didn't exactly understand what "this" was. In full transparency, more often than not, neither did I. I prostrate myself to Oshun Kolade and Ashogbolade for caring for my head with such grace, and to all those of Ile Ashe who taught me, in practice, the rites, rights, and responsibilities that go into constructing kinship ties that bind and uplift. These teachings have kept my life in vital spiritual perspective. Long talks over delicious meals with Sophia Davis and Sowj Kudva have made Durham feel like home.

Carlos: Thank you for continuing to be patient with me, day after day, when I've lost my patience, and my breath, which the hamster wheel that is this academic profession is prone to induce.

While this book began gestation first, Adisa beat it to the punch. In some sense, my daughter and this book are siblings. Their births have taught me different things about the dedication and daily sacrifice that go into giving life. And within all of that, I always receive more than I'll ever give, learn more than I'll ever teach, am appreciative of more than I'll ever be able to express in words.

INTRODUCTION

No electricity meant no fan to cut the humidity in the small living room–turned–makeshift dance studio where I trained under Jenny. In the September heat of 2013, the largely Black, inner-city neighborhood of Cayo Hueso was experiencing yet another blackout. In this run-down *solar* (tenement building) in the heart of the municipality of Centro Habana, the windows faced an inner courtyard, Havana's Black commons, where *rumbas* would have been "formed" (arranged, assembled, and given shape) by residents. "*Se formó la rumba!*" or "*La rumba se formó!*" is what practitioners exclaim to mark and describe the collective efforts that bring the danced music event into being. *Solares* (*solar*, pl.) are as much a credit to socialist housing policies as they are an artefact of endemic racial inequality and racialized class segregation (Hernández-Reguant 2006, 258). Forming rumba made these physical and figurative places, much like how Jovan Lewis speaks of "the yard" in Jamaica, into a geography of shared fate and communal striving, amid tensions and, in this case, increasing disillusionment (Lewis 2020, 2). During our dance classes, Jenny would shout, "This is not dancing for dancing's sake!" when I missed a musical cue, demanding I pay closer attention to the instruments with which my movements should be in dialogue. While learning to dance from this Black community of practice during a period of economic change, I came to an understanding about the stakes and the contours of what rumba itself gave form to. These lessons led me to theorize rumba as a space for an ongoing conversation about Black life, between the more-than-human and their kin, that started during slavery and has continued through revolution after revolution, reform after reform.

When my teacher yelled in the third-floor apartment where she gave her lessons, her voice echoed for all the neighbors to hear and feel. The acoustics in these urban courtyards allow sonic vibrations to permeate deep into the cracks of the walls, stovetop pressure cookers, and *soperas de santo*: ceramic vessels for stones that have been made into Lucumí divinities, called orishas, who live with their spiritual children in these overcrowded spaces of Black sociality. Centro Habana is known as a cradle for rumba and home to descendants of the enslaved who are initiated into these African-inspired ways of knowing themselves in time and place.

The electricity had gone out in Cayo Hueso the evening before, part of the rotating blackouts frequent that summer as the state attempted to protect its fragile electrical grid while preserving electrical supply to tourist areas. These uncertainties heightened people's sense of frustration as the country underwent its latest wave of economic reforms. Miriam Galvez Carbonel, affectionately nicknamed "Morcilla" (Blood Sausage) by Jenny and friends, had arranged for me to live in an attic apartment above a bodega in Cayo Hueso where the neighbors picked up their monthly state food rations. It was a short walk from the *solar* where she lived and where Jenny often held her private lessons. I had slept on the tile floor the night before to try to stay cool, even though it meant risking getting crawled on by roaches fattened by the mounds of sugar and rice stored below. When I woke up that morning to the still motionless electric fan, I called Jenny to ask if she would like to reschedule the class. She commuted to Centro Habana from San Miguel del Padrón, a predominantly Black working-poor municipality on the outskirts of Havana. I did not know how the outage would impact her ability or willingness to come. I had already paid for the lesson in advance, but these were extenuating circumstances, or so I thought. She was unfazed by the precariousness of the city's infrastructure. Residents of Havana's poorest neighborhoods had to acclimate to daily inconstancy.

Studying under Jenny, I learned that she attributed her ability to make a self-affirming livelihood amid economic change not to state support, but to her *fé* (faith). By faith, I refer to her sense of self in the world as kin to African diaspora divinities and ancestors. She belonged to a ritual family that invested in a shared web of rights and obligations with the living, the more-than-human, and the dead. Practitioners are "made Lucumí" or "re-made into Yoruba-diaspora religious bodies" through a process of spiritual birthing that entails "interarticulated body gestures" that "establish mutual living-ness" (Beliso-De Jesús 2014, 503). The term *Lucumí* refers to the enslaved Yoruba-speaking people trafficked to colonial Cuba and to the religious practices they inspired. As a Lucumí priestess, she counted on her relationship of "mutual living-ness" with multiple guiding energies to help her find a way to overcome daily challenges big and small. Aisha Beliso-De Jesús has called these energies "copresences," for they are "recognized as being on, around and within the practitioners' bodies" and are felt and sensed through embodiment linked to a racial consciousness (Beliso-De Jesús 2014, 504). In return for her religious labor with and for family, Jenny's *ángel de la guardia* (guardian angel) or *padre* (father), Elegguá, the orisha who opens and closes the roads, would clear her a path for where she wanted to go in life.

While the phrase *"la rumba se formó"* may imply an air of spontaneity, the expression recognizes that rumba coalesces only through the coordination of distinct actions in time, each of which exercises different kinds of embodied expertise and conjoins to construct something larger than the individual parts. This something larger is embodied through music and dance and is felt as Black.[1] *Rumberos*—those who form and are formed by rumba—invest financially, physically, and affectively in filial relations bound by faith to save themselves from otherwise unfavorable situations and dismal fates. Those who form and are formed by rumba take center stage in this study, as they purposefully mobilize Black popular culture with spiritually endowed significance and within gendered scripts.

This work is anchored by the sixteen members of the rumba ensemble Yoruba Andabo, in which Jenny was the dance director and a lead dancer, and their intergenerational community of followers. Their networks in Havana spanned numerous professional rumba ensembles that, by extension, also became my teachers. The concept of "communities of practice" (Wenger 1998), groups of people formed by collective learning in shared domains of human endeavor, is helpful for understanding the many people I encountered from 2009 to 2018 in Havana. In contrast to the typical scholarly focus of rumba, which centers those who play percussion and sing, by highlighting dance expertise within my study, I center an underappreciated element wherein women play a vital role.[2] The following pages were born from the lessons I learned, both directly and indirectly, from the parts of their lives this community of practice shared with me.

The rumberos I came to know would often claim that *la religión* (their term for Black Atlantic faith practices), like rumba, was "in their blood," and to perform rumba was to "defend" it. While some may interpret such statements as predicated on an essentialist understanding of race, I saw it as a rhetorical strategy to legitimate claims to inalienable rights and resources they felt they were entitled to as descendants of the enslaved. They traced these Black-identified practices to their ancestors, both known and unknown, through slavery. Without monetary inheritances to speak of, they asserted a sacred entitlement to use these practices, as did their African ancestors, as tools not just to survive, but to create more possibilities for their lives in the face of continued structural limitations and daily indignities. As I will elaborate in chapter 1, "defending rumba" was grounded in a Black politics of worldmaking against a long history of (neo)colonial enclosure.

As Jenny made clear to me in class on that hot September day, this was not dancing for dancing's sake. Yet, for what purpose and in whose interests did rumberos move? Or put differently, what moved them? And what did their movements form? *Defending Rumba in Havana: The Sacred and the Black Corporeal Undercommons* explores the stakes of rumba at a specific historical conjuncture: the period of Cuba's private-market expansion post-Fidel (2007–18), to "update" the Revolution for the twenty-first century. However, the post-Fidel period of economic change was only the most recent in successive reforms fueling racial stratification in Cuba (de la Fuente and Bailey 2021). Amid these restructurings, rumba has been mobilized by different sectors to either deny the persistence of racism or declare racial pride despite pervasive anti-Blackness (Bodenheimer 2013). Rumba references a long history of Black struggle alongside and around national development in the wake of slavery and within Cuban Socialism.

When I began doctoral fieldwork in the early 2010s, the Cuban state was decidedly "updating" its economic model to better attract foreign investment. The *actualización del modelo económico de la Revolución* (update to the economic model of the Revolution), under the leadership of Raúl Castro as president of the Republic and head of the Cuban Communist Party (PCC), intensified existing racialized class and gender inequality in Cuba. Yet, the state media deployed a discourse of "updating" (*actualización*) and "perfecting" (*perfeccionamiento*) the Revolution to evoke a sense of continuity with the direction of the Revolution under Fidel Castro. The state's vision of socialism for the twenty-first century might otherwise be characterized as neoliberal, given its simultaneous weakening of the social safety net, mass layoffs in the public sector, and other austerity measures that disproportionately affected Cuba's Black population. However, many insist that the state's retention of a planned economy and redistributive programs warrant its designation as "still-socialist." The degree to which the hostile geopolitical context of a punitive US embargo can fully explain the Cuban state's own economic mismanagement and inefficiencies is an ongoing debate among academics, politicians, and ordinary Cubans themselves. Labels aside, there is increasing consensus that socioeconomic inequalities in Cuba have steadily exacerbated and impacted the Black poor most acutely.

Concurrently, the 2010s were marked by the United Nations' Year of the Afrodescendant (2011) and Decade of the Afrodescendant (starting 2015),

tions (Carrazana Fuentes et al. 2011). Black communities were significantly limited as to how they could participate in the economy, mirroring their exclusion from certain places of commerce in the city. Local anti-racist activist-scholars waged critiques against the state for rampant employment discrimination in the private sector. The impunity such anti-Black practices were met with conveyed state neglect for the uneven prospects for the next generation along lines of race. These critiques were not new, but grew out of a longer history of anti-racist mobilization led by Black Cubans dedicated to challenging the dominant rhetoric of revolutionary exceptionalism regarding racism.[5] In this shifting socioeconomic landscape, the choices and resources rumberos perceived as being available to them were instructive in their particularity.

As occurred during the return of the Cuban tourist economy in the prior decades, religious affiliation was an informal form of social capital that rumberos leveraged to get access to much-needed hard currency (Hearn 2008). My study delves into how la religión, as a mode of community-based organizing, and being a *religioso* (a practitioner or devotee of African-inspired religion) as a category of racialized belonging and subjectivity provided a critical standpoint for strategically navigating exclusionary market relations. Similar to anti-racist activist-scholars, rumberos were critical of the way the state placed symbolic value on Black popular culture without paying cultural producers a living wage. However, unlike the activist-scholars who sought solutions by means of policy reform, through their faith, rumberos in Havana created other possibilities and places for themselves (Berry 2016). My aim is not to reify "religion" as a folkloric category that separates it from "secular modern" conceptions of law, science, and politics, as it is framed in Cuban state policies and everyday language, for this categorization relegates it to a primitive, timeless arena divorced from the politics of daily life (Asad 1993). Rather, rumba provides a window into how that which is marked as sacred, conventionally located within the domain of "religion," animates and legitimizes bottom-up mobilizations to form dignified lives within raced, classed, and gendered constraints.

Although the racial aspects of Cuba's emergent private sector have gained more scholarly attention, the gendering of racism in private-sector employment since 2010 has been less discussed.[6] The way the private sector capitalizes on the social constructions of Black masculinity and femininity in different ways (addressed in chapters 2 and 3, respectively) is important for understanding how rumberas and rumberos have fashioned dignified lives for themselves during the reforms. As state officials calibrated rumba's usefulness for the state when seen as patrimony within the revamped national project, rumberas like Jenny choreographed rumba to pursue greater life aspirations than had been afforded to Black women folkloric dancers (a point mapped historically in chapter 1 and elaborated ethnographically in chapter 2). I see the bottom-up maneuvers of this community of practice as important for understanding how Black experience among the urban poor is gendered and how religious significations of gender anchor their responses to the liberal logics of nation-building, which the economic "update" brings into sharp relief.

This project differs from a familiar focus in Cuban studies on how everyday Cubans struggle to make the socialist system work in a faltering welfare state. Other excellent scholarship has investigated how the Cuban state has leveraged the social capital and organizational capacity of grassroots networks of support maintained by religiosos, and the complexities of those collaborations around official development projects (Ayorinde 2004; Hearn 2008). However, the rumberos I learned from expressed ambivalence about what continued investment in state employment or trust in the emerging private sector could yield for their well-being. Grounding themselves in their own notion of development, *desenvolvimiento*, predicated on access to labor, goods, and services to which they were spiritually entitled, served to offset reliance on both the public and private sectors.

Wary of the extent to which market liberalization and regime change could solve their everyday problems, rumberos consciously distanced themselves from the explicitly oppositional political camps that the state deemed "counterrevolutionary." The spirit-based notion of development that rumberos defend elaborates its own critique of capitalism. Its ethic of relation hinges on a theory of the human that is co-constituted by and interdependent with the more-than-human. The centrality of the sacred to the life of rumba performance and performers, I insist, reveals how Black subjects critically assess and address their changing socioeconomic reality by fashioning an alternate sphere of relation and exchange that they construct through embodied practice.

Building on studies that analyze local conceptions of what is necessary to live a good life and who gets to determine what is adequate for whom, this ethnography shows how those determinations are lived by this Black community of practice in Havana. As Hanna Garth argues, notions of adequacy are "deeply entangled with desires to live in idealized ways in the face of change" and these commitments are also shaped by gendered and racialized expectations (2020, 7). In contrast to Garth's work on food in Cuba, my work centers a conception of entitlements beyond the purview of the state. As elaborated in chapter 4, these are *derechos* (rights) that are conferred through "religious work"; this term refers to an understanding of the rights of personhood and labor that rubs up against neoliberal modes of self-making. A focus on rumberos reveals a complex web of resource exchanges and solidarities—what is otherwise cursorily mentioned in Cuban studies as informal gifts or trades—wrought by one's membership within spiritual kinship networks. Where copresences provided the family ties necessary to weather the difficulties of more and more market liberalization, rumba formed a space for rights worth defending.

This "post-Fidel" context has shaped the stakes upon which rumberos perform dedicatedly practiced choreographies of exchange, devotion, and pleasure both "on stage" and in their daily lives. Practitioners defend a terrain wherein they perform a collective right, as heirs of the enslaved, to refuse the coercive logics of nation-building schemes and to enact socioeconomic relations otherwise. In this way, rumba communities form what I call a *Black corporeal undercommons*. Notably, sacred filiations and gender ideologies play crucial roles in navigating this space that rumberas and rumberos form through their bodies. My methodological route to this theorization employed dance training and performance analysis to grapple with rumba as a complex domain of human endeavor too often undertheorized by its relegation to folkloric dance. While this study insists that there is something to learn from rumberos, who are too easily overlooked because they are dancing, it also underscores the importance of embodied methodologies for Black study. To take rumba seriously as a way of knowing is to account for the embodied spiritual dimensions of Black political imagination.

The Black Corporeal Undercommons

"You have to know how to occupy the space," Julio César "El Gordo" (The Fat One) stated when I asked him to reflect on the key to Yoruba Andabo's success. He was a longtime percussionist in the group and responsible for repairing their conga drums and *cajones* (box drums) when they needed maintenance. He explained further with an illustrative example: "It's like this," pointing to the drums he had made himself beside the table where we sat. "If I didn't know how to do it, I would have to pay someone else to do it. Now I can do it my way, the way that I like it, and it comes out better. . . . And I do it with consciousness." He made sure to credit respected Black male elders for teaching him how to occupy "the space" with consciousness. As the only phenotypically white member of the ensemble, this deference was especially important. Before agreeing to our first interview, he made sure that Geovani del Pino, Yoruba Andabo's artistic director, had authorized him to speak. Only with the permission of elder Black rumberos was he granted belonging in this space, and thus worthy of the knowledge and material resources exchanged between spiritual kin.

While this was, in some sense, true for all rumberos, El Gordo's belonging, as a non-Black man, illustrates what Beliso-De Jesús has argued with regards to how African diaspora bodies are made through complex rituals that hail "blackened epistemologies" rather than relying on a notion of biological essence attributed to race. That is, regardless of racial identification, those who become entangled in these webs of mutual living-ness are transformed into African diaspora bodies. The entitlement to hail what Beliso-De Jesús calls "blackened agency" (2014, 515) is co-constructed through "initiatory genealogy" (Palmié 2013, 160). During initiation, subjects are reborn into ritual families, called *familias de piedra* (families of stone), as children of specific divine energies or sovereigns.[7] The ritual performance of bodily patterns enacts meanings apprehended through the body, which activate webs of relation that are then reaffirmed through material exchanges that constituting belonging (Mason 1994). Indebtedness to and reliance on a specific set of racialized, gendered, classed, and generational social relations keyed one's affective registers to a sense of historical memory that, in turn, marked El Gordo's racial corporeal schema (Beliso-De Jesús 2014). While he remained conscious of the weight of his extra burden of representation, as someone who was not born into rumba or la religión through his blood family, he could enact legitimate belonging to his "stone family" through consistent observance of the bodily techniques and duties of sacred lineage that necessarily exceed and precede the demarcated space-time of folkloric cultural display.[8]

Knowing how to occupy the space—as a non-essentialist, racially conscious, and racializing spatial practice of embodied relation—is even more significant given the exclusion of the Black poor from the emerging landscape of commerce in Havana. Rumberos claim a spiritually endorsed entitlement, as heirs of the enslaved and kin to African diasporic copresences, to inclusion in a protected space of dwelling and fair trade. The kind of spatial consciousness rumberos form has consistently been intertwined with the ways global capital propels movement and migration. Lisa Maya Knauer's (2009) study describes the processes of electronic media exchange between rumberos in Cuba and those residing in New York City in the 1990s. She conceptualizes rumba as a transnational subjectivity producing an alternate spatio-political realm, or "portable homelands" (161) that "resist both the territorially based constructions of *cubanidad* (Cubanness) articulated by Cuban nationalists before and after the 1959 Revolution, and the equally insular politically charged definitions promoted by 'exile' leadership" (165). Importantly, she remarks on how this alternate realm allows them to negotiate their relationship to the state from a position of racial marginalization, economic dispossession, and geographic dislocation. Rumberos in Cuba and in the United States both describe themselves as "defending" a shared space of exchange, signaling a challenge to capitalist exploitation *and* racial discrimination or marginalization (Knauer 2009, 166). In so doing, they are "producing and reproducing a sense of belonging not coterminous with national boundaries" (Knauer 2009, 160). I build on Knauer's attention to the alternate realm of belonging that rumberos produce through transnational relation, in contradistinction to the binary of statist vs. "exile" camps. My study tunes into the exchanges that happen across not only geographic space but also currency (CUP/MN, CUC), concept-metaphor (secular, sacred), and time (colonial era, republican era, revolutionary era), referring to the ancestral and more-than-human energies that populate rumba's diasporic political geographic imaginary.

This Black diasporic consciousness is performed in movement. Deborah Thomas has written about how the collaborative needs of Black popular dance inform our understanding of political life in the wake of the plantation. Given that Cuba was one of the last countries to abolish slavery, her insights are pertinent here. This was a political consciousness inhabited by putting their body in motion together with others (2019, 207). It came from the felt recognition of how the history of slavery bears on the present, just as copresences make themselves felt through the bodies of their kin. In those historical referents lay the guidance, bodily techniques, and communal practices for saving themselves. *"Yo te salvo a ti; tú me salvas a mí"* (I save you; you save me) is a refrain among religiosos that reflects a deeply embedded ethic of mutual aid for collective well-being rehearsed in religious practice and performed in other forms of community life. The way many rumberos described their performances as acts of defense—*"defendemos la rumba"* —attuned me to a contestatory politics of space invoked when referencing their lifesaving bodily practice. This consciousness inspired a geography unconstrained by national boundaries or restricted by liberal-secular temporality.

I call this space that rumberos defend a "Black corporeal undercommons"—a kind of Black geography found not in place but in choreography (*choreo/*

geography)—grounded by the spirited maneuvers of everyday Black people.[9] Through the mobilization of people throughout the city in rumba's defense, this racial spatial imaginary was made manifest. The *under* indexes their relegation to the bottom or to the margins of respectability, as well as their underestimation for critical thought. To be largely opaque to, which is to be unable to be grasped by, those who do not belong is to be powerfully unseen in plain sight (Glissant 1997). The notion of a *corporeal* undercommons is a recognition of the body's capacity to hold and transform space, while at the same time acknowledging how dance performance, as Thomas gracefully puts forth, "not only express[es] a political worldview but also enact[s] it" (2019, 207). This book fleshes out how rumberas and rumberos form a space that expresses a political worldview in gender-specific ways that we cannot understand outside of a rigorous engagement with the embodied politics and poetics of the sacred. Here faith in and indebtedness to ancestral spirits and African divinities are summoned to simultaneously underscore the salience of the history of slavery and carve out a place of autonomy from the state on those grounds.

The Black corporeal undercommons opens a deeper consideration of what Black people collectively moving on their own behalf have the potential to form and the will to defend. With the help of Stefano Harney and Fred Moten's (2013) concept of "the undercommons," I enter into critical dialogue with Fernando Ortiz's *hampa afro-cubana* (Afro-Cuban underworld) (Ortiz [1906] 1973, 1916). Following Harney and Moten, I challenge Ortiz's pejorative label for the domain of Black sociality to reconsider "the Afro-Cuban underworld" as a set of social relations (between the human and more-than-human) that enable the sharing of material, cultural, spiritual, and epistemological provisions within a larger project of Black well-being. The Black corporeal undercommons, therefore, highlights the role of bodily practice in reconstituting the literal and figurative spaces Black people occupy to sustain themselves.

This critical attention to how space is bodied forth has been a key contribution of dance studies and Black feminist geography (McKittrick 2006, 2011). Bridging these conversations within anthropology, in *Shapeshifters: Black Girls and the Choreography of Citizenship* (2015), Aimee Cox analyzes Black girls' creative practices of agency within constraint as a way to make space for themselves in a country where they are not deemed worthy of the rights of citizenship. Cox writes, "Choreography is concerned in a very fundamental sense with the ordering of bodies in space. . . . Choreography suggests that there is a map for movement or plan for how the body interacts with its environment, but it also suggests that by the body's place-ment in a space, the nature of that space changes" (2015, 28–29). Not least of all, "choreography, like culture, is a process of meaning making" (30). I contend that the social choreographies, to use Cox's phrasing, of rumbe-ras and rumberos are distinct and largely illegible to dominant regimes of seeing and knowing Black people dancing in the wake of slavery (see chap-ter 1). Taking rumba seriously as a way of knowing, we can feel the beat of a uniquely situated Black political imaginary articulated through the body in movement and its formation of a space to call their own.

This work looks to social spaces where most politics is lived, the "ordi-nary" activities of noncompliance or deviance that are rarely recognized as political (Cohen 2004; Kelley 1994). While it is tempting to label these activities as "resistance," scholars of Black politics across the diaspora cau-tioned against the facile application of that interpretive framework. Cohen urges us to pay attention to intent. She critiques how the counternorma-tive behaviors of Black people are overdetermined by the lens of "resistance," thereby conflating attempts to "fundamentally sway the distribution of power" with attempts to "create greater autonomy over one's life and make the best of limited life options" from outside normative structures (40). Deb-orah Thomas, on the other hand, insists that we contemplate the related-ness between hegemony and resistance, as "mutually constituting concep-tual tools rather than oppositional poles" (2004, 258). Instead of looking to neatly categorize aspects of cultural production as either challenges or ca-pitulations to dominant practices or ideologies, she argues that we might do better to take stock of how descendants of Africa throughout the Atlantic world have been forced to develop creative means of critiquing dominant structures through direct engagement with them (Thomas 2004, 257–62).

To be sure, the rumberos in this study make clear that they are not in-vested in a politics of "resistance" understood as opposition to the Commu-nist Party or revolutionary state. They do not intend to sway the fundamental distribution of power in the country through race-based reform—as other Cuban anti-racist activists did at the time (Zurbano 2014)—much less aspire to overturn the state or, in the case of contemporary Haiti, "make the state" on their own terms (Kivland 2020). Instead of assuming undeclared or latent resistance, what would it mean to take seriously how rumberos justify partic-ular actions on the basis of sacred subjectivity and religious duty? Their piety can readily fit within a folkloricized vision of Black culture dismissing their posture as, at best, comfortably apolitical if not primitive. At the same time, it may position them as deviant vis-à-vis an idealized construction of secular liberal subjecthood in that it insists on a social theory of relation that defies the political coordinates of the Party and the State. Either way, their collective vision and political orientation remains opaque to the platitudinous logics of the ideological disputes that have governed Cuba-US geopolitical relations.

This book illuminates the kinds of social spaces and possibilities that rumberos formed and defended at a key moment in history when the Cuban state was faced with weakened economic allies and plagued by continued US sanctions. The most recent revamping of the political economy of the revolution is part of a long-standing plight to sustain its project of national sovereignty. Anthropologists have demonstrated how research in the Caribbean context is uniquely positioned to demystify liberal constructs of the human upon which classical Westphalian conceptions of formal sovereignty are based (Thomas 2022). New theorizations of the limits and possibilities of human relation are inspired by the everyday practices, sensory regimes, and affective dimensions that produce other conceptualizations of worldmaking that are broader than formal politics (Masco and Thomas 2023). Like the region itself, rumberos in Cuba challenge the concept of a sovereign individual who speaks and acts autonomously and are suspect of the notion of a neoliberal entrepreneurial subject who acts according to rational individual choice in the market which Cuba's new development design fosters. Instead, they insist upon, building on Bonilla (2017), their nonsovereign nature, their interdependence with each other, and their critical reliance on the more-than-human to order their steps and shape their fate.

For poor Black youth discouraged by their dismal prospects in the economic landscape of the new Cuba, rumba groups like Yoruba Andabo modeled the affective and material payoff of creating their own means of subsistence rooted in African-inspired sacred epistemologies and coordinated through bodily techniques. The collective mobilization of blood and stone family, linked through ritual kinship to sacred energies, facilitated an ethic of community-based subsistence. This ethic implicitly called into question the moral integrity of the discourses surrounding the campaign to "perfect" Cuban Socialism privileging foreign investment and increased privatization. Thus, the Black corporeal undercommons represents an alternative to the state's design for progress by devising alternative terms of economic engagement and embodying more affirming practices of self-making.

This brings me to the tensions that animate the book's pages. One tension is how to honor the performativity of rumberos' politics of "defense" without clumsily adopting a rhetoric of "resistance" that the subjects of this book consciously do not espouse. While I am cognizant of the resonance

The politics of gender also carries terminological implications. Throughout the book, I privilege the terms practitioners used to describe themselves. This community of practice follows the conventions of Spanish language grammatical gender wherein all subjects are categorized as either masculine (often ending in -o; e.g., rumbero) or feminine (often ending in -a; e.g., rumbera). For the same reason, I refer to rumba practitioners as rumberos in the plural, following the convention of having the masculine gender represent a mixed-gender group. However, in the specific moments when I aim to highlight the *difference* gender makes for my analysis of the group, I go against the norm and instead list out "rumberas and rumberos." Both in writing and in movement, this Black feminist has wrestled with how to ethically navigate and ethnographically render a space that holds the binary sex-gender system dear. However, more work can and should be done focusing on when those conventions fall short in describing the fullness of sexuality, gender expression, and creative social maneuver among people formed by rumba.

These tensions get to the heart of an intellectual and ethical knot: how to highlight the political significance of this distinct spatial imaginary without falling into an uncritical romanticized discourse that would portray rumba, and thereby the Black corporeal undercommons by extension, as inherently or necessarily a site of political resistance, much less a feminist utopia? How to self-reflexively bring my own analytics as a Black feminist to bear, but in terms that are sensitive to how such work can be taken up by political projects to which the practitioners themselves do not uniformly ascribe, or worse, would render them more vulnerable to patriarchal-state power?

Ultimately, *Defending Rumba in Havana* represents an emphatic critique of the paternalistic terms upon which Black people have been interpellated into the nation-state project that rumba's nomination as national patrimony obscures. The ethnography brings Black feminist attention to creative maneuvers of differently gendered Black people in Cuba within constraints that are amplified by the inconvenient fact of ongoing racism within a nationalist project that, beginning before and leading through the current Cuban Revolution, has relied on the professed realization of racial harmony to distinguish itself from the US empire. Black Cuban feminists have indicted Cuban Communist Party leaders for constructing a paternalistic narrative that the Revolution *made* Black Cubans into people (Rodríguez López 2011, 201). That is to say, any dignity Black Cubans had was owed to the state, for which uncritical loyalty and gratitude was expected in return—as if "the Revolution" was somehow a disembodied entity apart from the people who presumably benefited from it (Farber 2011, 171). This same benevolently paternalistic discourse of top-down Black uplift emerges in dominant narratives of rumberos' journey from the slave barracks and the *solar* to the national stage.

Black Cuban Marxist scholars have coincided with Trouillot's estimation of another Caribbean island of iconic revolutionary proportion in saying that being written into the national narrative, becoming Cuban, has come with silences that reveal power inequalities (Carbonell 1961; Trouillot 2015). This is not to invisibilize the involvement and even leadership of Black people in Cuban revolutionary movements from colonialism to the present, or to diminish the radical social impact of revolutionary reforms on all poor Cubans, and Black Cubans especially. However, if to be a Cuban citizen is to be a secular-liberal subject of the nation-state, and an obedient and uncritical one at that, the Black corporeal undercommons unsettles the presupposition that this is what the formerly enslaved only ever wanted to become. A glimpse of this other horizon of belonging and being is revealed in the sense of Black pride that came from rumberos who saw their ancestral heritage as an asset for a more holistic kind of development predicated on spiritual resources that are inalienable to their bodies and shared among their kin (see chapter 4). In the pursuit of *desenvolvimiento*—a notion of development tied to spiritual obligation, potential, and interdependence— rumberos have formed a space that exceeds the nation-state's jurisdiction or definition of citizenship rights.

Rumberos have not limited themselves to the contrived stages of cultural display afforded by the state, nor have they internalized its nationalist interpellations and political ideologies wholesale. Instead, they have found ways of continually investing their labor in their own communities, from which they receive substantive dividends. In doing so, they have reclaimed sites of national spectacle and refashioned them as spaces of radical Black public assembly (see chapter 5). If not engaged in dancing for dancing's sake, following Jenny's assertion, the work of the Black corporeal undercommons might be to claim space for Black collectivity, with all its difference, and defend that ground.

These bottom-up maneuvers motion toward rumba as a way of knowing a commons wherein Black people in Havana dwell and exchange resources in self-affirming terms. Rather than striving for more inclusion in the national project to "update" and "perfect" the Cuban Revolution for the twenty-first century, rumba points us toward a sector of the Black urban poor that maintains a critical distance from statist logics and interpellations. In motion we can feel what Hanchard calls Black quotidian politics, the politics of everyday life, that beget Black community (Hanchard 2006). These quotidian practices create other possibilities than the kind political parties or capital "P" Politics afford. They ground an investment in the kinds of aspirations that the formerly enslaved had to disavow to become Cuban (see chapter 1). These are the very kinds of yearnings I see moving diasporic Black struggles today to go beyond the state and its party politics as their political horizon.

Rumba offers much for our understanding of Black political thought and embodied worldmaking in the Americas. At stake for the hemispheric movement for Black lives is appreciating in rumba what Soyini Madison has called "radical performances that violent constraint has provoked" (2014, viii). Indeed, this seems to be the direction in which the masses are already heading when they go marching in the streets. I am thinking with the diasporic mobilizations from Minneapolis to Rio de Janeiro asserting a moral gauge more legitimate and collective power higher than state authority—the transnational movements for Black lives that defend an audaciously irreverent stance toward the kind of respectability politics that has betrayed the working-class Black masses for so long. It is no coincidence that these movements are inspired and energized by what many have anecdotally described as a spiritual calling to defend their dead. It is no wonder that protesters are called to create makeshift altars in the street where they say the names of spirits in popular prayer who cannot rest because there is more work to be done by the living. It is in this broader sense that I invoke a spirit-based politics—not as a stand-in for religion, but as a shared, historically situated understanding of who we are collectively accountable to. It is an understanding that emboldens us to make different choices and feel justified in those actions. It is a different way of validating what we are supposed to be doing in the here and now, and for whom. It is at once a political and historical orientation to the world that is not always articulated in words but made visible in motion. It is a study in how to give to ourselves what a state cannot offer us.

Rather than a clenched fist in the air as their choreographic motif, rumberos shrug their shoulders, sway, and smile to a syncopated beat. A street protest for Black life is one way to perform that the dead are not gone, that we are responsible for making their spirits manifest, and that they have a message, directions, for the living. Rumba shows us that there are other ways that may be less recognizable, illegible to the state, because they are dancing.

Knowing the Sacred Place in Rumba

"Rumba" has been used in everyday Cuban discourse to signal a diversity of music and dance styles that have taken on new meanings over time. Dating to the mid-nineteenth century, rumba was a social event distinguished by live percussion, song, and dance, giving cultural expression to a social practice that linked Africans and people of African descent across "slave," "free," and "fugitive" status in colonial western Cuba. Although colonial Spanish law, unlike the British system, did allow Catholic marriage, social associations (*cabildos de nación*) loosely grouped by language spoken or colonially defined ethnicity, and self-purchase of freedom (*coartación*), under the caste regime (*régimen de castas*), even Black people who were "free" by law suffered numerous limitations on their economic and social advancement and did much of the same sorts of work as their enslaved and fugitive counterparts in the cities.[10] It is in this context that rumba is said to have established its function as a "social chronicle of the dispossessed" (Acosta 1991, 54). To be sure, the rumba centered in this book is distinct from the commercialized and whitened versions that circulated in cabarets and ballrooms throughout North America and Europe, which may be more familiar to a wider readership due to how the word *rumba* or *rhumba* traveled outside of Cuba in the 1930s attached to a mixture of dance movements and musical arrangements that bear little resemblance to popular rumba on the island (Daniel 2009; Moore 1997).

What would become the distinguishing characteristics of rumba in Cuba were consolidated in the urban slums of the western cities of Havana and Matanzas by the formerly enslaved (Urfé 1982). Since the 1500s, Havana had been an important trade hub for the Spanish Empire through which commodities, people, and ideas circulated. This circulation exploded after the Haitian Revolution, when Cuba (alongside Brazil and Puerto Rico) became the center for world sugar production and its enslaved population rapidly increased. Cuban planters eagerly filled the void in the world market left by the neighboring former French colony and established itself as one of the most capital-intensive plantation economies in the Americas in the nineteenth century. Historians estimate that roughly one million enslaved Africans were trafficked to the island as chattel, primarily from the regions of West Africa and Congo-Angola. Even as the slave trade ceased in other parts of the Atlantic under British interdiction, in Cuba it persisted in clandestine form until 1867. This contributed to the intensive transmission of African practices, languages, and beliefs from communities often captured en masse, and the formation of distinct cultural identities in different parts of the island. While the *régimen de castas* legally codified Cuba's majority Black and *mulato* population into a racially stratified society in which Blackness (African) and whiteness (Spanish) marked opposite poles of power and privilege (Wade 1995, 1997), at the same time, it created some paths for a degree of social mobility that were foreclosed in the British colonies, namely via "racial mixing" and the purchase of one's freedom. The sociodemographic landscape of Havana and Matanzas was dramatically transformed by the expansion of slavery; they became home to a majority Black population and several important rebellions in which cabildo membership played an instrumental role (Childs 2006; Finch 2015; Ferrer 2014). Furthermore, there was a rich tradition of *cimarronaje* (fugitivity) in both rural and urban areas. The density of *cimarrones urbanos* (urban maroons), finding refuge among their enslaved and "free" counterparts, made these Black neighborhoods into *palenques urbanos* (urban runaway communities) (Deschamps Chapeaux 1983, 6, 54). It is significant that rumba was practiced among the workers in the ports of Havana and Matanzas and was particularly associated with members of the male initiatory association Abakuá and their ritual music and dance. Indeed, international traffic in the port cities of Havana and Matanzas connected the enslaved, free, and fugitive Africans and people of African descent in a diasporic network of political thought and activity that shaped the kinds of freedom dreams that were elaborated in the Atlantic world (Dubois 2006; Scott 2018; Ferrer 2014).

It is difficult to know how rumba was played and danced in that period. Communal gatherings called rumbas were likely to host a complex of music structures and accompanying dances that served as a playful means of courtship and a corporeal means to affirm the kinds of solidarities that colonial elites bet against and actively sought to deter. These solidarities were expressed through the body in the register of pleasure and praise, and were underwritten by bonds limned in political, ancestral, and spiritual terms. In the twentieth century it became identified with three forms or music/dance subgenres, and today, *rumba* is an umbrella term that encompasses *guaguancó*, *yambú*, and *columbia*. Each indexes a particular historical dynamic of race, gender, sex, and class as it is rehearsed in relationship to contemporary conditions of anti-Black discrimination, heteropatriarchy, and poverty.

The first two forms, *rumba guaguancó* and *rumba yambú*, are typically danced by a male-female couple. In the popular Cuban imaginary, *rumba guaguancó* is defined as an encoded courtship dance representing the "ritualized enactment of sexual conquest" (Moore 1997, 168). The male "rooster" (*el rumbero*) attempting to chase his "hen" (*la rumbera*) is a cultural metaphor for male sexual pursuit as danced play. Masculine movements called *"vacunaos"* (vaccinations) are the sexual advances that the woman aims to block with gestures shielding her pelvis called *botaos* (from the verb *botar*—to throw away, kick out, knock down, or bounce off) (discussed further in chapter 2). Under the most widely accepted readings of *rumba guaguancó*, "vaccination [penetration] is the goal" (Daniel 1995, 69). In contrast, the much slower *yambú*, while also described as a flirtatious dialogue between an older male and a female, is defined by the absence of vaccination (penetration) (Daniel 1994). The third subgenre, *rumba columbia*, is a competitive and typically male solo dance thought to be the result of the gender imbalance of the slave population. It is aesthetically influenced by the dances of the Abakuá, with cultural, political, and religious dimensions (described in chapters 1 and 3) that were founded by enslaved African men near the ports in the colonial era. *Rumba de cajón* (box rumba) refers to the use of box drums, like those made from the crates used to transport codfish at the ports where many Abakuá men worked. Tabletops, dresser drawers, spoons, or other objects of daily life were also improvised instruments to supplant drums when they were outlawed. Although it is squarely located within the commercial centers of the colony, unlike *cimarrón* (maroon) communities in rural Cuba, rumba has been theorized as part of the genealogy of "maroon music" because it summoned the collective action of marginalized Black people, hiding in plain sight from colonial control (Vaughan 2012; Sublette 2004).

Hampa afro-cubana: Los negros brujos: Apuntes para un estudio de etnología criminal (The Afro-Cuban underworld: The black witches: Notes for a criminal ethnological study), published in 1906, by Fernando Ortiz, known as the "Father of Cuban Anthropology," was an account of the spaces in Cuban society that bred "dangerous atavism." He trained under Italian criminologist Cesar Lombroso, and using that analytical lens, during the height of what is now called "scientific racism," he meticulously describes the amalgamation of proto-delinquent practices in the Black slums of Havana that threatened to undermine Cuba's standing among the family of modern nations, among them the *rumba de solar*. In 1924, he defined rumba in his *Glosario de afronegrismos* ([1924] 1991) as, among many things, an "obscene partner dance" evidencing the "primitive psyche" of Blacks: "violent," "lascivious," "spontaneous" (387–88). *"Todo negro nace bailador"* (all Blacks are born dancers), he asserted (Ortiz [1924] 1991, 387), a sign of their innate proximity to savagery. Ortiz's definition of rumba reflected the anxieties that he and other white creole elites shared about establishing a viable national identity with a large Black population and under the racial pressures of two US military occupations (1898–1902, 1906–1909) (Dubois and Turits 2019). US politicians who sought justification to undermine Cuban sovereignty and control its politics instituted the Platt Amendment to the Cuban Constitution in 1901. It allowed US military intervention at signs of domestic political "disorder." On both sides of the Florida Strait, elites' anxieties about a politicized and rebellious Black Cuban citizenry were projected onto the appearance of Black people dancing and playing music.

Decades later, Ortiz's writings about rumba and Black popular culture more broadly presented a revised portrayal of Blacks and promoted their "culture" as part of Cuban modernity, giving rise to "Afro-Cuban studies." Like Ortiz's contemporary in the US academy, Franz Boas, his scholarship emphasized culture so as to debunk the theory of biological determinism to which he had once held. Emerging from that fraught intellectual genealogy, rumba came to be understood as an expression of cultural hybridity: a mixture or blend of different cultural forms primarily deriving from Africa and Europe. As in other Latin American nations founded on racial slavery, the discourse of cultural blending promoted by the intelligentsia, instantiated in Ortiz's *ajiaco* (stew) metaphor (1940), served a nationalist mission of ostensible inclusion and harmonious blending, and legitimized the myth of "racial democracy" (Freyre 1946). This myth strengthened an ideology of unity within national identity while simultaneously negating the pervasiveness of historical patterns of racial exclusion and hierarchy and downplaying structural racism, even while it ostensibly sought to upend them.

Robin D. Moore's (1994) critical analysis of Ortiz's body of work highlights how characterizations of Black artistic practice have long been embedded in social relations of power that give race meaning in Cuba. "Rumba is perhaps best understood as composed of both specific associations with music and dance styles and broad, historically derived associations with Cuba's black underclass, their lifestyles, attitudes, and culture" (1997, 169). He states that rumba circulates as a racial signifier, such that its invocation can perform both derogatory anti-Black sentiment and oppositional racial pride and belonging. Stuart Hall's claim that "race is the modality in which class is lived" speaks to the racialization of class in neighborhoods where rumbas are formed in Havana (Hall et al. 1978, 394). In short, rumba's Blackness indexes a lower urban class position mapped on to a racial geography rooted in slavery. It is either demeaned or defended on that basis.

After the 1959 triumph of the Cuban Revolution, radical changes in the political, economic, and social fabric of the country allowed poor and working-class Cubans unprecedented access to housing, education, health, land, and professional opportunities. Black Cubans, historically overrepresented in the lower socioeconomic sectors, experienced measurably significant gains in terms of life expectancy, quality of life, housing, schooling, and social mobility as a result (de la Fuente 1995). In turn, rumba went from being a social chronicle of the dispossessed to a social chronicle of the liberated (from capitalist oppression) via the triumph of socialism. Rumba gained a reputation for being a cultural symbol for revolutionary values of integration and egalitarianism (Daniel 1991, 1995, 2009).

The undeniable gains in a range of arenas that Black Cubans experienced due to the Revolution's restructuring of social and economic institutions help explain their widespread support of the project of Cuban socialism and their respect for Fidel Castro as a leader who addressed issues of poverty and national independence. However, an initial period of lively debate and cultural production that addressed racial issues was marked by US-backed military invasion, sabotage, and economic blockade, helping prompt a shutdown of virtually all critique; in 1961, Fidel Castro declared that racism had been eliminated by the state. A united front against US imperialism became paramount in the Cold War context of US aggression; this demand built on the nineteenth-century independence discourse of racial unity, encapsulated by the slogan "Not Blacks, not whites, only Cubans." Thereafter, claims that Black artists, intellectuals, and activists made about the continued salience of race, reproduction of structural racism, or impact of racial prejudice on their daily lives was actively silenced through government censorship, and suppressed as divisive and counterrevolutionary (Benson 2016).[11] However, despite Fidel Castro's proclamation, so-called color-blind socialism did not eradicate racism; nor did it make Black consciousness obsolete (Clealand 2017). The mid-1960s to the mid-1980s were characterized by "inclusionary discrimination" (Sawyer 2005, 19) that encompassed both social advances and restrictions, material improvements and cultural censorship.

The Cuban state declared itself officially atheist from the outset of the revolution. Religion was regarded as an "opiate of the masses," a maladaptation to capitalism, and thus no longer necessary under Cuban socialism. The state made religious affiliation of any kind grounds for exclusion from becoming a Communist Party member, for aspiring to certain professions, or to holding a higher government office, although this restriction fell more heavily on practitioners of African-inspired religions. Responding to the dogmatic Sovietization of every social realm during the 1970s, at the same time that Fidel Castro declared Cuba an "African Latin" nation, practitioners of African-inspired religions were criminalized and violently persecuted, and religious activities were restricted and stigmatized (Ayorinde 2004; Berry 2010). This pushed African-inspired religious practices further underground. Religiosos, especially those seeking professional advancement in state-subsidized sectors, had to hide their initiatory beads (*collares*), refrain from dressing in white during the year-long initiation, and conduct ceremonies clandestinely, among other restrictions, so as to not jeopardize their employment.

This racial democratic rhetoric and official atheism proved less tenable in the 1990s when the economic crisis prompted by the fall of the Soviet Union, which had subsidized Cuba's economy, and exacerbated by the US embargo severely limited the expansion of opportunities for Black Cubans. The "Special Period" of the 1990s laid bare the contradictions of officially silenced forms of ongoing racial discrimination and racial inequality. Large-scale economic collapse and severe food shortages made Cuban households more reliant on remittances from abroad. The saying *"hay que tener fé"* (you have to have faith) and all will be well, once a revolutionary slogan signaling that people were working in the underground to topple the US-backed Batista government, was now turned upside down to signal a bitter reminder of their failed hopes for what that revolution would bring (Hernández-Reguant 2002). *Fé* became an acronym for *"Familia en el Extranjero"* (family abroad). Given the early flight of the largely white Cuban elite and professional class, white Cubans who remained had greater access to this new economic lifeline that was now indispensable for economic survival.

In this dire context, many orthodoxies of the past were revised. Among them, the state shifted from sugar export to tourism as the major source of foreign exchange and created a dual currency system to facilitate foreign investment in strategic sectors. This resulted in a two-tiered system of spaces and goods to which only foreigners, or those few with exchangeable currency, had access. Additionally, recognizing its limited ability to meet popular material needs, the state revised the constitution in 1991, declaring itself secular rather than atheist. It thereby officially relinquished religious affiliation as a legitimate basis for overt discrimination and marginalization, even as old prejudices remained intact (Ayorinde 2004).

At the same time, the commodification of expressions of Black popular culture staged as a secular national resource played a key role in Cuba's post-Soviet economic future. The early revolutionary era of rumba's institutionalization lay the groundwork for its commodification in a new cultural market for foreigners. For religiosos seeking formal employment in the tourist sector, adopting a secularist discourse became a rubric for professional advancement and was advantageous for seizing economic opportunities (Hagedorn 2001; Ayorinde 2004; Daniel 2010). Therefore, folkloric performances became one of the few means for Black Cubans to circumvent the "tourist apartheid" created by the dual currency system (Roland 2011, 67; Sawyer 2005, 76).

By and large, touristic representations of rumba reinscribe a flattened image of Black people dancing and drumming, reducing rumba practitioners to their caricatured circulation in the popular imaginary. Even while rumba has been taken up as a secular symbol of national identity in the era of cultural tourism, it is still regarded as *"una cosa de negros* (a Black thing) and disparaged given racialized stereotypes that link the practice with *el bajo mundo* (the low life), excessive alcohol use, and violence" (Bodenheimer 2013, 177). That is to say, class is racialized to such an extent that dominant sectors have viewed rumba as the cultural expression of poverty. To that effect, rumberas and rumberos carry the projections of Blackness as delinquent, unruly, hypersexual, hedonist, and humble. This unsavory reputation has made rumba a paradox for Black identity politics and, specifically, for an "Afro-Cuban cultural movement" that seeks to critique and dismantle those very stereotypes (Berry 2016; de la Fuente 2008). Contemporary discourses around rumba emphatically expose the enduring entanglement of race, gender, and class oppression in socialist Cuba.

When I formally approached Geovani del Pino, the artistic director of Yoruba Andabo, to ask for his consent to include his ensemble in my study, he said that he was averse to foreign researchers but would grant me permission for four reasons: because I'm young, I'm Black, I'm religiosa, and we have a mutual friend from the US (also an anthropologist) who is very dear to him. His response gave a clear indication of what aspects of my identity he deemed most relevant, which in turn illuminates his own practices of self-making and how he positioned himself (or not) in relation to others. Notably, his race and his faith were paramount for ultimately deciding to talk to this wide-eyed young foreigner who was becoming an anthropologist. The questions I asked (and learned not to ask) over the years, as much as their responses, were necessarily informed by my "passport privilege," the extent of my body's racial interpellation, my gender expression, and the sacred meanings assigned to my subjectivity as a descendant of Africans enslaved in Cuba and kin to a family of stone (albeit based in NYC). Reflexive about my unique positionality in these exchanges with rumberas and rumberos, I came to know rumba differently. Paramount to that understanding was its sacred underpinnings.

Religiosos predominate among the ranks of professional rumberos. As musicologist and rumba promoter Ned Sublette asserts, "Almost all rumberos today practice Santería, and images and quotes from its santos appear in the text they sing" (2004, 267). Likewise, studies tracing the language of ritual songs to Africa, such as those of the Abakuá confraternities housed in cabildos to which rumberos have historically belonged, and then locating their traces in rumba music recordings, have made the case for the embeddedness of the sacred within this ostensibly secular Cuban popular cultural form. Documenting the "African roots" of Cuban popular music through etymological reconstruction of song lyrics has been one way to make the place of the sacred visible within Black cultural practices that have been officially categorized as secular (Miller 2000).

Nevertheless, a common sense persists, and official discourse insists, that rumba is a secular activity. This common sense is reflected in state policies and the everyday language that rumberos themselves deploy. Despite the importance of religious affiliation in Geovani's decisions concerning his relationship to my project, professional rumberos like himself routinely adopt a secularist discourse—"folklore is folklore; religion is religion"—as a rubric of professionalism, and as a protection from state interference, in exchange for a monthly salary paid by the state. Rather than take the connection between rumba and African diasporic religious practice as purely circumstantial, or make a point about its African roots, this book reveals why the sacred is important for situating this embodied practice within a larger Black emancipatory imaginary that is adjusting to the diminishing gains of secularism in a weakened welfare state. For rumberos, faith was key to self-authorizing the practices they devised on the ground so as to move beyond/around/under/through persistent socioeconomic constraints. Likewise, within Cuba, predominantly white writers since the twentieth century helped caricature rumberos as "salt-of-the-earth Black protagonists" or the humble poor (los humildes) in the cultural drama of an anti-US-empire Revolution (Schmidt 2016, 164), who were devoid of political and economic agency. To leave faith out of my analysis of rumba would be to deny a key framework that Black subjects use to understand themselves, interpret their conditions, direct their choices, and legitimate their claims in particular ways. Rumberos are strategically and consciously drawing on and gesturing toward shared understandings of the sacred in their performances and in their connections to each other to mediate this moment of economic change.

I.3 A *religiosa* cheers at a Yoruba Andabo performance at El Palacio de la Rumba. Photo by author.

As transnational feminist M. Jacqui Alexander (2005) reminds us, if we are serious about respecting Black subjects as producers of knowledge about their lives, we have something to learn from their "pedagogies of the sacred." Alexander calls this a "spirit-based politics." Her insistence on the interconnectedness of the spiritual and the political is characteristic of the Black feminist tradition that guides my theorization of the Black corporeal undercommons. Drawing specifically on Audre Lorde's ([1978] 1984) formulation of the erotic as the sensual bridge that connects the political and the spiritual, Lyndon Gill (2018) poignantly names the "political-sensual-spiritual" as his "principle interpretive posture" (xxv), thus making it possible to interpret, for instance, Black popular art and queer activism as an "eros driven critique of the nation" (16). Musing on these submerged connections, a metaphor for the underwater unity of the Caribbean archipelago itself, Gill reframes spirituality as, "at its core, a desire for a metasystem of accountability and larger continuity of existence" (Brathwaite 1975; Gill 2018, 10). My ethnography assumes such a political-sensual-spiritual posture and suggests that this move brings me in closer alignment with rumberos themselves. Therefore, this Black feminist orientation to anthropological study, one which refuses mind-body, spirit-politics divisions, is indispensable to my ethnographic rendering of this Black community of practice. It is key to understanding how those formed by rumba analyze the social, critically engage with a nation-state haunted both by slavery and Soviet orthodoxy, and fashion other systems of care and accountability that lie outside state jurisdiction.

The African diasporic sacred, as a vitally embodied epistemology, is also a bridge that connects my project to Black performance studies, allowing me to treat embodied articulations as sites of social theorization. A nonverbal correction given on the dance floor, a collective shift of weight, a reverential embrace, or a furtive glance are respected analytically as strategic exchanges between subjects deserving of critical engagement on their own terms. Learning to move and think through rumba was for me a means to better understand Black experience in Cuba at the specific political and economic conjuncture of the Raúl Castro presidency (2008–2018), when the national reforms that promised to secure the Revolution's socialist future in effect compromised the kind of guarantees that the Black working class had relied on.

Updating the Revolution

Whether Cuban society was changing for the better or for worse was an active debate during the period this book chronicles. The start of my research occurred just a year after Fidel Castro, the leader of the 26th of July Movement (Movimiento 26 de julio, or M-26-7) that overthrew the US-backed Batista regime in 1959, stepped down as president after nearly fifty years in office, due to declining health. When Raúl Castro, his younger brother, stepped in to fill the post, people wondered how the country would shift. The viability of the Soviet model, with its top-down, centralized, and dogmatic forms of control, had been challenged by the demands of increasing incorporation into global circuits of capital. Under Raúl, the Cuban state shifted gears to approximate a "Sino-Vietnamese" model of state capitalism: it retained a powerful single-party state that controls strategic sectors of the economy, while sharing other sectors with domestic and foreign private capitalists (Farber 2013). Raúl stated in his first speech as acting president in 2007: "Revolution means having a sense of our moment in history, it means changing all that ought to be changed." As pledged, adjustments were on the horizon.

The strategic plan issued by the PCC, titled *Los Lineamientos de la política económica y social del partido y la revolución* (The guidelines of economic and social policy of the party and the revolution, 2011), or *Los Lineamientos* (*The Guidelines*) for short, laid out a piecemeal yet significant path toward economic reform. *The Guidelines* prompted the implementation of 130 new policies, the publication of 344 new legal regulations, the modification of 555 existing regulations, and the elimination of 684 regulations that thereafter characterized Raúl Castro's stamp on Cuban history (Castro Ruz 2016). The discourse issuing from the PCC, also headed by Raúl, asserted that these adjustments aimed "to perfect Cuban socialism" for the twenty-first century. With "perfecting" came the solicitation of foreign investment, the expansion of the private market, the adoption of elements of economic rationality to increase "discipline" and "efficiency," and with that, the consolidation and normalization of economic inequality. My eighteen months of sustained doctoral fieldwork in Havana from 2012 to 2014 coincided with the launch of Raúl's *actualización* (update) to the economic model of the Revolution. Five postdoctoral research trips between 2016 and 2018 bore witness to its denouement. Fidel Castro's death in 2016 sealed Raúl's presidency as the symbolic end of one era and the birth of another.

Legal reforms at the national level were articulated alongside changes in international law. Raúl's pledge to bring change to the country was pronounced the same year as the "Law of Historical Memory" was passed in Spain. Under the 2007 law, any Cuban national able to trace a grandparent or great-grandparent in their family to Spain was eligible to establish citizenship based on jus sanguinis, the right of the blood. White Cubans capitalizing on their new birthright to dual citizenship had an advantage as the reforms took effect. The Spanish Consulate in Havana received more than 25,000 applications within the first months of taking effect. They were the descendants of an estimated one million Spaniards who emigrated to Cuba at beginning of the twentieth century, including Fidel and Raúl's father. Of the 500,000 applicants worldwide, 40.7 percent were Cubans, most of whom were phenotypically white (Hansing 2017, 340). Those of Spanish descent with an EU passport found a slew of possibilities for class mobility, including ease of travel abroad without a visa; the option to legally emigrate to Europe while continuing to own property in Cuba, work abroad, and send remittances to their families still living on the island; and the ability to enroll their children in private international schools once restricted to the families of diplomats (Bastian 2018). On the day the first passports were issued in February of 2009, recipients were quoted as being grateful that their ancestors had given them this opportunity, and shouting "Long live Spain!" (Israel 2009), words that would have been socially scorned in the days of revolutionary fervor under Fidel. When the first Cuban to be granted dual citizenship enthusiastically readied himself to retrace the voyage across the Atlantic that his grandfather made in 1916, Cubans of African descent braced for a reversion of different kind. By and large, Black Cubans experienced the "update" as a regression to pre-revolutionary racialized class stratification, logics of competition, and individualistic values that disproportionately favored the already structurally advantaged.

Cubans of African descent had been among the biggest beneficiaries of the Revolution's centralized reordering of society in the 1960s under Fidel. The policy changes of the revolutionary regime, which overhauled the logic of supply and demand to nationalize the productive sectors of the economy, greatly benefited Cuba's poor, among whom Blacks were disproportionately represented. Later, under a survival mode of operation in the 1990s—called the Período Especial en Tiempo de Paz (Special Period [of Wartime Austerity] in Times of Peace)—everyday Cubans needed to constantly *luchar* (to struggle, to fight) to find alternative avenues to acquire hard currency or hustle by any means to survive (Hernández-Reguant 2010). Economic reforms to reopen and fortify the tourist industry resulted in moderate allowances for joint ventures and family-run private businesses, such as hotels, small *paladares* (home-based restaurants), and *casas particulares* (room rentals). As Daniel (2010) notes, in 1991, reports indicated that tourism had even returned to its pre-revolutionary levels, when Cuba was considered the US's backyard playground in the 1950s (Economist Intelligence Unit 1991, 21). Scholars have marked this post-1990 period as one of "recreating racism" or the "erosion of racial equality" in revolutionary Cuba (de la Fuente 2001b, 2001a; Blue 2007; Zurbano 2013). During this time, which some economists refer to as the late socialist era, severe material scarcity and socioeconomic inequalities that prior reforms had sought to upend resurged. The term *tourist apartheid* describes how flows of capital were consolidated in the hands of white Cubans while the forms of *la lucha* practiced by Black Cubans lacking access to remittances were disproportionately criminalized (Fusco 1998; de la Fuente 2001b; Sawyer 2005; Roland 2013). Few Black Cubans had the means to establish tourist-facing businesses of their own. Moreover, they were systematically kept out of more lucrative jobs in the state-run or joint-venture tourism industry on the pretext that foreigners preferred contact with white Cubans or that Black Cubans simply lacked the "good presence" (*buena presencia*) required for such professions (de la

Fuente 2001a). At the same time, a stigma was disproportionately attached to the informal way Black people "hustled" to make a living, labeled *jineterismo* and widely associated with prostitution.

Black people gained limited entry to spaces of commerce as the folkloric entertainment that performed Cuban cultural authenticity, or as Daniel aptly puts it, as "a commodity literally 'in motion'" (2010, 21). Dance floors became market spaces for erotic economies in what Jafari Allen has called "the triangle trade of desire" (2011, 160). Faced with constrained socioeconomic possibilities, men and women of color relied on their ability to perform racialized and gendered tropes in exchange for foreign currency. Blackness functioned as a sign of cultural authenticity, and professional rumba performance satisfied the tropicalist expectations of international consumers (Jottar 2013). In effect, the spotlight on rumba in state tourism coincided with the increased visibility of gendered anti-Blackness and racialized class restratification in revolutionary Cuba.

The state ignored or rationalized these changes in the social fabric of the Revolution—granting impunity for overt forms of anti-Blackness and profiteering—as necessary evils to survive against all odds and protect the revolutionary project from foreign incursion. Those who worked in legal family-owned businesses operated with a *"doble moral"*: on the one hand their economic activities were encouraged by the cash-strapped state, but they were also stigmatized due to the association between private enterprise and capitalist greed (Bastian 2018).

In contrast to Fidel, Raúl Castro's leadership has been described as one of "managerial practicality, dispensing with some anti-market orthodoxies of old" (Bustamante 2018). Notably, mass layoffs in the public sector were paired with the promotion of self-employment, and the significant reduction of state subsidies coincided with an aggressive courting of foreign investment. Hope Bastian (2018) notes in her ethnography on Cubans' everyday adjustments to the economic reforms, "From 2008–2011, state spending for social welfare decreased by $386.2 million" (13). The PCC framed these changes not as a turn toward neoliberalism, but as needed "updates" to the Revolution's economic model.

The update required that Cuban citizens revise their understanding of the state's role, change their "mentalities" and behaviors, and adjust their relationship to each other accordingly (Pañellas Álvarez 2015). In order to relieve the "burden" of the "bloated" state payroll (Frank 2010), Cubans were encouraged to become small, private-business owners (*cuentapropistas*) and entrepreneurs (*emprendedores*). *Granma*, the official newspaper of the PCC, steadily covered the private sector, echoing the broader state discourse promoting the value of individual initiative and personal responsibility, counting on yourself or working on your own behalf (*por su propia cuenta*), rather than for the government. In a special series on the emergent sector (*Granma* 2010), a prominent segment about self-employment (*trabajo por cuenta propria*) boasted the headline, "*La cuenta propia, no la ajena*," which roughly translates as "Self-employment, don't miss out!"[12] Listed in the newspaper were the 178 new forms of legal private occupations, including eighty-three that allowed one to hire their own employees. While these were relatively minor occupations and did not include wholesale activities, people were allowed to hold licenses for multiple occupations at once and thus multiply their revenue streams. Within six months, all licensed occupations were allowed to hire their own employees. In the emergent private sector, *cuentapropistas* would have to answer to their bosses, and those bosses to their investors, all responding to competition, which would ostensibly ensure quality of service, diversity of consumer options, and increase opportunities for consumption for all. In exchange for their salary (determined by what the market would bear), employees were expected to be obedient and submissive to their boss (Pañellas Álvarez 2015, 176). This reproduced relationships of power and exploitation that had been deemed antithetical to the achievement of human dignity under socialism, as stated in the Cuban Constitution (Bastian 2018, 10, 144).

Between 2010 and 2011, according to the Cuban National Statistics Office, the number of private-sector workers rose from 147,400 to 391,500 (Bastian 2018, 12). Given the lingering mistrust around what official registration would entail in the long term, it is safe to assume that the actual number of people informally working in the private sector was much higher. In political speeches and state-controlled mass media, Cubans were ordered to let go of the "laziness" enabled by the inefficiencies and "paternalism" of the prior system and its "unnecessary" state subsidies. Through taxation on official licensing, income, sales, and social security, private-sector actors would contribute their fair share to el pueblo (the people). To realize the projected economic development of the nation, citizens were encouraged to undergo self-reform and become more ambitious, self-sufficient economic agents. While this would be called *neoliberal* in other contexts, that term was not part of the official discourse (Bastian 2018, 7).

The nationwide call for personal reform eerily recalled the 1960s, when Ernesto "Che" Guevara established a template for revolutionary self-making in the figure of "El hombre nuevo" (The New Man) (Guevara [1965]

1967). The central figure of the 1959 Revolution was implicitly a man without class position, racial identification, or religious affiliation. The New Man was driven by concern for the collective good rather than material incentives. His cultivation was supported by new social programs that sought to expunge perceived "impurities" from the body politic. As other scholars have noted, those programs disproportionately targeted Black men and women labeled "deviant" for their racial consciousness and religious affiliation (Benson 2016; Ayorinde 2004). In the case of Black people who were same-gender-loving, Allen asserts, "gender inappropriateness is [was] charged" (2011, 106).

The New Man 2.0 is the term I use to refer to the central actor of the post-Fidel reforms; it similarly implies a racialized and gendered ideal type. He is the entrepreneur featured in local and international media stories that characterize Cuba's move toward national development by focusing on personal drive, hard work, and innovation. In her ethnography of neoliberalism in the Caribbean, Carla Freeman identifies the entrepreneur as the embodiment par excellence of neoliberal reworkings of selfhood in its image (2014). In a similar vein, the self-employed entrepreneur became the new noble revolutionary figure to "perfect" Cuban socialism in the 2010s. Able to generate his own income, the New Man 2.0 did not rely on government rations and thus relieved the state of the "burden" of his welfare. He absorbed risk, wielded technology to compete responsibly in the market, and employed other Cubans to work under his supervision. He knew how to effectively govern his subordinates and provided for his family by responsibly competing with other men in the global marketplace. The *cuentapropista*, as the name suggests, counts on himself.

Notably, this idealized entrepreneurial subject was overwhelmingly white and male. As Bastian (2018) reports, increasingly segregated social networks have led to an overrepresentation of white male, professional, and middle-aged employers in the private sector, a group largely unfettered by labor laws and regulations as they exploit the labor of others. These entrepreneurs either had family abroad, dual citizenship, or were the "son or grandson of" someone with a "historic salary" (middle-class professionals who were allowed to keep their pre-revolutionary salaries to mitigate the brain drain in the 1960s) (Bastian 2018). Alternatively, they were the "son or grandson of" people in leadership positions within the state apparatus, and therefore had what Bastian (2018) calls "revolutionary cultural capital," and thus were put in charge of large-scale joint ventures with foreign investors. In both cases, they were the progeny of those Spaniards whose race licensed them to travel on the decks of the ships crossing the Atlantic, not packed like sardines in their bowels. In these New Man 2.0 discourses, the successful capitalization of neocolonial structures of racial hierarchies, generational wealth, and transnational social networks of access to capital were recoded as virtuous revolutionary business acumen.

Raúl's campaign proved effective in addressing Cubans' consumer desires, fueled by their exposure to the services and goods that tourists could afford, and the agency they wielded, when visiting the island. As Daybel Pañellas Álvarez found in her study of the psychological impact of the reforms, interest in the private sector is related to the sense of autonomy (from the state) that it offers and that many youth crave (Pañellas Álvarez 2015, 176; Bastian 2018, 142). Cuban youth had grown increasingly disenchanted with the project of the socialist revolution due to the devastating economic crises. If they didn't have the means to leave (officially considered as defection), they found ways to survive either through extralegal forms of "struggle" (la lucha) or remittances (Hernández-Reguant 2010). Younger generations of Cubans grew cautiously optimistic about how the emergent economy might improve the quality of life for those who chose to stay. Renewed hope on the part of white Cuban youth was no doubt afforded by family networks abroad, inherited resources, and racial privilege.

Black youth, on the other hand, had compounded reasons to feel frustrated by their limited prospects of social mobility in a plan that normalized conspicuous consumption as moral and rationalized the individualistic market logics and racialized inequality it represents as "progressive" Cuban socialism. This neoliberal discourse diminished the fact that families of African descent were disproportionately dependent on state subsidies due to long-standing structural inequalities. Lack of large monetary inheritances or gifts for startup funds, property ownership, and exclusion from lucrative social networks means that they were systematically least able to insert themselves into the emerging economy and become new New Men and Women. The Guidelines effectively put white families at a structural advantage in terms of access to the funds and resources needed for successful entrepreneurship, creating a new consumer class from which Black Cubans were systematically excluded.

Understandably, when the Ministry of Culture officially recognized rumba as national patrimony in 2012 and state media presented it as part of the government's actions to align with the 2011 United Nation's Year of the Afrodescendant for the benefit of people of African descent, young rumberos viewed the designation cynically. As with previous moments of promoting rumba during times of political and economic crisis, the 2012 nomination of rumba as national patrimony meant that rumba groups like Yoruba Andabo received invitations to perform in more venues throughout the city. However, this heightened emphasis on rumba in the Cuban tourist sector did not bring the kind of material benefits for Black performers themselves that citizens were being encouraged to seize in the marketplace. Rumberos' salaries did not increase even as the cost of living in the capital rose.

When I asked Jenny's goddaughter Tailyn why she thought the genre was receiving a renewed degree of attention from the state at that moment, she rubbed her thumb and pointer finger together and replied, "Because it's good for business." She noted the widespread frustration her peers felt about the struggle of Black cultural producers to benefit from their labor within the public (subsidized)- and private (unsubsidized)-market channels alike. We spoke in Morcilla's living room after one of my lessons as she prepared lunch for Jenny. Tailyn Duperey was a member of the all-female group Rumba Morena, which performed at El Callejón de Hamel (Hamel Alleyway), a venue in the heart of Centro Habana's Cayo Hueso neighborhood that hosted a rumba every Sunday. Morcilla also worked there. El Callejón is an independently managed outdoor performance space and art center, set between walls painted with murals that refer to African-diasporic religious aesthetics. It caters to visitors who wish to experience "Afro-Cuba" in situ (Allen 2011). Performers make money by selling CDs to tourists after their shows. But, Tailyn explained, such sales were never guaranteed and had to be split between all nine members. Sometimes the tourists would load back on their buses without purchasing anything, content with the video and images they captured on their phones as their souvenir. These losses were even more pronounced for groups like hers who did not have access to the same amount of performance venues as their male-led counterparts. From Tailyn's vantage point, the remedy to her dissatisfaction was not resolved through more "access and inclusion" to the private market. Instead, she was skeptical of whose interests private ventures ultimately served. The state's championing of entrepreneurialism stigmatized those, like Tailyn, who doubted its potential as "lazy" and stuck in the past. Ignoring rampant race- and gender-based employment discrimination and the uneven benefits of tourism, failure to thrive in the updated economy, as it was in the Special Period, could be attributed to deep-seated "culture of poverty" rationales rooted in essentialized notions of Black inferiority (de la Fuente 2001b).

After Raúl Castro and Barack Obama's historic simultaneous announcement in 2014 of imminent diplomatic normalization between the two countries, and Obama's impactful visit to the island in 2016 (the first sitting US president to do so since 1928), international news agencies began reporting on racial inequality in the private sector. In a 2017 report by Public Radio International (PRI), "Havana's Business Boom Exposes a Stark Racial Divide," Cuban historian Alejandro de la Fuente stated, "The lack of Black business owners is leading to a stark economic divide between white and Black Cubans, something the socialist government worked hard to erase" (D. Fernandes 2017). Indeed, save for a few exceptions, well known in part because of their rarity, successful Black business owners are few and far between (Rodriguez 2015). Following the lead of anti-racist scholar-activists relentlessly organizing within and beyond state institutions in Cuba, social scientists on both sides of the Florida Strait have taken to studying the worsening of pre-established systems of racialized class stratification (Carrazana Fuentes et al. 2011; Hansing and Hoffmann 2019; de la Fuente 2019). The legal freedom to employ other Cubans (outside of immediate family) in private businesses expanded what Black Cuban anti-racist activist Roberto Zurbano has termed "(neo-)racism" (2011). Although statistical data regarding employment discrimination is difficult to obtain, the language common in employment ads was telling. The return to the coded language of "good presence" was indicative of overt racially biased selection.

While editorials have clearly identified racism, and to a lesser degree sexism, as deleterious consequences of Cuba's market reforms, less ethnographic attention has been brought to bear on how both racism and sexism mutually constitute lived experiences of class oppression on the ground. This intersectional lens allows us to better appreciate the significance of the surge of ads looking for wait staff in revolico.com (the Cuban Craigslist) for the new private restaurants often explicitly specifying that only young white women or *trigueñas* (olive-skin brunettes) need apply, thus reinforcing Eurocentric standards of feminine beauty. In his *New York Times* op-ed, de la Fuente (2019) cites a prime example of the openly sexist and racist job ads that circulate with impunity: "Seeking qualified experienced personnel: waitstaff (good-looking blond or brunette women, who speak foreign languages) and security and protection (strong men of color)." Notably, the growing demand for a burly Black man to flank private businesses and, essentially, keep Black patrons out, epitomized the return to pre-revolutionary practices of de facto segregation and their gendered maintenance. The different constraints and opportunities under which Black women and men labor in the emerging market highlight the gendered nature of the racialized employment barriers and tracking that peso-poor people contended with more broadly post-Fidel. When comparing the differential returns for their labor in updating Cuba, what was "good for business," using Tailyn's words, wasn't necessarily good for all.

Defending Rumba in Havana contributes to our understanding of this moment of post-Fidel "neo-racism" by turning to the analytical frameworks, historical referents, and embodied strategies that poor Black subjects use to negotiate gendered and racialized expectations and exclusions arising from Cuba's development schemes. The "sense of our moment in history" that Raúl referenced in his inaugural speech about the course the Revolution needed to take was quite different from the one rumberas and rumberos shared. Jenny's historical framing was felt in the piercing look she delivered at me with her chastisement: "And as Black women, we have to give ourselves value! Because no one else gives us value." With it, she gestured toward a specific kind of racialized *and* gendered injury that deprived Black women of more dignified life chances at the very moment of Cuban socialism's proclaimed "perfecting." These differential orientations to the history of Cuban nation-building correspond to unique senses about what conditions needed to change in the present and why, and from where power could be derived to legitimize those assertions. A Black feminist lens is paramount for teasing apart the gendered specificity of the corrections, recollections, frustrations, and aspirations conveyed to me by the people I danced alongside.

Worth Defending

"La Gozadera" by Yoruba Andabo was the rumba anthem during this period of socioeconomic change. Yoruba Andabo performances were events that Black inner-city youth in the capital flocked to at every opportunity. Just as the lyrics suggested, "When Yoruba Andabo hits the dance floor, you have to run, you have to run [to get there]." Word spread quickly about the song from those who experienced Yoruba Andabo in person, whether at their weekly matinee at a nightclub in Centro Habana or at a post-ceremony party at a *casa-templo* (household-temple) in neighborhoods throughout the city. It became a hit on the streets well before the release of the group's 2015 recording that would blast on the radio, out of bicitaxis, and at house parties throughout the country. The chorus rang, "*Pon te pa lo tuyo que hasta tú tienes problemas!*" which roughly translates as "Mind your business because even you have problems!" These lyrics may have spoken to how people jealously measured themselves up against others in a heightened competitive

I.4 Yoruba Andabo performance at La Tropical. *From left to right:* Lázaro Monteagudo Lara, Jennyselt Galata, Ronald González Cobas, and Geovani del Pino. Photo by author.

society. However, the reason for the song's popularity, I argue, cannot be derived from the words alone. Embodied methodologies and performance analysis allow us to understand how embodied practice produces its own meaning that, especially in Cuba where state surveillance looms large, necessarily exceeds what is spoken (Guerra 2014).

Geovani's wife was preparing coffee for the group while Yerilú and I sat together to talk at the kitchen table. Yerilú had joined Yoruba Andabo just four months before. She grew up dancing in the storied *comparsa* La Jardinera of the Jesús María neighborhood in Old Havana. Although the comparsas bear the stigma of the same racialized stereotypes assigned to rumba, she took pride in being the descendant of generations of musicians, dancers, and singers who kept alive the traditions of the cabildo processions started by Africans during *el tiempo de la colonia* (colonial times). She excitedly showed me pictures on her phone of her baby girl, who she would likewise raise to carry on her family's cabildo legacy. After slowly moving up the ranks in the comparsa, she eventually joined the Conjunto Folklórico Nacional de Cuba (the National Folkloric Dance Company of Cuba, CFN).

Yerilú attributed her decision to ultimately leave the CFN to her frustration as a new mom and as a dutiful "daughter" of orishas. The demands of working for the state folkloric company left little time and resources to care for her daughter or work ceremonies in her ritual community. She was honored to have been given the opportunity to belong to such an important cultural institution and recalled how she developed as a performing artist on the way to achieving the status of principal singer. She was even able to choreograph parts of the repertory and was proud to have left her mark. But she also felt stunted artistically as she was required to perform in a formulaic fashion, making monotonous what was otherwise a dynamic creative process in ceremony. "In the Conjunto they always ask you to do the same thing. . . . And I realized that I wasn't advancing."

She vividly recounted the day she knew she needed to change professional course to have desenvolvimiento in her life. She was conducting a ritual feeding of her orisha around the time of the anniversary of her initiation into Lucumí priesthood. A message from Eleggúa came demanding that she dedicate herself to performing for religious ceremonies or she would lose her voice and never sing again. Leaving the CFN to join Yoruba Andabo, another state-subsidized ensemble, after returning from maternity leave, represented a way to still work as a professional artist while heeding Eleggúa's call to also prioritize serving her stone family. It was Yoruba Andabo's reputation for being active ritual performers and respected within her religious community that convinced her that the more holistically beneficial path to which she was being divinely guided lay with them.

Although it was delivered in the form of a threat, the message she took away was that devotion to religious labor was the key to saving both the integrity of her voice and her family. Her sense of spiritual and financial well-being was intimately tied to the claim divine forces had on her body, causing her to take the message seriously. "Do you know what I feel every time I sing? It's like a magnetic field around my body. A field in which the only thing that exists is the percussion, the dancer, and myself. A field that covers us, that protects us." Performing with Yoruba Andabo, Yerilú felt her body situated in the same realm of refuge that her ritual kin create for themselves during ceremony in Matanzas, where her family was from. The feeling of protection was what rumba and ceremony formed for her. It also connected her to a social network linking Black neighborhoods throughout the city and new possibilities to care for herself and her family. She'd later invite me to one such ceremony where she was hired to perform as an *akpwón* (lead singer), so I could see, and hopefully feel, what she described.

Similar invitations by other members of Yoruba Andabo would lead me to travel to neighborhoods across Havana where the protective and connective choreo/geography Yerilú attested to was also formed. Directions were always given to me using the public bus routes, so that is how I primarily traveled. Although waiting times were long and unpredictable, causing overcrowding, it was the most affordable way to move throughout the city and therefore the way that was most familiar to them. That is how I came to know coordinates of the capital city far off the tourist map.

The bus stop nearest to where Lekiam Aguilar, a percussionist, lived in Pogolotti was across from a store dedicated to selling the all-white clothing required for the yearlong process of Lucumí priesthood initiation. Pogolotti was a historically working-class Black neighborhood in the municipality of Marianao, renowned for its religiosos. Its reputation grew after the publication of now canonical texts written on the subject by Cuban ethnographer Lydia Cabrera, who conducted her research there in the 1930s and 1940s (Cabrera 1940, 1948, 1954, 1957). Cabrera came from an elite white Havana family and was first exposed to Black culture through her servants, and in particular, her nanny. I found myself walking along the same blocks as Cabrera once did some eighty years later to also conduct ethnography. But rather than being connected through servitude, Lekiam, a drummer in Yoruba Andabo, and I were related by faith. My distant cousin was initiated as a Lucumí priestess in his casa-templo years prior. Lekiam and others in his blood and stone family in Pogolotti taught her husband the sacred batá drums, and taught her the ritual songs that she would later perform as an akpwón for ceremonies in New York City.

When I arrived at the door, a dark-skinned bald woman answered. Her face was full of worry. I introduced myself and politely inquired if I was at the right house. "Does Lekiam live here?" I asked. Just then he appeared from a room in the back. He put his arm around his mother's shoulders and invited me inside. "So, you found it okay?" Given his mother's expression, I couldn't help but wonder if something awful had occurred right before my arrival. Seeing my concern he explained, "She always gets like this when I travel." He was packing for a trip to Mexico to teach a series of percussion master classes. He and his brother, an akpwón, both earned money for the family performing for religious ceremonies throughout the city. Their connections to ritual family around the world led to trips abroad, where they earned money playing at ceremonies and teaching their craft to others. That money would go toward the care of his two children, Arkeli and Aliya, named after his favorite R&B singers. As sure as his mother was that our ancestors were responsible for guiding my cousin and me, although under different pretexts, to their door, she knew that ancestral forces were guiding her son abroad. What she couldn't be sure of was if the spirit guides who had made her son's trip possible had put him on a path that would lead him away from home permanently. She hoped that the spirits would continue to keep him planted here, with her, in Pogolotti.

Lekiam hoped to one day open a music school in his neighborhood for the local boys to formally learn percussion. "The dream for Afro-Cuban culture is that it doesn't lose vitality, and that people continue to defend it," he shared in our conversation. For Lekiam, the music had more than just an artistic value; it was an inheritance that would ensure the well-being of future generations, a benefaction that only they could give to themselves, and that they must protect. In contrast to the Spanish Law of Historical Memory, this inheritance was not written into international law nor linked to nation-state membership. Nonetheless, Lekiam asserted that Black Cubans should value their exclusive claim to the cultural legacy of the cabildos as descendants of the enslaved. It would help them to, like Lekiam, care for their families.

Lekiam stated that this was not the first time that Black Cubans disproportionately bore the brunt of large-scale pivots to strengthen the Cuban economy. As people of African descent, Lekiam asserted, they had a birthright and a timely need to continue to do the same. "In this moment in the world, we are in a situation where the economy is very imbalanced. . . . Our society is losing a lot of our human values. People of color [of African descent] have suffered a lot to achieve what we have, and we have to take care of what we have achieved up until now," he urged. Especially now, with so much else out of reach in society, Black people couldn't afford to take what they had for granted. The embodied wisdom of their enslaved ancestors was an inheritance worth defending. His active relationship with copresences equipped him with a racial consciousness that he used to analyze the current economic inequities. Like Yerilú, Lekiam's faith ultimately provided the analytical framework, networks, and resources for navigating, and even mitigating, the update's pernicious trappings. Perhaps this ancestral vocation was the business signaled in the lyrics that Yoruba Andabo's followers were inspired to mind.

Yet, this refuge should not be construed as an egalitarian utopia of another kind. As much as the sacred is central to assertions of dignity, more often compensation for labor, not equality, is the goal. Along the way, it also reproduces power imbalances, exclusions, and tensions across difference that I try to lay bare and grapple with. For instance, in chapter two, we

The second chapter, "Black Feminist Aptitudes," takes dance pedagogy as a point of entry into how Black women theorize their movements and the relationship of those improvisations to broader structural constraints. Although I was a paying foreign student, my own body was often appraised by the same colonial heterosexist logics as those of my teachers. I think with the constrained improvisational techniques I was coached to master, to flesh out how rumberas experience and understand their uniquely raced and gendered position in the market vis-à-vis fellow rumberos, state administrators, private-business owners, and tourists. The conscious rehearsal of essentialized tropes of Black womanhood sedimented in slavery inspired me to consider rumba as a technique of dissemblance, situating its choreographies of seduction and refusal within a Black feminist tradition. Sacred epistemological and choreographic repertoires become critical tools for negotiating power, mitigating risk, asserting self-worth, and demanding compensation.

Chapter 3, "Sacred Swagger and Its Social Order," explores how sacred choreographies of Black masculinity and conceptualizations of sovereign territory coded during slavery are conjured and linked in rumba. The way rumba groups showcase the genre's Abakuá heritage, and the controversary of its simultaneous popular appeal for Black male youth and rejection by dominant white society, highlights the politics of virtuous manhood and social order in Cuba. These old contentions were heightened as New Man 2.0 discourses normalized claims to private property that protect forms of racialized economic exclusion. The swagger of Abakuá sacred fraternities is theorized as repositioning Black male youth vis-à-vis structural economic barriers and their essentialized association with social danger.

While market-oriented reforms put Black peso-poor households at a systemic disadvantage, religious duties and networks afford rumberos resources to "save their families." In chapter 4, "Moving Labor across Markets," I analyze how rumberas and rumberos maximize their economic agency by moving between folkloric display and ritual duty. This close analysis of how rumberas and rumberos labor across normative conceptions of sacred and the profane, public and private, also reveals how gendered norms of embodied devotion and divine reciprocity shape the different capacities poor Black people leverage to navigate shifting market logics. Desenvolvimiento, I argue, provides a bottom-up counterpoint to the national development plan (*plan de desarrollo*), rather than arguing for more inclusion within it.

Chapter 5 is a meditation on the choreographies of fugitive assembly that rumba inspires in public. "Underworld Assembly" situates an atypical (though far from singular) night at a public theater within the changing social landscape of "updating" Havana. Wherein middle-class whites increasingly flee to burgeoning private-business establishments, the possibility of spiritual immanence in the state-owned venues accessible to peso-poor Blacks beckons deeper consideration of a Black radical imaginary and praxis beyond "resistance." A dance analytics allows for consideration of these constrained improvisations in broader hemispheric relation and their Black feminist potentialities.

The concluding chapter looks to the process behind the nomination of rumba to the UNESCO Representative List of Intangible Cultural Heritage of Humanity as a way to return to some of the main contributions and commitments of the Black corporeal undercommons. It also draws out the necessary attunements a Black feminist posture is poised to practice in Cuba and beyond.

The epilogue, a narrative of my reunion with Jenny in 2022, presents recent developments since the onset of the COVID-19 pandemic and connects them to people introduced and themes raised in the ethnography.

1 BLACK INCLUSION, BLACK ENCLOSURE

Cuban artists, particularly rumberos,
need and deserve ... a loose hold.

YVONNE DANIEL, *Rumba*

"The Song of the Fatherland Is Our Song," announced Monday's headline in the cultural section of *Granma* on March 3, 2014 (de la Hoz 2014). The article described the welcome-home concert for Fernando González, the most recently released political prisoner of the "Cuban Five" who were sentenced for espionage in the United States.[1] The concert, billed as "El Concierto por los Cinco" (Concert for the Five), honored the five men who, revered in Cuba as national heroes, had become household names. The televised spectacle also served as an international demonstration of the strength and conviction of Cuba's next generation to similarly defend the revolutionary cause with their lives. "Everything was said, as it should be, Saturday night on the university grand staircase," the article began. "From culture came the call and to culture it went." The journalist, Pedro de la Hoz, head of *Granma*'s Culture Department, described the free open-air concert featuring rock, *trova*, spoken word, rumba, *son*, and *timba* as a reaffirmation of the "unbeaten tune of the Fatherland." While the article praised the other live performers for their artistry and even cited their lyrics, which poetically spoke to the momentous occasion, the mention of the rumba act was markedly different. "Rumba sent off spears into the night with Yoruba Andabo," it started.

Watching the concert live on TV from the apartment where I lived in Centro Habana, the racialized connotation of metaphorical "spears," a symbol of the primitive, was not lost on me. Centro Habana was categorized as a "disadvantaged neighborhood" by the Cuban Center for Psychological and Sociological Research (CIPS), illustrating how Blackness fell within the geographical segregation of class in the city (Espina Prieto et al. 2004; Martín Posada and Núñez Moreno 2013). "You have to see how they project themselves and act," the *Granma* article continued. But rather than following with a concrete description of the rumberos' actual actions that night on stage, it drew attention to their symbolic value as "women and men of the people," followed by the projection of thoughts onto their artistic director: "It is almost certain that Geovani del Pino, their director, is remembering their days of blood and sweat on the productive fronts and in the fight to dignify the great humility of their origin." The exact temporal location of his presumed memory of "blood and sweat" was left ambiguously open, but the article succeeded in framing the rumberos as of, if not in, the past. On the concert stage curated to project Cuba's unbeaten strength to the world, they embodied, it would seem, the triumphant underdog narrative of the proletariat under socialism: "Women and men of the people," humble of origin yet dignified through the productivity of their grueling physical labors for the nation. This depiction of rumberos redeemed through their physical sacrifice is, in Ann Stoler's (2002) words, "easy to think" because it had been sedimented into the popular Cuban imaginary long before through the (neo)colonial archive (100). This ostensibly self-evident televised spectacle of Black inclusion underscored the virtue of the Cuban Five's mission to protect the Fatherland from imperialist sabotage. Like the sonic spear thrown into the night air, rumba has been situated as a trace of the African past in Cuba's revolutionary present—a dark past that is conditionally absolved by its utility for nation-building.

Granma's write-up about Yoruba Andabo on the iconic steps of the University of Havana harkens back to one of the dominant ways in which Black people, and by extension, their dances, have been called, or rather "hailed," into Cuban cultural nationalism, subjects of its ideological state apparatus. For the Cuban creole elite, Black people dancing rumba gained social legitimacy (and legibility) over time through their use-value for nation-building. By 2014, amid Cuba's economic "update" for the twenty-first century, the inclusion of rumba on a high-profile occasion like a national hero's homecoming could only evidence the Cuban Revolution's full inclusion of the formerly oppressed "humble masses": an embodiment of a progressive racial politics which can be traced back through Cuba's protracted struggle for sovereignty. Geovani, Yoruba Andabo's artistic director, himself a resident of Centro Habana, was an auspicious vessel for this noble national narrative.

Later that same week, I spoke with one of the rumberos who performed that night. I wondered what it must have felt like to perform rumba on such

1.1–1.2 Watching "El Concierto por los Cinco." Photos by author.

a huge platform, knowing the whole nation was watching. We had both arrived early and were waiting for the rest of the group to show up to perform at their weekly matinee showcase at Cabaret Las Vegas in Centro Habana. When I asked about his experience of the nationally televised welcome-home concert, he smirked and blew out cigarette smoke in a slow exhale. Far from reminiscing nostalgically about their blood and sweat for the nation, he replied, "You know they didn't pay us for that. We had important [religious] work that we had to cancel." What they called *trabajos diplomáticos* (diplomatic gigs), performances for the government, felt like onerous, if not exploitative, obligations. For him, as well as other rumba performers, these symbolic national demonstrations paled in comparison to the material importance of performing at religious ceremonies in their neighborhoods.

Nationalistic tropes about rumba circulating in official discourse maintain the kind of tight hermeneutical hold on rumberos that Yvonne Daniel laments. Importantly, they have silenced other meaningful aspects of rumba's relationship to the project of Cuban nation-building that have also been salient for the practitioners themselves. Daniel (2011) affirms that this is not unique to Cuba. In the Caribbean more broadly, what gets chosen as nationally representative dance culture says more about what those in power think about themselves in relationship to what certain values symbolize in specific historical conditions (92). Even if done with the best of intentions, it remains challenging to discern and integrate the views and estimations of the powerless within those preferences (91). In the context of Cuba's latest market-oriented reforms, the official discourse defining rumba as the embodiment, par excellence, of Cuban racial democracy rang even more dissonant. Dancing for the nation, as the *Granma* article purported, represented a limited view of the purpose their embodied labor fulfilled. It was clear to me that, contrary to what the PCC newspaper claimed, everything was *not* said about Yoruba Andabo's performance that spring night in 2014. Instead, only a partial, popularized story about rumba was repeated from the perspective of those most invested in "the nation" as a social and political construct.

I make the case that although rumberos may have sung aloud on stage that night, that which did not adhere to a familiar, hegemonic story about the Cuban national project as their sole raison d'être remained inaudible. Inclusion of rumberos into the national body politic has prompted both pride and ambivalence. This ambivalence registers the contradictory history of racial politics in Cuba, even long before the 1959 Revolution, which has followed a pattern of "inclusionary discrimination" (Sawyer 2005). In other words, racial hierarchy determines the terms of inclusion such that improvements occur alongside enduring discrimination (19). Indeed, national belonging has continually hinged on a strategic disavowal of Black affective ties and political vision in exchange for citizenship and secular-liberal personhood. Yet, and still, the practice of rumba, and its embodiment of a Black corporeal undercommons, has always destabilized official discourses and mapped its own coordinates of belonging. The perpetuation of the grand narrative of Black inclusion into the national fold, afforded by a rebel, racially progressive state, obscures how rumberos have had to navigate their own belonging to and defense of communities that exceed the liberal, statist political project.[2]

This chapter puts rumberos' contemporary negotiations with the figurative use-value of their physical labor for Cuban nation-building into the context of a larger history of enclosure. I build on Damien Sojoyner's (2017) formulation of "enclosed space" to reference the punitive containment of the Black corporeal undercommons by elites, literally and figuratively, to incorporate obedient and nonthreatening constructions of racial, gender, and sex difference, through the normalization of limiting tropes. Importantly, as Sojoyner emphasizes in relationship to the public educational system in the United States, this process of forced containment, which accompanies a process of evisceration, happens under the guise of liberal beneficence. Thinking about the nationalization of rumba as a process of Black enclosure, rather than "uplift," allows us to historically situate the compulsory and fraught performance of allegiance that state performances also represent for rumberos. I do this by examining the social and political conditions in which certain enduring tropes of Black people dancing were produced and normalized by white elites. At the same time, I illustrate how Africans and their descendants often capitalized on the biases, misrecognitions, and ignorance of those in power to hide the social meanings and political purposes of their dances, maintaining loyalties to sacred Black community in plain sight. Just as Sojoyner does in thinking through the Black radical planning and action that inform the counterweight to enclosure, I turn to Tina Campt's (2017) Black feminist notion of fugitivity, "not as an act of flight or escape or strategy of resistance," but foremost as a quotidian, creative "practice of refusing the terms of negation and dispossession" (96). In short, Black practitioners made daily calculated exchanges, taking up without internalizing the dominant semiotic coding of their embodied labor for strategic material gain. We can then productively appreciate rumba as a fugitive cultural repertoire born from the ways that poor and working-class Black people creatively danced with Cuban statecraft. This social choreography, to build on Cox (2015), protected the Black corporeal undercommons from evisceration.

An effort to defuse the threat of Black autonomy undergirds appraisals of Black popular dance from the nineteenth century to the present. Descriptions of the dances of the Black corporeal undercommons abound in nineteenth-century accounts of the Día de Los Reyes, Kings Day, festivals on January 6, when the enslaved were permitted to take to the streets in music, dance, and song. Colonial functionaries and elites derided these Black spectacles as monotonous and savage, yet allowed them as necessary for the prevention of slave rebellion. The criminological diagnosis of an "Afro-Cuban underworld" that threatened the social health of the nascent Cuban Republic gave way in the 1920s and 1930s to the valorization of selected aesthetic elements from the Black domain that were deemed to be "cultural" and thus of value for the construction of an autochthonous *cubanidad*.

However, there has been little recognition that the state's secular liberal politics of racial inclusion was deeply at odds with the practitioners' understanding of their artistry as forming part of a broader diasporic political community spanning time and space. These constrained and calculated terms of inclusion reified colonial constructions of racialized gender and downplayed the role of the sacred in underwriting a distinctive sense of personhood, place, and belonging. Effectively, in nationalizing rumba, to extend Robin D. Moore's (1997) productive formulation, the embodied practice was distanced from the politics of sacred subjectivity, a characterization that continued into the post-1959 revolutionary era. Yoruba Andabo is most directly linked to this history of Black enclosure through tracing the specific gendered tensions attendant with incorporating the dances of the "Carabalí" African cabildos into the Cuban racial state.[3] Enclosed within a national trope, practitioners today still contend with the enduring common sense about what rumba means.

In analyzing through a Black feminist lens how Black people dancing have been understood and policed accordingly at key points in the trajectory of Cuban nation-building, this chapter highlights the importance of the relationship between epistemology and power in mapping the Black corporeal undercommons.[4] More specifically, this chapter thinks through, as Tariq Jazeel (2014) has argued, how the universalizing concept-metaphor of the sacred-secular binary obscures radical political geographies. Indeed, the modern system of sacred-secular classification and state formation has structured disciplinary thinking about rumba in Cuba, allowing it to be understood as a secular expression of national patrimony. Crucial for troubling this common sense is Saba Mahmood's poignant call to scrutinize the precise form that embodied actions take for the way they contribute to a particular kind of political subject, and for how such scrutiny reveals the terms of discourse through which politics can be understood (Mahmood 2004, 24). Therefore, I tease out the raced, gendered, and secularist terms of discourse applied to rumba throughout Cuban history to make a case for understanding what rumba practitioners form beyond the spatial imagination of the nation-state project.

"The Illusion of Freedom" in Colonial Cuba

Perhaps the most frequent adjective used to describe the dances of the enslaved in the nineteenth century was "monotonous." Dolores María Ximeno y Cruz, born in 1866 to a wealthy family in the Matanzas region of Cuba, penned one of the earliest descriptions of a street rumba during a Kings Day festival in Matanzas. In her "Memorias de Lola Maria," she writes, "The cabildo went out in the streets playing music and dancing beneath the windows of rich people's houses. The dances were done in pairs, the woman with her skirt pulled up with both hands, making dashes and leaps and escapes . . . culminating in an unbridled dance of jumps and skips or falling in the other extreme, an enervating monotony" (Martínez Rodríguez 1995, 140). Whereas I relish this early record of a rumbera's artistic virtuosity, she is eclipsed by the gaze of the writer who reduces her movements to a waste of energy, thus inscribing her in the colonial archive. What whites considered to be the repetitive and haphazard movements of Blacks to relentlessly chaotic rhythms were tantamount to madness.

The disdain for Black people and their "African cultural baggage" is palpable in the writing of this era. Fernando Ortiz culls these nineteenth-century newspapers, memoirs, and travelogues, and quotes them at length in his twentieth-century studies of what he later terms "Afro-Cuban culture." In the colonial era, Black music and dance was, in many ways, the clearest sign of an essential difference between Europeans and Africans. An account from 1866 denotes how the sight of Black people dancing was anathema for the civilized: "All half-naked . . . in their different groups, form the most repugnant sight possible to the eyes of civilized man. . . . Some play the discordant instruments already mentioned above, that are damaging to the hearing, while other wretches dance feverishly, contorting their bodies in such a way as to be offensive to the sight" (Ortiz [1920] 2001, 9). Black expressive culture was viewed as an assault on the senses, both on hearing and on sight, the privileged tool for meaning making since the Enlightenment.

At the same time, it was primarily through sight that white onlookers sought to rationalize the utility of this form of Black assembly within the world order they sought to maintain. "It is easy to see, just by looking, the state the bodies of these individuals are in after twelve hours of continuous exercise so strenuous that many cannot continue into the afternoon. And yet they all get something out of it and enjoy themselves in their own way, even if only one day of the year" (Ortiz [1920] 2001, 8). These words, published in the *Prensa de la Habana* on January 6, 1859, and quoted by Ortiz, represent how white onlookers attempted to make sense of—which is to make peace with—the sight of enslaved people dancing at the yearly Día de Los Reyes festival in Havana. On this one day of the year, the cabildos de nación were permitted to flood the streets of the city and enjoy "above all the illusion of freedom, in an orgy of ritual, dance, music, song, and cane spirit" (Ortiz [1920] 2001, 1). The comparsas or processions of the cabildos fueled the white elites' imagination and projections of their lewd fantasies and awesome fears. One journalist in 1842 reported on "the sumptuousness of the negro women of the nation" (Ortiz [1920] 2001, 11), while another writer noted that "all the gross and barbaric imagination of the African tribes was carried to the extreme with the *ñáñigo* [pejorative nomination for the male member of a cabildo Carabalí] . . . [who] did as they pleased" (5). If monotonous, the rhythms had a way of raising gendered racial anxieties of Black women and men run amok.

Masters in the New World knew that Africans were not a homogenous, undifferentiated mass. In contrast to the British slave system, Spanish law allowed for the organization of associations by free and enslaved Blacks. The cabildos, modeled after the Spanish *cofradías* (religious brotherhoods or fraternities), were given the names *Lucumí* (encompassing the Yoruba-speaking people), *Congo* (referencing the Kikongo-speaking people of Bantu origin), and *Carabalí* (referring to the Efik-speaking people hailing from the Cross-River Delta region), to name the most prominent associations. By grouping Africans who shared a degree of language and approximate region of origin, authorities established a means of officializing cultural difference and distinct identities in the New World. For the planter class in Cuba, which drew on colonial practices of the Catholic Church, cabildos were a mechanism of social control: divide and conquer (Barcia Zequeira, Rodríguez Reyes, and Niebla Delgado 2012). They buttressed a notion of distinct African ethnic identities, "each in their different groups," in the effort to deter the bonds of solidarity necessary for mass revolt. The public processions of the cabildos were seen as instrumental in sustaining the naturalized colonial order of things. Dancing with one's own kind, it would seem, made the body more docile to racial domination.

While the physical condition of their bodies, brutalized by slave labor, was "easy to see, just by looking," the motivation behind engaging in such "feverish" movement was seemingly also self-evident. "The negros in Cuba have no greater joy at any other time in the year than the Day of Holy Kings. They spill out in all directions *like a black cloud over the city*. . . . [S]lave servants . . . those who have achieved their freedom also partake. . . . [A]ll, in short, snatch these moments of madness from the heavy yoke that is their fate. *Because man . . . needs a certain palliative to strengthen the spirit as to bear the bitterness of existence*" (Ortiz [1920] 2001, 9–10, emphasis added). These accounts tell of Black people, both enslaved and free, wreaking havoc on European aesthetic sensibilities. They made raucous noise and contorted their bodies in ways that qualitatively transformed—darkened—the built environment of the streets of Havana, "like a black cloud over the city." And yet, these repugnant cultural spectacles would ensure the release of a pressure valve, so that they could continue to bear their bitter existence. According to this logic, curtailing such moments of cathartic identitarian expression could have devastating repercussions for maintaining Cuban slave society.

Once the Cuban planter class arose as the major world producer of sugar after enslaved and free Blacks overthrew the French colonial regime in Saint-Domingue, it did not want to risk prohibiting Blacks this "illusion of freedom." Since they saw the Haitian Revolution as a reaction to a regime that excessively curbed forms of social outlet, Cuban colonial functionaries permitted these contained yearly occasions for public Black assembly to continue (Childs 2006). As early as 1790, Diego Miguel de Moya wrote to His Majesty that the Blacks are inclined to "dance in the barbarous styles of their countries . . . and if this [right] is denied them, it will cause irresistible pain and produce bad consequences" (Childs 2006, 106). Miguel de Moya was able to gather the signatures of "almost all of the masters of sugar plantations in this jurisdiction" in his petition to give the enslaved the right to celebrate such holidays on the explicit grounds of saving themselves, the planters, from the enslaved's collective resentment (Childs 2006, 36). If not given this illusion of freedom, Blacks would—as in Haiti—make their freedom real.

When circulated in writing, the discourse of protecting the recreational release mechanism of the enslaved enclosed the meaning of Black popular dance within colonial bounds of reason. A limited sense of autonomy and a strong sense of ethnic difference, they concluded, would stave off rebellion. Ortiz, quoting a passage from 1843, noted that the Blacks were free for a day "and yet none forgetful of his respective duty [to his master]" ([1920] 2001, 8–9). In effect, this colonial archive inscribed a common sense about how to understand the fact of Black people dancing in a way that supported racial slavery. To the white elites' imagination, the subordination of the enslaved and free people of color alike would be bearable if they were allowed corporeal expression.

The collective political imaginary of cabildo membership, however, far exceeded what the colonial regime had calculated. Contrary to what masters could perceive, cabildo processions were not moments of distraction from structural oppression, but instead served political, ideological, economic, and spiritual purposes for their constituencies. Far from dampening Black aspirations, they saw their participation in the cabildo as a pathway to both individual and collective liberation (Childs 2006, 36). Cabildo dance functions played a key role in forging solidarity among and across divisions of ethnicity, color (Black or *mulato/a*, meaning mixed-race, as delineated in the *régimen de castas*), Cuban (*criollo*) versus African-born (*bozal*), slave, free, and fugitive status. Within the cabildo governance structure, the importance placed on knowledge of African language and customs, and specifically the social value placed on being African-born, reversed the colonial structure of social hierarchy that privileged proximity to whiteness. Moreover, cabildo functions were occasions for fundraising, collecting fees and donations from members and spectators alike, to meet the material needs of the "nation." Cabildos effectively operated as mutual aid societies providing health care, boarding, burial expenses, and funds for *coartación* (self-paid manumission), and networks for the refuge of fugitives. African ancestry and African-inspired practices of praise became political, spiritual, and financial resources for Black self-organization.

In short, practices of self-making were grounded in spirit-based, embodied belief systems of the Black Atlantic diaspora. "Dancing wisdom" is what Daniel (2005) calls these Black diasporic vernacular systems of knowledge espoused in Cuba (as well as Haiti and Brazil) encoded in bodily techniques and aesthetic patterns. The dances of the cabildos cultivated and celebrated alternative ways of knowing through the body and modes of kinship relation through rites of initiation. Aesthetics and kinesthetics efficaciously communicated across the borders of the human and more-than-human, bridging bloodlines decimated by the slave trade, and creating viable networks of support and accountability. Songs, rhythms, and movement connected humans, ancestors, nature, and divine forces in a sense of homeland sedimented through social relations of reciprocity. Of course, white observers were skeptical, stated a journalist in 1842, of "the veneer of religious solemnity they give to these profane acts" (Ortiz [1920] 2001, 11).

Importantly, these embodied, spiritual epistemologies affirmed alternate ways for racially subordinated people to know themselves and recognize each other beyond their colonial status designations designed to divide and dominate the majority non-white populace under white supremacy (Concha-Holmes 2013; Childs 2006). Cabildo members initiated each other into networks of support, families of stone, that sustained Black life in the New World (Barcia Zequeira 2003, 2012). They formed the basis for a sense of identity on their own terms and for their own ends. The cabildo processions publicly displayed these spiritual affiliations and, in so doing, mapped the contours of this terrain they laid claim to through their bodies. Moments of danced drumming during enslavement such as these, as in Brazil, have been called "spaces of refuge in thunder" or alternative spaces of Blackness (Harding 2003).

On this basis, I understand the dances of the cabildos as being the earliest markers of a Black corporeal undercommons. As a set of social relations, rather than a physical site (Harney and Moten 2013), the Black corporeal undercommons extended beyond the walls of the cabildo or the temporal delineation of the comparsa proper, to more generally include the choreo/geography of cooperative Black sociality over time. While the processions of the cabildos on Kings Day may have ephemerally remapped the streets of the capital, momentarily changing the sense of the place for whites ("like a black cloud over the city"), the dancing wisdom cultivated through the cabildos themselves allowed the formerly enslaved to situate themselves differently in place and in relation to each other. Katherine McKittrick (2011) calls this a Black sense of place. This embodied mapping practice also afforded them material resources to pursue possibilities that the hegemonic design for Black life in the New World had depreciated. In this formulation, popular dance cues us to an alternate space in which Black people dwelled in colonial Cuba. The Black corporeal undercommons engendered a more affirming relation among Africans and people of African descent during slavery, and simultaneously embodied the specter of slavery's undoing.

Indeed, as historians have shown, cabildos were not only sites of Black diasporic self-making, but key hubs in the formation of racial solidarity and organizing of antislavery rebellion (Childs 2006; Finch 2015). Cabildo networks were critical for providing refuge and other forms of aid to fugitives (Deschamps Chapeaux 1983). As Matt D. Childs (2006) shows in his history of the 1812 Aponte Rebellion, the fact that Cuban-born people of African descent would voluntarily participate in associations led by the African-born troubled the slaveowners' belief that subsequent generations of people of color would consider themselves culturally removed from Africa, and therefore have no stake in building common cause in antislavery rebellion (98–99). In her study of the *La Escalera* conspiracy of 1843–1844, Aisha Finch (2015) argues that it was the whites' "colonial myopia" that led them to perceive these dances as simply indulgent fantasy "play," when in fact the makings of rebellion were on full display. For instance, cabildos would elect leadership, bestowing them with royal titles like "king" or "queen," often based on specific roles in conspiracies in the making (160–161). Then they would unveil these insurgent roles to those in the know during the public processions.[5]

Scholarship within the field of Black diaspora studies has argued that Black cultural politics in the 1800s was constituted by a sense of shared subjectivity conditioned by relative proximity to the brutality of plantation life. By the same token, it can be defined through a "consciousness of kind" or "diasporic identification" forged through common struggle against the racial oppression of colonial slave society (Howard 1998; Gordon and Anderson 1999). Anthropologists of Yoruba-inspired religion have likened this Black Atlantic cultural politics practiced in the Americas to Ong's (1999) notion of a "transnational cultural citizenry" (Concha-Holmes 2013; Castor 2017). However, I propose that the secular-liberal notion of "citizenship" is tied too narrowly to the logics of the nation-state, thus inadvertently dwarfing what was a more uniquely diasporic conception of political consciousness and belonging animated by copresences (Beliso-De Jesús 2014) that defy modern geopolitical concept-metaphors.

The formerly enslaved's critical engagement with the promises of modern statehood might be taken seriously as a feminist pedagogy of crossing (Alexander 2005). After all, women had an important role in the cabildos, often constituting a decisive force in internal elections of cabildo leadership (with the exception of the cabildos Carabalí, discussed below) (Childs 2006). This calls us to consider the gendered grounds upon which cabildo conceptions of polity were constituted. It also urges us, as Finch argues, to reconsider the gendered terrain of political organization more broadly. Knowing the role of cabildo dances in antislavery rebellion, and the importance of copresences and women therein, we might be inclined to think back on Ximeno y Cruz's colonial account of the Black woman, "with her skirt pulled up with both hands, making dashes and leaps and escapes" as a rehearsal of fugitive choreography "beneath the windows of rich people's houses" or rather, beyond what the white gaze was positioned to see.

Black people dancing together both concealed and revealed the kinds of insurgent possibilities they sought to change their terrible fate. Rumba, then, becomes a way to trace the markers of the Black corporeal undercommons to the spaces that Black people bodied forth for themselves during slavery, be it in the clearings in the cane fields, in the slave barracks, at the ports, or on the city streets (Sublette 2004). The disparate positionalities from which their repetitive movements were observed in Cuban slave society established the tensions at play when Black people and their dances were officially included within the project of Cuban nationalism.

The Afro-Cuban Underworld

In the years before official abolition in 1886, thousands of freed Blacks flooded to the major cities seeking to escape their servitude in the countryside. The ruling elites foresaw the need to tame the illusion of freedom granted to the cabildos. They ordered cabildos to "divest themselves of their African names, paraphernalia, and rituals and to reconstitute themselves as Spanish-style mutual aid societies or social clubs," and "break the longstanding links between the cabildos and the African-based religions of Abakuá, Santería, and Palo Monte" (Andrews 2004, 122). Toward this end, in 1884, they were banned from drumming, dancing, and parading publicly. However, to the dismay of the Cuban political elite, "Africa" had already moved into the capital's urban slums. After Cuba won its independence from Spain in 1898, when Black comparsas took to the streets, they were a testament to the endurance of cabildo cultures among the Black working-class. These "repugnant African spectacles" linked Cuba with its colonial past and detracted from the "civility" of the modern nation that elites sought to assert.

Havana's Black slums, hubs of rumba, became one focal point of negrophobic anxiety. Echoed in the social science of the day, the dances of the Black corporeal undercommons were a signifier of African backwardness and invited the continued negation of the formerly enslaved's full humanity after emancipation. Newspaper articles and editorials called for an end to Cuba's "Africanization." A 1916 editorial penned by one military officer, Castillo Boloy, succinctly captures the sentiment of white elites in the early Cuban

Republic: Blacks who knew how to prove "I am a human being, I am not a thing" (referencing those who fought on the battlefields of the Independence Wars) knew that "rights are not achieved in rumbas nor in comparsas . . . but rather in becoming cultured" (Moore 1997, 71). The assertion juxtaposes two orientations that Blacks assumed after emancipation: an ostensibly iniquitous politics of Black cultural difference versus an ostensibly virtuous politics of cultural assimilation to Euro-Western norms. Rumberos represented the former: those Blacks who stubbornly maintained identification with and allegiances to their African "nations" of origin. They refused the virtuous path of "civilization," which was to reserve their bodies exclusively for service to Cuban nation-building. While entrenched anti-Blackness set the terms of citizenship in the Cuban Republic, rumba was a marker of the Black corporeal undercommons, that which produced the kind of social relations that exceeded the bounds of the white-led secular liberal racial state.

Praise of rumberos in the twenty-first century that use allusions to Black people's laboring bodies as virtuously productive for nation-building, as in the *Granma* article that opens this chapter, must be understood within this dichotomy established during Cuba's unique path to abolition and independence, between the "wayward labor" (Harney and Moten 2013, 32) of the maroon versus the dignifying labor of the citizen. The path for Blacks to dignity was indelibly charted by a minority white ruling class reliant on Black manpower, and thus forced to adopt a politics of racial inclusion. Despite white people's fear of losing political hegemony, when José Martí, a white man of Spanish parentage, argued in the late nineteenth century that Cuba's then majority Black population was the insurgent nation's secret weapon in the fight for freedom from Spain, the effort to include Blackness within the body politic became paramount for Cuban independence. His thesis was that any racial resentments Black men retained from slavery would dissolve by fighting side by side with whites on the battlefield (Ferrer 1999). Desperately, in 1868, planter elites in Cuba's western territories freed their enslaved in exchange for Black male enlistment in the Liberation Army, promising them citizenship and suffrage in the new nation. Some attest that as many as 60–75 percent of the soldiers in the Liberation Army were Black or mulato, and they were represented in even the highest echelons of military hierarchy after proving their skill and bravery in battle (Ferrer 1999, 204; Moore 1997, 21). Spain also granted freedom to the enslaved as part of its own military recruitment campaign. As a result, most of the male enslaved population in Cuba gained freedom by fighting in the Wars of Cuban Independence, greatly accelerating legal abolition in 1886, sixteen years prior to the official dawn of the new Republic in 1902. Whereas for whites it became undeniable that Black participation was vital to achieving Cuban sovereignty, for the enslaved nation-building was the most viable pathway to emancipation (Ferrer 1999).

At the same time, Black political aspirations had to be kept in their rightful place. The "race problem" made Cuba politically vulnerable to imperial overtures from the United States. Serious limitations on Cuba's sovereignty had already been inscribed in the Cuban Constitution via the Platt Amendment. The *miedo al negro* (fear of the Black), a holdover from the colonial era haunted by the specter of the Haitian Revolution, evolved into a fear of being perceived as a "Black Republic" by the "Family of Nations" within which Cuban political elites sought belonging (Helg 1995). Ridding Cuba of the "stain of Africa" was key for proving the viability of the Cuban nation-state as a project.

Coming out of slavery with a majority Black population as a result of the massive scale of the plantation economy, the ruling class doubled its efforts to "whiten" the population and culture (Andrews 2004). After gaining independence, Cuba joined countries such as Argentina, Brazil, Venezuela, and Uruguay in waging a "whitening" campaign, wherein lawmakers instituted immigration reform to subsidize the relocation of whites from Spain and other parts of Europe to Latin America. These policies guaranteed newly arrived Europeans land ownership, employment, and political representation at the expense of Black Cubans (Andrews 2004). Black Cubans, on the other hand, were relegated to the least skilled and most poorly paid positions and were treated as second-class citizens. This Social Darwinist effort to engineer the population complemented the policy of suppression of Black popular culture, classified as "witchcraft" (*brujería*). In conjunction with other urban reforms to "modernize" the cities' infrastructure, Cuba publicly demonstrated its fitness for self-rule.

The homosocial vision of racial harmony among men under Cuban nationalism that Martí inspired effectively endeavored to keep the dangerous excesses of Black strength at bay, predicated on the reproduction of the colonial racial hierarchy. Therefore, Cuba's progressive history of racial inclusion from its birth as a nation—granting voting rights to Black men and deciding against de jure segregation—goes hand in hand with concerted efforts to diminish, manage, and actively suppress African identification and thus to enclose Black political will under white leadership.

Much scholarship has documented the rich culture of self-organization and activism Black Cubans fashioned to meet their needs and pursue their own political aspirations in the face of continued structural racism after independence (Fernández Robaina 1994; Helg 1995; de la Fuente 2001a; Guridy 2010; Pappademos 2011). Those needs and aspirations were far from homogenous and often differed along lines of class, culture, gender, and region. In the process, they forged diasporic communities of exchange and dialogue that solidified a sense of supra-national identification in the shadow of US empire, what Frank Guridy (2010) calls diaspora in action. Black political communities in the twentieth century were diverse in strategy and included those who worked within, challenged, and moved beyond the structures of the liberal democratic institutions of the Cuban state (Pappademos 2011).

In the words of Jafari Allen, Black mutual aid societies (those extending from cabildos, such as Abakuá societies, in particular) gained their power among Black popular classes precisely because "they stood in the gap where the state had failed" (2011, 124). To this I would add, not only did they stand in that gap, they danced. In some ways, we might perceive the Black corporeal undercommons in the dances hosted by the *sociedades de color*. Dances facilitated these societies' ability to carry out the social functions that cabildos de nación once served in terms of providing social services, loans, money for burials, and a safe space of respite from the onslaught of indignities experienced in a white-dominant society that de jure citizenship did not remedy (Fernández Robaina 1994; Helg 1995; Brock and Castañeda Fuertes 1998; de la Fuente 2001a; Guridy 2010; Pappademos 2011). However, the mostly middle-class constituents of *sociedades de color* subscribed to the discourse of "civilization" promoted by white elites that distanced them from the "African atavisms" associated with slavery. They vehemently rejected rumba and instead opted for dance genres of higher cultural prestige, such as the *danzón*. Furthermore, they fashioned themselves as decidedly secular social and recreational enterprises and sought to gain socioeconomic resources through assimilation and patronage politics (Pappademos 2011).

But following the bloody 1912 Black massacre of alleged supporters of the Partido Independiente de Color (Independent People of Color Party, PIC), direct challenges to the racial balance of power from within Cuba's liberal democratic institutions proved to be a dead end.[6] The members of the Cuban National Army as well as the white militias who carried out the massacre could cite Martí's declaration in his famous essay "Mi Raza" (My race, 1893), "The Negro who proclaims his race . . . justifies and provokes the white racist" (Martí 1963). Silence regarding anti-Black racism became the only viable means to participate in the political system. The divergent meanings ascribed to Black people dancing in the Republic carry the dread and hope of what collective Black sociality had the potential to manifest.

On the other hand, Africanist civic societies, many of which were extensions of the colonial cabildos, emphasized African ethnic allegiance and claimed a birthright to political autonomy from, instead of political inclusion within, the Cuban state apparatus.[7] Their members "claimed kith and kin in Africa," and in some cases their claims of connection to an African body politic extended to even organizing bids for repatriation (Pappademos 2011, 92–95). However, in the main, they engaged in mutual aid, problem-solving around daily trials and tribulations, and cultural transmission. Importantly, their claims to self-determination were substantiated by their generational subscription to African religious practices. A large sector of the Black poor and working class continued to invest in these associations that espoused a more diasporic vision defined in religious and ancestral terms. Thus, "Africanness" was a politicized category of belonging, and anti-Africanist policies, Pappademos maintains, must be understood as an attempt to discredit Black political mobilization (2011, 109). Given the centrality of African ancestry and belonging to the discursive construction of an autonomous political sphere, and the privileging of spiritual epistemology within that vision, Africanist societies and the *casas de santo* or *casa-templos* of the urban slums, whose origins have been directly traced back to the cabildos (Barcia Zequiera 2012), were perhaps the most paradigmatic nodes for the expression of the Black corporeal undercommons after emancipation.

Indeed, the sacred arts nourished an autonomous, haptic epistemological standpoint from which working-class Black people knew themselves not just as Cubans, but as people of African descent accountable to African sovereigns, ancestors, and by extension to each other. The *casa-templos* inhabited by spiritually defined kin "blurred the boundaries of religions, economy, society, folklore, and politics" and personhood (Concha-Holmes 2013, 495). The social networks of these "houses" were created in and through embodied knowledge systems and, as such, music and dance continued to be vital mechanisms for collective Black mobilization, subjectivity, political thought, and alternative social organization. "Community members could become leaders in the community and attain prestige despite state-sanctioned racism and discrimination" that otherwise limited social mobility (Concha-Holmes 2013, 494). The shared positive investment in sacred relation created the basis for Black diasporic identification and Black pride. Black people dancing together, moving in common, afforded neighbors a collective identity beyond the nation-state and cultivated a sense of dignity not wedded to creole elite interests.

The historically Black neighborhoods in Havana known for rumba today index the legacy and vitality of danced drumming and its creation of an alternate space of Black belonging and becoming that did not disappear after emancipation. Rumba was a popular modality of working-class Black assembly and rehearsed a choreo/geography of refuge from white domination. The central courtyards typical of the *solares*, urban slum collective residences, where rumbas were most commonly formed, such as in Cayo Hueso and Colón in Centro Habana, and Belén and Jesús María in Old Havana, brought together constituencies from overlapping *casa-templos*—kin networks of blood and/or stone, related via consanguinity and/or initiation. Rumba was critical to fashioning more dignified spaces of urban dwelling for the formerly enslaved, expressed through coordinated physical movement in praise, pleasure, and mutual aid. The choreo/geography of rumba made the confined spaces of tenement courtyards and cramped living rooms into alternative Black political headquarters. Inasmuch as rumbas formed in Havana's Black enclaves are important markers of the Black corporeal undercommons in the Republic, they were also prime sites for Black criminalization.

With an eye for where culture met the law, Fernando Ortiz's scholarship, and those of his peers in jurisprudence during this period (Roche y Monteagudo 1908), provided a framework for understanding "the Afro-Cuban underworld" (*el hampa afro-cubana*), a term that he coined. Born in Cuba to a well-to-do white family and raised in Spain, Ortiz earned a PhD in law. He specialized in the prevailing criminology of the time that advocated racialist thought in biological terms and the association between race and criminal behavior. According to the Italian thinker who led criminological thought at the time, Cesare Lombroso, criminals had specific inherited traits and behaviors that were most prevalent in inferior peoples (those who had yet to evolve past a primitive state of civilization). Ortiz's canonical 1906 ethnography, *The Afro-Cuban Underworld: The Black Witches: Notes for a Criminal Ethnological Study*, endeavored to describe the cultural markers of Afro-Cuban criminality. Unsurprisingly, the young intellectual was a passionate proponent of white immigration. In 1906, he stated that "race is perhaps the most fundamental aspect that should be considered in the immigrant," claiming that Blacks had proven themselves delinquent relative to whites (de la Fuente 1996; Andrews 2004, 119).

Framed in Social Darwinist and criminological discourses of public health and safety, "scientific" studies like Ortiz's provided evidence that the spaces of Blackness born from African primitives who failed (or stubbornly refused) "upliftment" through Euro-Western refinement constituted a social problem (Bronfman 2004). The forms of Black sociality associated with rumba were, according to Ortiz, symptomatic of *la mala vida cubana* (Cuban criminal life), a delinquent anachronism. Ortiz's detailed descriptions of "Afro-Cuban religion" and "Afro-Cuban music and dance" became empirical evidence for the stigmatizing claims that Black peoples and practices were naturally at odds with progress and, thus, needed policing. His work was vital to the effort to "disinfect" the Cuban social body of the contagion of *atraso*, the backward African primitive psyche, which could easily contaminate the white working class. Ortiz resolved that it was the white man's burden, "one aspect of the responsibilities that social progress requires of the ruling classes," to inspect, surveil, and reform these savages lest Cuba forever be stalled in its colonial past ([1906] 1973, 64).

Thus, the social legibility of Black people dancing after slavery was circumscribed by the limits of nation-state interests relying on a heuristic of Euro-Western categorization: religious or secular, primitive or modern, criminal or healthy, African or Cuban. Ortiz writes, "One truly antisocial and savage phenomenon entails the dances associated with *brujo* cults. This applies to convulsive dances that induce hypnosis and produce an epileptic state. . . . It is also true of the lascivious dances found in both religious and secular festivals, even if they do not always manifest such markedly antisocial character" (Ortiz [1906] 2018, 49). The modern construct of "religion" and its primitive distortion, "witchcraft," was an instrumental, capacious Western conceptual framework for the diverse complexity of embodied practices linked to African-inspired systems of belief. For him, even if the drumming appeared to be nothing more than a source of innocent diversion (read: secular) it created a context for the transmission of backward beliefs (read: witchcraft) (66). Ortiz's ethnographic work described in detail the unrelenting "psychic atavisms of primitive peoples," including their expressive arts and religious systems, and the unruly interconnectedness of the two.

Eventually, in the 1920s and into the 1930s, Ortiz took an active role in Cuban politics and matters of the economy and lawmaking to contain the "Afro-Cuban underworld." State violence was enlisted to uphold laws targeting comparsas but applied equally to policing traditional rumba performance within the intimate spheres of Black neighborhoods. In 1913, in the wake of the 1912 massacre to suppress Black political mobilization, the mayor of Havana declared that the comparsas would only be permitted if they left their "African" instruments at home. Groups were also "forbidden to 'dance or make movements with the body to the rhythm of the music'" (Ortiz and Vasconcelos 1946, 140, cited in Moore 1997, 71). In 1925, President Gerardo Machado signed a national ordinance outlawing any sort of public African drumming and dancing, which he described as "bodily contortions that offended morality" (Moore 1997, 72). The hard-won yet so precarious cause of national sovereignty, in the shadow of the US empire, helped to justify continued white political rule, de facto racial segregation, surveillance of Black neighborhoods, and the evisceration of the vestiges of a Black corporeal undercommons. Yet in the decades to come, white artists and intellectuals would be at the helm of a cultural movement that institutionalized the terms through which rumba could be valued as representative of a vanguard culturally mulata nation.

Becoming Cuban, Becoming Folklore

The expressive culture of the Black corporeal undercommons was eventually included in the conception of Cuban cultural nationalism through a literary and music movement called *Afrocubanismo*, which blossomed in the context of expanding US political, cultural, economic, and military encroachment. Since US disparagements of Cuba's fitness for self-governance were rationalized through racial thinking privileging "purity," "it became imperative to reconceptualize the relationship between race and nation" (de la Fuente 2001a, 176). Whereas in the early years of the Republic, *cubanidad* hinged on eliminating the African *atraso* entirely, by the 1940s, the Cuban intelligentsia, led by Ortiz, advocated a "transcultural" construction of Cuban identity that celebrated its racial plurality.[8] Emboldened by the vogue of Black diaspora cultures via the European avant-garde, the "jazz craze" that emerged worldwide in the late 1920s and 1930s, and the fervent quest by intellectuals and artists within the broader Latin American region to create national identities inspired by indigenous elements, mostly white Cuban intellectuals, writers, visual artists, and composers endeavored to produce a distinctive national literature, theater, and sound by incorporating stylized traditions of the urban Black "underclass." The *Afrocubanismo* movement expressed an affirming, patriotic vision of Cuban cultural modernity inspired by its autochthonous primitive Other (Moore 1997; Maguire 2011). As Moore (1997) writes, "Ultimately, a qualified acceptance of Black expression was the only recourse of intellectuals and performers desirous of creating ideological unity in a country so heavily influenced by Africa" (220).

Afrocubanistas could reference the proposition of the Society of Cuban Folklore (founded in 1923 and led by Fernando Ortiz) that Cubans should define themselves in terms of mixed cultural heritage rather than a shared ancestry (del Morro 1929, cited in Moore 1997, 133). This was in line with a progressive shift away from biological determinism within the discipline of anthropology in an attempt to counter the rise of fascism in Europe. The scientific separation of race from culture, and the adoption of race as a social construction, promoted in the US academy by the concerted efforts of Franz Boas, allowed white middle-class subjects to appropriate Black working-class aesthetics in the name of Cuban ethno-nationalism.

The "rumba craze" of the 1930s marked a boom in appropriating Black popular culture for nationalist ends. Predominantly white, middle-class performers took advantage of the international market for Black entertainment in France and the United States to create their own commercial rumba, which bore little resemblance to the noncommercial practices of the Black working class. Instead, they built on the stock figures of "El Negrito" and "La Mulata" from the *teatro bufo* (Cuban vernacular "blackface" theater) tradition developed at the start of the First War of Independence (Moore 1997, 172–73; Lane 2005). *Rumba guaguancó* was rendered most frequently in the performance and literary musings of *Afrocubanismo* artists (Moore 1997, 168). While ostensibly "orgiastic rumbas" had once been deemed a danger to civil society, those very same elements were emphasized in the cabaret acts from the 1930s through the 1950s. At the same time, the writers of *poesía afrocubana*, also called *poesía negrista* (Black poetry), a term coined by white Puerto Rican poet Luis Palés Matos, although influenced by the Harlem Renaissance, for the most part, were not Black. In fact, they belonged to the white middle and upper classes and were socially removed from everyday Black experience. Some Black writers and performers, like Nicolás Guillén and Eusebia Cosme, rose to fame during this time. But they stood as rare exceptions in a sea of white artists whose work took up themes from working-class Black expressive culture, rendering them more palatable to the dominant white audience. The arts gave visual and sonic expression to a political and social movement in the 1930s that privileged the mixing of Spanish and African elements in opposition to the growing Americanization of the island. In short, mining the Black corporeal undercommons for artistic source material became the mark of the new Cuban "mulato" patriotism.

This led to a paradoxical abundance of texts about "Black themes," relative to a scarcity of narratives authored by Black people. Cuban poets like Emilio Ballagas relied heavily on Ortiz's studies for inspiration, although the anthropologist did not have much direct exposure to Black enclaves at that time. Even so, Ballagas and his peers often used the first-person narrative voice in their writings on Black culture, inspired by Ortiz's evocative descriptions. This asymmetrical and ventriloquized expression of cross-racial politics in Latin American and the Caribean, which Jossianna Arroyo (2003) terms "cultural drag" (*travestismo cultural*), normalized a white masculinist standpoint for knowledge production about Blackness in general, and Black cultural forms like rumba specifically.

Emblematic of this white masculinist standpoint, the figure of the *mulata rumbera* became a prop for fulfilling erotic fantasies of seduction and rape, and for establishing homosocial solidarity between white and Black Cuban men in opposition to US incursions (Kutzinski 1993). Pivoting on essentialized tropes of women of African descent, the woman of color dancing rumba was a metaphor for racial mixture, her phenotype the congenial amalgamation of otherwise incompatible or antagonistic social differences, in a post-slavery society. The pendulum sway of the hips and buttocks of women of color dancing rumba spans a wide array of performance, prose, poetry, and visual art. White cabaret performers like Ninón Sevilla attained notoriety in Mexico by exporting this representation of mulata Cuban culture through exaggerated choreographies that parodied Black femininity (Gutiérrez 2010, 113; Blanco Borelli 2009; Castro Ricalde 2020). Abstracting the mulata from her lived experience within Black social life, rumba spectacles became overdetermined as classically Cuban scenarios where white women performed as seductive women of color for male enjoyment. In his definitive work, *La Música en Cuba* (1946), esteemed novelist, essayist, and musicologist Alejo Carpentier illustrates the salience of the hypersexualized tropes of Black womanhood that the rumba craze reified: "It is no small wonder that the word *rumba* has passed into the language of Cubans *as a synonym for noisy partying, licentious dancing, boogying with loose women*" (Carpentier 1946, 226, emphasis mine). Yet, Black female subjects themselves—and the dreams, frustrations, ambivalences, and spiritual endowments they also expressed through their movements—remained largely absent or ventriloquized through white cultural drag. Rumbera moves were ultimately interpreted as anthropological evidence of Black and mulata women's inherent eroticism, attributed to their African ancestry (Arnedo 1997; Blanco Borelli 2016). In *Afrocubanismo*'s "cult of the mulata," her inherently sexual rumba moves aroused a white Cuban masculinity anxious to shore up patriarchal rule over a "mixed-race" nation.

Robin Moore notes the striking tension between the Afrocubanista creations made by primarily white, middle-class artists, geared toward mainstream consumption, and those of Black Cubans themselves at that time. "This distinction was a conscious one, recognized by all in the music establishment," Moore continues, and the process of commercial transformation was described through a benevolent discourse of "'purify' (*depurar*), 'make sophisticated' (*sofisticar*), 'dress with elegance' (*vestir con elegancia*), and 'universalize' (*universalizar*)" (1997, 134–35). The process of what Moore terms "nationalizing blackness" reveals how the "inclusionary" project of Cuban cultural nationalism went hand in hand with anti-Black racism, rather than being opposing forces.

Nationalizing the dances of the Black corporeal undercommons came attendant with a strict policing of its excesses. Notably, in 1934, authorities instated a curated version of the comparsa for tourist audiences in Old Havana. Later, in 1937, after Havana mayor Antonio Beruff Mendieta wrote to Ortiz asking if the event made the country look favorable or unbecoming in the eyes of foreigners, cabildo-led comparsas were reauthorized with the condition that the streets be flanked with police along their route "to prevent disorder" (Moore 1997, 82–84; Bronfman 2004; Schwall 2021, 40–41). That same year, later in May, Ortiz staged the first public demonstration of *batá* drumming and dancing. At the same time, white middle-class writers' renderings of rumba betrayed more spiritual meaning than they avowed. As Carpentier claimed, "[Rumba] is more than a genre, it is an atmosphere" (1946, 226). Recalling the descriptions of the "black cloud over the city" from the colonial era, they sensed that there was more to rumba than met the eye.

Thanks to the broad circulation of Afrocubanista cultural production in the decades leading up to the triumph of the 1959 Revolution, terms like *the dances of our Blacks* and *Afro-Cuban dance and music* as *Cuban folklore* were well sedimented in mainstream Cuban discourse when it came time to refashion Cuban national identity in step with that revolutionary makeover. What better than the popular dances of the formerly enslaved to represent *the folk* who freed themselves from the shackles of US foreign rule? Rumba's historical association with the figurative "commons" of the Black working class made it well suited to represent the country's anti-colonial and anti-imperial cultural remaking in the construction of Cuban socialism (Daniel 1991). Economic changes spearheaded by Fidel Castro's M-26-7 were mirrored in the cultural realm. Culture was transformed from a commodity to a right whose distribution and consumption the government subsidized

(Moore 2006). Once again, Black popular music and dance, and rumba specifically, were enlisted to pronounce Cuba's newly revolutionized national character to its citizens and the world (Daniel 1995). Nevertheless, scholars of race relations in Cuba have underscored that the early 1960s is best characterized as a period of dynamic social change during which official antiracism and anti-Blackness coexisted (Benson 2016). Officially, the music and dances of "*our* Blacks," as the expressive culture of "the humblest," were the target of "preservation" and "upliftment" to the newly nationalized stages. Cuban revolutionary leaders relied on ethnographic research from the first half of the twentieth century to support this narrative.

However, the increased representation of Black music and dance, and even increased presence of Black people in the spotlight, concealed the endurance of colonial ideologies of race in revolutionary Cuba both on and off stage (Berry 2010). State actors downplayed rumba's historical relationship to religious and political Black self-making. Instead, Black popular dance became regarded as the secular cultural capital upon which to base the nation's distinctive authenticity in a burgeoning Cold War world market for "folk music and dance."[9] The category of *folklore* became an umbrella term referencing the choreographic repertoire that *used to* be connected to the African-inspired religious beliefs (Hagedorn 2001). Cuban folklore's subgenre, "traditional popular dance," where rumba was slotted, contained those dances of the Black working class that ostensibly were never sacred to begin with.

Tellingly, the National Folkloric Dance Company (El Conjunto Folklórico Nacional, CFN) was founded in 1962, the year after Fidel declared that racism had been eradicated after only three short years of the state's racial antidiscrimination campaign (insisted upon by Black intellectuals and activists). Any mention of ongoing anti-Black racism was taboo, and any mention of the continued salience of race was deemed counterrevolutionary (Benson 2016).

While working-class Black women and men made professional careers for themselves and received universalized social services that were unimaginable prior to 1959, "upliftment" for Black working-class rumberos came with strings attached. Following the persistent pattern of "inclusionary discrimination" (Sawyer 2005), bureaucrats and administrators viewed and related to Black dancers and musicians according to a colonial division of labor between brains and brawn. Governmental discourses referred to the role of "the anonymous artists of the people" as "informants" (Schwall 2017), implicitly signaling that they were not to be the authors of the artistic creation. The CFN administrators, choreographers, and costume designers, who saw themselves as ethnographers, were almost exclusively white (except for Rogelio Martínez Furé, CFN cofounder and advisor), while the informants were exclusively Black and mulato. Indeed, Argeliers León, the leading figure in Cuban musicology during the early years of the Revolution, had previously studied ethnology and folklore under Ortiz. León was appointed leader of the departamentos de Folklore y Musicología (Departments of Folklore and Musicology) at the Teatro Nacional de Cuba (Cuban National Theater) and director of the Instituto Nacional de Etnología y Folklore (Institute of Ethnology and Folklore) at the Academia de Ciencias de Cuba (Academy of Sciences of Cuba). In 1961, he declared that his research team was taking a "scientific" approach to working with "informants," while also doing the "careful work of revolutionary indoctrination" (León 1961, cited in Schwall 2017, 40). The same year, atheism became a central pillar within the creation of the new revolutionary subject following Fidel Castro's official proclamation of adherence to Marxist-Leninism. Along with homosexuality and prostitution, faith in African-inspired systems of belief was considered a social ill exacerbated by capitalistic systems of exploitation that needed to be wiped out from the body politic (Allen 2011). Overwhelmingly, artists of African descent were regarded as purveyors of "raw data" and a brute force to be organized by enlightened authorities and assessed based on their potential "use-value" within the socialist cultural remaking of *cubanidad*.

The CFN began performing a weekly show called Rumba Saturday (Sábado de la Rumba) in 1975 (Schwall 2021, 149). The outdoor patio attached to the CFN headquarters, where Rumba Saturdays were held, was named El Palenque, the Spanish word for maroon village in colonial slave society. The 1959 revolutionary government's celebration of the music and dances associated with marronage was not necessarily shared by the general populace. Moore records how Rogelio Martínez Furé encountered much opposition from the neighbors in middle-class Vedado, where El Palenque was located, due to their discomfort with Black people dancing and playing drums near their homes. He writes, "Once [Sábados de la Rumba] were established, residents grudgingly accepted the gatherings. Even so, critics suggested that their primary benefit to the community was not cultural, but rather that they 'kept all the [Black] delinquents off the street for a while,' and in a single location where their actions could be monitored" (1997, 169). The expressed need for containment and surveillance was not without basis. In its redefinition of Cuban heritage, color-blind ideology written into the law rendered illegal the Black mutual aid societies that formed the cohesive fabric of Black communities and criminalized Black consciousness.[10] The targeted dissolution of Black organizations, social institutions, and belief systems undermined the state's symbolic celebration of practices and spaces of Black autonomy on Cuban soil.

Political leaders predicted that the "religious myths" the Black performers embodied would eventually disappear. Recalling the early twentieth-century precedent of ethnographic research's criminological application, the knowledge acquired through state-funded ethnological studies was used against living devotees to better identify and persecute them. Although all religious practice was shunned, Afro-religious practice, most prevalent among the Black working class, was criminalized and persecuted in particularly violent ways.[11] Practitioners took to hiding their initiatory beads and their altars out of sight for fear of persecution. León avowed that through the informants' participation in the strategic theatricalization of their culture, divorced from its context, they would be converted to "more materialistic attitudes and [separated] from metaphysic situations that their beliefs implicitly carry" (Schwall 2019, 40). While Black religious practitioners themselves were being targeted by the state, the ethnographic pursuit of the CFN would preserve and showcase the traces of the *africanía* (Africanism) left behind (Berry 2010).

Informants of the CFN expressed resentment and dissatisfaction with how aspects of their traditions were being staged without their consent and how their labor was consistently undervalued and grossly underpaid. "Interactions between performers, researchers, choreographers, administrators, and bureaucrats ranged from synergistic to antagonistic" (Schwall 2019, 38). Various forms of disrespect, at times, resulted in work stoppages and outright violent confrontation between the performers and CFN administration behind the scenes (Hagedorn 2001; Schwall 2019). The racial character of the discrimination they experienced was especially apparent relative to the higher wages that dancers of Cuba's predominantly white national modern dance and ballet companies made at that time (Schwall 2019, 41–42).[12] These fraught internal dynamics of the CFN reflect the frictions produced when the Black corporeal undercommons rubbed up against the confines of revolutionary paternalism.

In becoming folklore, forms of Black self-making germane to Black enclaves were scrutinized and measured against a rubric of revolutionary subjecthood devised by the predominantly white and middle-class vanguard leaders. Repackaged pseudoscientific beliefs about "the Afro-Cuban underworld" became part of the revolutionary common sense, justifying the urgent need for continued state intervention in the Black neighborhoods where rumbas formed. Census records taken by the Tourism Police in 1959 in neighborhoods known as rumba hotbeds in Havana, like Barrio Colón, Barrio Atarés, El Cerro, and La Victoria in Centro Habana, further legitimated these criminological perceptions and justified future state interventions in Black communities (Hynson 2015, 134). The curated spectacle of "the folk" on stage both exemplified and mirrored how the state instructed Black subjects to model themselves after better organized, "improved" versions of themselves offstage (Berry 2010).

This enclosure of Blackness within a limited definition of revolutionary cultural nationalism played out in gendered terms. In the 1970s, when Cuba sent troops to support African struggles for independence, government discourses described the largely Black and mulato Cuban forces as making an ancestral homecoming to African soil. Studies of Afro-Cuban dance were encouraged to take an approach that explicitly benefited the Revolution's political agenda. The all-male form of rumba, called *rumba columbia*, aimed at "perfection of form and style, interchange, bravado, and competition" (Daniel 1995, 69), was staged in state-sponsored performances to underscore combative Black masculinity as virtuous when in the service of national interests. Recalling Black male bodies' utility during the independence wars, folkloric dances that CFN performed worldwide representing the African divinity of war, Ogún, showcased the discipline, strength, and precise unison of Cuba's Black men primed for military action (Berry 2010). While the otherwise denigrated masculine rumba performance was appropriated on stage as virtuous for its patriotic fervor, the state-sponsored reformists treated offstage rumba dancing by women as a social problem.

Although Black women folkloric dancers were being praised as national symbols, offstage rumberas always fell short of the white middle-class standards of respectability to which they were held. They regarded the dance form as the cultural lubrication that kept Black women and sex work, a vestige of capitalist debauchery, in slippery proximity. A national campaign aimed at ridding society of feminized social ills disproportionately targeted Black women from the outset and escalated in severity from 1959 into the 1970s.[13] As one white Cuban dance instructor, Teresa González, was quoted in conversation with Mexican dancer Alma Guillermoprieto in 1970, "All the boys who went up to Sierra Maestra with Fidel believed that rumba and prostitution were the same thing" (Guillermoprieto 2004, 60, quoted in Hynson 2015). The rhetoric and strategies the reformers deployed relied on colonial ideologies about the sexuality of women of African descent and the enduring rumbera trope from the Republican era (Hynson 2015, 126). The Black places where rumberas dwelled, and the Black practices they embodied, were taken as corroboration for the other as pathological.[14] Any woman "perceived as sexually available" (by her skin color and/or walking down the street unescorted) living in a neighborhood "perceived to be ridden by vice" (i.e., a historically working-class Black enclave) was subject to state intervention and continued surveillance. Thus, revolutionary reformists predisposed to seeing Black and mulata women as sexually available made that population that much more vulnerable to policing (136).

Prostitute reeducation centers, to improve non-virtuous (read: Black) women by inculcating them in white middle-class mores of dress, speech, and bodily comportment (Guerra 2014, 222–23), became sites where Black women strategically choreographed rumba to critique the anti-Blackness of the ostensibly color-blind revolutionary reformers. Devyn Spence Benson details a scene at one such labor camp in Camagüey, taken from news footage by a correspondent in the 1970s: "As a well-dressed white female revolutionary leader looked on, a *mulata* woman started singing impromptu rumba lyrics while Black women drummed and acted as a chorus. The spontaneous song celebrated Castro's leadership, communism, and the Revolution. Nevertheless, in a fascinating Black reinterpretation of national rhetoric, the *mulata* brushed her forearm with her other hand, to refer to Blacks, while saying . . . 'We are the revolutionaries'" (Benson 2016, 238). Benson describes this scene as portraying the contradictions within revolutionary pledges of paternalistic equality, as well as Black counternarratives of refusal to see themselves as pathological. Similar centers instituted across the country, like the famous Granja América Libre (Free America Farm), run out of a confiscated estate in the wealthy Havana suburb of Miramar, represent how working-class Black women's own feminist expressions were distinct (a topic I explore more deeply in chapter 2) and not neatly consonant with the kind of gender politics advanced by the National Women's Federation.

In a 1979 essay, Cuban ethnographer and self-identified "disciple of Ortiz" Miguel Barnet penned an ode to the CFN's lead informant, Nieves Fresneda, in honor of her retirement. In it he described the "small body of this septuagenarian woman" as "an anthropological symbol of our culture, its owner of its uniqueness, its synthesis" (Barnet 1979). Ventriloquizing thoughts he assigned to her, just as the *Granma* journalist did to Yoruba Andabo's director in 2014, he concluded, "I am folklore." When given pride of place in the national spotlight, like Yoruba Andabo almost forty years later, Black people dancing become receptacles for anti-imperial projection. Although Barnet intended to honor Fresneda's talent, his words essentialized her body in the socially virtuous terms available to her as a Black woman past her sexual prime. As Schwall argues, by collapsing this dignified Black woman into a national sign, Barnet simultaneously granted himself, as ethnographer, the authority to speak in her voice, undermining her personal agency (2019, 49). The license Afrocubanistas assumed to speak for—by speaking as—rumberos, as if literary figures in an anti-imperialist national fable, echoed in the coverage of the Cuban Five homecoming. This mode of folkloric representational enclosure forecloses the virtue of narratives about Black people dancing that exceed national use-value. In order to be dignified, rumberas and rumberos must always be dancing for the nation.

"Underworld Thugs"

This history of Black enclosure alongside national inclusion can be most directly linked to Yoruba Andabo by attending to the uniquely fraught history of the cabildos Carabalí, from whence the Abakuá brotherhood emerged. In many ways, the case of the Abakuá is paradigmatic in how it highlights the intimate interplay of the politics of race, gender, and the sacred as integral to the conceptualization of being and belonging in the Black corporeal undercommons. By the same token, the Abakuá bring to the fore a distinctive strategy elaborated by the formerly enslaved to defend a unique vision of sovereignty that nimbly moved within and around Cuban nation-building.

Abakuá societies are all-male, esoteric, initiatic mutual aid brotherhoods founded in the cities of Havana, Matanzas, and Cárdenas since at least 1836 by enslaved Africans to resist slavery. Although initially membership was restricted to the African-born, for Carabalí associations to survive, creole (Cuban-born) Black men became eligible for initiation. Carabalí referred to Calabar, the main port city of the Efik-speaking Cross-River Delta region in West Africa that straddles present-day Nigeria and Cameroon (D. H. Brown 2003; Miller 2009). In addition to providing needed services to their membership through mutual aid, the Carabalí cabildos, modeled after the Ékpè-Efik Leopard societies of Calabar, espoused principles of self-governance over sacred territory by way of a parallel political structure, posing a latent threat to Spanish colonial rule (Pappademos 2011).[15] Since at least the late 1800s, Abakuá initiates have been described in print in disparaging terms, namely, "little devils" (*diablitos*) and *ñáñigos*. Their annual processions expressed an irreverent attitude of self-determination. As one 1891 account published in *La Habana Elegante* noted, "ñáñigos did as they pleased" (Meza 1891).

Whereas autonomous maroon communities were established by fleeing slavery and escaping to isolated, rural spaces set apart from the dominant society, Abakuá societies were embedded in the urban landscape; in particular, its ports. For its members, these societies and the territory they variously refer to as *lands* (*tierras*) or *powers* (*potencias*) effectively reconstituted the colonial cartography. Self-identification as a Carabalí people, mutual aid, self-governance, and a historical view that conceptualizes citizenship before enslavement (thus before the birth of the Cuban Republic), undergird Abakuá conceptions of sovereignty. For their membership, the Abakuá "evoke qualities of masculine virility, spiritual authority, and political prowess" (Routon 2005, 387). Perhaps for this reason, the figure of the "Black criminal" dominated white perceptions of Abakuá men.

In an account from 1891 quoted in an essay by Fernando Ortiz about the Día de Los Reyes (Ortiz [1920] 2001), Abakuá dancing epitomized the savage: "All the gross and barbaric imagination of the African tribes was carried to an extreme with the ñáñigo . . . highly repugnant. . . . The other tribes drew attention to their picturesque, exotic song, costume and dance: everything about the ñáñigos was wild, somber, and nauseous . . . incessant in their offensive convulsions, shaking the many bells tied around their waists" (5). The noted shaking of the hips to sound bells hung around the waist signal the performance of the Ireme, an ancestral spirit, to which I will return in chapter 3. The narration continues, "They would always be declaring war on one another, the war would be on and in the fighting there would ensue ferociously cruel wounds and killings" (5). Fights between different Abakuá cabildos over urban territory led to bloodshed and to their overrepresentation in the prison population, corroborating the prevalent associations made between Black men and "darkness," violence, and social deviance (Schmidt 2016). Their militant defense of political autonomy on sacred grounds espoused a Black sovereignty via placemaking that challenged the monopoly of white patriarchal authority over colonial territory. To use the words of anthropologist Kenneth Routon, the Abakuá "threatened the order of civil society" (2005, 372), and many whites feared them as a result.

After the Spanish crown outlawed the Abakuá societies in 1875 to consolidate white rule over colonial territory, the brotherhood began inducting white men into their secret lodges, capitalizing on preexisting relationships with white elites as former slave traders in Africa to build strategic cross-racial initiatory relationships (Miller 2009). By selectively initiating white men occupying positions of power, Abakuá men were able to extend influence over the fate of initiates and, to some degree, the fate of other enslaved people. Once *ecobios* (brothers by initiation), Abakuá men could bargain for freedom and more lucrative jobs in the ports, where rumba also flourished. Although this tactic became a source of much internal controversy and divisions among the cabildos, the calculated initiation of white men provided a channel for Abakuá members to secure a hold in the hubs of commerce (Miller 2004). In a slave society governed by racial logics of white supremacy, I contend, heteropatriarchal rule was a lingua franca that connected Africanist and white systems of sovereignty, allowing for diplomatic exchange and control over resources. In essence, homosocial bonds forged in the slave trade were a bridge enabling Black men to gain unofficial bargaining rights in a white-dominated public sphere and to absorb the power of the state into their underground system of governance.

After the island-nation gained formal independence in 1898, Abakuá societies continued to uphold their alternative sense of citizenship, decentering Cubanness as the sole category of civil personhood. Unsurprisingly, in 1903, the Abakuá were officially re-criminalized while rumba was persecuted. By the 1920s, the Abakuá had a virtual monopoly on the distribution of jobs in the port, practically functioning as a labor union for Black men who were barred from official trade-union membership. In the context of political instability after Cuban independence, the Abakuá posed an enduring threat to the consolidation of power over labor and territory in the hands of white political elites.

Ethnographic writings about *diablitos ñáñigos* serve as a rich archive of white Cuban patriarchy's enduring fraught attraction-repulsion to the Black male body(-politic) within its own political vision of homosocial national becoming (Arroyo 2003). In his early work, Fernando Ortiz described Abakuá initiates as "underworld thugs" (*hampones*), reinforcing their lasting association with incivility located in the "Afro-Cuban underworld" (*hampa afro-cubana*) ([1906] 1973). Armed with the research Ortiz, Roche y Monteagudo, and others conducted linking Blackness, *brujería*, and criminality, police targeted Abakuá port workers for arrest when playing rumba.

The close historical links between Abakuá societies and rumba have been well documented in studies that trace Abakuá affiliations among the most well-known rumberos, as well as similarities in the musical forms

(Miller 2000). Indeed, Yoruba Andabo's founding members were all Abakuá initiates who worked in the Port of Havana. Abakuá port workers often sang, danced, and played rumba on the docks during their breaks with improvised instruments like box crates and spoons (called *rumba de cajón*). These working-class expressions of rumba, tied to devotional, political, and economic desires, raised white anxieties about Black masculinity unyoked from white rule and the kinds of social problems that made Cuba more vulnerable to US intervention post-independence (Bronfman 2004).

Knowledgeable about the white elite's ideological investments in the utility of Black brawn for advancing nationalist agendas, Abakuá initiates strategically utilized nationalist rhetoric as camouflage. Ned Sublette describes such a scene on the docks where *ecobios* worked and played rumba, "They couldn't pretend these *tambores de rumba* were just barrels, but they got around it by giving the bigger one the name of *mambisa*—as in *mambí*, a Liberation Army soldier. It was a bogus name, of course, because they didn't play these drums during the War for Independence. But no, sir, Mr. Policeman. These aren't African witchcraft drums. These are patriotic Cuban barrel drums—mambisas!" (2004, 265).[16] Nonetheless, substantiated by the criminological claims about African pathology, targeted arrests of Black men undermined the Abakuá's hold on the ports by the 1940s (Booth 1976). Ortiz's later publications on Afro-Cuban popular culture and the Abakuá, in particular, describing the brotherhood in more respectful terms as an "an Afro-Cuban version of Freemasonry" or an "all-male secret society" (Ortiz 1950), did little to reverse the criminalized stigma of Black sovereignty that the brotherhood espoused.

The figure of the *ñáñigo* and his rebellious stance—doing as he pleased—was co-opted over time by white political elites, eviscerating its original meaning to instead signify Cubanness vis-à-vis US imperial power.[17] Nevertheless, Abakuá initiates, similar to rumberas offstage, fell short of white regimes of public decency elaborated under Cuban socialism. Citing the study of Natalia Bolívar and Román Orozco entitled *Cuba Santa: Comunistas, santeros y cristianos en la isla de Fidel Castro* (1998), Jalane Schmidt writes, "Internally circulated memos of state security bureaus singled out Abakuá members as 'antisocial elements' and recorded the 1968 arrest and jailing of 458 of the society's members in Havana alone" (2016, 176). Although much of the Abakuá hold on the ports was diminished by the 1940s, Christine Ayorinde documents claims of labor organizing by Abakuá stevedores at the Port of Havana even in the 1960s (2004, 125), pointing to the persistent gap between the revolutionary government's political vision and the hopes of the Black working class. Rumberos' historical linkages to the brotherhood were to be carefully managed for symbolic inclusion within Cuban folkloric spectacle.

Real or imagined, the brotherhood's historical association with the capacity to wield unlawful influence over labor and land has continued to stain the group. Even if today Abakuá are dispersed throughout many occupational sectors, they are still associated with a particular working-class Black masculinity tied to spatialized control over historically "dangerous" neighborhoods (often, but not exclusively, proximate to ports) presumed to still function as seats of illicit power. This criminal designation has made the Abakuá fall under the jurisdiction of the Ministry of the Interior, whereas rumba falls under the purview of the Ministry of Culture. Since the Special Period, the ñáñigo has certainly been absorbed into what Allen (2011) has called the "'triangle trade' of desire" (160), meeting the demand in the tourist market for the "tropicalist thug fantasy" (171). Nevertheless, the brotherhood's continued stigmatization in dominant Cuban society, outside the demarcated space-time of folkloric cultural display, I insist and elaborate in chapter 3, cannot be understood outside of the ongoing struggles waged between differently racialized emancipatory imaginaries in the New World.

Meanwhile, characteristic of the Africanist civic societies they exemplify, Abakuá members themselves maintain that their organizing principles are above all African and religious in nature. The Abakuá highlight the ways that descendants of the cabildos continue to enlist the sacred to negotiate a terrain where white political geography has sought hegemony. This history invites us to theorize the coordinates plotted through the bodily practices of the cabildos, the salience of sacred gendered scripts to its articulation of sovereignty, and the danger it represents to modern secular liberalism. Importantly, the heteropatriarchal grammar of American social order in the wake of slavery positioned the Abakuá to capitalize on the currency of homosocial desire to defend their land.

As rumba is showcased in contemporary Cuba as a cultural sign for a rebellious island under the persistent shadow of imperial threat, what Geovani del Pino calls "the Abakuá inside rumba" (to be discussed in chapter 3) both conceals and reveals the unwavering defense of a polity of their own that rumberos continue to form. What is at stake in the resentments that accompany being called to perform "diplomatic gigs," to the extent that it obstructs fulfillment of the community-based "religious work" that Yoruba Andabo members also perform, might be more fully appreciated if viewed in relation to this history of Abakuá's punitive containment within the project of Cuban nationalism.

Religion Is Religion and Folklore Is Folklore

"You know they didn't pay us for that [diplomatic gig]. We had important [religious] work that we had to cancel": Rather than take the remark made outside Cabaret Las Vegas that day as evidence of wholesale adherence to a secularist separation between the sacred and the profane, or "religion" and "politics," I see it as signaling the ongoing tensions between the various callings that rumberos' embodied labor service, the differing political geographies they are enlisted to body forth, and the material desires and possibilities they enable or foreclose. The respectability of Black popular dance within Cuban revolutionary nationalism has hinged on rumba's conceptual separation from "religion," divorcing it from its ceremonial, community organizing, and space-making capacities, in effect depoliticizing it as purely recreation and entertainment. This process has relied on a willingness on the part of practitioners to be reshaped by this authoritative discourse (Asad 1993). Certainly, the fundamental changes in access that Black working-class people experienced after 1959, in terms of housing, education, health, land, and professional opportunities, further motivated that willingness, at least publicly. When prompted, rumberos indeed perform fluency in a binary taxonomical system that underwrites the terms of their inclusion as folkloric professionals fit to represent an ethno-national secular body-politic. With that comes a rhetorical disavowal of rumba's connection to a Black corporeal undercommons wherein such neat divisions maintain an unruly intimacy.

In her ethnography of rumba in the 1980s, Daniel tries to make sense of the ways in which rumba is imbricated within African-inspired religious practice in contrast to the pervasive, officially promoted common sense that it is distinct and separate from "religion." In a chapter on the symbolic aspects of rumba, she remarks that respected rumberos "acknowledge a long association between rumba music and [religious] music of the orishas. They sing Santería chants with Yoruba words and explain how these fit into rumba clave and how they are used quite frequently, in fact with some regularity, in the programs of most traditional rumba groups" (Daniel 1995, 133). She notes: "Many informants also say that orishas can request that a Rumba be performed. And a *santero*, or priest, can organize a Rumba (if a petitioner has requested a favor or a particular blessing and in return has promised a fiesta or party for the orisha who is believed responsible for granting the favor or request). In this context, the Rumba is commonly called *bembé*" (133). Yet, Daniel notes a sense of discomfort that arises when rumberos narrate these connections, leading to their subsequent disavowal. She deduces: "Despite these connections, the reason most Cubans say there is no relationship between rumba and orisha music/dance is that historically the two traditions have been categorized separately and Cubans have heard years of repeated rhetoric about separate arenas" (133).

The felt need to explain away the lived experiences of "information out of place," Stoler argues, "underscores what categories matter" (Stoler 2002, 107). At the time of Daniel's fieldwork, a decade that many remember as the "golden years" of the Revolution, when no one worried about money and there was always enough to go around, Cuba was still an officially "atheist state." This meant that Communist Party membership and thus professional advancement was closed off to people who maintained religious affiliations. Backed by the economic support of the Soviet Union, the fruits of the state's redistributive policies changed the socioeconomic landscape and qualitatively improved the life chances and choices for the Black working class. For working-class Black Cubans who had been closed off from professional careers before 1959, the opportunities and material benefits of playing into the apolitical, secular, folkloric slot assigned to rumba were significant.

Daniel follows with an illustrative anecdote of a dancer she interviewed in the late 1980s who said there was no relationship between orishas and rumba, thereby positioning her embodiment of orisha motifs within rumba choreography as her own artistic innovation. Nonetheless, Daniel herself could attest that this "blending" of genres had been a commonplace occurrence even in the early 1970s (when religious practice was at the height of criminalization). Indeed, the rumbera's framing situates her own creative choices within the institutionalized body of scholarship about rumba, of which Daniel would be aware. However, this rendering necessarily entailed a certain forgetting of commonly known and long-maintained practices that had heretofore resisted the secular logics of modern classification. This exchange underscores the ongoing politics of rumberos publicly acknowledging and performing an unruly intimacy with the sacred.

If indeed the material benefits gained from the revolutionary state in its heyday made rumberos willing participants in tacitly forgetting that which exceeded the national agenda, the diminishing returns for the Black working class since the 1990s explain the subsequent renegotiation of the terms of race and nation. The fall of the Soviet Bloc had decisive repercussions for racialized lived experience, racialized class inequality, and race relations on the island (de la Fuente 2001b; Sawyer 2005). Unable to ensure the same kinds of return in goods and social services to its citizens in the Special Period, the state initiated a series of modifications to the prior Soviet-style revolutionary orthodoxy, opening the country to tourism as the main source of national revenue and making some allowances for home-based family businesses, and alongside those, the principle of religious freedom. The reform of the constitution in 1991, which changed Cuba from being officially atheist to an officially secular state (meaning religious affiliation was no longer legal grounds for discrimination), certainly created more room for public expressions of religiosity in Cuban civil society, even if prejudices continued (Ayorinde 2004).

In the 1990s, rumberos, along with Black working-class devotees more broadly, slowly started wearing their sacred initiatory adornments in public with less fear of state recrimination. Moreover, with the advent of *santurismo*—a tourist market catering to foreigners who wish to learn about and even initiate into sacred kinship networks for inflated fees (Hagedorn 2001; Argyriadis 2008)—Afro-religious practice became a tangible way to improve one's economic situation. State-sponsored rumba ensembles, like Yoruba Andabo, gained a reputation for highlighting their dual proficiency in rumba *and* the repertoires clearly associated with embodied worship, making their close proximity once again public in a way that was previously foreclosed by hegemonic norms of revolutionary propriety. In the Special Period political economy, rumba became an avenue for entering the tourist market and a synecdoche for faith-based, working-class Black cultural politics in the late twentieth century.

Characteristic of Black Atlantic cultural politics more broadly, rumba transformed in relationship to "popular social needs, organizational and religious goals, and to political contexts" (Concha-Holmes 2013, 491). The spatial imagination of rumberos transgressed geopolitical boundaries and included localities as distant as Cayo Hueso, the Bronx, NYC Central Park, and Calabar within a shared diasporic consciousness (Knauer 2009; Jottar 2009a). Paradoxically, the Black diasporic racial identification and Afro-centric spiritual devotion rumberos ascribed to privately before the Special Period resurfaced as a sign of Cuban authenticity and a crucial means of material survival thereafter. In this sense, the uses of rumba by Black working-class practitioners in the Special Period, at once spiritual and useful for pragmatic ends, recalled how their enslaved ancestors had negotiated the push and pull of Black inclusion over one hundred years prior.

Still, over a decade later in Havana in the early 2000s, I witnessed the same rote repetition of claims to an unequivocally separate sacred and secular realm that were not sustained in the practices I observed or in follow-up questions in semi-structured interviews with rumberos. While taking full advantage of the market opening for faith-inspired spectacles, rumberos engaged in a mix of strategic displays and disavowals of their faith when performing for the public in state venues. Memories of religious persecution and prior norms of artistic professionalism loomed large in their interactions with state bureaucracy, motivating them to tread carefully depending on the audience.

My first group of interviews with Yoruba Andabo members in the spring of 2013 made clear that these metaphorical discursive dances only thinly veiled a more complex understanding of the relationship between rumba, race, knowledge, and power. Geovani facilitated a convening in his home, a *solar* in Centro Habana, where I could formally introduce my study one-on-one to each member in an intimate setting. When I arrived, on the living room TV, placed next to a large Lucumí altar, a DVD of the controversial documentary *Raza (Race)* (Corvalán 2008) was playing. Geovani insisted that everyone pay attention to its message. The documentary, an exposé of the legacy of anti-Blackness in post-revolutionary Cuba featuring leading Black activist-scholars and artists, was banned from Cuban movie theaters after the popularity of its opening night. The film began as a student thesis that would not have received permission to be made from the director's supervisors at the Cuban *Instituto Superior de Arte* (Institute of Higher Art, ISA), if not for the advocacy of key figures featured in the film. No doubt, the documentary delivered a strong critique of white hegemony in Cuba within the spheres of commerce, tourism, education, and the performing arts. Geovani had somehow acquired a personal copy through his social networks and thought it important for the members of the group to watch it. It was not long before the rumberos started discussing how the content resonated with their own experience. While informal debate about the film occurred in the living room, I conducted preliminary interviews with each member, either one by one or in pairs, next door in the kitchen.[18]

I began by asking about the members' artistic background and their journey to becoming members of Yoruba Andabo. My interview with Didier Acosta, the youngest of the group, has stayed with me. Geovani made sure to let me know that Didier was the newest member, and it was his first time ever being interviewed. The disclaimer put me at ease. I sympathized with him, as it was only my first time conducting such an interview with the group and I, too, was anxious about leaving a good impression. After we talked about his upbringing in a devout household, from a family of religiosos, and his training as a young boy playing at ceremonies in his neighborhood—a common theme in all the interviews—he mentioned that there was not always a clear separation of secular from sacred when it came to how he thinks about his drumming. Geovani, who was listening in on our conversation from the living room, immediately interjected to "correct" the statement: "Religion is religion and folklore is folklore." Geovani proceeded to apologize to me on the young man's behalf, reminding me that he was not used to speaking to anthropologists. The young man raised his eyebrows in surprise at what just happened, and then, with a laugh, agreed that I should not listen to him because he does not know much about these things.

It seemed that the artistic director, a veteran "informant" since the 1980s when Yoruba Andabo was "discovered" at a showcase at the Union of Cuban Writers and Artists, saw the occasion as a professional development opportunity for the newer members of the group. While talent for the group was intentionally scouted from ceremonies in their community-based *casa-templos*, part of the education they received as professional "folkloric artists" was to learn the rules of professional self-representation vis-à-vis academic institutions, official organizations, and the media. While on the one hand, Geovani's investment in keeping the group abreast of the discourse of anti-racist activism in Cuban society demonstrated an unmistakable degree of racial consciousness, as the director of a state-sponsored rumba ensemble he had to ensure that members also knew how to talk about their craft in alignment with the legitimizing truths circulating about them in the academy that institutionalized their bodily practices as folklore. Geovani knew very well that I was religiosa too; in our first conversation about my doctoral study, he noted this as one of the few reasons why he agreed to participate. However, because my research visa was sponsored by the Cuban Ministry of Culture, which I disclosed upfront, I believe that he was also sensitive to how my own professionalism as an anthropologist would be appraised. This was a professional development opportunity for me too. The Cuban common sense about rumba built into everything from scholarship to state policies and everyday language may not line up neatly with the meanings practitioners assigned to their own embodied labor. Someone like Didier who grew up drumming these specific rhythms his entire life and was clearly respected for this talent could be easily dismissed as uninformed or lacking sufficient expertise. Being a professional rumbero meant becoming adept at code-switching to make one's movements legible in different ways to different audiences when it mattered.

The fluid movements of the Black corporeal undercommons that desta-bilized modern taxonomy were as unruly for the purposes of the (predomi-nantly white and atheist) Cuban revolutionary vanguard as they were for nineteenth-century elites. The paternalistic (and maternalistic) attitude of the revolutionary vanguard toward "*their* Blacks" pulsed beneath rumba's "upliftment" to the national stage in Soviet-Cuba. It was the (not always so silent) call that Didier, and I, as Black (religioso/a) professionals had to learn to hear and respond to when necessary. When the historic gains for the poor eroded in the post-Soviet era, the disavowals that Black inclusion wrought proved harder to contain. At the onset of Cuba's most recent wave of economic reform, when my fieldwork began, the cumulative effect of these unspoken trade-offs, and their gendered discontents, formed the terrain on which Black subjects articulated their own investment in rumba.

Dancing beyond the Nation

Tracing the systematic process of punitive containment that has accom-panied rumba's trajectory to pride of place on the national stage makes thinkable a Black political geography, a Black sense of place, that was never seamlessly coterminous with Cuban nation-building. On the one hand, rumberos and Black popular culture more broadly have been lifted up as embodiments of the successive iterations of revolutionary vision of the future. On the other hand, identifying as Black, self-organizing as Black people, and expressing loyalties to African-inspired sovereigns have been seen as savage, anachronous, and counterrevolutionary (Ayorinde 2004). As Fidel Castro stated in his widely cited speech of June 30, 1961, "Words to the Intellectuals," "Within the Revolution, everything, outside the Revo-lution, nothing." The Black corporeal undercommons is a way to map and think with the forms of Black self-making that continue to form subjects "outside" national use-value; and by exceeding, refuse to be refused.

Fernando González Llort, the guest of honor, stood beside then vice president (now president) of Cuba Miguel Díaz-Canel in the front row of the concert for the Cuban Five. Tellingly, the dignitaries did not understand the rhythms of the music. They clumsily clapped out an even 4–4 beat rather than the core, orienting 2–3 *clave* rhythm that rumberos mark in unison. Before long, Zulema Pedroso and Vladimir took center stage to demonstrate some basic steps and warm up the crowd. The TV cameras shifted between the rumberos on stage, the smiling faces of the white dignitaries in the front row, and the cheering sea of people filling the street below extending into the night. A gigantic Cuban flag waved high above the masses.

The prime-time television broadcast showed Yoruba Andabo in the spotlight, perched on the outdoor stage constructed at the University of Havana, the site where Ortiz had hosted public lecture-demonstrations with Black informants decades earlier. In both instances, rumberos contended with the biases, misrecognitions, and ignorance of those in power while being simultaneously praised as national patrimony. The patriotic role assigned to rumba, as exemplified by the article in the official newspaper of the Cuban Communist Party's coverage of the 2014 "Concierto por los Cinco," coincides with a particular way Black people dancing has been appraised and staged throughout Cuban history. The newspaper echoed the meanings that have been ascribed to rumberos' bodies by those most invested in Cuban nation-building all along, framing Blackness as a natural resource made of blood and sweat, performing an autochthonous original source for a mulata nation and a rebel root for an anti-imperial state.

Despite the written account in the newspaper that will stand as archival record, the rumberos of Yoruba Andabo were far from congealed in a national past and far from restricted to a territorially bound sense of belonging delineated by nation-state sovereignty. They opened their set with a traditional *guaguancó* song, yet their self-presentation signaled a particular vision of Black diasporic modernity akin to what Deborah Thomas (2004) terms "modern blackness" for working-class Jamaicans negotiating capitalist globalization. This sense of selfhood is distinct from the institutionalized "folk" or "revolutionary" formulations of belonging historically tied to postcolonial nation-building and is also a framework for evaluating future and present possibilities (Thomas 2004, 231, 243). Instead of donning the colors of the Cuban flag—red, white, and blue—they wore distressed jeans and bright yellow T-shirts with the words "Yoruba Andabo" on the front in red and green. When the camera zoomed in close, those looking for it would have noticed their beaded initiatory bracelets showing their devotion to their respective Lucumí sovereigns. Their gold chains, dark sunglasses, and door-knocker earrings, shared by the top reggaeton artists of the day, appealed to their loyal young Black following across the island and beyond, from the inner-city neighborhoods of Cayo Hueso to the Bronx. While I certainly don't mean to suggest that Yoruba Andabo members are unpatriotic, or "feigning" patriotism to Cuba, these aesthetic choices squarely pronounce yet another proud self-identification with a Black diasporic dancing body-politic that is too often blocked out in favor of an official one that is easier to think. Only if separated from Black self-making can the dances of the "Afro-Cuban underworld" be a virtuous essence of *cubanidad*.

Recent studies about the early history of racial politics in the 1959 Revolution provide a needed counterbalance to hegemonic characterizations that simplistically render "Cuban culture" and "the Cuban people" as a unified homogenous front vis-à-vis imminent threats to state sovereignty. I concur with Schwall's proposal that the process of Black dance's nationalization post-1959, and Black social inclusion writ large, might be more accurately described as a collaborative process between a majority-white revolutionary vanguard and Black subjects, albeit "undeniably built on the fraught foundations of racial inequality and paternalistic reform" (Schwall 2019, 37). Ultimately, I propose that the construct of (Afro-)Cuban (folkloric) dance and the *rumba genre* that it includes refer to the collective practices Black people have embodied while navigating complex libidinal attachments to nation-building amid conditions of US imperialism, capitalist globalization, and racial and gender inequality.

The enlistment of rumba to do "diplomatic work" for the nation-state represents much more than the "dignification" of the Black race through its labor. It also evokes the continued interest in containing the productive force, legible form, and aims of Black people dancing and drumming within the bounds of the nation-state. What would it mean to loosen the nationalist grip on rumba and afford its practitioners the kind of space that they endeavor to form with their more-than-human kin? That is to say, how might the rumba portion of the open-air concert have been described differently in *Granma* if it were politically viable to appreciate the copresences that animate their movements? And, even so, Black people quotidianly push beyond the given geopolitical and epistemological borders for their own sake. How might we think with the quotidian desires, dispositions, memories, and spaces that rumba helped form during Raúl's update to the economic model of the Revolution? These fugitive practices beyond nation-building are what this book endeavors to honor in the following chapters.

2 BLACK FEMINIST APTITUDES

Female postures paralleled the social position of women; body orientation became standard in low level, not just slightly but deeply bent downward, yet alert, flexed, or ready to move. . . . Females watch, discover, respond, and initiate occasionally, according to their own strategies.

YVONNE DANIEL, *Rumba*

"¡En el torso no esta' haciendo na'!" (You ain't doin' nothin' in your torso!) was the correction that Jenny gave me most often in class. I suppose this had a lot to do with the lack of dexterity in that part of my body, but it also says something about how critical these muscle isolations were to the form. Yvonne Daniel described the movement of the torso in rumba as an almost constant "undulation of the spine": "Her torso can be divided into upper and lower sections and moves in forward to back swing energy. Her rib cage lifts with the undulation and alternates from side to side. Her knees are flexed and shift softly from side to side accommodating the polyrhythms above the feet" (1995, 77). The flexibility in the torso is facilitated by the *muelleo* (from *muelle*, or "spring") in the knees, a softly bent constant springing motion that anchors the weight downward with the pulse of the music while opening space for the articulation of the hips in coordination with the torso. ". . . And your *muelleo*, Maya!" was the correction that came in a close second.

The fine-tuned articulation between the woman's torso and her knees fades from view in the literature about rumba. Widely characterized as a dancing metaphor for courtship, descriptions of rumba guaguancó narrate a man playfully chasing the woman with the aim of "vaccinating" her—a double entendre for sexual penetration. In this portrayal, rumberas are reduced to thrusting breasts and swaying hips, leading to associations with serpentine animality. Her dancing, the ostensibly natural by-product of some innate racialized essence, casts a hypnotic spell on the (male) viewer, enticing his *vacunaos* (vaccinations).[1] But my teachers emphasized the aspects least mentioned in the prevailing discourse about the dance. How could these bodily techniques so crucial from a practice perspective be completely absent from descriptions about rumberas in the popular Cuban imaginary?

The meticulous polyrhythmic movements that rumberas must master are so subtle that it is almost imperceptible to an eye that is not equally conditioned to appreciate them. Anatomically speaking, the pulling in and down of the shoulder blades, which creates the undulation in the torso, is contrary to the way the scapula operates. Rumberas rehearse this movement to make it appear as natural as breathing. It is this same dorsal dexterity and softness in the knees required when dancing in prayer to the orisha divinities. This resonance in the dancing body, in praise and in pleasure, makes rumba and the dances of the orisha linked rather than disparate bodily techniques. On the contrary, these two "folkloric dances" are institutionally categorized as discrete according to a sacred-profane binary carried over from classical anthropological taxonomy. Long-term commitment to dance training forced me to develop a greater awareness of those and other unseen and unacknowledged connections between seemingly disparate analytical realms.[2]

Private dance lessons are unique interpersonal encounters for transmission. They reveal that what we—as an audience—perceive as natural or spontaneous is actually a structured improvisation honed with precise intention. Similar to how Judith Butler (1990) has theorized gender performance more broadly, the performance of femininity in rumba is taught and rehearsed in the everyday. It is as quotidian as it is risky. That is to say, there are stakes to the way rumberas learn to move in their bodies. Jenny insisted that to take up the rumbera role responsibly when dancing in public it was critical for me to understand how my body, as a Black woman, was perceived. For this, I had to develop a sense of attunement for how my proprioception keyed in to social constructions and copresences.

We had our lessons without mirrors, so I could not rely on my reflection, my outward appearance, for guidance. I had to find the correct feeling in myself. In "real life," there were no mirrors to tell us how we should feel about our dancing, she reasoned. All I have is me. Besides, the small living rooms converted to dance studios in Centro Habana where she trained me did not have large mirrors. Wide, full-length mirrors were an expensive luxury—a discreet status symbol more common in the home decor of the middle and upper classes. I had to learn to recall in public that same feeling of the movement I had rehearsed with her. However, this was not a straightforward lesson in how to cultivate a positive self-image independent from an external gaze. After all, rumba is a social dance; you never dance by yourself. You have to infer how to occupy the space in relation to others around you, and how the placement of your body parts in space produces social meaning.

Her corrections to my improper execution of the dance prompted conversations that added more clarity to the aptitude being transmitted. Jenny's stern words to me made it clear that this was not dancing for dancing's sake. Dancing, she instructed, is a way Black women could confer added "value" upon our bodies in an exclusionary market that would not grant us our due worth. To be sure, rumberas count on their sexualized interpellation as the *mulata* trope as a kind of stock in the "triangle trade of desire" in which Cuba, and the Caribbean more broadly, is located (Allen 2011). Not unlike the Cuban state itself, rumberas perform for foreign investment, largely relying on the "natural resources" within their reach to enact degrees of agency. She coached me out of falling into certain choreographic "exaggerations" that I had picked up from watching younger rumberas *en la calle* (in the street). These movements commonly signified sexual looseness. "Don't lift your arms up so high, remember you are holding an imaginary skirt and you don't want to show everyone your *chocha* [pussy]!" or "Don't spread your legs so wide, it makes you look easy!" Rumberas trained me to see the difference between women who *defienden la esencia* (defend the essence) in rumba guaguancó's danced pursuit of the woman's sex, versus women with "poor technique." "Poor technique" referred to those who pandered to cheap notions of sexiness or were inappropriately influenced by the theatricalization of rumba adopted by institutions of higher learning. Whereas to defend the essence meant dancing in a way that honored the female ancestors who danced in this role before them. Ancestral reverence was conveyed in the elaborate and creative ways women dancers shield their *chocha* from male possession. Maintaining feet in parallel position, hip-width apart, was an assertion of dignity in that it gave one access to the widest range of evasions from his vacunaos. These evasions were called *botaos*. Dancing rumba professionally warranted an agile, defensive posture, which meant also being alert to the possessive colonial gaze.

While some may attribute these protective motions to a "politics of respectability" (Higginbotham 1993), la rumbera, by virtue of participating in this form of play at all, already dances beyond purity's borders. As detailed in chapter 1, historically rumberas posed a challenge to white middle-class standards of femininity and respectability promoted by revolutionary leaders. Instead, much like their Black lower-class counterparts in other parts of the Caribbean, rumberas endeavor to defend their dignity by leaning in to timeworn tropes of racialized hypersexuality waged against their female ancestors (Thomas 2004). Affording rumberas a feminist consciousness allows "the hipped enunciations [to shift] . . . from being erotic suggestions for the patriarchal gaze to becoming historicizing declarations" about and for Black women's lives and labor (Blanco Borelli 2009, 230). The Black feminist analytical framework of "dissemblance" might help approximate this strategy of creating the illusion of openness while protecting an inner psychic space developed by Black women in response to the ordinariness of the threat of sexual violence (Clark Hine 1989).[3] This reckoning with Black women's sexual vulnerability through the practice of Black popular dance speaks to the lasting legacy of the sexual economy of slavery (Davis 2002).

Although we never directly discussed the legacy of racial slavery, Jenny's teachings were clear about that history's weight on a present condition that we shared. Being a Black woman in the Americas means needing to demand respect for one's body in nations whose wealth has relied on the negation of our bodily autonomy in a way that devalues our being and diminishes our ability to materially care for our families. What is more, the pursuit of self-worth and a living wage in a context of persistent sexual vulnerability makes it imperative that we develop creative strategies to reclaim agency.[4] I would learn from Jenny and other rumberas with whom I studied that the cultivation of "value" or dignity that comes from demanding material compensation for their labor could entail risky exchanges.

In this moment, when poor Black women are trying to find their footing in a historic period of private-market expansion, what would it mean to understand certain recognizable tropes of Black womanhood associated with rumba as Black feminist aptitude for dissemblance? Again, I mean, conscious choreographic choices conveying a sense of openness that strategically protects the sanctity of an inner psychic space within constraint. Like the Black women during the Great Migration who Darlene Clark analyzes in the United States, rumberas' quest for respect and access to well-paying employment that is not domestic servitude motivated their movements and is tied to the desire to control their own sexuality. Thinking with Black feminism alongside dance frames of analysis, I consider the *choreographic aptitude* required of Black women whose bodies are appraised as sexual-cultural commodities (Berry 2021). These "constrained improvisations" (Cox 2015) point to an awareness of structural raced and gendered power relations that have direct material implications for their lives in an "updating" Cuban economy.

This line of analysis affords rumberas a feminist consciousness they have not been granted in the popular Cuban imaginary. Instead, the rumbera figure is commonly hailed as an object of desire: a Black(-ish) woman in a bent-over posture, seductively swinging her hips to a pulsing rhythm, as a by-product of an essentialized "tropicalism" rooted in a biologized "African" inheritance. According to Gustavo Ribeiro's definition of "tropicalism," happiness and sensuality are core tropes associated with this kind of Orientalism, which is most often applied to sites in Latin America and the Caribbean with large Black populations (Ribeiro 2019, 765). The rumbera stands in to represent a signature "mulata" or "Cuban femininity" coded as Black in all its primitive sensuality, discursively fashioned as a sign of unbridled sexuality (Blanco Borelli 2016; Kutzinski 1993). As a diligent student of my teachers, I strived to become more attuned to the nuances of the intersectional analysis they actively demonstrated in their movements while negotiating the possessive attempts of a heteropatriarchal colonial gaze and their own claims to possession by copresences.

Rumberas turned to sources of wisdom they cast as sacred to devise strategies for countering the diminishment of their dignity and worth. To echo Daniel's (1990) reflections on the women who ushered her through her fieldwork in the 1980s, "They were also stunning examples of the successes as well as the problems of the Cuban revolutionary government in forwarding female liberation" (16). This approach to studying rumba attends to the pressures for peso-poor Black women to perform the fantasy projected onto them in increasingly exclusionary markets. The spiritually inflected Black feminist consciousness expressed in rumba during the reforms becomes critical for situating Black working-class women's investment in rumba as a profession for, in Jenny's words, giving themselves value.

Before and After the Music Played

The sonic landscape of Cayo Hueso, where I had lessons in small living rooms with the furniture pushed back, was broken up by Jenny's screams of disapproval at my execution. The *solar* residents had a front seat to my chastisements twice a week for an hour to ninety minutes in the peak of the afternoon's heat. Jenny's screams would echo through the central courtyard, inviting people to glance over to satisfy their momentary curiosity as they carried out their daily chores. Jenny and her posse of women affectionately called the man who lived directly across the courtyard "El Vecino" (The Neighbor). El Vecino was a soft-spoken, somewhat stout, dark-skinned Black man from the countryside, and they playfully teased him on all those grounds. He would eventually divulge that he befriended me mostly out of pity. He thought I was a *guajira*, a girl from the countryside, who, like many (including himself) migrated to Havana (illegally) in search of economic opportunity.[5] He knew girls from his village who came to Havana to try their luck in the big city in hopes of sending money back home to their family. The higher concentration of tourists in the city meant higher potential access to hard currency. Maybe they would become professional artists and get hired in tourism one day, or maybe they would catch the attention of a foreigner they would eventually marry. My unstylish, bland, and modest clothes clearly marked me as either too poor or too provincial to keep up with the Havana fashion that city girls flaunted with sass. In stark contrast to Jenny and her friends, I was not irreverent and quick-tongued. I was polite and soft-spoken, much like El Vecino himself. *"Pobrecita"* (poor thing), he admitted he would say to himself, as he peeked through the window to see Jenny verbally shoot me down once again.

He offered much unsolicited counsel: "Your teacher does it like it should be done. She yells at you, but it's for your own good." My skin was a darker shade of brown, like Jenny's, but pretty enough, El Vecino assessed, to let my talent shine if I listened to and applied myself to copying her behavior. I had a lot to learn about making the most of being a woman of my complexion in Havana's competitive market for tropicalist fantasy made flesh. El Vecino was wrong about my motivation for learning from Jenny. However, we could agree that private lessons were transactions of different kinds of capital, driven by the convergence of various desires for value in an uneven field of exchange. He was not wrong to assess that, for the Black women from humble origins whom I resembled, tropicalist typecasting made folkloric dance a viable career avenue in a competitive and exclusionary economic landscape. The way I looked might have engendered his pity, but I could potentially use the choreographic aptitude I was learning to negotiate the social expectations assigned to my body and exercise some agency.

Jenny was, in many ways, such a success story. She came from a peso-poor Black family, in the far outer borough of San Miguel del Padrón, for whom the Revolution provided an unprecedented means to get a formal education. As a young Black Cuban woman, when she entered the National School of the Arts in the 1990s, Jenny was tracked to be certified in folkloric dance. Her degree opened doors for a career that was founded during the unique era when the state was incorporating "Afro-Cuban culture" as part of its revolutionary remaking. In the past, ethnographers might have ventured out into religious homes like hers to extract raw aesthetic material from the "Afro-Cuban underworld" that would be secularized and refined to fit a new modern mulato ethno-nationalism. Her father, who went by the nickname Chacho, was a highly respected *oba* (master of ceremonies) within the religioso community. *Obases* (*oba*, pl.) throughout the city considered him to be the highest authority on even the most arcane of liturgical intricacies to fulfill their duties as ceremonial officiants in the household temples they were hired to serve. At a major transit hub in Centro Habana, you could tell any taxi driver, "Take me to *Padrino* (Godfather) Chacho's house," and they would automatically know your exact destination. Jenny still lived with her parents, sister, and aunt. Jenny did not take lightly her role as a custodian for the dance traditions she inherited from her ancestors. But to legally work professionally as a dancer, she needed the credentials issued from state institutions of higher learning to endorse her secularized expertise in "folkloric dance."

Although officially employed as a performer and dance director of Yoruba Andabo, Jenny's primary source of income came from teaching *clases particulares* (private lessons). She was careful not to abandon her professional obligations to the group, but sometimes a teaching gig required her to travel abroad and miss scheduled performances in Cuba. On these occasions, she needed permission from the artistic director of Yoruba Andabo to authorize her temporary absence so that she could legally leave and return to the island.

In 2010, the occupation of "Folkloric dance artist" was written into law, along with 178 new categories of legalized self-employment, under the new economic reforms. Like many dancers who made a living teaching privately outside of formal educational institutions, she refused to apply for the license. Recognizing themselves as not only cultural experts but rightful inheritors of an ancestral legacy, these women sought to be their own brokers. In Jenny's case, asserting her independence from the kind of patriarchal authority endorsed by the state enabled her more latitude in allowing her copresences to order her steps. Following the paths Elegguá opened for her paid off.

When it came to money, Jenny was a savvy, no-nonsense businesswoman. She did not disclose how much she earned, but she could afford to renovate her family's house in San Miguel, the latest i-gadget from abroad, a fresh pedicure and manicure with nail extensions every week, and a fresh weave every few months. Her earnings also allowed her to take private taxis wherever she traveled in the city, so she never needed to rely on the unreliable city buses. Private transportation also meant that she could get to her teaching gigs on time. Punctuality was a quality she and her students valued. Most of all, she never needed to rely on a man to give her and her family the stability they required and comforts they desired. In 2012, with the constitutional reform allowing Cuban citizens to travel without permission from the government, Jenny was able to make the most of her network of students abroad. In turn, she became less beholden to the male directorship of the state-sponsored ensemble that heretofore granted her a formal salary. At the time, it was rare in the industry for a rumbera to secure invitations to travel internationally as an individual. But Jenny had a strong reputation among Afro-Cuban dance aficionados and religiosos around the world for her exceptional interpretation of the dances of Yemayá.

Jenny taught dance to both Cubans and foreigners alike, at different rates, of course, and with different stakes involved. Her Cuban students mostly came to her for additional training to help them pass qualifying exams under the Ministry of Culture, for which she was a jurist, or to stand out in future auditions while pursuing their dance careers. Foreign students came from all over the world to train with her as well. They could have encountered her for the first time in an international festival (mostly in Eastern Europe and Mexico), where she was flown in to give master classes, or maybe they operated "Latin dance" studios in their countries of origin and sought professional development. She was paid in cash in exchange for imbuing her students with embodied knowledge that had transferable value in a cultural market for Cuban folkloric dance. Nimbly, she factored in those calculations every time she taught, offering a customized learning experience at market rate. Jenny told me that I was the only foreigner she did not charge full price. For those who cannot rely on mass media channels for promotion, a well-trained student like me was a valuable marketing tool. This wasn't dancing for dancing's sake, after all.

In my case, the fact that I was also a Black woman, and of Cuban descent, gave her added material to raise the stakes of my study. "You have to channel that rumbera inside you from La Hata!" she'd say, referencing a tough community infamous for its strong Abakuá presence in the working-class Black neighborhood of Guanabacoa, where my great-grandfather was born. Her pedagogy aimed to capitalize on the affective force of my ancestral kinship ties, thinking it might bring out the movement quality she desired when I reached my growing edge. When I achieved a certain level of proficiency, she would invite friends or her other Cuban students to watch my classes. She took special pride in revealing that although I may have resembled someone born in Cuba, I was foreign, a fact that was meant to surprise the viewer. My "passing" for a local while dancing was, for her, a testament to her pedagogical expertise.

   . The way my body looked mattered outside of dance class, too. I was most often interpreted, by Cubans and foreigners alike, to be part of the local landscape. As such, I would be cast in quotidian roles seemingly congruent with my race, gender, and class. On the one hand, this "passing" allowed me to blend more easily into the Black spaces where rumba practitioners dwelled, affording a level of presumed belonging that might function as protection. On the other hand, "passing" as Cuban also positioned me as an object of hypervisibility and desire, exposing me to unwanted advances. The more proficient I became as a dancer, as my body schema seemed to change, the more frequent these interpellations occurred.

   These hailings did not stop at the perimeter of the dance floor. I was reminded of my casting when foreign men, tourists, would make advances at me while on my way to an interview or the store, or when security guards would refuse me entrance into the hotels where I bought internet cards—the presumption being that I was yet another *jinetera* (a hustler or prostitute) they had to protect their decent patrons from. There was no presumed need to ask me any clarifying questions before relating to me according to the dominant social script. The onus was on me to learn its logics, understand the systems that undergirded its reproduction, and maneuver astutely so I could get from point A to point B.

   Both before and after the triumph of the 1959 Revolution, dominant discourses about rumberas projected the desires of the male gaze onto Black women. As in other former slave societies, particularly in the Caribbean, darker-skinned (dancing) women signify lewd commodities to be consumed rather than heard from (Kempadoo 2004; Alexander 2005; Ruiz 2007; Álvarez Ramírez 2008). The movements specific to women dancing rumba have largely been interpreted in ways that corroborate that perspective. As I recounted in chapter 1, rumberas have been a mainstay in the white male imagination, abundantly reflected in literature as objects of male desire and metaphors for Cuba's unique mulata culture. Descriptions of the genre before and during the *Afrocubanismo* movement relied on the authority of ethnographic accounts to fuel their erotic narratives based on miscegenation fantasies (Arroyo 2003). During the "rumba craze" of the 1930s through the 1950s, white Cuban writers and artists represented rumberas as a "sex toy for white men who 'discover' her on the streets" (Moore 1997, 187). The *mulata rumbera* trope maintained its currency in the early 1960s, evidencing the need for revolutionary leaders to save Black women from waywardness, prostitution, and *la mala vida* (Hynson 2020). Then, in the 1990s Special Period, state officials sought to market rumba as a tourist attraction. Studies about the relationship between sexuality and chattel slavery in the Americas have shown that "desire marks the place of colonial access" (Spillers 1987). In other words, rather than desire evidencing the absence of racism, racism can just as well order desire (Holland 2012). Although acquiring new meanings according to the particular historical moment in which she danced, the ways rumberas have been written into Cuban cultural sense over time have nonetheless reified Black dancing women as natural, if not rightful, objects of male consumption.

The mulata rumbera is framed in discourse as both victim of her own sexual surplus and instigator of her sexual assault, prey and co-conspirator. In the danced chase of rumba guaguancó, while the rumbera shields her *chocha*, the coveted target of male penetration between her legs, she instigates her own pursuit. Her seductive hips, so they say, portray an enticement of further attempts. By extension, the defensive refusals of Black women on or off stage, if the women seem to fit the description, are always already understood as erotic openings. This hypersexualized reading of rumberas provides a palatable culturalist rationale for these everyday expressions of anti-Black heteropatriarchy. In such a way, the partner dance can be interpreted as affectionately heteropatriarchal and authentically Cuban. There is an old, built-in market for these kinds of performances of benign mestizo heteropatriarchy and erotic play. No doubt, many tourists come to Cuba to experience it in living color. *She Is Cuba*, as Melissa Blanco Borelli (2016) so aptly titles her treatise on the *mulata rumbera*. These "Cuban" readings of rumba not only reinscribe the nostalgia and promise of sexual access to Black female flesh, but dangerously underappreciate the meanings Black women assign to their own improvisatory practice (Berry 2021).

Jenny and her posse of rumberas (confidants, sisters and daughters of stone) would coach me in how to handle the circumstances I encountered around rumba events as women who looked like them. I will never forget the time Morcilla swooped in to disentangle me from the groping hands of a tourist on the dance floor at El Palacio de la Rumba. Even though she was a good many years senior to Jenny, she would become Jenny's *ahijada* (goddaughter) years later after a serious health scare that she survived thanks to the *trabajo religioso* (religious work) of Jenny and their family of stone.

Morcilla was the daughter of a well-respected rumbera singer who crossed over into the cabaret and mainstream entertainment industry back in her day. By day Morcilla worked at Callejón de Hamel, and by night she went with Jenny to venues where rumba groups performed. She was very dark-skinned, thin, and short. Her legs were her favorite attribute, so she always wore a mini skirt and heels to show off their tone. She was also a self-identified alcoholic and taught me how to check the bottom of beer cans for the red, yellow, or green color dots that indicated if the alcohol percentage was above, below, or standard, so I could buy for her wisely. "If you are poor and an alcoholic, you have to know how to make your money stretch," she said matter-of-factly. No matter how inebriated she became, whether at Callejón de Hamel or El Palacio de la Rumba, she maintained a vigilance to unwanted male advances.

That night on the dance floor I had made several attempts to politely refuse a white man who insisted on dancing too closely. He was Mexican, so there was no language barrier to understanding my verbal refusals in Spanish. He was either too drunk to care or had chosen to interpret my "no's" (which I said with a smile only to not incite anger) as coy "yes's." At his level of inebriation, I sensed that laughter could easily turn to aggression on a dime if he felt offended. As I receded, he stepped in closer, legs wide, establishing a grip around my waist. I leaned back, trying to reestablish distance. Internally, my mind was racing and my heart was pounding. Suddenly, Morcilla strutted over and, without making any eye contact or even saying a word, pried his hands from around my back in one deliberate and continuous motion—all without interrupting the fluttering of her fan in the other hand. Caught by surprise, he stumbled over to the floor while I was carried by the momentum of her free hand back to our table. "The Mexicans and the Italians can be the worst with that sort of thing. They come here and get too drunk and want their fantasy. You look like one of us, so they don't know [you are a foreigner]. If you don't want to [be with them], you'll have to learn how to protect yourself and make yourself understood," she counseled me. The posse had a good laugh, nodded, and continued swaying steadily to the clave.[6] They understood that words were often futile for countering the expectation that El Palacio de la Rumba seemed to advertise to foreigners, promising a night of tropicalist sexual conquest. The logo on the marquis showed silhouettes of a rumbera and a rumbero on opposite sides of a conga drum. The rumbera held an ambiguous pose, legs together bent at the knees, leaning ever so lightly away. The rumbero held both arms up high and one leg off the floor about to thrust. Inside, these same figures straddled the stage in larger-than-life proportion, framing the action on the dance floor.

As I moved throughout the city, I was repeatedly reminded how Black women's bodies were cast in an ongoing story about us that preceded us, framing our social interactions. But that was not the entire story. While the way we looked may evoke a fraught genealogy of social meanings, Black women devised strategies to move with spiritually endowed dignity within the essentialized bodies they occupied (Blanco Borelli 2016, 17). Morcilla demonstrated how a simple yet deliberate choreographic intervention could get one's message across the gender, race, and class divide better than words: a precisely timed sweeping gesture could make a man fall under his own weight without ever missing a beat. Rumberas' choreographic choices entailed making the most of their social casting to assert agency in a market with no guarantees.

Calculated Transactions

One morning in July, a flashy red rental car pulled up to the curb in front of the bodega below my window. Thanks to Morcilla's connections with the neighborhood *bodeguero* (*bodega* worker or grocer), I was renting the apartment above just a skip away from El Palacio de la Rumba and a jump down from the Callejón de Hamel. The *bodeguero* decided it was safe to tell the neighbors that I was his little cousin who, as a favor to my mother, would stay there while I completed my studies. The apartment had a living room spacious enough to dance in when we pushed the furniture back. As if the car itself did not already stand out enough on its own in this neighborhood, the two pale men, dressed in all Black, lugging expensive camera equipment, added to the stark contrast. A French film crew was doing a documentary on "Cuban femininity," Jenny told me. The filmmaker wanted footage of Jenny teaching a class. I was her only active student at the time, so she asked for my consent to let them film one of our private classes, which, after getting the okay from the *bodeguero*, I granted. "Just make sure they don't touch my orishas," he demanded. I gave him my word that the divinities, who rested in pots on shelves in the living room, would not be disturbed during the filming. The class would be free of charge, Jenny clarified, since I was doing her a favor. As they climbed up the steps to the living room, Jenny immediately told them that I was a foreigner and I danced very well. I hoped, as always, not to let her down. This documentary could serve to promote her expertise to a French viewing audience. I had butter-flies in my stomach as they walked around to find the best light.

When Jenny positioned us in front of a mid-sized mirror hanging on the wall, I could tell that this class was going to be different. Jenny played some recorded music from her iPod with portable speakers and quickly demonstrated a routine that I would repeat. Shortly after we began dancing, the cameraman and the director exchanged comments in French under their breath. Jenny must have stuck out the tip of her tongue at one point, her signature move evoking her own enjoyment in her body. The gesture clearly captured the filmmaker's attention. He wanted to see it again. "The tongue, show your tongue," the director made out in his broken Spanish. She obliged without missing a beat of the choreography. Wanting to make sure that the cameraman captured a close-up of her tongue peeking out her mouth, the director gave Jenny another command, "Again." She obliged. Although the premise was to record a typical dance class, this was anything but typical. Rather than hearing the punctuation of her vocal commands and corrections to me over the music, the Frenchman gave cues to coach *her* into a script for a dance class that catered to a marketable fantasy. The cameraman knelt and crouched tightly around the kinesphere Jenny and I shared, exploring different angles. "Again. More tongue," his voice became more severe as he focused the zoom lens. My body was moving but I was frozen, trapped by their gaze.

When the song ended, we took a short pause. Jenny performed the part of what a dance teacher would say: "Very good. Now, from the top. This time with more feeling." After the first sequence, she began to stick out her tongue without his command to add emphasis in the places he had indicated. She was a professional and could memorize choreographic changes and perform them seamlessly as if they were second nature. Not daring to embarrass my teacher by noncompliance, I went through the prescribed motions. I may have even shimmied my shoulders for added flurry. Averting eye contact with the camera now below my waist, I tried to mentally escape the camera's production of its object, my flesh. I zeroed in on the reflection of my torso's pulse in the mirror. Class was short that day. After two songs they had gotten all the footage they needed. Two sets of sensual, swaying hips: check. The tongue was a windfall, perfect for a plotline about the art of Cuban seduction.

After packing up their equipment, they invited us to lunch. Our choice, they said; anywhere not too far from here. At first, I politely declined. I had lost my appetite and wanted some distance from their company. Jenny pulled me aside and insisted that I not leave her alone with them. After seeing her perform the sexiness they ordered with such apparent ease, it had not occurred to me that she, too, would have reservations about being alone in their company. But this social exchange after the music played was part of the job, too. It had, no doubt, served her well in the past. As they descended the steps back to where the *bodeguero* and the neighbors were watching the car, Jenny told me privately that she knew just where to take them, one of the most expensive restaurants in the Chinatown district. "One day, you'll learn how to manage these circumstances." Perhaps that was the real lesson of the day. She could tap into and reflect the filmmaker's desire, and in doing so create openings to fulfill her own. Without time to change out of my dance clothes, I grabbed my purse and followed Jenny down the stairs.

When we entered the restaurant, the waitstaff greeted us like we were familiar faces. I had never been there before. I resented their knowing smiles. This was not the first time a pair of white foreign men entered with two Black women (in spandex no less!) at their side. Jenny made no move to disclose my foreignness to the onlookers at that moment. I watched myself being watched and being understood as if reenacting a cliché scenario. Life imitating art, imitating a colonial miscegenation fantasy. Two Afro-Cuban seductresses, professional rumberas no doubt, steering their prey—or so went the script.

At the table, the director shared how much he loved Cuba and preferred to be here than in his home country. He began to complain about "the Arab problem" in France and how they were invading the country, committing crimes, and refusing to assimilate. He expressed resentment about the fact that Arab women covered themselves and that their men got aggressive when French men looked at them. Cuban women, by contrast were the complete opposite. They were more open to foreigners, which he greatly preferred. The director, whose name I later learned was Daniel Lainé, was reciting his working hypothesis about Cuban femininity that, I would only years later learn, is what drove the film he was making. Rumberas were a key example for supporting his thesis, and Jenny was a case study.

Enraged by the conversation, I silently pretended to peruse the expensive menu and waited to take my cue from Jenny to storm out. Except she, too, was looking down at the menu. "Yes, yes, Cuban women, we are very different," she repeated rote while nodding slowly in agreement. Then she lifted her gaze ever so slightly to shoot a demure smile my way. The smile was of a woman who knew the benefit of the part afforded to her in that moment. The film's reach would raise her social capital as a sought-after expert. I could not help but wonder if this is what she meant when she said that as Black women we needed to give ourselves value. If so, I learned that "added value" may come at an emotional cost. The averted gaze and smile were adornments that I could put on to mask my discontent when dealing in these calculated transactions.

Five years later, I reminisced with Jenny about that night over dinner at a new restaurant in Centro Habana I wanted to try. She told me that the documentary had been released and it came out great. I even appeared in the final cut. She arranged for her *ahijado* (godson) to burn me a copy so I could watch it; he was a young dancer and met us at the Palacio de la Rumba late the next night after one of his hotel cabaret gigs. It was almost another year before I finally watched the documentary. I had put it off out of fear of what I would find—my dancing body staged as corroborating evidence in an erotic fantasy of Cuban femininity made to order.

"Cuba: The Flavor of the Caribbean" would be one part in a five-part film series by the same director called *Les Chemins de la Beauté* (The routes of beauty), covering "the art of seduction and feminine beauty around the world" (Lainé and Combroux 2013).[7] The opening scene started in a typical fashion for foreign films about Cuba: a Havana street scene showing the panoramic view of the bay, then the hustle and bustle of the city and old cars from the 1950s, and finally zeroing in on women walking, standing, or sitting as ornaments of this nostalgic landscape. The narrator acts as a guide for the viewer, interpreting the scene as one of carefree suffering: "Cuba is a place out of time and out of fashion with a disconcerting tranquility. No advertisements. . . . Here we find the most beautiful women of the Caribbean."[8] Women of African descent show the extent of the country's natural, if irrational, joie de vivre. Their sex drive, we are later told, is a by-product of the "hot" tropical environment. Double entendres referring to nature and animals are sprinkled throughout.

Suddenly, the sound of drums creeps in over the cityscape and we move from the street to a close-up of a laughing Black woman's face in thick makeup. The camera pans to others in the room, also Black, laughing along, as the woman dances in an elaborate yellow costume to live drumming. This is a religious ceremony in someone's home and establishes the filmmaker's insider access to a behind-the-scenes view that entices tourists to this exotic, "forbidden," "wild" island. If you looked closely, you could see one young Black woman who is not laughing. Instead, she is intently watching. That young Black woman was me.

I was immediately brought back to the day Jenny had invited me to attend the staging of a *tambor* for Ochún at her house that she planned for the film. Her father's *cumpleaños de santo* (saint birthday or anniversary of initiation) as a priest of Ochún, was the same day, June 24, so the altar room would be set up in full regalia for that annual occasion. She may have sensed my reticence about being in the company of the French men again. I could learn something, she insisted. She always encouraged me to go to *tambores* to study how the orishas manifest on earth and bring that understanding to my own dancing. She would be dancing for an orisha who I was currently studying in our classes: Ochún, the divinity syncretized with the patron saint of Cuba, Our Virgin Lady of Charity. Although people of any gender could figuratively "wear Ochún's crown," the divinity was often hailed in the literature as a metaphor for all Cuban women and depicted as a mulata. Rumberas often incorporated the movement vernacular of Ochún praise dances into their stylings when dancing guaguancó. While I was prohibited from filming drummed ceremonies at her house, Jenny encouraged me to come prepared with my camera this time since it was not real, "*de verdad.*" The divinity was not coming to the filming. However, based on my prior experience with the filmmakers, I came emotionally prepared for much more than the study of music and steps.

When I arrived, I saw that she had recruited a bunch of her friends to come out so that there would be a good turnout for the filmed simulation. Some I had met before at ceremonies or rumba shows as friends and members of her blood and stone family. Others I saw for the first time. With the furniture removed, the living room became the stage. People brought cell phones to take pictures of Jenny and themselves "on set." Jenny entered the living room from the kitchen in full stage makeup and with a big smile. She had on an elaborate costume: the one she reserved for when she performed Ochún on large proscenium stages. I felt awkward seeing her activate this level of stage presence in the intimacy of her home. There was such a stark contrast from how I had seen her show up among family during ceremonies they had hosted for themselves. There was no attempt to bear any resemblance. This was a promotional video for the French men and the monied European audience they represented.

I am not sure if the French men knew that the ceremony was staged, rather than serving an actual religious function for the community, or if it even would have mattered. The director was visibly excited by the spectacle. He gave quick commands to his cameraman to get shots of the attendees gathered around the living room in a circle as Jenny danced in the center in front of the double set of *batá* drums. After being drilled on these very rhythm sequences and songs in our class, I was proud that I could perceive her execution of complex decision-making in her steps with the music. Just as I had seen her dance in rumba guaguancó, she skillfully accommodated the men's unpredictable movement in the tight space, adjusting as they circled around her, rotating her facing to keep them in her peripheral view. She accounted for them seamlessly in her choreographic improvisation. All this while maintaining a smooth effort quality, steadied by the never-ceasing pulse in her torso. She showed a high degree of somatic astuteness. She was a true professional. I knew that these sophisticated calculations were invisible to the French men. On the movie screen, Jenny's movements appeared spontaneous. Her skilled performance would be used as evidence of some innate, raw sensual surplus natural to tropical women of her kind. In the film, her body would corroborate that Cuban femininity "tastes" like a dancing mulata. She is "hot," inviting the male gaze into the intimacy of her home and body—she was Cuba.

The filmmakers loved the remote community ambience as a backdrop to their star, a rumbera performing the dances of an "African goddess"—a perfect synecdoche for the Cuban femininity that sells. This insider access to private ritual would anchor the documentary's theory about Cuban women's innate openness to other forms of penetration, a sensual essence ostensibly anchored in ancient African cosmology. However, the crowd of people filming the filming with their cell phones, creating their own souvenir of being "on set," disrupted the chronotope (space-time), in the Bakhtinian sense, that the filmmakers were hoping to conjure. The director, visibly irritated, yelled at everyone to put away their cameras immediately: "No photos! No photos!" The locals were weakening the force of the performance. Or rather, their behavior revealed the scene's constructedness for the camera, breaking the tacit agreement that everyone present would participate in the performance of a particular figuration of "Afro-Cuba" exclusively for his camera. This figuration relies on a naturalization of a colonial imaginary of Blackness as anachronistic, perpetually in the past (Wirtz 2014).

At that moment, Jenny delivered a hyper-theatricalized laugh, an embellishment of Ochún's signature expression, one of her tools to quell conflict. Mouth and eyes wide, her laugh incited her audience to laugh in kind. I was not sure if they were laughing in homage to the divinity's signature cunning or laughing at the director who felt entitled to take control of the looking. In any case, Jenny's affectation of levity expertly diffused the mounting tension between the filmmakers and the attendees and allowed the show to go on. What happened next did not make the final cut.

When the dance demonstration was over, the French men asked to do an interview with Jenny in the adjacent altar room. The elaborate fabrics and

2.1 Jennyselt Galata as Ochún in a screen grab from the film *Cuba: La Saveur des Caraïbes*. Photo by author.

food offerings, decorated from floor to ceiling, made for a great backdrop for their star. While the rest of the attendees stayed out in the living room, she asked me to enter the altar room and stay close nearby. Aware that I spoke French, this time she asked me to act as her translator. Specifically, she asked me to translate for her what the French men were saying between each other. Whatever had happened between her and the filmmakers since my last encounter seemed to warrant additional suspicion on her part about their internal exchanges. Jenny stayed in character as Ochún.

The director started the interview by asking her to tell him who or what Ochún is. "Ochún is the patron saint of Cuba and the divinity of feminine sensuality and eros," she began. He nodded with satisfaction at her response. Then he asked her to characterize Cuban femininity. In the same sweet voice, she responded, "When are you going to pay me? I want my money," never breaking her flirtatious smile. Her sister, who had been sitting to her side adjusting the fan of the costume's skirt across the altar, broke out into laughter. Jenny delivered the same affectatious laugh as before. This time a tinge of dark humor came through unequivocally. The director, again visibly irritated, waited in silence for the moment to pass. Then she looked straight at me, "Translate me," she ordered, as if taking his silence to mean that there was a language barrier. I knew he had heard her the first time, perhaps she did too, but I dutifully obliged. "She wants to know when you are going to pay her," I said in French. The director shot me a piercing dirty look and shooed me off with his hand as if I were a pesky fly, yet another nuisance ruining the scene.

She began a monologue: "Just like in many countries, we have highs and lows; but it's about having lots of love, passion, lots of sensuality. Like Ochún, we must always smile. She can be committing murder, and as she kills you, she stays smiling. Like how I'm smiling at you now, see?" Jenny made her point. She narrated the mechanics of her cunning performance as a learned behavior that strategically disarms her assailant—a tool to navigate the political economy of Black femininity amid conditions of power asymmetry. "Ochún teaches us that you must don a feminine charm, a charisma, even when you are hungry, exhausted, and ridden with grief. No matter how bad things are you must always maintain a resplendent and graceful expression on your face and in your mannerism." She performed this mannerism of dissemblance as she described it, revealing it as a "tropicalist" role she was consciously playing with. Happiness and sensuality in the face of precarity are the main tropes associated with this kind of Orientalism (Ribeiro 2019). "You must always wear a flirtatious smile. That's why Europeans like you come here looking for us Cuban women, right?" Jenny retorted, "Beautiful like me: a mulata!" She smiled and stuck out her tongue to punctuate the end of her monologue, then broke out in another laugh.

In all the years I have known Jenny, she had always self-identified as *negra* (Black), and proudly so. Her self-identification as mulata in that moment situated her squarely as the rightful representative subject of the French man's film. This conscious fashioning of selfhood comments on *mulataje* (mixedness) as a learned racialized and gendered performance of identity adopted strategically for a particular kind of recognition in a market-space of coloniality (Quijano 2000; Blanco Borelli 2016).[9] She showed herself as an expert of colonial projections onto her body and reflected it back to the French man in spades, for which she expected to be remunerated. Once again, she flipped the looking glass and implicated the viewer as someone she had been watching and studying all along. She had been collecting his desirous projections onto her body as data. Again. And again. With more tongue, she situated his own erotic fantasy of her as a construct that framed their terms of engagement. In doing so, she revealed her own self-awareness of how the force of colonial desire shaped her own performance of racialized gender expression all along. However, there are other influential forces also bearing on her present that legitimize her claims. Indeed, within Ochún's sacred dance repertoire was a mirror with the power to reflect back what the viewer needs to see, when they need to see it. The altar seemed to embolden Jenny to speak with the force of divinities who demand recognition and reciprocation from the living. Within Ochún's sacred choreography were mechanisms to dispel conflict and ensure accountability, positioning Jenny, and her family by extension, to negotiate these calculated transactions on different footing, equipped with other tools of persuasion, protection, and praise.

Little from that day's filming would make it past the editing floor. A close-up shot of my face in silence leaning against the entrance of the altar room with bated breath made it in somehow. The moment when Jenny brought her elderly father up to dance with her in front of the drums would be of no interest to the director. Padrino Chacho, a respected child of Ochún, twirled effortlessly to his divine mother's rhythm, vividly evoking an imaginary skirt around his waist with stunning grace. These scenes representing the dynamism and complexity of everyday choreographies of Black femininity in Cuba that were not ruled by sex would be deleted as pesky anomalies. What Padrino Chacho might teach them about the divine feminine was a distraction from the hours of other footage corroborating the thesis that Cuban women's voracious sexual appetite was rooted in the hot weather, the absence of Catholic repression, and the trace of Africa. Hips swaying side to side down the street, buttocks and breasts peeking out from bikinis at the beach, spandex-covered pelvises gyrating on stage, and rhythmic seductresses dancing rumba on a patio would stand as empirical evidence for the thesis about Black women that dated back to the colonial era. A *trigueña* woman boasting about the unique eroticism of "our Blacks," ostensibly due to the history of cultural miscegenation, concluded the film.

However, as Jenny's student, I gained a different vantage point that the film's focus and framing could not capture. From where I stood, between Jenny and the camera, I could appreciate her sophisticated construction of a persuasive ideal type, choreographed in such a way to gain access to needed resources in a market for a fantasy in high demand. Ochún did not need to be incarnate for her sacred repertoire to provide the tools, and the license, to insist upon her children's material compensation. Learning to dance rumba with an awareness of who I resembled allowed me to appreciate the everyday art and imperative of moving in a way that was attuned to the geopolitics of trade in the afterlife of slavery.

For rumberas, harnessing the signifying power of their own body, that which they did not choose, to steer a man's fall under the weight of his own fantasy, had its risks. These were some of the variables that Black women, structurally undervalued by society, calculated daily. Theirs was a skillful art that, as someone whose body fit the description, I had no choice but to pay attention to and take seriously. My body was always already implicated in the script, as was my profession as an anthropologist, within the ongoing traffic between fact, fantasy, desire, and violence (Hartman 2008, 5). These lessons were perhaps exceptional, while they also testified to the broader challenges Black women faced as they harnessed the sacred repertoires available to them to accrue added value as the Cuban economy updated. While interpellated by the rumbera trope, rumberas hailed Ochún—on and off camera, in Chinatown restaurants, and at the altar—to push against the constraints of their socioeconomic conditions, legitimize spirited actions, and claim other possibilities.

The Silent Gendering of "Racismo Profesional"

I was pulled in at the last minute to interpret for a rumba music-and-dance-class series taught by the members of Grupo AfroAmérica. They were hired to teach a group of Americans from the United States as part of an educational tour to Havana in 2018. Grupo AfroAmérica's gender composition distinguished itself from other rumba groups in that it was a male-led ensemble but with a female cast of percussionists. When I expressed an eagerness to know more about the gendered aspects of the careers of the women in the ensemble, Silvia Cabrera Sarria, the dance director, enthusiastically recruited Mercedes Lay Bravo and Amelia Mesa González, both percussionists, to participate as well. Silvia and I had the same dark brown complexion and stature. She wore a Catholic cross around her neck and an *ide* (initiatory beaded bracelet) around her left wrist. Her hair was pulled back in a high ponytail that framed her heart-shaped face. Amelia would be read in Cuba as mulata for her light brown skin, but she identified unequivocally as Black. She was tall and wore her hair in pigtails with a middle part and a white ribbon around her forehead to match her white tank top, white jeans, and white sneakers. Mercedes wore her hair proudly in a beautifully coiffed afro. She also donned a white outfit, more modest than Amelia's, and paired it with a mustard-colored shawl and slippers to match. We convened after the last class for lunch on the patio of *La Casa de la Amistad* (The House of Friendship) where the classes were held. I let the voice recorder run in the middle of the table while we drank and ate, talking over the recorded music to which the waitstaff hummed.

2.2 Silvia Martiza Cabrera Sarria teaching rumba guaguancó. Photo by author.

By then our voices were sore from screaming over the live drumming during the class. But that did not dull the conversation. To each question they interjected answers in quick succession. While the conversation progressed, Amelia excused herself intermittently to check her phone, which was plugged into an outlet nearby; it would not keep a charge, and she was worried that a German tourist she had exchanged numbers with days prior would think she was ignoring his love messages. She sometimes read his messages aloud to us for laughs and for help with their interpretation. When one struggled with how to articulate an idea to me, the others would finish the sentence, even illustrating their points with bodily reenactments until they were satisfied that the message had come through. The fluidness and force of the exchange could be attributed to their closeness. I would learn that this bond was also forged through the process of fostering each other's professional development against gendered adversity. They were part of a grassroots intergenerational network of women spanning the city, seeking to gain a foothold in rumba's male-dominated industry.

One of the main concerns that the women of AfroAmérica expressed revolved around their limited job opportunities as professional rumberas.

They told stories of their own experiences of social intimidation by men who effectively steered them away from higher-paying roles, like drumming and artistic directorship. These limitations in how women could earn a living for their talent discouraged them from competing with men for power and resources. At the same time, they were ushered into dancing roles that relied on their sexual desirability. It was often the case that in rumba ensembles dancers were treated as auxiliary members, sometimes contracted on a case-by-case basis to "adorn" the musical act. In short, women's access to wages through rumba was relatively limited, unstable, and reliant on male leadership and erotic choice.

The pace of the conversation sped up as the women of Grupo AfroAmérica traded anecdotes about how male chauvinism and market logics had played out in their lives and those of other rumberas who were deemed to step out of their "natural" roles as women. Mercedes and Amelia both spoke of the day when Obini Batá debuted as an all-female percussion ensemble. Their "gender-bending" was a scandal. They played at the National Folkloric Dance Company (CFN)'s annual Father's Day Celebration in 1992. The women who founded Obini Batá started their professional careers as dancers in CFN. Even though the drums they played were unconsecrated and therefore did not serve to communicate with the divinity like in ceremony, many religiosos were disturbed by women playing drums, a role traditionally assigned to men. Amelia, too, began as a dancer but was inspired by Obini Batá to develop her artistry in percussion. When she showed up to an Obini Batá audition, even without any prior drumming experience, she quickly discovered that she had a knack for it and, in her words, *"me enganché"* (I got hooked). Religious doctrine aside, being barred from drumming had financial repercussions (discussed in chapter 4). Either implicitly or explicitly, it was made clear to rumberas that dancing—not drumming and certainly not directing—was the woman's rightful role and thus where her talents were assigned social value.

Mercedes and Amelia relayed story after story of men sabotaging their mastery of the drums, either by intentionally teaching them incorrectly or incompletely.[10] "They'll say 'yeah, that's it [correct].' But it's not really [correct]." Most men in their communities were anxious to see women drummers fail as evidence of their innate biological difference. Rather than confronting the men head on, women who wanted to advance in the craft took on the extra labor of cross-referencing everything they learned from men with multiple teachers, and then triangulating those lessons with what they saw in live performance to verify the accuracy of what they

2.3 Members of Grupo AfroAmérica. *From left to right:* Justo Pelladito Hernández, Amelia Mesa González, and Mercedes Esperanza Lay Bravo, on percussion. Photo by author.

were taught. Along their journey to find trusted teachers, they established their own learning networks where they exchanged their independent research and began to train other women and girls also seeking to learn. This journey led Mercedes to Justo Pelladito, a founding member of the CFN and the son of a cofounder of the famous rumba group Los Muñequitos de Matanzas. In 1993, greatly benefited by Justo's credibility, they eventually cofounded Grupo AfroAmérica. But finding men like Justo who were willing to teach and drum alongside women was rare.

Fed up with the hazing they endured to prove themselves to male gatekeepers, other women ventured to form their own all-female rumba ensembles where they could exercise full leadership and control. Notably, both Silvia and Mercedes had daughters who were percussionists in all-female ensembles. Amelia gave private percussion lessons to other girls for free in her neighborhood. Although the women agreed that in the 2010s there were more female percussionists and all-female ensembles than ever before, there were still relatively few, and they had difficulty getting hired to perform. They attributed the added professional exclusion all-female rumba ensembles faced to "Cuban machismo" and men being overrepresented in the decision-making roles for managing and booking talent.

In effect, more likely than not, if women were to be valued in rumba, they had to be dancing (or alternatively, singing). If indeed men ultimately determined the direction of money flows, Black women had reason to invest in self-fashionings that positioned them as squarely representative of limiting definitions of "Cuban femininity." If they didn't, they risked compromising their foothold in the market. During the update, then, rumberas developed their artistic talents with an acute awareness that economic opportunities were shaped by heteropatriarchy. More often than not, rumberos incentivized rumberas to build careers whereby the expected performances of racialized gender were reinforced. This also resulted in women being positioned in competition with other women for limited roles.

Silvia insisted that the gender discrimination rumberas faced was uniquely harmful for darker-skinned women. She summed up the unfair playing field in the entertainment industry in two words, drawn out for emphasis: "*rac-is-mo pro-fes-sion-al*" (employment racism). To bring home the point, Silvia put on a deep voice, stuck out her chest and widened her elbows to imitate a man in charge, "No [shooing me away as a darker-skinned woman], get me a tall mulata!" In auditions, they were measured against other women based on whose body had the potential to fulfill the mulata rumbera trope that appealed to the imagined desires of the most (heterosexual male) consumers. Her statement made me recall Jenny's cool calculation of the French filmmakers and her pragmatic self-nomination as *mulata* when it could make a positive difference. Competing for paid dance parts in nightclubs and cabarets crystalized rumberas' experience of the silent gendering of employment racism in Havana.

To the extent that the economic reforms granted New Men 2.0 more autonomy in talent booking driven by profit speculation, rumberas had to contend with a constrained range for their artistry and gender expression. "The new trend of dancing rumba with high arms is because of rumba's staging in cabarets, when rumba was being done by models who didn't know the tradition but fit the beauty standard. . . . And now the young girls are copying that commercial distortion," Silvia complained. Amelia, the youngest in the group, defended rumberas of her generation, emphasizing that the rising cost of living in Cuba could not be ignored. "Cuba today isn't the Cuba of yesterday," she reminded the others. They had inherited an economic reality of rising inequality and needed to pursue viable career pathways that could support their families. Structural conditions of economic exclusion have long reinforced persistent notions about Black female sexuality (Fernandez 1999), which rumberas, as seen in the French film, calculated. Silvia's invocation of the term *employment racism* shows how she situated rumberas' specific challenges in attaining gainful employment within a broader discourse from below about the discriminatory wage-labor landscape during the economic reforms under Raúl Castro.

For Black women and girls, this "updating" economic field meant a return to, or intensification of, particular kinds of raced and gendered labor seen before the 1959 Revolution, specifically, domestic service. The resurgence of this occupation has been accompanied by exploitative working conditions at the hands of small-business owners, who are overwhelmingly white middle- and upper-class men. In these positions, women are disproportionately vulnerable to gender discrimination and sexual harassment. As Anasa Hicks writes, "Notions of domestic service as the natural lot of women, especially women of African descent, were so deeply embedded into Cuban culture that the work emerged untransformed from such dramatic historical moments as slave emancipation, the 1933 Revolution, and the ratification of the 1940 Constitution" (Hicks 2019, 264). Once regarded as a vestige of Cuba's slave society, revolutionary leaders had long celebrated the eradication of domestic service after 1959, when social programs empowered women to labor for the state (Hynson 2020). In the "updating" Cuba post-Fidel, legal private placement agencies freely catered to heterosexist requests for female servants grounded in enduring colonial associations of Blackness with promiscuity (Hicks 2019).

While Amelia and others make a distinction between the constraints on the choices that rumba professionals must make today versus before, situating rumba within a long history of Black enclosure allows us to see important historical continuities. That is to say, rumba allows us to see the stakes of code-switching in one's body, of modifying one's performance on cue in relationship to how commonsense appraisals of racial and sexual identity impacted one's external valuation within an "erotic economy" (Cabezas 2009; Allen 2011; Stout 2014). What is unique to the post-Fidel period, however, is how rumberas' calculations with regard to how to navigate essentialized ideologies applied to their bodies heightened their consciousness of the contingencies and constraints of their access to an ostensibly "opening" economy where Cubans were encouraged to seek out individual prosperity. At the onset of the reforms in the early 2010s, as Jottar (2013) attests, rumbera choreography may have asserted women's capacity for economic independence invigorated by the promise of what the new economic landscape could bring.

After all, state discourses painted the expanded private market as more "efficient" because, unlike in the public sector, jobs were ostensibly attained through a logic of competition (versus equal distribution), and compensation was based on profit and individual merit (versus citizenship entitlement). However, economic opportunity proved particularly constrained for the Black women and girls these rumberas knew. One might determine that a degree of "strategic essentialism" (Spivak 1988) while dancing was necessary lest the update route her back toward forms of servitude once socially denigrated as a vestige of the colonial era.

We can then better understand why rumberas could explicitly identify "employment racism" as the cause of their professional strife, without necessarily rebuking the way foreign men's erotic fetish for the Other also shaped their possibilities. Rather, foreign men's erotic preference to consume the mulata rumbera was praised for positioning Black women at a rare relative advantage over white women for job selection. "Their vision of Cubans is that we are Black, and that Black people dance with more flavor," Silvia explained. Amelia finished Silvia's thought, endorsing its validity, "[White Cubans] dance with a white flavor." "There's a difference!" agreed Silvia. Amelia jumped in, "They don't have this [putting her left hand on her chest to draw attention to the pulsing motion of the torso Jenny had insisted on in our classes]." Silvia continued welling up with emotion, "I am not against a white woman who dances our folklore. . . . But sometimes when I see that my traditions [are being sold], that which came from Africa . . . and I see a white woman [given preferential treatment], I say *zapatero, a su zapato* [stick with what you know]. Because it's distorting a tradition that is mine and doing what you want with it, without knowing where it comes from, without knowing anything!"

In this analysis, the stereotyped vision of "authentic" Cuban femininity as a fetishized Black Other was a saving grace for Black peso-poor women seeking solvent careers. While they resented the negative repercussions of essentialist, colonial renderings of their womanhood, they still doubled down on those same essentialized ideologies of race and biology to make a claim for Black women's exclusive right to be given preference for paid dance parts. Marc Perry (2016) makes a similar argument about the "eroticized market for blackness" in Cuba that hip-hop artists also seize (46). He writes, "while a sexualized commodification of blackness may operate globally as a site of consumptive desire, it may simultaneously allow some darker-skinned Cubans spaces and gendered modalities of labor within a market economy in which Afro-Cubans are structurally marginal" (47). Melissa Blanco Borelli offers a way to attend to how the mulata choreographs herself into being, an analytics that she terms "hip(g)nosis": "By choosing to perform whatever aspect of '*mulata* identity' necessary for some recognition, a *mulata* enacting hip(g)nosis has some agency in how she is perceived" (Blanco Borelli 2016, 20). Indeed, rumberas used choreography as a pragmatic tool to reinforce myths about them in order to gain advantage against white women for limited resources. If coerced by men into dancing, the money allocated for those roles, they argued, was their ancestral birthright. Without faith in the promises of market rationalism, rumberas asserted an ancestral entitlement to limited benefits owed to them, hard-earned by their enslaved female ancestors.

The discussion after class on the patio gave me yet another important critical vantage for understanding the raced and gendered dimensions of Cuba's economic reforms, and how rumberas maneuvered within its logics. Along with the demand for rumba performance came narrow opportunities and competition with other women. This labor market marked the point of colonial access; the systematic forms of sexual violence visited upon women of African descent from slavery. Not all peso-poor Black women felt they could afford to opt out of this well-established hard-currency revenue stream. Instead, women flocked from the countryside to Havana with their dreams hitched to the promise of its payoff. As Hope Bastian puts it in her ethnography of the same period, it is economic capital, not "the right type of political attitude," that "increasingly allows individuals to pay their own way, or pay their way around obstacles" (2018, 27, 42). In other words, if you widen your leg stance, raise your arms high, and break at the wrists, you may not be dancing rumba "correctly," but you will get paid. And justifiably so. For resembling the mulata rumbera trope comes with its own risks, which deserve compensation. Essentialized, colonial projections upon their bodies were at once costly and valuable.

For Black working-class women, securing viable sources of remuneration came with calculated transactions. Dancing rumba positioned them to evade some of the risks attendant with private sector employment, such as those incurred in domestic servitude, even if it meant doubling down on the kinds of racialized and gendered expectations that reified similarly limiting renderings of Black womanhood on stage. A particular choreographic aptitude, buttressed by sacred repertoires, allowed rumberas who "defended the essence" to strategically negotiate these external projections upon their bodies and still provide for their families. Intimate conversations with rumberas helped me appreciate the stakes of the choreographic aptitude my teachers imparted and how they reconciled its tensions.

Not the Entire Story; Something Else

To help me better understand her frustrations with being a rumbera in the society in which her daughter now moved, Silvia shared her earliest memories of dancing. She located her first dance steps in the lifeworld of the cabildos in her neighborhood of Palmeras, in the city of Cienfuegos. She began, "Palmeras, they'd say, was the *pueblo* (town/people) of the three industries: *mujeres fáciles* (easy women), *la raspadura* (a sugar cane-based dessert), and *la brujería* (witchcraft)." It struck me that she rooted her basis for artistic creativity in relationship to anti-Black and sexist archetypes sedimented in the popular Cuban imaginary during slavery: the heterosexist trope of Black women as hypersexual and the pathologizing of African-inspired spiritual epistemologies. These "industries" were listed alongside a dessert directly tied to plantation labor, positioning all three as inextricably conjoined in the afterlife of slavery. This rendering racialized and feminized Palmeras, the place and its people, within Cuba's political geography. "Palmeras was a small pueblo, but what made it grand were its [cabildos] temples," she countered with pride.

Palmeras was home to numerous cabildos, each dedicated to a different African-inspired divinity. Women played a central role in the maintenance of these community-based Black organizations dating back to slavery. The men in her family, she noted with intensity, were Abakuá. Her great-grandmother, Antonia Trujillo, on the other hand, inherited the responsibility of maintaining the temple for Oya—the feminine warrior divinity of the wind and owner of the cemetery gates—and was a respected *espiritista* (spirit medium). "*Sus ancestros la tenían muy posesionada*" (Her ancestors had a strong hold on her), Silvia said with pride. To be "possessed," in this sense, was to be both claimed and accompanied by spirits. It bequeathed vital resources to the person—resources foreclosed by the dominant society. Until the day she died, at the age of 108, Antonia in turn provided spiritual guidance to everyone in their family, even extended relatives, counseling them on how to live their best lives using the wisdom she received from spirits on their behalf. *Sea santísmo, sea* (Be it sanctified, so be it).

Tellingly, growing up with the example of sanctified Black women leadership in her community helped Silvia develop an affirming understanding of her Blackness in relationship to her gender, birthplace, and faith, countering the limiting, dominant tropes assigned to them. To carry oneself as a woman "possessed," grounded by a consciousness of being laid claim to by copresences, was considered honorable and auspicious for one's entire family. In this recounting of "the essence" of rumba, she conveyed a logics of divine belonging, accompaniment, and reciprocity that she learned was worth defending during childhood. In Silvia's depiction, complementarily gendered realms of sacred authority mutually governed the life chances and choices of the people in her blood and stone family, enabling them to collectively save themselves. I link this to a vision of individual and collective well-being, desenvolvimiento, taken up further in chapter 4. One can imagine that for a young Silvia, these sacred epistemologies that shaped her sense of self in place provided a critical counter-thesis for her social worth, resisting her objectification as a commodity in "the three industries." When the greater society simply labeled girls like her and her daughter "easy," and when she may have been granted professional opportunities based on that estimation, Silvia made sure I knew this was not the entire story. To acknowledge the currency of those projections did not mean that those labels defined them or delimited their agency.

Although during her dance class with the foreigners Silvia explained guaguancó in line with the institutionalized phallocentric definition—as a seductive game of sexual pursuit—in the group conversation among women, she put forth a different interpretive framework for understanding the dance as teaching the values of Black self-organization, communication, cooperation, and spiritual communion. She described rumba as a conversation between different parts of a whole, akin to the way ritual drumming is understood as a conversation between a family and the divine. Learning to dance rumba is akin to learning a grammar oriented around the clave rhythm. Within this grammar there are specific social conventions of call and response that dictate where and when each person enters a collective dialogue and expresses concepts through a poetics of gesture. To form rumba is to assemble a shared repertoire of signs to convey and receive meaning in a live exchange about quotidian Black dramas. Dance partners represent proverbial gendered figures—the man on da street, the woman round da way—living together while Black in the daily condition of the formerly enslaved.

In this rendering, rumba was defined by its capacity to hold an ongoing conversation between blood and stone kin about how to live together with dignity. To sustain this conversation, everyone played a different vital and necessary role. In this allegory, rumberas represented all (god)daughters/ (god)sisters/(god)mothers/(god)grandmothers creatively rehearsing their collective right to refuse what they have been apportioned and using ancestral, embodied wisdom to publicly subvert everyday moments of social dispossession. In guaguancó, a Black woman "possessed" was valued for wielding wisdom beyond individual life experience in secular space-time. In this alternative framework, lead singer, chorus, drummers, and dancers performed best when listening to each other, waiting their turn, knowing when to enter, and learning how to creatively contribute to a constructive group discussion. Rumba poetics formed such a Black sense of place. In it the community bore witness to Black women accompanied by a sacred force to be reckoned with, improvising.

Silvia's Black feminist reading of the meaning of rumba, and rumbera choreography therein, is exceptional only to the extent that it has been muted by the dominant ideological scaffolding of "Afro-Cuban studies." In contrast to the prevailing representation of guaguancó as "a masculine chase . . . climaxing in his pelvic thrust," thus portraying women as a passive, enticing object of male desire, rumberas described themselves as engaging in an improvisatory dialogue between performers conveying more horizontal relations. Her likening rumba to a conversation resonates with the way other rumberas taught me to dance it.

For another rumbera of Silvia's same generation, Maria Elena Gomez, women's moves in guaguancó are best understood as feminist critiques of patriarchy rooted in slavery. On screen in the French film on Cuban femininity, she is introduced as a rumbera and musicologist. Her hair is pulled back off her toasted brown face. She wears a bright yellow dress, a gold pendant of the Virgin Our Lady of Charity around her neck, and a smile. She maintains a meditative air of calm in her eyes as she delicately weaves improvised trails in the air with the hem of her dress, creating an obstacle course for her dance partner's red handkerchief should he dare to venture toward her. She explains, "Man has always dominated since the time of slavery. . . . He is the one who works outside the home and earns money, and the woman takes care of domestic matters. It's always the man that was in charge and laid down the law. . . . But in rumba, women show their ability to halt masculine domination, and that is what you see in the dance." Her narration continues, "In the dance, the man tries to dominate, and the woman tries to not let him penetrate her. That attempt to penetrate the woman, and her resistance to that penetration, is what characterizes guaguancó. The women protects herself from this act of copulation." In Maria

Elena's account, *botaos* are not just evasions; they are critical counterassertions. Rather than passive or knee-jerk reactions, Maria Elena conveys an agentive and active stance toward patriarchal forces aimed at exerting power over Black women's bodily autonomy.

Maria Elena's commentary in the documentary is spliced with footage of her dancing at a rumba in the patio of the iconic Egrem Recording Studio. The camera then cuts to Maria Elena sitting in the audience, acting as a witness for other women's equally witty *botaos*. Maria Elena accompanies her surrogate dancer by tapping the beat of the clave on her hands. She studies the movements of the women who dance before and after her. Jenny and other women sitting at other tables are shown doing the same. Collectively, they bear witness to the ever-expanding choreographic repertoire of Black feminist refusals that characterize rumbera improvisation. They sway to the clave as they study for when it's their turn to dance.

Just as Maria Elena and Jenny watched each other, other women and girls would be attentively watching my moves when I danced. After I eventually memorized the basic steps, their variations, and how to make logical transitions between phrases, my classes would turn toward teaching me how to think coherently on my feet in different scenarios that operated as case studies for the quotidian analysis of patriarchy in motion. My skill was measured by my ability to anticipate and wittily respond to the assertions of the men I would encounter on the dance floor with counterassertions. They would be watching for how I would elaborate a narrative all my own. The goal of my dance classes, then, if the French men had ever cared to ask, was never about mastering a prescribed, sexy routine. Rather, my teachers aimed to instill in me the proficiency to enter into a conversation that has been going on since slavery about the way descendants of Africans live together while Black. How their assemblies are interpreted by an external gaze and valued within a broader libidinal economy is part of the conversation.

Jenny put me in contact with Yamilé so that I could continue my training during her stints abroad teaching master classes. I was admittedly starstruck when she entered the threshold to Morcilla's living room where our classes took place. She wore high-top sneakers, spandex pants, a baseball cap, and yellow-ish gold shades that brought out the color of her thick yellow and white *ide* bracelet on her left wrist, pronouncing the divinity to which she was crowned. Yamilé was a priestess of Ochún (and El Gordo's *ahijada*). She could certainly fit the description of the mulata rumbera archetype: caramel skin, an hourglass figure. However, my prior training with Jenny attuned me to appreciate her immense technical virtuosity. In 2011, I came across a YouTube video where she appeared (Gingerfilm Latin 2011). The music video promoted the newly established rumba group El Solar de los 6. Yamilé was an official member of the legendary rumba group Clave y Guaguancó; like Yoruba Andabo, it was subsidized by the Ministry of Culture. However, she was regularly hired to dance with other groups, such as Yoruba Andabo, as well. Jenny would become El Solar de los 6's dance director, and they would later rebrand themselves as Osain del Monte. (At which point, Jenny would leave Yoruba Andabo, and thus relinquish her subsidized status.) I had watched the YouTube video no less than fifty times, each time in utter fascination with how she commanded the music. She danced opposite Vladimir, a son of Changó, also a dancer in Yoruba Andabo. Her performance of sensuality came from a nuanced ear for how the clave brought together all the other parts of the musical instrumentation, and from that she fashioned a signature utterance. I was mesmerized by how her *muelleo* seemingly bent the clave beat to her will.

As in the video, she exuded confidence in her stride. I imagined her commute to our class escorted by many eyes that took her in while she passed, just as El Vecino did then from his window across the patio. Morcilla said that Yamilé was a master in *rumba a la antigua* (the old-school style of rumba), what others called "the essence," that was sadly falling out of fashion. As usual, we danced without mirrors. I stood beside her, using my peripheral vision, building my proprioception to match her shifts of weight, the timing of her *muelleo*, the pulse in her torso, the effort quality of her arms, and the coordination of all the parts. Then she sat down on a stool in front of the one oscillating fan to observe how much I was able to retain if dancing alone. The air tingled the beads of sweat on her brow as she pressed the button to replay the same song again.

After a few of these rotations, Yamilé lowered the volume on the recorded music and took a breath. By then I had convinced her that I more or less had a handle on how to make logical transitions in my footwork phrasing and evade the inevitable male advances using different *botaos*. However, she determined that I was still missing something—"*te falta una cosa*"—something else available to me that I had not yet explored. Although the climactic moments of attempted penetration always loomed as a latent threat, if dancing with a seasoned partner, they would actually be few and far between. Rather than dance reactively, in a state of bated suspense of his initiations, the most sophisticated rumberas were adept at curating the more anticlimactic realm of dialogic exchange. To assert my own voice while dancing with a male partner, I needed to learn to establish a critical distance from his desire. Turning away from the more spectacular moments of "vaccination," these interstitial moments of relational improvisation were the gray matter our lessons then turned to.

To convey this "something" else, she demonstrated different scenarios that I might encounter while dancing with a partner, and the different decisions available to me in my body. She narrated the thought process behind her movements while simulating them in real time: "When he starts to move really fast and you see that he is using the attention to show off and make himself seem big, don't try to compete with him for attention by mirroring his same energy. Even if the drummers speed up, you are not going to play their [the man's] game. Instead, you do *you*." She changed from mirroring a quick paced and percussive effort quality to suddenly slowing down and marking her steps at half-tempo. The contrast was striking and gave the effect of dancing in slow motion. Her cadence bordered dangerously on being late, or behind the music, yet never quite breaking the pact with the clave. "You are saying, I'm not going to break a sweat for him and be ruled by his whim. You take your time and use the space in the music to articulate your body more fully, at your own pace." She raised her right eyebrow and looked away from her imagined partner completely. "You see? Your ease and comfort in your body makes his effort look erratic . . . ridiculous, even." She was teaching me how to identify the fragility that undergirded masculine assertions of virility, exposing men's need for validation from other men. It was the difference between unconsciously reacting to his stimulus and delivering my own critical evaluation that called the stimulus itself into question. "Enjoy it," she encouraged as she shaped her face to show the internal satisfaction to be had in revealing his flashy attention-grabbing moves as hiding a deep insecurity. For the remainder of our class that day she coached me in applying this critical aptitude to the ways in which certain rumba performances of masculinity bear on women's behaviors, and to locate pleasure in the capacity to interrogate them through my own improvisatory phrasing.

Subversions of the male partner's nonverbal command to simulate housework while dancing was another scenario ripe for critical decision-making, particularly salient given the recent resurgence of domestic servitude in the city. Three years later, I would be translating for Silvia's class when she mimed the same scenario of domestic servitude for the foreigners. The move is initiated by the man throwing his handkerchief on the floor, which cues the woman to get down on all fours and mimic scrubbing the floor by hand in a circular motion. "And now ladies you have to wash around . . . and around . . . and around . . ." The circular motion would extend from her hand to her waist, gyrating in the opposing circular direction. The labor of her buttocks in the air would act as an extension of the domestic labor she sumptuously reenacted. Following Silvia's lesson, it would seem that Cuban cultural norms conditioned Black women to unequivocally embrace this expected gender role. Submission never looked so inviting, so pleasurable. At first, the foreign women giggled with nervous hesitation. Making eye contact, they then slowly lowered down to the floor. Perhaps equal parts embarrassed and titillated, they mimicked the act of racialized sexualized submission.

However, in my class with Yamilé, she insisted that in practice rumberas could and did respond in a range of ways to the expectation that they should uncritically fulfill the domestic-sexual labor historically assigned to them, both on and off stage. In the moment of role-play in my private lesson, Yamilé paused before turning to see the imaginary handkerchief on the floor. Instead of rushing to the handkerchief, she visibly exuded an air of resentment toward it. "When the man throws his handkerchief on the floor for you to get on all fours and clean, what many women do now is just pick it up and toss it in an imaginary washing machine and walk away." Yamilé acted out the way the gesture should look. She sauntered over to the spot calmly, unhurried, and slowly bent down at the waist as if to pick it up. With one graceful motion she turned and dropped the cloth in an imaginary receptacle as she walked away, almost as if to exit the dance floor entirely. Then, not a moment before her own accord, she melted back into the basic rumba step, merging yet again with the clave rhythm. "Or, what I do is toss it right back at him as if to say, 'here, wash it yourself.' And then I walk away." Then she gave her imaginary partner a head-to-toe scan, as if to say, "you tried to humiliate me to make yourself look powerful. Now look at yourself, dirty and alone." By maintaining her fidelity to the syntax of clave that keeps all rumberas and rumberos in sync, her defiant refusals of sexist expectation were accepted as fair arguments within the conversation. "You see?" she asked with a smile. I nodded and chuckled. In this way, she encouraged me to study in rumba how patriarchy coerces women's behaviors, and to also look for ways to create space, insist even, for alternative terms of social relation.

Similar to Maria Elena, Yamilé was taking stock of these threads of argumentation about gender, race, and power being initiated by women across the city and was invested in continuing the conversation by transmitting them to me as her student. We met later in the week at El Palacio de la Rumba so she could assess how I applied this aptitude in practice on the dance floor.

That night and thereafter, I danced knowing that my witty somatic retorts were performed more for other women to see than even for my male dance partner. Just as Yamilé smiled and clapped when observing me apply her lessons on the dance floor, Black women spectators across the African Diaspora have long found pleasure in seeing each other interrogating gender expectations and devising creative ways to move otherwise under the phallocentric gaze (hooks 2014). Black women spectators of rumba laughed and cheered on their surrogates, taking pride in the way men were put on the spot to grapple with their repeated failure to figuratively penetrate her *chocha* or her psyche. This choreographic aptitude denoted a critical distance from the dominant patriarchal definition of the rumbera's limiting binary role as passive/defensive and seductive/accessible. When afforded a Black feminist consciousness, guaguancó rehearsed and displayed a range of possibilities devised by Black women for other women living a shared condition of intersecting oppressions. As in life, creative negotiation with power was an art. In that art was a politics, a pleasure, and praise for those who danced before them and through their bodies, that had its own value.

Rumba was the soundtrack to their choreography of girlhood into womanhood. When reflecting on their lives in open-ended interviews over the course of my fieldwork, women repeatedly recalled memories of growing up singing to rumba while sweeping, drumming rumba while washing, and dancing rumba while cooking. These anecdotes signaled how their artistic training was inextricable from their socialization into gender expectations. And still, in these everyday rehearsals they created opportunities to experiment with choreographies of refusal. Rumba was both the music playing in the background while learning to perform the rules of gender and the bracketed-off space for moments of critical attention where women actively imagined otherwise. Rumba was a site where race and gender expectations were reinstated, but it was also the space where women actively tried to cultivate the courage to perform differently through their bodies in relation to men and for other women. When afforded a Black feminist consciousness, rumberas' movements theorized the potential for more liberatory possibilities for them all.

Indeed, Black feminism demands that the tropes assigned to Black women must not be mistaken as the entire story. Rather than see myself solely from the standpoint of the male gaze, as an object for the onslaught of his *vacunaos*, rumba, I learned, opened up a space for conversation in which I could cultivate my own feminist voice in motion. I could study for the cracks and contradictions in the social choreography of hegemonic masculinity that are obscured by its iterative performance. Perhaps the characteristic "seductive attitude" the rumberas ostensibly donned tells us more about the pleasure this theorizing produces for themselves. Or, recalling Jenny's lesson at the staged *tambor*, perhaps the wisdom embodied in Ochún's dances advised her to use her smile as a tool of dissemblance when audaciously demanding to be compensated for what she was owed.

While we might wonder if the debt owed Black women can ever be repaid, taking seriously rumberas' own interpretive frameworks for their movements offers a more nuanced appreciation for their continued investment in the space rumba forms. To be sure, rumbera choreographies embody a Black feminist vision that is both radical and pragmatic.[11] La mulata rumbera mobilizes her interpellated status to advance her own economic ambitions, enacting agency in how she is perceived by men. And that is not the entire story. What Black feminist performance theorists have often described as "reading against the grain," a counterhegemonic looking relation that offers its own pleasure and politics (Fleetwood 2011), is key for grasping statements they may never write down on paper. Maria Elena's definition of rumba guaguancó establishes their danced improvisation as a Black feminist critique of the centuries of sexual exploitation institutionalized in Cuban slave society, and the Americas more broadly, as much as an indictment of that which made "easy (Black) women" a so-called industry. That is to say, she saw in the form a way to publicly historicize and condemn the low returns in social value for Black women in everyday life. If Silvia's spiritual groundings, Yamilé's insistence on creating new openings, and Jenny's virtuosic application of the two are taken seriously, we might begin to understand the feminist discourses that populate the Black corporeal undercommons. These Black feminist theorizations of rumba may appear anomalous only to the extent that they are foreclosed by the phallocentric gaze and have historically eluded white patriarchal national interests in Black popular dance.

Rather than a masculine chase, we might recast rumba as a communal conversation practiced across generations proudly "possessed." It is a dance that trains young Black girls with the tools to sense everyday divine accompaniment, and to think quickly on their feet in the face of pervasive attempts to transgress their bodily autonomy or diminish their sense of self-worth. Such theorizations by rumberas about the meaning of their movements largely go unseen and unheard in exchange for becoming a national symbol. Although the dominant, institutionalized definitions of Black dancing women in the literature still reign supreme, rumberas' alternate theorizations of what and why they dance point to a Black feminist politics of interpretation in motion. Their creative improvisations within the rumba vernacular, bending the beat to their will, inspire other ways of knowing themselves in their bodies, even as they calculate how they can survive materially through colonial desire. For every rumbera who dances on the national stage, an intergenerational multitude bears witness and makes forms of more dignified relation imaginable that we would do well not to discount and explain away, shoo off.

"The Smile We Wear When We Dance"

"No! Again," Jenny commanded. Each time I repeated the dance phrase, I felt weaker, gradually more defeated and betrayed by my years of meticulous study and good intentions. When, repetition after repetition, I attempted to make the correction in my body and apparently failed to get her approval, over and over again, I knew that I had reached my growing edge. In that moment, the edge felt like a cement wall, like the kind that keeps Centro Habana from falling into the bay. Despite all my might, I couldn't break through. "And as Black women we have to give ourselves value! Because no one else gives us value." By the time Jenny barked this addendum to her chastisement of me, the tears had started running down my face. Maybe it was the humidity that day—the lack of new air to cleanse my muscles when I inhaled to return the feeling of fresh possibility. She looked me straight in the eyes and went on,

> We have to believe in ourselves and know our worth. I was taught that, and I had to learn that, and you have to, too. And you have to know that you are better so that you can make other people know and respect you. Because we both want to be someone in life, people that are respected for our knowledge in our field. And we both carry this in our blood. And because we both have talent and potential. If I didn't think you had it in you, I wouldn't yell at you to bring it out. . . . So, I am going to continue to yell at you! Because look at all you have learned from my yells! And when you start crying, I'll say okay, fine but I won't let you do it incorrectly. And if you do it incorrectly, I'll yell at you again. I'm never going to stop teaching you. But you also have to get out there and do your part. You have to do your homework, get books, study the vocabulary, internalize the steps. Because that's what I did. When I started at

the National School for the Arts, I had to change a lot. And I got yelled at a lot and cried and cried. When I say that you are going to perform on stage, you can't tell me, "No, I can't." You have to rise to the occasion and face the public, because that is the only way you are going to overcome your fears, is by facing them. You can't stay forever *en la bobería* [in dat bullshit].

Jenny had just threatened to put me on stage to perform with Yoruba Andabo. She believed it would raise the stakes of my concentration in class, and ultimately raise my sense of self-assuredness, what she diagnosed I was lacking. The ambivalence I felt about dancing only grew the more I danced. The prospect of being appraised by a paying audience was mortifying enough, but perhaps equal to the discomfort I felt being caught in the colonial gaze, subsumed under the rumbera trope. Perhaps my ambivalence was what blocked me from the breakthrough she tried to coax out of me. The irony of studying harder so that I *wouldn't* perform on stage was not lost on Jenny. She called it *bobería*. I was trying to escape the inevitable, rather than equip myself to face it head on.

Now, I reflect upon my desire to maintain a critical distance as a researcher, using that profession as a form of protection. What does it mean, as an anthropologist, to actively resist making myself vulnerable to the kinds of appraisals that form such a meaningful part of rumberas' professional lives? Saidiya Hartman captures the particular stakes of the research endeavor for Black women studying Black women in the archive: "This writing is personal because this history has engendered me, 'because the knowledge of the other marks me' because of the pain experienced in my encounter with the scraps of the archive" (2008, 4). Similarly, the specific ways in which my body and its movement were seen during fieldwork and read by various audiences (my teachers, other rumberos, Cuban and foreign men) made me attuned to the tacit demands put on rumberas' bodies. All these (mis)recognitions left marks. I knew too well, from personal experience, that being presumed an Afro-Cuban seductress could sanction nonconsensual sexual advances (Berry et al. 2017). Despite diligent rehearsal, off the dance floor, when there is no clave to anchor the conversation in spiritual communion, *botaos* are not always respected as credible utterances. Morcilla would not always be there to step in when refusals failed. Rumba made visible the quotidian threat of gender violence that silently accompanies Black women. And maybe that was part of what Jenny was trying to prepare me for, the inevitability of looking easy to consume, which is to be easy to think as worthless.

2.4 Members of Rumba Morena. Photo by author.

Dance classes taught me the analytical tools for competency and discernment that would allow me to appreciate the kinds of choices seized when stepping into that representative role of Black womanhood. Through elaborating a Black feminist discourse in movement, I came to understand a Black feminist consciousness hidden in plain sight. Its traces could be sensed in the divine inspiration they bring to calculated transactions and constrained improvisations. Again and again, rumberas turned to sacred epistemologies—figures of divine proportion and ancestral importance—to counter their objectification and expand their repertoires for successfully negotiating unequal terrain. This choreographic aptitude was hard won for the women who mobilized it.

Black women experienced the economic "update" as a specific kind of constrained possibility, wherein men colluded to withhold resources and extract profit and pleasure from their bodies. The space of ongoing conversation that rumba produces creates its own kinesthetic archival entries, its own embodied record of reckoning with the diasporic afterlives of slavery, and the means hopefully to make ends meet. Rumba allows us to know a way that Black women defend the ability to imagine and body forth more empowering modes of gendered relation both on and off stage. The other women nodded in agreement when Silvia said, "Now we are fighting so that that essence doesn't get lost. It all depends on us [Black women] and how we are going to defend ourselves, and I mean in the sense of really defending our tradition." By situating the tradition of rumba in the cabildos where she grew up, Silvia defended an ongoing conversation led by women "possessed," laid claim to by spirits who guided their steps and for whom they cared in return. How might this standpoint of divine possession have created the critical distance necessary to trouble the value offered by state licensure to teach that to which they already had rightful claim? How might the sense of sacred accompaniment unsettle the conceit of needing managerial permission to travel where their steps are divinely led? How might the ethic of divine reciprocity buttress refusals to labor without due compensation? What if rumba choreography developed to protect this aptitude for dissemblance, which has been sacred to Black women alongside the project of nation-building over the *longue durée*?

As a form of conclusion to our group conversation on the patio of The House of Friendship, Silvia lamented, "People don't understand that the smile we wear when we dance is a product of effort." In recognizing the labor, study, training, and attunement entailed in embodying the mulata rumbera, we might more deeply appreciate why Black women may invest in maintaining an exclusive claim to the wages for which this colonial fantasy is exchanged. These fantasies were shaped by intersecting forces of gender oppression, racial hierarchy, capitalism, and desire. Even if only subtly apparent in the pulse of the torso, the bend of the knee, and the tip of the tongue, the rumberas I learned from defend these hailings into racialized tropes alongside the inalienable worth of and creative possibility latent in sacred filial relation. Rumba indexed the art of Black feminist refusal acknowledged within knowing glances, whenever and wherever they be. This choreographic aptitude is, too, the tradition of the Black corporeal undercommons and worth defending. Perhaps the "flirtatious smile" ostensibly donned by rumberas tells us more about the persistent conditions that warrant this kind of protection. These are the same conditions that leave their feminist critiques hidden in plain sight.

3 SACRED SWAGGER AND ITS SOCIAL ORDER

Guapo is courageous, valiant, bold, daring, resolute, enterpris-
ing, good-looking, handsome, neat, elegant, ostentatious, vain
or in another sense, a dandy or a bully. It is associated with the
behavior of tough, street-wise men of the taverns, bars, ports,
marinas and *solares* or the nineteenth and early twentieth
centuries. It is especially associated with *los negros curros*,
free blacks and mulattos who wore a specific style of dress
(very decorated, fancy and reminiscent of Rumba costuming
today), spoke a particular dialect and were reputed to be very
daring and challenging, even to the death.

YVONNE DANIEL, "Race, Gender, and Class Embodied in Cuban Dance"

It was a warm November night in 2018 during the "Rumbazo #2" festival
featuring the hottest rumba groups from around the country.[1] Osain del
Monte, one of the newest groups of the "rumba renaissance," took the stage
at La Tropical, located in the borough of Marianao. La Tropical is an open-
air, state-managed dance hall infamous for attracting "unruly" audiences
from Havana's Black inner-city neighborhoods. The only time I have ever
witnessed a delayed performance due to the police lining up all the ticket
holders and patting them down, one by one, before permitting entry, was
at a rumba show at La Tropical several years prior. The lineup of rumberos that night made their mark, showing off their *sello*, their unique stamp
on the genre, and their ability to move the crowd. The members of Osain
del Monte took the stage with swagger. Adonis Panter Calderón (a former
member of Yoruba Andabo) formed the group in 2013. Full of youthful zeal,
Adonis and Osain del Monte had already acquired a reputation for pushing
the category of folklore to its edge. The group embraced, sought out even,

3.1 Percussionists of Osain del Monte on stage at La Tropical. Photo by David Garten.

opportunities to perform rumba in venues far beyond the conventional folkloric circuit. Their collaborations with the Rolling Stones and Madonna, for instance, rivaled the most successful reggaeton and popular dance music artists of the day.[2] They sported embellished jeans, high-top sneakers, logo T-shirts, gold chains, dreadlocks with side shaves, cornrows under fitted caps, and dark sunglasses. Their self-presentation matched their primary audience, belonging to overlapping Black diasporic urban counterpublics fashioned by *timba*, hip-hop and reggaeton aesthetics of Black affirmation.

Before long, Rubén, a lead singer and their only white member (who I knew only by his given nickname "El Blanquito"), screamed into the mic, "*This* is our folklore!" The command catalyzed the signature rhythm of metallic clanging signaling the Abakuá order. His emphasis announced a deviation from the folkloric status quo, while it also evoked the religious brotherhood's recurrent hailing into Cuban cultural nationalism. Sure enough, an *Ireme* soon emerged in a full costume and the crowd obediently made way. The Ireme is the founding spirit said to be present when a "spiritual feeling of solidarity is summoned through collective expressions of music and dance" (Miller 2004, 210–11). The Ireme always emerged from a place hidden from view, covered from head to ankle in an elaborate cone-headed costume with a pair of eyes painted on the front. Only exposed bare feet betrayed a human form concealed underneath. Smooth, agile strokes of the masked figure's handheld broom cleansed its shoulders, neck, back, and stomach. These cleansing strokes were followed by the isolated shaking of the pelvis where a belt of bells dangled. As if on cue, several circular openings were formed among the crowd, centering elder Abakuá men who identified themselves by showing off their fluency in the Ireme's complex gestural speech. Substituting handkerchiefs for the broomlike object, they shifted their weight diagonally off-center right and left. They donned no bells around their waist, but the "acoustic gesture" of shaking of their pelvises echoed just the same (Jottar 2009a, 18). Young Black men watched along, attentively studying their graceful flurries, or took out their camera-phones to capture the beauty of the choreography and later showcase their own bodily proximity to its grace. To the colonial gaze, this picture of Black manhood for and with his own has always looked like social danger.[3]

When the Abakuá brotherhood was established in colonial Cuba by enslaved African men, as an elder of high rank in the brotherhood once explained to me, each Abakuá territory had a municipal government to which the cabildos (in this case, also called temples) in that territory were linked. This formed an infrastructure that connected all the brotherhoods in Cuba to each other. The complex system of African-inspired governance, considered religious by its subjects, essentially remapped the cities, provinces, and the country. Rather than a project rooted in nostalgia for "Africa," this tradition of worldmaking was sustained by the collective desire to craft a contemporaneous space of autonomy from state power in Cuba (Routon 2005). In the sacred Abakuá territories still defended today in inner-city neighborhoods of Havana, Matanzas, and Cárdenas, tightly choreographed bodily scripts gendered this sanctified Black sovereignty.

Young Black rumberos embodying this sacred swagger cue us to reckon with the Black political desires that stand outside of state-endorsed visions of revolutionary manhood and social order. These desires for Black sovereignty, articulated collectively through the body, accompanied a critical shift from an earlier hegemonic utopic masculinity established in the 1960s—the socialist color-blind New Man—to a neoliberal white masculinity I've termed the *New Man 2.0*. In both eras, men who did not fit the limited definitions of manhood endorsed by the state were rendered undesirable excess to the nation-building project at hand. Although distinct in some of their ideological scaffolding, both state-endorsed ideals excluded Black-identified men who worshipped, or pledged allegiance to, "their own." After all, autonomous visions of place, power, and belonging were deemed counterrevolutionary. Triggering racialized fear in some and racial pride in others, Abakuá societies represent a moral stance on what it means to "be a (good) man" beyond white paternalism and capital accumulation. For its members, they advance a sanctified vision for a more just model of political and economic self-determination. I contend that the popularity of Abakuá choreography among Havana's Black urban poor youth is best understood within this "Calabar" spatial, political imaginary of sacred social order in but not of Cuba. That Black peso-poor men's investment in the Abakuá "roots" of rumba embodies a strategy of positive self-affirmation in the face of the systemic inequities and racial indignities wrought by Cuba's "update" is what this chapter explores.

When rumberos collectively submit to Abakuá governance in dance, they chart and defend a polity that the enslaved from the West African Cross-River Delta region conceived. As the leading scholar of Abakuá societies, Ivor Miller, states, "Abakuá groups consider themselves sovereign lands (*tierras*) whose primary allegiance is to the *Ékue* [sacred drum]" (2000, 166). Here sovereignty does not refer to the classical Westphalian political model undergirding juridical relations between nation-states. Instead, it refers to a broader political imaginary of collective self-determination that subordinated subjects have taken up. The territorial claims made by the formerly enslaved often demand legitimized control over one's physical body as the basic unit of political community. Corporeal movement can thus be understood as a Black vernacular tool used to claim political subjectivity and defend ancestral territory.

Moreover, the Abakuá express their sovereignty through a politics and performativity of opacity. Similar to other initiatic communities of the Black Atlantic, the "Abakuá world" is a "sacred-secret space," whose power is reliant on the public acknowledgement of restricted knowledge that most can never acquire (Johnson 2022). Accordingly, rather than attempt to expose secret meaning, I explore the affect that is produced at the borders of what noninitiates are entitled to understand about the sodality, and thereby endeavor to glean its broader appeal and social relevance for those that go through its motions at rumba events. This non-initiate status is one I share with the majority of present-day Yoruba Andabo members and their following, even if my own particular positioning is distinct due to my nationality or gender. In this sense, I contemplate the "affective terrain" of the Black corporeal undercommons and its crafting of "moments of attention that lock a body into a larger frame of reference that matters" (Masco and Thomas 2023, 22). In short, this chapter explores the performativity of this choreography of

Black sovereignty as it is taken up by and for rumberos. In considering the epistemic power of bodily scripts coded during slavery for mapping a polity otherwise, I reorient the dominant analytical framework applied to rumba that has been too narrowly wed to Cuban nation-building.

Other scholars have shown that those whose formal means to assert sovereignty are precluded by modern state apparatus leverage racialized gender performance to index authority. This work builds on these examinations of the role of style, dress, and performance in how racialized peoples fashion their own sovereign political subjecthood in the Americas (Brooks 2006; Negrón-Muntaner 2015), while taking up Yarimar Bonilla's call to understand "sovereignty as an uneven and fragmented performance, rather than a stable capacity" (2017, 333). Here I also think with Jafari Allen's (2011) analysis of the politics of everyday expressive practices "for a larger freedom" in Cuba. In this same vein, as scholars of Black geographies have argued, we need to recognize the specific conditions that produce Black geographical expressions and make their attendant visions of liberation unique (McKittrick 2011). The wake of slavery informs the specific ways in which Black sovereignty is performed in place and time (Bledsoe and Wright 2019). To that end, I demonstrate how rumberos conjure sacred epistemologies conceived in resistance to slavery to compete with evolving systemic configurations of space, labor, and power.

The way in which the recent economic reforms heightened already persistent systems of pre-revolutionary racialized class inequality created an important conjuncture within which these sovereignty claims were embodied. In 2011, small private businesses were given jurisdiction over property for capital accumulation, thus sanctioning practices of racial exclusion and consolidating power and resources in the hands of white middle- and upper-class men (Bastian 2018, 142). The increased attraction of Black peso-poor youth to displays of Abakuá heritage, I suggest, can be understood as a distinctly racialized and gendered affront to the increasingly neoliberal ideals of twenty-first century Cuban socialism. This phenomenon certainly bears resemblances with the way Black male youth took up *timba* music as a strategy of social mobility during the 1990s when the state, crippled by the loss of Soviet support, reopened itself to some participation in capitalist markets (Hernández-Reguant 2006). In both cases, dance music is a space for "soft" critique of revolutionary discourses by Black disenfranchised youth when outright dissent is not viable. Critiques waged in *timba* "took into account the reconfiguration of life horizons for inner-city Afro-Cuban youth" due to economic reform (Hernández-Reguant 2006, 272). Similarly, these critiques in rumba were waged from a decidedly Black male-centered stand-point seeking empowerment vis-à-vis a white Cuban middle class, white men, in particular, and Black women, by extension. However, whereas *timba* performance "situated the Black male on top" by virtue of his hypersexuality, in the rumba case, performing proximity (if not belonging) to Abakuá *tierras* was grounds for moral superiority (Hernández-Reguant 2006, 251).

Rather than adopting rumba as a strategy for inclusion within capital-ist globalization, I maintain that rumberos defended an entitlement to a different kind of prestige, a sanctified "goodness," not calibrated by capi-tal. Sought in rumba was the swagger of sovereignty. On the one hand, this practice aligns with dominant heteropatriarchal norms of masculine rule over territory in modernity. On the other hand, the sovereign domain rum-beros formed was a provisional space of respite from collective inferioriza-tion vis-à-vis an exclusionary vision of virtuous manhood, the New Man 2.0, which the state conjured for national development in the twenty-first century, not as a means of inclusion within it.

My interest in the history of Abakuá societies and their ceremonial cho-reography came from wanting to sociohistorically situate the unique affec-tive intensity of young Black men's participation at public rumba events. In contrast to my study with rumberas, in these instances my own gendered body would circumscribe the extent to which I could approximate that affec-tive terrain. One night at the Callejón de Hamel (Hamel Alleyway), a popular open-air community project for rumba performance in Centro Habana, the master of ceremonies invited me to dance rumba guaguancó. The MC was a young, charismatic Black man charged with rousing up the crowd. He often drew foreign women into the shaded area cleared for performers. It was no secret that these overtures to dance could lead to courtships off the dance floor. I cannot remember if by that point I had made explicitly clear to him that my interest in dance was not a pretext for some thinly veiled desire for romance, which was a well-proven hypothesis about tourists in rumba spaces. I remember being intimidated by the personal attention that came with his invitation. I reticently obliged, not wanting to disappoint Jenny, seated nearby, who had been nagging me to display the fruits of my labor (and her pedagogy) in public. She may have even put him up to it. Although I tried to make my outward expression match the air of delight in the cy-pher around me, internally I concentrated on my form, the cadence of my steps, and those of my partner.

Ironically, my nervousness about the steps distracted me from recog-nizing the seemingly sudden musical transition from guaguancó clave

3.2 Ireme entering Callejón de Hamel. Photo by author.

seamlessly into an Abakuá rhythm.[4] Upon hearing the metallic resonance from the *ekón* bell that cued this new choreographic order, I erroneously heightened my corporeal response, embellishing the shimmied release of my shoulders as I sank my hips into the downbeat. I should have become still and promptly exited the dance floor altogether. My dance partner shook his head sternly, motioning me to stop, and escorted me back to a seat among Jenny and her posse at the clearing's perimeter. I had breached the code for feminine gender performance; by dancing (boldly at that) to this rhythm, I had trespassed into sacred masculine territory.

If I had defied the social conventions of *rumba columbia* traditionally reserved for male solo dancing, it could have been dismissed as feminist audacity (a move assumed by more rumberas, including Jenny herself). However, especially among rumberos, not abiding by the Abakuá social order for gender dictated by its rhythms was sacrilege. Imagining my teacher's disappointment, I obediently sat down while the mc ceremoniously cleared a path through the audience for the masked Ireme figure to make its stately entrance. Even though the mc was not an Abakuá initiate himself, he had a role to play, as we all did. The rhythm choreographed bodies into a prescribed way of occupying the space according to sex and initiatory status.

Rumberos at the Callejón de Hamel were charged with defending a living history of the brotherhood's sovereignty. Theirs was a contested Africanist self-governing community nested in Cuba, a politics of Black refusal sustained by their spiritual kin.[5]

"Not Legal but Legitimate"

Although initially membership was restricted to the African-born, as I explained in chapter 1, for the societies to survive, creole (Cuban-born) Black men became eligible for initiation. These days, to qualify for enlistment, typically a neophyte still undergoes long-term observation by elder brothers to monitor his adherence to "Calabar" codes of morally configured ideal manhood: "good husband, good father, good son, good brother" (as their saying goes). Implied in these attributes of "good" masculinity is heterosexuality and the capacity to defend "one's own," writ large.[6] Failing to uphold this code of strict moral rectitude dishonors their land and betrays the secret to their powers.

Serafin "Tato" Quiñones, a writer, activist, and elder Abakuá initiate, often talked about the brotherhood's legacy of inspiring Black self-determination in contemporary Havana. In 2017, at a special convening at Harvard University hosted by the Hutchins Center for African and African American Research, over thirty Black Cuban activists, intellectuals, artists, and academics were invited to discuss the history, gains, and lessons of the "Afro-Cuban Movement" against racism in Cuba. Tato spoke about the Abakuá public memorial ceremonies, jointly organized by different Abakuá lodges every November 27. He highlighted the symbolic impact of the annual popular tradition commemorating the five Abakuá who were murdered by the Spanish colonial government on November 27, 1871, after trying to save eight white medical-student insurgents. The five Abakuá and the eight medical students were executed. Every year on that day, Black Cubans from around the city gathered at the sacred ceiba tree in Old Havana to show solidarity with the Abakuá cause by honoring their fallen. The tree is located on the corner of Morro and Colón streets in Old Havana, which they consider sacred territory.

This grassroots ritual of remembrance is a powerful counterpoint to the national memorial service that takes place on the same day to commemorate the medical students as revolutionary martyrs. The state's memorial service celebrates the students as symbols of anti-colonial patriotism yet ignores the Abakuá completely. Although both events pay homage to young men who died defending their principles, they bear little resemblance to one another. The nationally televised service for the white students on the famous stairs of the University of Havana contrasts sharply with the intimate Abakuá memorial at the foot of the ceiba tree. Typically, ceremonial drumming is an essential part of the memorial, for Abakuá tributes are not complete without the dancing Ireme's towering presence. The conversation between the drum and song lures out the masked spirit to preside over the ritual. The spirit is blind and mute, hearing only through song and speaking only through coded gestural language (García Velasco 2016). The Moruá Yuánsa, as singing dignitary, serenades a report of all action, to which the Ireme gesturally responds. Holding a small wooden staff, the Ireme interrogates and gives approval with precision. A broomlike object in the other hand purifies the space with poised flicks of the wrist. A belt of clanking bells resounds from the groin area with each series of controlled swishes of the pelvis, calling all to order and attention. The cleansing motion of the Ireme's coded gestures references the ancestral power to create space for and divinely sanction collective acts that exceed colonial endorsement. Although mute, the Ireme's silent speech is socially audible and commands the living. Yet only the initiated can understand the coded dialogue occurring in plain view.

In a matter-of-fact tone, Tato said of the memorial, "It wasn't legal, but it was legitimate." Tato emphasized that the independent nature of the event is an important part of its ability to raise Black consciousness and self-esteem in the Black community more broadly. To be sure, many of the Black activists and community organizers present at the panel faithfully attend the ceremony annually and recognize it as a symbol of Black autonomy that has endured despite the 1959 Revolution's centralization of civil society. Recognized as more than just music to dance to, as one rumbero shared with me after a performance, "the Abakuá is a beautiful concept."

However, garnering government endorsement of the November 27th memorial service, to mitigate state suspicion, has entailed compromising the way they publicly remember. The presence of ceremonial drumming and dancing for the Ireme spirit was a particular point of contention. In 2012, I attended one such state-sanctioned ceremony when drumming was excised from the event. Although it was not publicly advertised to foreigners, I learned of it through my involvement with Black Cuban anti-racist activists and scholars who religiously attended the ceremony. That year it had been shortened to accommodate participation by members of the Federation of University Students (FEU) and cadets in military uniform from the Superior Institute of the Ministry of the Interior (MININT). Instead of proceeding to drum for the Ireme, attendees solemnly migrated from the ceiba tree to the statue commemorating the medical students in the plaza where Prado Avenue meets the bay. Attendees were greeted by eight FEU representatives who stood in formation beside large bouquets of flowers and cadets, holding a flagpole with the Cuban flag waving in the sea breeze. Then the Abakuá men were ceremoniously handed the bouquets and flag, anointing them with the national symbols. After granting the floor to an elder white Abakuá who made a short speech regarding Cuba's indebtedness to the valor of Abakuá men in the history of the nation, the eight cadets marched to place flowers on the statue. Although the military-grade funeral service was supposed to symbolize the Cuban nation's gratitude to Abakuá societies, the absence of drumming and dance, for Tato, signaled the sanitization of their tradition in exchange for state recognition as men worthy of honor.

The grassroots annual ceremonies, characteristically devoid of state recognition and approval, Tato asserted, formed a core element of the ritualized mourning's layered significance as a collective refusal of (neo-)colonial regimes of law and order. Importantly, it honored a vision of legitimate personhood that was not beholden to the Cuban state and its benevolence. The dancing Ireme spirit, in a sense, doubled as a physical pronouncement of sacred, rather than state-sanctioned, legitimacy to publicly honor their dead and dignify themselves on their own terms. "Based on that legitimacy we did it and we will continue to do so," Tato vowed.

Rather than seeing Black cultural forms as products of the passive repetition of an original African essence in a "mixed" nation, I attend to the willful imaginings of Africa in faith-based practices shared in situated contexts of racialized struggle and prohibition (Beliso-De Jesús 2015; Jottar 2009b; Ochoa 2010). As Tato preached in his presentation, the Abakuá tradition is an important antidote, even a beautiful counter, to the growing demoralization caused by the unfulfilled promise of full social equality for Black Cubans since the 1959 Revolution, and the loss of former gains. While earlier generations of Abakuá men received the brunt of pseudoscience campaigns as Cuba came of age as a nation, since 2010, peso-poor Black men have been further stigmatized through the newest campaign for national progress. Rumberos reassert this sacred claim to goodness, contesting the hegemonic way that meanings have been socially ascribed to their bodies. Exploiting the gap between signifiers and re-coded signs, rumberos engaged in what scholars of African American culture have termed "signifyin'" (Gates 1988), often dismissed as *guapería*.

3.3 Youth imitating Ireme at Rumbazo festival. Photo by David Garten.

The Abakuá inside Rumba, or What Looks Like *Guapería*

When rumberos played songs featuring Abakuá music and dance, as Osain del Monte did at La Tropical, Black youth filled the venue, established a border with their bodies, and studied the choreography of the Abakuá elders and Ireme dancers attentively. I was taken aback by how distinctly the dance floor operated during these songs of Abakuá pride: the deliberate focus and intentionality that created physical clearings in the space. No matter the group performing, when the rhythmic *ekón* bell ringing began, a tone of seriousness, discipline, and reverence set in. On these occasions, rhythm does the popular organizing work that lyrics don't necessarily disclose. Looking to lyrics for discursive meaning is useful if one is well-versed in Abakuá's esoteric ritual speech. Here popular meaning, shared among non-initiates, is routed through choreography. The performativity of the sacred-secret is crucial to understanding how rumba defends the emancipatory imaginary that the Black corporeal undercommons forms.

In an interview with Valentín, the production assistant and a longtime follower of Yoruba Andabo, I remarked on the unique energy and sense of spatial order that took place when they played Abakuá music. I had known Valentín longer than any member of Yoruba Andabo. He was the one who invited me to see one of their shows for the first time. We were introduced through a mutual friend during a trip to Cuba before I embarked on my doctoral degree. He arranged for his nephew to escort me to the show and back home safely. I had since developed a close relationship with his family. Perhaps it was the *confianza* (trust) we had cultivated over the years that allowed for his candor on that day. His face suddenly turned very serious. The topic seemed to have struck a nerve. "Others may not be willing to talk about it," he warned, "but if you were to ask the elders, they would share the truth." The founders of Yoruba Andabo were port workers, all Abakuá initiates if not direct descendants. He continued, "In truth, there was a prohibition [by the government]. . . . For many people, to speak of Abakuá was something bad, '. . . because the Abakuá are murderers, because they kill, because this or that . . . they steal . . .' So, the Abakuá were prohibited." Valentín spoke about how the sensibilities of government officials constrained what kinds of rumba performances were socially acceptable in "public space." Although the genealogies of Abakuá brotherhoods and the rumba ensembles were inextricable, it was a controversial heritage to openly proclaim.

Abakuá heritage constitutes a central part of Yoruba Andabo's group identity, as it does for many rumba ensembles (Miller 2000). Whether individual performers are initiated into the brotherhood themselves or not, rumberos have a long tradition of drawing on Abakuá references to espouse Black pride and promote Black self-determination (Miller 2000, 170). During an interview, Geovani explained to me that the group's mission includes showcasing "the Abakuá inside rumba," and the group's target audience for that message is "the youth." By highlighting "the Abakuá inside rumba," Yoruba Andabo contests the possibility of separating rumba from this particular religious heritage, just as it refuses to conform to the hegemonic construction of *cubanidad* that selectively incorporates Blackness under norms of white secular civility. The Abakuá-inspired songs in their rumba repertoire promote the principles of pride and autonomy based in a willful association with Africa and rightful collective rule of people of African descent over territory in the New World. Thanks, in part, to rumba groups like Yoruba Andabo, "the youth" show respect for and allegiance to these principles through highly choreographed responses to Abakuá rhythms that, to a white statist gaze, look like *guapería*.

The terms *guapo* and *guapería* (and their synonyms) were often used to index the "something bad" that Abakuá heritage conjured. Whereas in other Spanish-speaking countries, *guapo* means handsome or beautiful, in

Cuba, *guapos* are "tough guys," and *guapería* has been translated as "macho aggression" (Routon 2005, 374) or "knife-carrying black youth" (Hernández-Reguant 2006, 264). Guapería, in this sense, was a gendered way of being that could contaminate the body politic if allowed to encroach on public space untethered by the rules of folkloric (de-politicized, secular) consumption. Corporeal practices labeled *guapo* in Cuba, as seen in rumberos' obeisance to Abakuá rhythms, cannot be disentangled from their historical association with a particular kind of rebellious *Black* manhood. This masculinity is linked to the Africanist civic communities whose separatist political imaginaries were deemed threatening to the Cuban Republic's white elite social order. Abakuá fraternities, while afforded a certain prestige (relative to women) under patriarchy and cachet (relative to Black cultural forms with direct links to the United States, such as hip-hop) under anti-US imperial ideology, similarly challenge the dominant ideal of raceless revolutionary masculinity. In a country where Black manhood has long been a source of anxiety for the white political establishment, rumberos seize Abakuá bodily scripts to index a sacred-secret kind of Black masculine achievement and collective self-sufficiency that looks like guapería.

With regard to the association between guapería and rumba, Yvonne Daniel states that "the male rumbero personifies Cuban maleness and perhaps Cuba itself; he is guapo" (1994, 78). She defines guapo as, among other things, courageous, valiant, bold, daring, challenging, and resolute even to the death. Yet, I insist that the term's specific racialized application to rumberos—signaling *Black* masculinity insubordinate to white patriarchal (state) power—is important for understanding why young, peso-poor, urban, Black men express racial pride through its choreography. In other words, Abakuá repertoires of sacred masculinity resonate among Black urban peso-poor male youth as a cultural politics of resistance against dominant Cuban prescriptions for what it means to be a "good man." As of late, that included the kind of man who was capable of accumulating capital via entrepreneurship and relieving the state of the "burden" of his welfare.

Directed by Valentín's earlier provocation to ask the elders, I arranged to speak with Juan Campos Cárdenas, known to all as "Chan." In his late seventies at the time of the interview, he was the eldest Abakuá member of Yoruba Andabo. While sitting in his living room one April afternoon in 2014 in the Regla municipality of Havana, across the bay from where he used to work and live, he recounted how he and his fellow Abakuá brothers played rumba on the docks during their work breaks. Before achieving professional status as a performing artist in the 1980s, Chan and the other

3.4 Juan "Chan" Campos Cárdenas leading song in Yoruba Andabo performance of "Protesta Carabalí." Photo courtesy of Juan Campos Cárdenas.

founding members of Yoruba Andabo worked at the Port of Havana. Chan looked back fondly upon their days beating rhythms out of drums made of wooden shipping crates with metal spoons. He began working on the docks at the age of six in the early 1940s as a water boy (*aguador*) while living in the Solar África in Centro Habana, which had a local reputation for its rumbas. He later grew up to become a stevedore and was initiated into the brotherhood. Animated by his own memories from his youth, Chan clapped a clave rhythm softly with his hands and marked the downbeat on the tile floor with his right heel. He whispered a sweet *diana* into the air over the syncopation of his own making.[7] He cut into his demonstration to explain how being Abakuá determined his professional trajectory since childhood, from the docks to the stage. He recalled with great pride Abakuá's "dominance" before the 1959 Revolution: "The Abakuá world dominated the Port of Havana. . . . They were foremen, head of ports, head of ships. . . . Blacks helped the whites. The whites helped the Blacks. We exchanged judgments . . . way before the [1959] Revolution. . . . That is why in the ports of Havana, all the leaders became Abakuá." As I discussed earlier, one of the primary ways Abakuá acquired control over hiring dockworkers was by initiating white men into the Abakuá brotherhoods. Racial integration, as a strategy of self-determination, came at a calculated price in, as Chan called it, the "Abakuá world" (Booth 1976; Miller 2009).

Abakuá members today will boast about their historic self-integration *before* the revolutionary vanguard's command to desegregate schools, workplaces, social clubs, and public spaces in 1959. Although the brotherhood's racial integration is often framed within the Martían nationalist discourse of "racial fraternity"—harmonious brotherhood among white and Black men facing a common imperial enemy—it must be contextualized within the political machinations necessary at the time for men of African descent to secure influence over valuable territory controlled by whites (Guerra 2005; Pappademos 2011). These interracial relations did not evidence a transcendence of racial significance, nor did they remove the brotherhood's racialized stain. Chan viewed their self-integration and diplomatic dealings with white men as peers as a brazen assertion of agency and prescient political acumen, rather than assimilation to the values of a predominantly white revolutionary vanguard. The capacity to self-determine their fate versus deferring to government mandate was a controversial legacy to uphold after 1959, when the revolutionary project effectively centralized civil society through the creation of mass organizations.[8]

In 1961, the revolutionary government attempted to raise morale and productivity by creating music competitions between different labor sectors in Havana. Their group of Abakuá port workers that played rumba informally together became officially known as Grupo Marítimo Portuario. The members of Grupo Marítimo Portuario leveraged their vast performance experience playing at informal gatherings in their neighborhoods. Chan, Geovani, and their fellow Black port workers had long been mainstays of live music events in their neighborhood that encompassed praise, politics, and pleasure. They consistently won first place in the Festival de Aficionados until the competitions were suspended in 1965. However, their public exposure as a music ensemble in service to the nation-building effort accompanied new professional openings for secularized forms of Black popular culture in Cuban society at that time.

In the 1980s, Eloy Machado, a poet and Abakuá initiate himself, was tasked with organizing bimonthly showcases of Cuban culture on the patio of the National Union of Cuban Artists and Writers (UNEAC) headquarters in Vedado.[9] In 1985, he invited his *ecobios* of Grupo Marítimo Portuario to perform. There, Pablo Milanés, then a famous *nueva trova* singer (and former UMAP detainee), "discovered" the group. When Milanés asked for their group's name, Geovani recalls pausing in panic, unsure what to say. He re-enacted the moment for me with much animation. Searching around for an answer, he glanced down at the box drum of one of their members, Pancho Quinto. The box drum bore the name of Pancho's ritual drumming ensemble, "Yoruba Andabo" (meaning friend or follower of the Yoruba people, he told me). "Yoruba Andabo is our name," Geovani dramatically recalled blurting out with a chuckle. That is how they were introduced at their Karl Marx Theatre debut when Milanés invited them to open for him at the prestigious theater.

Geovani remembered how nervous they felt, performing for the first time on a mega proscenium stage. It was the largest cinema and live theater venue in Havana that, before the Revolution, was reserved for the white elites and aptly boasted the name *Teatro Blanquita* (Little White Theater). "We didn't have costumes," he said, "so we decided to wear all-white attire, to at least look uniform."[10] Uncertain how the audience would respond to rumba music, they were amazed when they received multiple standing ovations. They were such a hit that Milanés took the men to a big warehouse to buy their first set of factory-made drums as a gift. The UNEAC patio became their regular public performance venue. The rest, as they say, is history. Notably, the re-counting of both Chan and Geovani about their joint professional trajectory, from the docks to the stage, credits the Abakuá brotherhood as their central benefactor, not the revolutionary state, as is commonly repeated in the official narrative of Cuban rumba. Abakuá networks enabled *ecobios* to create openings for each other during the nation's remaking.

When I met the group in 2009, their biweekly showcases at UNEAC were a thing of the past. Valentín and several other older members of Yoruba Andabo disclosed how UNEAC officials pressured them to discontinue their Abakuá songs because they aroused *social dangerousness* (*peligrosidad social*). This provision in the penal code gained traction in the 1970s and has been applied systematically in ways that support a racialized perception of crime leading to the disproportionate incarceration of Black people on the basis of exhibiting "precriminal behaviors" (de la Fuente 2001a, 315; Sawyer 2005; Guerra 2014). The historical criminalization of the sacred brotherhoods since colonialism, and their continued stigmatization ever since, rendered rumberos playing Abakuá rhythms readily suspect of latent criminality. For this reason, to echo Valentín from earlier, "The Abakuá were prohibited." Pancho Quinto (1997) would later sing about the social scorn they received during their time playing at UNEAC: "They criticize me when I go to UNEAC . . . for hanging with people born in marginalized neighborhoods. . . . they criticize the Cuban who defends his roots. . . . Stop talking [about us]!" (translation mine).[11] In my conversations with older members of Yoruba Andabo, they recounted that UNEAC administrators had informed them about complaints the institution had supposedly received from neighbors in Vedado regarding the disruption caused by the *ambientales* (riffraff) that their music attracted. *Ambiente* (figuratively, a spatialized unruly atmosphere) was the dominant characterization of the guapo affective charge, cultivated in both Abakuá and rumba spaces alike, that rendered otherwise civil spaces suddenly dangerous.[12]

When I pressed for specific dates of these occurrences in our conversations, the elders, perhaps wary of incriminating anyone in particular, only testified to a more generalized disapproval for this controversial part of their vast African cultural repertoire that rendered them out of line with dominant, Soviet-era conceptions of "socialist morality." Jalane Schmidt found that in the revolutionary government's fashioning of a folkloric identity packageable for "ethno-business" during the Special Period, the secrecy of the brotherhood and fierce loyalty to each other made it appear impervious to state directives. Schmidt makes the case that these elements, considered "thuggish," do not readily lend themselves to the obligatory cheerfulness of public folkloric performance, what David Guss calls, "the hegemony of the smile" (2000, 205). Schmidt continues, "Many present-day ecobios are still regarded as hoodlums whose activities warrant government surveillance" (2016, 176).

UNEAC's selective support of Black popular performance exposed how parts of rumba's cultural heritage deemed not useful for the Cuban nation-building project had to be left offstage. This conditional acceptance of rumba and rumberos in public space belied an underlying distaste, on the part of institutional leaders and white Cuban society, for the Black pride that rumberos themselves revered as sacred and inextricable from the genre. That is to say, the "Abakuá inside rumba" undergirded rumberos' enduring claim to a sense of belonging that exceeded (or paralleled) Cuban nationality. Abakuá societies' fraught condition of disputed Black sovereignty in Cuba accompanies its sonic and gestural repertoire in popular rumba performance. Rumberos' decision to publicly embody Abakuá choreography and pay homage to its founding spirit of solidarity was an act of defense, an expression of allegiance to their sacred right to collective Black self-determination.

At first Yoruba Andabo obliged UNEAC and stopped playing Abakuá rhythms in public, but in recent years they had resurrected "Protesta Carabalí." I noticed that typically they incorporated Iremes when the show was for predominantly local Black audiences rather than diplomatic occasions or higher profile performances in mainstream venues, however. By comparison, the newly founded Osain del Monte rumba group was not subsidized by the state and thus not called to do formal cultural diplomacy work. They showcased Abakuá music and dance liberally, to much enthusiasm from their largely young, Black, and male following.

Newer, younger members of Yoruba Andabo were not aware of the specifics regarding the group's history of being pressured to suspend Abakuá music, yet they were familiar with the racial logics. Lekiam, a newly joined drummer in 2013, said that the area in Vedado where UNEAC was located was home to mostly middle-class white families who were not friendly to rumberos like him from Pogolotti, a disadvantaged, historically Black, working-class neighborhood in Marianao. When explaining the underlying social dynamics of the prohibition of Abakuá rhythms, Lekiam and other members would use their index fingers to brush their forearm, a nonverbal indication of race being a salient factor in the story. Someone would say, "You know how they [brushing forearm] are," and then brush that same index finger up the tip of his nose, signaling elitism. In these exchanges, "they" referred to Cubans who, rumberos believed, looked down on Blackness unfiltered by white interests in national folklore. Yoruba Andabo members critiqued the racialized perception of the audience's conduct during Abakuá songs as potentially violent, exhibiting a low level of culture, and lacking etiquette or manners (*educación*).[13] "They think we are *ambientales* . . . that when Abakuá comes on, we are guapo," echoed the youngest male member, Didier, with a smirk. Espousing racial pride in the legacy of an autonomous African polity induced fear for ostensibly engendering incivility and social dangerousness: guapería. This negative association was readily critiqued but, on some level, also relished.

Other anthropologists of race and gender in Cuba have alluded to the subtext *guapería* takes on when imposed on, then taken up by, Black men. Aisha Beliso-De Jesús translates *guapo* as "roughneck" (2013, 62), while Jafari

Allen elaborates that *guapo* is "also resonant with so-called cool pose or the aesthetics of flossin' and swagger" (2011, 49). *Guapo* and *guapería* function much like *thug* in the United States. On the one hand, these racially coded words assign latent aggressive criminality to Black male bodies. Yet simultaneously, Black men positively recuperate the thug label as *gangsta*, a criminalized swagger worn with defiant pride as a cultural politics of resistance (Gordon 1997; Henry 2004). Throughout the African diaspora, individuals find ways to resignify dominant ideologies and terminological practices in order to resituate themselves as powerful actors within their own social spheres (Thomas 2004, 251).

"The Abakuá inside rumba" instills panic for some and grandeur for others, both negatively perceived and positively felt in racial terms. In postperformance interviews in 2013, several rumberos recognized the stigma attached to these controversial rhythmic incorporations and defended their moral superiority regardless. One drummer said, "That has to do with the country. Politics [that are] somewhat against these types of manifestations. The Abakuá is created to be a good husband for your wife, a good father for your children, a good son for your parents. . . . Goodness, it's an understanding that is being devalued. . . . Abakuá were conceived as having bad blood. . . . And that's not how it [really] is. The Abakuá is a very beautiful concept." A singer agreed, "Because sometimes you put on a rumba and put on an Abakuá rhythm and the people . . . they get panicked, scared. . . . But it's very good. It is very beautiful because no one knows the transmission it has, the one who dances it, the one who sings it, the one who plays it."

Yoruba Andabo members' emphasis on Abakuá goodness spoke back to the durability of colonial renderings of Abakuá men as innately delinquent. More than a hundred years after Ortiz published his infamous treatise of the "Afro-Cuban Underworld," it would seem that Abakuá rhythms still activated the pseudoscientific belief that criminal aggression was latent within Black men's "blood." These testimonies by rumberos evidence the enduring anti-Black fears casting Black men as inherently dangerous to society. In Hope Bastian's ethnographic account, a white man from a privileged family of the self-identified "Military Oligarchy/Revolutionary Elite," defined the "lower class" as "that guy who has no other way and breaks in and robs your house" (2018, 69). While not mentioning race in explicit terms, he asserts a belief shared among privileged, white respondents, that class status and class mobility is hereditary and cannot actually be achieved through hard work or ingenuity (69–70, 88). The class resentment of Havana's have-nots was personified through the figure of a guy trespassing onto property where he has no right to be, where he does not belong, to take that which he has no lawful claim to. Fears of Black men were also a veiled acknowledgment of the extent to which this sector of society was excluded from the means to accumulate wealth and unable to participate in particular modes of consumption. Rather than confront the contradiction of systemic barriers to class mobility in a revolution that ostensibly eliminated class conflict—which is to reckon with why "that guy [. . .] has no other way"—an African fraternity that espouses a sanctified claim to territory, beyond the law, gets easily rationalized as organized crime.

A rhythm that honors the collective capacity to remap spatial coordinates and impose an alternate social order is a dangerous legacy to claim. Well aware that their corporeal expressions in step of Abakuá rhythms will look like guapería, rumberos nevertheless showcase their positive investment in this criminalized repertoire. They resignify this "unruly" masculinity as "good" and "beautiful" in and through their proudly dancing bodies. Sacred swagger, I propose, is the corporeal idiom that Abakuá rhythms offer men eager to assert a sanctified legitimate claim to space. Flippin' the script of dispossession and exclusion, they embody a sacred choreography of Black sovereignty. In the grand narrative about Cuban rumba, the "discovery" of musical talent in humble workers and their appreciation by a Cuban mainstream audience on the national stage reflected the state's anti-imperialist project of "upliftment" and "inclusion." For those port workers-turned-professional artists, sacred affiliation was no less crucial at every juncture of their career trajectory. From the docks to the stage, they engaged in careful negotiation of their bodies' capacity to slip back and forth between socially virtuous and socially delinquent, attraction and repulsion, Cuban nationalist and Black, at the sound of a drum. During rumba events in the 2010s, young men rehearsed this choreography of sovereignty historically coded as a defiant guapo force to be reckoned with. If social mobility during the update was an inherited trait, then sacred swagger projected the bequeathment of a moral value beyond capital.

The New Man 2.0, the Negrón, and the Ñáñigo

As trends in private-sector job listings reveal, Black men are visible fixtures in the new economic landscape in one increasingly important occupation: bouncers, who serve to keep Black people out of commercial spaces. The blog Negra Cubana tenía que ser, by Black Cuban feminist scholar and activist Sandra

Heidl Ramírez (formerly Abd'Allah-Álvarez Ramírez), began reposting articles about the dearth of Black business ownership and employment in the private sector, anticipating formal scholarship on the topic. In chorus with Silvia's indictment of *"racismo profesional"* (chapter 2), Angel Márquez Dolz (reposted in Abd'Allah-Álvarez Ramírez 2016) used the term "racial casting" in an article entitled "Negrón de discoteca: ¿Nuevas formas de racismo en Cuba?" to describe one of many new forms of racism seen in Havana since the private-market boom. Similarly, Sandra has highlighted how hiring in the tourism sector based on racial stereotypes intersected with gender (Álvarez Ramírez 2011). The article reported on the growing pattern of hiring burly Black men in bouncer positions to guard business establishments like exclusive hotels, hard currency stores, nightclubs, and restaurants. The nickname developed for these men, *"Negrón de"* (Burly Black Man of . . .) [name of business establishment], spoke to the growing normalcy of this racialized and gendered figure in the capital city's landscape. De la Fuente draws attention to the case of a Black nightclub bouncer named Yúnior who had a college degree in accounting and finance from the University of Havana and secured a public teaching position at the university, only to find that the meager CUC $20 monthly salary was insufficient to survive on. "So he went to work in the private sector where his physical attributes—especially those society attributes to his skin color—were more valuable than his education. Blackness is equated with brute force. Accounting and finance are for white people" (de la Fuente 2019). I would add that the characteristics society attributes to *Black masculinity*, specifically, is what de la Fuente's account alludes to.

The way conceptions of virtuous manhood under "perfecting" socialism converge with anti-Black coloniality is key to decoding the employment patterns that colored the economic landscape of a city on the up-and-up. Sandra astutely noted, in her preface to the article, that white business owners banked on the historic "fear of the Black" (*el miedo al negro*) in Cuban society to maintain order via intimidation. These qualities make Black men the bouncers of choice for protecting private property and enforcing arbitrary rules of entrance through the ever-present threat of brute force.[14] The hiring of Black men as bouncers assisted what I am calling New Men 2.0 in exercising their right to rule over their private commercial domain. The *Negrón* (obedient to and reliant upon the New Man 2.0) does not own the property as a proper patriarch would, but as an extension of the white patriarch's property himself protects its border. While dutifully guarding white capital accumulation, he simultaneously rebukes Black solidarity and upholds the racialized social order of global capital. The advent of the *Negrón*/Burly Black figure evidences the social belief in Black men's unique propensity for violence and lack of intellectual acumen, regardless of education level. It also shows the normalization of their status as property, belonging to a corporate entity (i.e., *Negrón de discoteca* / Burly Black man *of* [belonging to] the nightclub). This disparaging designation for the Black male subject relies on the same kinds of beliefs about inherently aggressive Black masculinity that the *ñáñigos* represented in the nineteenth century (chapter 1). Only in this iteration, the *Negrón* does *not* do as he pleases. Instead, Black bouncers are expected to carry out the will of the private business owner, which typically entailed racially profiling potential clients to deny entrance to Black people presumed not to have inherited the means to lawfully consume in private establishments. The *Negrón* keeps guapos, like himself, off the premises. Here guapería is only an asset to national development when in subservience to white supremacist capitalist patriarchal rule over territory.[15]

Thus, in "updating" Havana, the *Negrón de discoteca* fulfilled a social function that eerily recalled the social practices of de facto racial segregation enforcement in recreational centers that the Cuban Revolution ostensibly swept away.[16] Black bouncers hired to police the borders of private businesses functioned in similar ways to Havana's largely Black police force, widely known since the Special Period to racially profile citizens in touristic areas in the name of complying with racially coded state mandates to keep the public space safe from "social dangerousness" (de la Fuente 2001a; de la Fuente 2001b; Sawyer 2005). Delimiting Black people's presence within New Man 2.0 territory was essentially sanctioned by the impunity with which PCC leaders regarded the worsening of racialized class stratification within Cuban society at that time.

Oriented around a New Man 2.0—a white patriarch with access to (foreign) capital to exploit the labor of others—the new revolutionary masculinity poses a challenge for Black men seeking validation as patriarchs themselves or, perhaps more threatening to the new (and old) social order, seeking in Black sovereignty a more just space to determine their fate. For rumberos in "updating" Cuba, positive investment in sacred swagger, what looks like guapería, pronounces an embodied political positioning of antagonism against normative scripts for virtuous manhood and their embedded racial hierarchies and geographies. For young Black men cast to the borders of commercial spaces, Abakuá bodily repertoires reimagine masculine prowess beyond its expression in individual capital accrual. We can think of peso-poor rumberos as embodying an alternate, sanctified vision of power over property, labor, and resources: the foundational elements of patriarchal sovereigns in modernity (I. Perry 2018). Rather than distancing themselves from allegiances to Black community or lamenting a lack of inherited wealth, rumba provided a public space to map a sacred entitlement to sovereign terrain and self-recognition as morally superior men, good and beautiful to the ones who dance it. While one could argue that the same demographic of disenchanted youth targeted by Yoruba Andabo's transmission of cultural pride swelled the ranks of Abakuá lodges, "eager to prove their masculinity" (Routon 2005, 374), I contend that what looked like defiant macho aggression might be more accurately understood as a Black masculine performance of moral superiority enlisted to negotiate the gendered indignities of race and class oppression.

These nuances get collapsed when rumberos (or guapos) are hailed as stand-ins for universal Cuban identity. What is more, the underlying economic forces and political ideologies that construct new social figures like the *Negrón* get erased and thus normalized within the PCC's vision of a more perfect Cuban Socialism. Charging those who embodied the Abakuá inside rumba with guapería is a deflection from dealing with the systemic causes of the unmet material desires of black youth. Yoruba Andabo's performances of "Protesta Carabalí" (Calabar Protest) daringly call attention to this public secret. Whether rumberos were initiated into the brotherhood or not, public commemorations of a sacred heritage of Black self-determination were as gratifying to black youth as they were threatening to white norms of revolutionary respectability. While frustrated by how their race, class, and gender largely limited their participation in the private market as subordinates to white patriarchy, in a collective power stance, rumberos mapped a sacred dominion.

Calabar Protest

The cold air in the dark nightclub venue was typically cloudy with cigarette smoke. For those of us relegated to the back due to late arrival, we heard Yoruba Andabo before we saw them. Geovani stood behind a microphone hitting the familiar syncopated stream of hollow cracks with wooden clave sticks. The song "Protesta Carabalí" (Calabar Protest) opened with a traditional guaguancó rhythmic structure. Characteristic of small nightclub performances by ensembles in the "rumba renaissance," Black youth from Havana's inner-city neighborhoods predominated in the space. In the second verse, without missing a beat, Geovani lowered his hands to the

3.5 Ireme enters in Yoruba Andabo "Protesta Carabalí" performance. Photo by author.

ground, smoothly replacing one wooden stick with an *ekón* bell, similar to a cowbell, that lay waiting at his feet. While maintaining the same rhythm, he changed the timbre of the time-line pattern from a hollow knocking to a metallic clanging. The percussive clangs sonically punctuated a shift in the space. On this cue, a percussionist moved his drum from the upright position to a diagonal tilt. He balanced the bottom edge of the drum on the floor, securing it in place between his thighs. These small modifications in the musical format orchestrated a transition to a faster-paced rumba for male solo dancing. As Daniel attests, rumba columbia "features the male dancer in all his glory and provides the forum for danced competition" (1995, 69). However, this particular clave rhythm, marked with an *ekón*, is derived from the Abakuá ceremonial repertoire. The sonic shift registered in the focus of both the artists and the audience. This musical change called for a distinct form of bodily engagement. And with the tonal, affective, and corporeal re-arrangement, they remapped the space.

Detaching his microphone from the row of stands in the chorus, Chan moved with charisma to center stage. He carried his frail, mahogany frame with a dignified elegance that commanded respect. Liberating himself from his still choral posture behind the line of microphone stands, Chan assumed his ritual role as Moruá (Yuánsa), the Abakuá singing dignitary. The crowd shuffled in place to get a straight view of Chan. He took over the stage with a certain playful savoir faire and low-effort quality that can be best summed up as swagger. The former lead singer of the opening gua-guancó portion obediently receded from the spotlight to join the chorus stepping in place. The transfer of power to Chan, so to speak, performed an important displacement of the previous order and accompanied the daring transformation this Calabar Protest was known for. Some men in the audience shifted their weight from right to left, joining the chorus in the steady marching pattern. Traveling in place referenced the processional character of Abakuá music. Abakuá songs are called *marchas* (marches) because they are ceremoniously played in motion. They reference colonial times when ca-bildos were only allowed to parade with their drums on Kings Day. Chan stayed in motion, traversing the stage back and forth, and then suddenly shifting his weight by inclining his torso on diagonals, showing a signature mastery of balance off-center. Chan's improvisational gestural flurries foreshadowed the sacred Ireme spirit's entrance. Two professional dancers dressed in full Ireme costumes would soon emerge, answering his summons.

Chan sounded out a prolonged "Ya-yoooo!" before singing the solo verse in Spanish. This first interjection of Abakuá *dialecto* (a prestige tongue spoken between initiates) punctuated the new rhythmic state with spiritual grandeur. The lyrics in Spanish followed, "I'm going to delve deeply/ into the struggle of Cuba/ so you can learn to respect it." Yet Chan's insertion of Ireme gestural tropes, interspersed throughout his lyrical storytelling, complicated the seemingly straightforward patriotic narrative. His coordinated leg extensions drew smooth curves on the ground. Tilted torso postures played off arms creating juxtaposing sharp angles bent at the elbow. The smooth, charismatic grace of his crisp citational flurries, woven in and out, played counterpoint to the spoken chronicle about the white independence leader Carlos Manuel de Céspedes. Indeed, Kristina Wirtz attunes us to consider Carabalí songs as performative, invoking a vision of solidarity, belonging, and cultural resistance through historical vignettes (Wirtz 2016, 365).

Carlos Manuel de Céspedes is revered in Cuba's official history as the revolutionary white creole who freed the enslaved on his plantation in 1868, sparking the independence wars against Spain.[17] Although this insurgent figure of white benevolence is the ostensible protagonist of the verse's lyrics, Chan's charisma constantly overshadowed him. The call in the song for people to remember the *"Grito de Yara"*—Céspedes's rallying cry that freed the enslaved—echoed from Chan to the chorus, performatively catalyzing another call to action in the present moment. Chan's virtuosic choreographic assemblages conditioned the spatiotemporal terrain that the audience and the professional Ireme dancers would momentarily chart beyond the dominant discourse of Black indebtedness to white paternalism. Recalling the history of Abakuá incorporation of white initiates to extend their own political influence over Black fate, here the movement sequence incorporated the figure of a powerful white man from the landowning elite into a narrative about a freedom struggle on *their own* terms. Chan's solo dance, for one, competed for sensorial focus over the patriotic lyrics in Spanish and won easily, making the way for the Iremes to soon take center stage.

Chan sang the third, final, and longest section of the song, the *montuno* (the repetitive call-and-response section), completely in *dialecto*. Scholars of Abakuá have argued that, after the Spanish verses mentioning Céspedes, "the track moves into Abakuá music and language underlining the fact that Abakuá was established in Cuba to defend and liberate Black slaves" (Miller 2000, 178). However, the majority of those present in rumba spaces were non-initiates and thus could not know the ritual language's hidden message. Yet even non-initiates should sense the rise in the temperature of the music. This was the section where Ireme dancers and audience participation was foregrounded. Lyrics aside, the social choreography prescribed by the rhythm made everyone complicit in its defiant historicizing and place-making pursuit.

The acceleration of speed in the rhythm created dramatic tension as Yoruba Andabo's two professional male dancers, Vladimir and Lázaro, appeared from a door at the side or back of the venue. The densely packed crowd nonverbally complied with the imperative to reorder the space, allowing them entrance. For the audience, the rhythmic intensification rendered the kinesphere thinner and less resistant, or more pliant to quicker movement. As if from a portal connecting to another plane of existence, the two dancers emerged stealthily, fully masked in red-white-and-blue Ireme costumes, referencing the Cuban flag, made to both impress and conceal. The steady marching in place contrasted with the masked figures' slow leg lunges. They recalled the graceful movements of a leopard, the sacred animal of the Ékpè-Efik "Leopard Societies" where Abakuá brotherhoods trace their origins (R. F. Thompson 1984). Bare, calloused feet, their soles caked with cigarette soot, were the only sign that human flesh supported the slow-moving frames. Although low to the ground, the men towered over the crowd with otherworldly presence. Long, low, and deliberate strides propelled the dancers smoothly through the crowd toward Chan, who sang a report in coded *dialecto*. Audience members adjusted and readjusted quickly to avoid causing the masked dancers to break their steady forward motion. Exuding the same grace of isolated muscle control that Chan foreshadowed in his opening, the minimalist and controlled choreography of their limbs expressed what Robert Farris Thompson aptly describes as "manful self-assertion" (1984, 252). The juxtaposition between the quick and steady marching in place of the crowd, clearing a way for the Ireme spirit's passage in slow motion, marked the dynamic temporal contours of this sacred landscape.

In ceremony, the ancestor spirit, as a pure being from another plane, not only cleared the path for ritual events to take place but cleansed any bad habits of the men who participate (García Velasco 2016). The Ireme brushed the men with deft licks of a handheld broomlike object called a *tongue*, a play on the expressive power laden in a mute spirit who speaks only through gesture. Neither of the dancers were initiated, yet they executed the sacred strokes of the tongue with dutiful precision. Only men in the audience offered themselves to be purified by the Ireme's smooth licks along the way, accepting the gesture's power to cleanse and also affirm their manhood. After one last shake of the pelvis, sounding the bells hanging around their waist, they reached their tongues diagonally up into the sky in an extended lunge. Vladimir and Lázaro aimed for seamless unison, although the masks meant to convey the Ireme's blindness apparently hampered the peripheral vision that would be required to do so. Their movement phrase concluded in the low lunge, a grandiose pose of manful prowess, in succession.

In typical rumba songs, the *montuno* section signals the "break" of the rumba, opening the floor for male-female pairs to dance. However, under Abakuá order, after the Ireme dancers finished their set routine, only initiated men in the audience could dare enter center stage. They identified themselves as Abakuá by stepping forward. More purifying strokes of the tongue were applied to their bodies. The *ecobios* from the audience engaged in embodied conversation with Chan, as Moruá, exhibiting their proficiency in the coded, gestural language only they could understand. Dancing Ireme choreography liberated the body from linear time, collapsing present and past selfhood, man and ancestor, here and there, in locomotion. As the Abakuá saying goes, "My body is in Cuba, but my mind is in Africa" (Miller 2009, 37). Bodily practice effectively unsettled the temporal-spatial logics of the state-run performance venue. This counter-choreography of sovereignty otherwise routed the body toward an imagined place of Abakuá dominion, moving in place.

To experience these performances of Abakuá liturgy as a non-initiated rumbero or rumbera is to bear witness to a polity's self-endowed claim to opacity, to not fully understand. Rumberos claimed no special access as Cubans to "the secret" of the brotherhood. Uninitiated rumberos were likely to say, "I don't know what it means" rather than offer a personal interpretation. Even Yoruba Andabo singers themselves were not taught the secret meanings of the choruses they chanted, nor were the drummers told what the confluence of their rhythmic accompaniment achieved in a ritual setting. As one singer told me after a rehearsal, "Folklorically, anyone can sing it. Here [in Yoruba Andabo] they don't say what the vocals mean, what the rhythms mean, no, no, no. . . . Perhaps if the person singing is Abakuá, yes. But if the person singing does not belong to that religion, there shouldn't be any reason to know what one thing or the other means. That teaching is not given here."

Beyond risking a "wrong" interpretation, for the uninitiated to produce discursive meaning would be to assert unauthorized political belonging to the Abakuá world. As in Caribbean Freemasonry, "for the initiate to know and interpret the word is a way of crossing a threshold from outsider to insider" (Arroyo 2013, 26–27). Trespassing this threshold would be an affront to the brotherhood's sovereignty. These testimonies of interpretive restraint defended a politics of "ethnographic refusal," when respondents deem "enough" has been revealed. Paramount becomes respecting the "representational territory" gained from hindering the colonial drive of total ethnographic description as required for governance (Simpson 2007, 78). Just as membership to this polity was not a natural birthright, interpretation was a privilege that must be earned through initiation and long-term study under authorized elders. While state-endorsed folkloric paradigms superimposed Cuban cultural nationalism as the core of rumba's meaning, to acknowledge the Abakuá inside rumba was to refuse colonial arrest by representation in words.

These rumba events pronounced obeisance to the sanctity of what cannot be known in language yet must be respected in motion. Located within this "spectacular opacity" (Brooks 2006) lay the homosocial intimacy of public strokes between men—the graceful lick of tongue on skin that cleanses the spirit.[18] In subservience to Abakuá rule, non-initiates, myself included, willfully narrowed the breadth of our interpretation and moved in step. Corporeal meaning, vital here, was neither endlessly contingent (relative to the individual) nor generalizable to *cubanidad*. Abakuá regulatory regimes exercised sanctified power over the order of the senses and the sense of order.

If embodied practice is taken as seriously as practitioners of this faith do, "Protesta Carabalí" moves from a figurative device to a performative enactment.[19] "Calabar Protest" suggests a declaration of a "we" loyal to an Africanist political community. This sacred repertoire uniquely beckons adherence to an alternative arrangement of the social in public space, which is to publicly affirm the relevance of a spirit summoned by the kind of solidarity forged before nationalism's hold on the enslaved. It is a protest in but not of Cuba. Kristina Wirtz argues that affectively charged "coordinated, agentful, even choreographed movement" in space, what she terms "micro-mobilities," enacts a distinct collective space that marks racial difference (2017, 59). Similarly, live performances of Abakuá choreography invited rumba aficionados to act in accordance with a prescribed repertoire of gesture, tone, rhythm, responsorial chant, and bodily scripts that guide an alternate ordering and racializing of space. I underscore the gendering of this racialized placemaking as sovereign territory.

Yoruba Andabo's performance of "Calabar Protest" was, surely, remarkable, but not rare. Choreographic invocations of the Ireme spirit's gestural speech, made with an imaginary brush in hand or handkerchief, reappeared with regularity in moments of dance improvisation by both initiated and uninitiated young Black men in rumba guaguancó and rumba columbia more generally. Given the politics of interpretation at play, perhaps the question should not be, what does it mean (theological or otherwise), but what does Ireme mimicry do? What does it do to mimic or bear witness to the signature physical commands of the Ireme given other figurations of Black manhood in circulation? What Saba Mahmood (2004) would call "affective embodied experience," conditioning a differential mode of being-in-the-body, might get us closer to approximating what sacred swagger enacts. From where I stand outside the threshold, I can only respectfully offer that we might be compelled to humbly bear witness to the swagger of Black sovereignty with our whole bodies. For those who seek such a belonging, respect for the cues in the rhythm could bind a Black body politic to a power higher than state authority, to a place beyond the nation. After attending an Abakuá public ceremony escorted by Chan, I learned how Calabar Protest performances in nightclubs would prepare me to think with the limits of my right to understand in other clearings.

The Choreography of Sovereignty, or Sacred Swagger

It was an early Sunday morning in December 2016 and my first time attending an Abakuá ceremony—a *plante*. The word *plante*, from the verb *to plant*, evokes the ritually edifying claim to land. Chan, who was eager to nurture my growing interest in Yoruba Andabo's Abakuá repertoire, escorted me. He took pride in his ability to grant me exclusive offstage access as an elder in the brotherhood. To get to this cabildo from downtown Havana, you take a ferry across the bay to the municipality of Regla, then a local bus, then hike. He told me to meet him at the docks of Regla first thing in the morning. More specifically, we would meet under the tree in front of the Church of the Virgen de Regla (a Black Madonna syncretized with the Lucumí divinity Yemayá) that overlooks the bay. The numerous times I had visited him in Regla before, I always called him from my cell phone when I was at the ferry on the Old Havana side. He insisted on this to help him gauge when to leave his house, a slow ten-minute walk away. While I felt awkward causing him to make this extra physical effort because of his age, for the same reason I felt it impolite to insist otherwise. I had similarly given up trying to convince him that he need not call me to make sure I arrived home safely after our visits. Ensuring my safe arrival was, for him, part of what it meant to be a good man. Although he suffered from his fair share of physical ailments, his slow and steady gait projected the same air of swagger he performed on stage. He carried his weight like a man in command of his surroundings. This time, rather than making the left toward his house, we turned right toward the bus stop.

While waiting for the bus to arrive, I asked him if he belonged to the cabildo where we would be going. He replied no; but, since he lived in the vicinity, he always had an open invitation to participate in their ceremonies. He told me that the plante had started at 11 p.m. the night before. It was common for alcohol consumption to accompany these all-nighters to strengthen the men's stamina while completing the extensive ceremonial labor. His *ángel de la guardia* or *madre* (mother), Ochún, forbade him from drinking alcohol, to preserve his health in his advanced age. A good son, he respected her orders. This was partly why Chan stopped participating in plantes regularly, or only attended specific portions, like the part I would witness that day. Chan had timed our morning arrival to coincide with a climax in the public pageantry that would take place outside the house he called *cabildo* or *temple* interchangeably. *Cabildo* could refer to both the group of people who belonged to the house as well as the physical structure of the temple itself, which was a collectively purchased property passed down within the brotherhood over generations to conduct their ceremonies. Unbeknownst to me at that point, I would see ceremonial Iremes bringing the highest-ranking initiate into the cabildo. Then, away from public view, the brothers would continue conducting rituals for hours into the next night.

At plantes, Abakuá perform their cultural history. In ritual, theater, song, gesture, and symbols are used pedagogically to prepare the next generation for leadership, transmitting knowledge incrementally through the body (Miller 2009, 4; Miller 2000, 167). Miller refers to Abakuá art as "kaleidoscopic," revealing multiple layers of hidden meaning that are transmitted through the overlapping media (sonic, verbal, imagery, gesture), cloaking messages in semiotic webs (2009, 154). My conversation with Chan, as he escorted me to the plante that morning, already revealed the embeddedness of the kaleidoscopic use of coded signs to talk about their practice. It also foreshadowed the power of sacred performance for conjuring authority over territory.

The nearest local bus stop left me and Chan at the base of a settlement of rudimentary dwellings tucked up on the hills of a neighborhood called La Sierra Chiquita. We then started our hike to the place where the cabildo stood. I followed behind his slow and surefooted steps. Even though La Sierra Chiquita was technically in a municipality within the capital's city limits, the narrow dirt footpaths leading to the cabildo made it feel rural. We began to hear the faint sound of drums as we climbed deeper and higher into the settlement. I turned my head to gaze at the clear view of Regla down below to the left. It was serene. The sound of the drums grew stronger as we climbed. A uniformed policeman stood at the opening of the clearing just ahead.

Approaching the top of the hill, Chan turned to me and murmured, "We will pay tribute to Fidel Castro, the President of the Republic." I was confused. Just days earlier, Fidel Castro's corpse had been very publicly buried. His brother, Raúl, had succeeded him as president as early as 2006. After years of knowing Chan, one thing I knew for sure was that the years had not dulled his cognition even a bit. His memory rivaled that of any person in their prime, and he could recall even the smallest of details and dates with precision. Fearing that the window for clarification was soon fleeting with the clearing now almost in sight, I managed to utter, "But Chan, Fidel is no longer president." "The President of the *Republic*," he insisted. I racked my brain for an appropriate way to form a more pointed follow-up question. He paused, realizing that his explanation was grossly insufficient. Then he turned back to me to explain how the Abakuá have their own constitution, their own president, governors, vice president, "all of the things that a republic needs. It's a republic [*Es una república*]."

In contrast to the mainstream stigmatization of Abakuá societies as thugs (or at least "thuggish"), Chan's framing of what I was going to see as an act of patriotism invoked a political structure that was both sovereign and legitimate. Just as Yoruba Andabo's Ireme costumes bore the colors of the Cuban flag, Chan's deployment of the normative statist terminology both impressed and concealed. In laying claim to their own republic nested in Cuba, enslaved Abakuá men effectively recoded powerful symbols of the nation-state. This discursive move recalled the tactics Abakuá port workers deployed in the early twentieth century, camouflaging their rumba drums in the available patriotic terms necessary to avoid arrest ("No, sir, Mr. Policeman. These aren't African witchcraft drums. These are patriotic Cuban barrel drums—*mambisas!*") (Sublette 2004, 265). In a similar fashion, rather than use the ritual title for the cabildo's political head, Chan referred to him as "Fidel." This tradition of semiotic play has been critical for protecting "their own" in hostile political terrain.

Emerging from the shaded trail, we finally reached an opening—a semi-wide concrete area lined with houses. The sun, still hours from midday, was already beaming at full force. The first thing I noticed was the multitude of men in small groupings, milling around, drinking on the front stoops of the homes surrounding the courtyard. The second thing that immediately caught my attention was a thick trail of smeared blood scorched on the concrete. The long, red smear led to a central focal point of soot and painted inscriptions on the ground outside the door of a house around which most of the action was assembled. The masked Ireme, covered from head to ankle, stood on this "stage." The Ireme adjudicated the purity of the environment holding a live rooster in one hand—flapping wings did the cleansing work in this ceremony—and a staff in the other to chastise.

Throughout the bulk of the time I was present, mostly young Black men gathered to drink and talk, seemingly waiting or just resting. After the long series of ceremonial activities had taken place through the night, this was a moment of recess for some before the long day and night of ritual work ahead. There was a Black woman with a basin of ice selling beer under the only umbrella for shade. She had some customers, but maybe would have had more if the men were not also passing around their own bottles of rum. Out of the cabildo came a man who distributed small cups of brothy soup. Chan passed a cup to me. The liquid tasted slightly sour, but I drank it anyway to be polite. As I sipped slowly, men approached Chan individually and greeted him, sometimes offering rum. He declined obediently. I trailed behind Chan as he surveilled the area. Across the perimeter there was another Black woman sitting on a bench where other men also sat. She did not seem to be interacting with those around her. Unlike the men chatting in her vicinity, she was quiet. The other women and girls looked on from the front porches of the houses surrounding the courtyard. Around the corner, down the block, the "President of the Republic" sat on a stump, bare-chested and rotund, awaiting his grand entrance. He was accompanied by more men and another Ireme standing guard. The Ireme was positioned in a way that partially impeded the policeman's view of their head of state. I found it poetic that just days after Fidel Castro's nationally televised funeral, this "Fidel" was awaiting his big entrance, guarded by a Calabar ancestor.

I wondered how long the policeman had been standing by and what role his presence played in their scenario of sacred law and order. I imagined how the looming gaze of the law, a fixture since slavery, might have been incorporated into this ritual scene. "They have to be there," he answered after I asked about the visible police presence at the plante. Chan explained the due process with diplomatic poise. When members want to have a plante, they tell "the president," who then tells the local police precinct to get official permission. According to Chan, the police always grant permission, but they post a few officers to make sure things do not get out of hand.[20] This reminded me of the 1930s, when cabildo-led comparsas were flanked with police "to prevent disorder" (chapter 1). The presumption is that a group of Abakuá men gathered for long hours drinking is a recipe for delinquency. Therefore, police officers in uniform typically stand guard beyond the perimeter of Abakuá gatherings, not to interfere but rather to ensure "public safety."

The Abakuá had their own guards posted too, strategically positioned to protect *their own* resources. Muscular, towering Black men took turns standing guard at the door of the temple. Taking a stance reminiscent of the bouncers so often seen on Havana's "updating" city streets, their crossed arms accentuated broad shoulders blocking the entrance. No amount of money could be exchanged for access here. The cabildo guards exuded a dignified, foreboding posture, warning anyone who would dare enter without sanctified authorization. As a site of militantly guarded opacity, the temple hid the secret to their powers. In this scenario, the policemen, the cabildo guards, and the Iremes formed a striking constellation of men on duty employing surveillance and threat of force as a mechanism of gendered power. Security officers deployed by their respective sovereigns ensured respective notions of social order in ways that were nonetheless mutually legible as underwritten by higher authority.

This was an unambiguously masculine space. Unlike the Ireme, who is vocally mute yet gesturally audible, in this scenario rehearsed across both rumba events and plantes, women follow prescriptive choreographies of muted expression. Diana Taylor (2003) makes the case that cultural repertoires can discipline an audience into defined modes of reception. Similar to how women at nightclubs acted as still witnesses, the women at plantes stand quietly, acting as the "unseeing audience" (Gagliardi 2018, 747), physically present for but shut out from the activities inside the cabildo. These choreographies for feminine corporeal address—unmoving and unseeing— physically delineate gender and territory. I was hard-pressed to speak with a rumbera who did not readily accept the sacred grounds for their gender's exclusion. When I chatted with women afterward or apart from the performance, they would often proudly share that their fathers and grandfathers were Abakuá, or they were close to people who were, whom they respected. Having been raised in households and in community with Abakuá men, these women largely endorsed the sanctity of Abakuá sovereignty.

At a house party in Centro Habana with Jenny and members of Rumba Morena several years prior, I once incorporated Ireme stylings into my rumba improvisation. Perhaps I thought Jenny would be impressed by my initiative, picking up moves on my own that she did not teach me. She crossed her arms and, staring right at me, rotated slightly toward one of the other rumberas and called me *una atrevida* (insolent) loud enough for me to hear. My *atrevimiento* was embodying the specific gestures of the Ireme; in other words, not knowing my place in relationship to Abakuá choreo/geographic territory, from which I should keep a respectful distance. Even in the intimate company of mostly women and no Abakuá present, I had committed trespassing by daring to mimic that sacred masculine gestural speech. I never did it again. There were reasons why certain dances were not taught to me, and I didn't have to understand the theology in order to know better. In this scenario, Black women's willful unseeing and still presence had a role to play too.[21]

Once I sensed an opening, I asked Chan if all the men at the plante were Abakuá. He answered no. Most of the young men were there because they aspired to be sworn in some day. I questioned how he knew who was an *ecobio* already as opposed to who wanted to be one. He simply answered, "They identify themselves," but did not divulge the sign. Abakuá brotherhoods rely on virtuosic repetition of esoteric embodied scripts to uphold and demonstrate their belonging, ceremoniously using theater, song, gesture, and symbols to clandestinely convey Carabalí history to their polity. I was reminded how certain men would come up to Chan to greet him and give him a special handshake. Perhaps that was some indication of Abakuá citizenship. If nothing else, I had learned that to pry further would be to trespass into contested territory. Here, on consecrated land, I showed respect by not daring to overstep.

Chan exchanged one such handshake with a man similar in age to himself. The man's olive-skinned complexion would place him in the Cuban racial category of *trigueño*, literally a wheat-colored man. He wore bright blue trousers held up to his navel with a woven leather belt. A bright white *bolshevike* hat topped off the ensemble, matching his white dress shoes. His skin color and style of dress contrasted with the young Black men surrounding him in the latest threads of urban cool: baseball caps, muscle tees, ripped jeans, gold chains, and sneakers. Chan and the *trigueño* resembled each other in age and dress, but unlike Chan, the latter was sworn in to the Abakuá brotherhood in the 1970s. He was the eldest member present from this particular lodge. He would later tell me that he was responsible for ensuring that all of the outdoor activities were going according to ritual protocol. Chan looked at his watch and began to get restless. The grouping of elders remarked among themselves that the procession should have begun by now.

Chan asked his *ecobio trigueño* to stand with me on the perimeter of the courtyard so that he could check on the progress of the rituals being performed inside the temple. While awaiting Chan's return, the elder engaged me in conversation, explaining that I was in a territory called the *birthland of Abakuá (tierra nacida de Abakuá)*, where the first cabildo was formed. "Everything has a name," he said. Then he proceeded to identify different objects in quick succession, pointing with his index finger. The words that rolled off his tongue in *dialecto* were so foreign sounding to my ear for Cuban Spanish, and said so quickly, that I could not make them out. "The performance of Abakuá language is a key element to leadership in the society" (Miller 2000, 167). I gathered that the point was not for me to remember, much less understand, the words but for him to perform linguistic proficiency, signaling his rightful belonging to and leadership in that territory.

He shared how the Abakuá in Cuba see themselves as the global protectors of this secret religion that was lost in Africa due to colonization. "In the period of slavery, Africans came from Calabar, and they brought this religion to Cuba," he said. "And now, wouldn't you know that Nigerians come to Cuba to learn what this is, because they were colonized by the Muslims and so they lost this. So, you see, we in Cuba have to keep this going." The conversation was yet another of many indications that although Abakuá men trace the ancestral origins of their practice to a distinct location in Africa,

they do not see their practice as a Cuban derivative of an African original (Routon 2005). Despite a history of uprootedness and displacement,
they take pride in having figuratively planted themselves on this side of
the Atlantic through ritual and having successfully defended their territory
against Muslim influence, Spanish authorities, and their creole successors,
revolution after revolution. By transmitting this choreography of refusal
over generations, they dwelled in a sacred land nested within but not of Cuba's geopolitical borders. As such, they claimed "a privileged source of autonomous power" independent from the nation-state (Routon 2005, 372).
Indeed, their bodies may appear to be in Cuba, but they were in "Africa."

We stood for some moments in silence, awaiting Chan's return. Careful not to trespass by probing for answers, I patiently waited for the *trigueño*
to initiate conversation. He looked at the clumped groupings of young men
under the increasingly hot sun with a sigh. "The youth today don't know the
language; they don't know how to play the music, they aren't interested in
learning," he suddenly uttered. "Before, the cabildo used to be a mutual aid
society. Not anymore. Now all they are about is guapería." He had discerned
that identifiably Abakuá bodily scripts resonated with the youth, yet the choreography had often taken primacy over commitment to serving the membership of this alternate polity in practice. Subsequent discussions with
other Abakuá elders supported a prevalent sense that while outward displays
of Abakuá aesthetics (i.e., tattoos and dance choreography) had increased in
popularity among inner-city youth, the kinds of social systems, duties, and
ethics that grounded the "Abakuá world" was fading.[22] Most of the men at the
Abakuá public ceremonies could not claim initiatory status that would make
them privy to the secret knowledge necessary for leadership or transmission.
To this elder's discerning eye, young men adopting Abakuá-inspired gestures
and bodily markers, during rumba or otherwise, but devoid of study from
and moral duty to elders, was just guapería. In this view, the youth's attraction to celebrations of Abakuá cultural heritage in rumba has more to do with
the social currency of such expressions of belonging rather than the actual
maintenance of the institution to which one could belong.

A little while later, Chan returned and the Iremes finally escorted "Fidel"
into the temple in a grand procession. At the front, a man held a tall pole
with a cross perched on top, reminiscent of drawings of the colonial Kings
Day ceremonies. The prominent display of the infamous Catholic symbol
here was yet another tool of strategic concealment . Promptly thereafter,
Chan beckoned me to leave with him right away. Yoruba Andabo was performing on the other side of the city, and we had to rush to make it back to

the ferry on time. Besides, he said, from that point on the *ecobios* would be inside the cabildo conducting their secret rituals for hours into the night. Unlike the security guards at the state-run nightclub where Yoruba Andabo performs, the man guarding the cabildo would not permit me to enter.

The long historical arc of Abakuá performance, audaciously staging their autonomy in public yet coded in secrecy, takes space within a colonial field of vision contoured by Cuba's history of anti-Blackness, gender dominance, political dispossession, and capital accumulation. To take seriously the political imagination, bodily scripts, and coded gestures that form the boundaries of the Abakuá world is to better appreciate the social currency of their incorporation within contemporary rumba performance. For poor rumberos in Cuba's "updating" economic landscape, the ability to shape their own fate and establish their own sense of order in public space, even if only fleetingly, was powerful heritage to claim. However, this stature could not be inherited, only earned. Short of initiation, perhaps it was the swagger of Black sovereignty they were after. Inasmuch as patriarchy, white supremacy, property, and capital continue to underwrite the New Man 2.0's ability to index legitimate power and authority in post-Fidel Cuba, these scenarios of sacred swagger will continue to represent timely claims felt far beyond their cabildos' walls and membership. To the extent that the Abakuá inside rumba continues to stand in for social danger, such performances of sanctified Black masculine prowess affirm a power higher than state authority and moral value higher than neoliberal development.

Dancing around Territory

The gendering of sovereign spaces created by Black public processions are by no means unique to Cuba. Black confraternities in Mexico, for instance, functioned as social safety nets for Africans in the sixteenth and seventeenth centuries (Valerio 2022, 11), which also created an alternative political geography and an alternative horizon of political possibility grounded in collective memory of Africa transmitted through performance. Building on Imani Perry (2020), Miguel Valerio insists that festive confraternity performances during colonialism speak directly to contemporary political conditions that impel the collective construction of sites of/for defiant Black joy: the joy that exists through pain and suffering, not absent from it. To echo the words of one rumbero, "The Abakuá is a beautiful concept." Seeing beauty and goodness where others see guapería confers defiant joy to those young men who dance it, even if the majority may only be going through its motions.

Despite official proclamations adopting rumba as national heritage and even Abakuá as folklore, the pointedly anti-Black shroud that has covered Abakuá societies since colonialism also cloaks rumberos, marking the genre pejoratively as "a Black thing" (*una cosa de negros*) with the potential to attract guapos (Bodenheimer 2013). Thus rumberos and Abakuá alike can be understood as racialized communities of practice conjoined discursively by the shared denigration of their bodily expression under prevailing white regimes that cast them as both folkloric others (Godreau 2006) and social pariahs (D. H. Brown 2003).

Underscoring the controversy around the performance of "Protesta Carabalí" vis-à-vis the Cuban status quo, Valentín exclaimed, "Look at how the Abakuá is telling history! . . . They were born in the age of *cimarrones* (maroons). They lived and they defended themselves. . . . *Qué arreglo de humanidad* (What an ordering of humanity)! . . . *That* is the song." As he alludes in his synthesis of what the song means to him, by giving Abakuá heritage pride of place, rumba shows cast a spotlight on a tradition of urban Black fugitivity. To the extent that public displays of Abakuá heritage create a space to collectively dance around the notion of Black collective self-determination, these performances are met with the fears of white society as well as the desires of Black youth. Both projections form the basis of the sense of controversial pride that constitutes the Black corporeal undercommons' unique affective terrain. As discussed in chapter 1, the *ñáñigo* and Ireme have long personified white elite anxieties around Black masculinity unyoked from the rules of social order. The conscious decision to highlight the Abakuá's living legacy inside rumba suggests a timely, positive reinvestment in a fugitive polity that exceeds the bounds of national folklore even as it conceals itself in its discourses.

Dancing with/as an Ireme in public constitutes a profound choreographic tradition of fugitivity, refusing the terms of Black political dispossession. From the Enlightenment, the public domain, Perry asserts, "provided theaters of patriarchal domination that included nonpersons" (2018, 27). For instance, slave auctions were theatrical instantiations of sovereignty where personhood versus nonpersonhood status was displayed (Perry 2018, 26; Brooks 2006). In this case, the Ireme, while a nonperson, was also much more than that. This sacred personality for the enslaved and their descendants was deemed unlawful and yet wielded an authority that came from another plane, a place purer than the one constituted by conquest and the transatlantic slave trade, the Republic, and even the Revolution. The ancestral spirit both gesturally summons and is summoned by the kind of solidarity capable of defending an alternative kind of personhood and place in anti-Black terrain.

As recent anthropological debates about sovereignty have raised, these psychic and affective dimensions of historical experience tell us something about how a notion of sovereignty gets activated and shapes the form of agency and self-formation that are possible in particular moments (Masco and Thomas 2023, 22). Like Joseph Masco and Deborah Thomas, this chapter's discussion of sacred swagger and guapería as important affective registers of sovereignty "move[s] beyond a political economy frame to attend to the psychic and affective dimensions of historical experience" (2023, 22). In this broader moment of competing claims over territories in the Global South, the imperatives to *be a man*, and a particularly entrepreneurial one at that, always for the sake of global capital couched as national defense, crystallize how sovereignty becomes imaginable in capitalist modernity and performed on the ground in the everyday. As was the case when Che summoned the New Man into becoming, Cuba's sovereignty is once again under imperial surveillance and deliberate attack (Escuela 2019). Rumberos remind us of the role that race and gender performance play in shaping notions of the idealized citizen-subject and his property amid competing neocolonial claims to legitimacy in the Americas.

This node of the Black corporeal undercommons highlights the moral configuration of Black identities and the gendered configurations of sovereignties in postcolonial emancipatory imaginations (Williams 1996; Price 2009). Unlike in other sites in the Caribbean, the appeal of the "Abakuá inside rumba" works against the logics of capital to define one's manhood through economic productivity (Chevannes 2002; Lewis 2020). With sacred swagger, one confronts one's limited opportunities for capital accrual on different footing, from a position of moral superiority. This element distinguishes the political imaginary emerging from the Black corporeal undercommons from contemporaneous calls for, for instance, loans for more Black-owned businesses to bolster against the harms of "neo-racism" in Cuba. Accentuating the Abakuá inside rumba perhaps invokes a morality purer than the present Party vanguard to determine what forms sovereignty can take, a morality that nonetheless privileges manhood, and certain men over others.

The Abakuá inside rumba also reminds us how heteropatriarchal ideologies form bonds and maintain boundaries within the intimacy of Black spaces. Rather than criminalize the men who feel "beautiful" and "good" while dancing gracefully in step to sacred rhythms and with each other, I historically situate their morally configured self-fashionings within a constellation of men on duty to defend forms of property produced through the colonial encounter. Not unlike the template for idealized manhood defended by the revolutionary vanguard, homophobia and misogyny are, as other Black Cuban feminists have argued, fundamental to bolstering Abakuá conceptions of "good manhood."[23] The New Man and his 2.0 version, the *Negrón* and the *ñáñigo*, the policeman and the Ireme, all trade in homosociality's shared association with order and rightful rule over territory. When political imaginaries collide, heteropatriarchy has proven to be an efficacious lingua franca leveraged by the (formerly) enslaved to maneuver within hierarchies, engage in diplomatic relations, and decide upon which claims to territory are observed. As Chan so matter-of-factly reasoned, they had to be there. Imani Perry argues in her exegesis on patriarchy and the conditions of modernity that regimes of civil order have been predicated on exclusionary laws of personhood, sovereignty, and property, shaping asymmetrical relations of power since the age of conquest and the transatlantic slave trade (2018, 9–10). Thus, these seemingly straightforward spectacles dismissed as guapería productively beckon us to contemplate what sovereignty can look like in the Black popular imagination in the wake globally.

From my place standing still at the border, I silently ponder what precludes the summoning of a spirit of Black solidarity that dares to chart a future beyond property, personhood, and sovereignty defined through heteropatriarchal logics? Could such a spirit make the terms of belonging for Black cis and trans women, and Black queer people of all genders, feel less threatening? From where does that spirit derive legitimacy and the right to protection? When rumba is released from its overdetermination as a secular symbol for Cuban cultural nationalism, it is free for us to reckon with how these broader questions affect its practitioners, and all of us, most urgently and most intimately. We can then more critically consider how norms, feelings, and imaginaries of sovereignty emerge and are sustained, and the kind of aspirations toward order they enable and disavow (Bonilla 2017, 334). For the latter, I am reminded how the gestures, postures, and positionings of men of African descent become prime sources of inspiration in contrast to how other models of social relation (perhaps beyond gender binary paradigms of social order) more easily fall out of the national imagination and ancestral memory, and are less likely to be defended.

4 MOVING LABOR ACROSS MARKETS

As rumba and the Rumba event are analyzed in their national showcase, what began as the redemption of cultural dance traditions appears as a commodity and the nexus among foreign consumers in an international market. In this manner, dance, an aesthetic system, interacts with the economic arena of Cuban social relations.

YVONNE DANIEL, *Rumba*

Cabaret Las Vegas was located on the border of Centro Habana and Vedado. Centro Habana is a densely populated, marginalized, historically Black neighborhood, with high unemployment (a social worker told me that the main cause of death there is building collapse), whereas Vedado is a neighborhood where wide tree-lined promenades boast large houses and academic institutions, now known for being at the heart of the city's *emerging economy* (*economía emergente*) of private businesses. Tourists are less likely to frequent these small state-owned nightclubs unless they are part of a cultural itinerary organized by the state-owned tourist agencies. In general, tourists expecting "five-star service" frequent the newly opened private nightclubs and bars that owners have renovated using funds from either well-to-do family members in Miami or other foreign backers and business partners. This "emerging" nightlife doesn't cater to Black "peso-poor" clientele who earn in Cuban pesos and save up for a night on the town. As we have seen in chapter 3, they are more likely to actively bar Black people from entry.

At the entrance to Cabaret Las Vegas, an easel announced 50 CUP/MN (for Cubans); CUC $2 for foreigners. The dual fees signaled the stark differences that have coexisted in the country since the economic crisis of the Special Period. The cost of admission was equivalent in the two Cuban currencies, symbols of what economists have referred to as Cuba's "dual economy": consisting of subsidized and unsubsidized markets. *Pesos cubanos* (Cuban pesos, CUP), also referred to as *moneda nacional* (national money, MN), is the currency those in the public sector earn, which only has exchange value on the island. It is through this local currency that the state promotes its socialist welfare system to ensure state workers' access to subsidized basic food staples, utilities, and services. *Pesos cubanos convertibles* (CUC) or Cuban convertible pesos are the hard currency that can be exchanged for foreign bills. Remittances from abroad are withdrawn in this currency, as are salaries and profits from joint business ventures with foreigners that deal to tourists or Cubans who buy and sell in the private, unsubsidized market. The PCC's *Guidelines* (2011) have steered individuals and institutions alike to find ways to become self-sufficient, decreasing reliance on government subsidies, and attract capital from abroad to sustain an evolving vision of Cuban socialism upon which the nation's sovereignty relies.

Yoruba Andabo's weekly *peña* (showcase) at Cabaret Las Vegas was a testament to the group's loyal following. Yoruba Andabo's professional status as a state-subsidized (*subvencionado*) group ensures them a steady year-round salary in CUP/MN equivalent to roughly CUC $20 per month. It also authorizes the group to be eligible to perform in any public venue, including the state-run nightclub where they had their weekly matinee *peña*. The state entertainment industry allows Cuban patrons to pay the entrance fee in CUP/MN but relies on alcohol sold in CUC to turn a profit. Their production manager, Gilberto, once bragged that the Cabaret had to stock up on additional cases of beer when Yoruba Andabo performed to meet their audience's high demand. The group filled all the venues they performed in to capacity, so even though revenue from the entrance fees was relatively low (at 50 CUP/MN or CUC $2 per person), the high sales from alcohol made Yoruba Andabo good for state-run business.

In these arrangements negotiated by the Empresa de Música Popular (Popular Music Agency), the state agency that legally endorses Yoruba Andabo as professional artists, the performers themselves receive the same monthly flat rate regardless of profits from consumption. Like other public-sector workers, they might receive small bonuses in CUC. Regardless, living on a public-sector salary alone was very difficult, if not impossible, in Havana, particularly given the simultaneous rise in cost of living and cuts to subsidized basic services and goods (Bastian 2018, 110). It is a long-held open secret that public workers often expect "gifts" in appreciation for their work. Adjusting to the higher cost of living has meant that outright bribes or under-the-table payments are increasingly necessary to get public workers to do services that are designed to be government subsidized (Bastian 2018, 115). These public workers are trying to escape peso-poverty (Weinreb 2009; Cabezas 2009). As the Revolution "updated" its economic model, Cubans were driven to improve their family's economic situation by keeping pace with what the market could bear. For Yoruba Andabo, faith was essential for escaping peso-poverty.

When Yoruba Andabo proudly affirmed that their fanbase was largely from humble economic standings but was also *demasiado* (overwhelmingly) devout, what was framed as religious excess was actually at the core of their livelihood. After leaving the Cabaret, the group traveled to casa-templos where they made in one hour what they earned in one month from the state. Laboring for family of stone was a sacred matter, and all the more powerful for its ability to circumvent both state jurisdiction and private market exclusions.

This chapter examines the ways rumberos made a living by moving across various labor markets. The reliance on the commercialization of their labor in the name of religion confounds the dominant assumptions about the degenerative relationship between commercialization and Black popular culture, as Cornel West (1988) critiques when he argues that "cooptation" by commercial interests entails a distancing from Black popular music's roots in a religious lifeworld. A similar sentiment has been articulated by Cuban cultural critics who admonish the way that Afro-religious arts became an economic lifeline for both state institutions and practitioners through its integration into the tourism industry in the 1990s (Martínez Furé 2001). Then again, the monetized life of rumba also highlights the grassroots social welfare activities that constitute a core aspect of the kind of solidarity attributed to cabildo heritage that practitioners hold dear and upon which they materially rely (Hearn 2008, 32, 54). While tourist-facing folkloric performances permeate the context in which rumberos live and work, the focus here are economic transactions between Cuban religious kin, not foreign tourists. I suggest that rumberos privilege religious norms and networks oriented around logics of reciprocity and interdependence between kin to fulfill their economic ambitions. These informal, community-based economic maneuvers between (or beneath) formal markets bring new analytical attention to rumba as a form of gendered labor that, despite its own logics of inequality and exclusion, feels more fair relative to the options available for Black workers in Cuba's subsidized or unsubsidized formal markets. As such, rumba poignantly reveals the importance of sacred filiation for saving each other.

The labor dimensions of rumba call for a different conceptualization of Cuba's shifting political economy than is typically considered in scholarly and popular debates. With it comes a material understanding beyond rumberos' symbolic value indexing tropes of the nation's folkloric past or as commodities for foreign consumption. Both pragmatic economic actors and devout kin to copresences, rumberos are negotiating complexly structured and uneven terrain. I take their creative strategy of active movement between revenue streams they differentiate as sacred or secular as a point of departure to explore how peso-poor practitioners enact economic agency within a shifting Cuban economy. The meanings assigned to gender difference, divine agency, and the norms of sacred entitlement—by that I mean, the right to financial compensation for religious labor owed copresences—converge to determine how individual economic agency is enacted. The pursuit of economic salvation through *derechos* (rights or cash entitlements) for the fulfilment of ceremonial services illuminates alternative designs for development from the ground up.

The Black corporeal undercommons indexes the ways in which differently gendered rumberos endeavor to build sustainable livelihoods by crafting a realm of exchange they call their own. Little attention has been paid to how gender makes a difference economically in poor Black people's lives outside (sex) tourism. An April night in 2014 provides a paradigmatic example of the way rumberos nimbly and astutely labor across markets.

In the Name of God, *Ay Dios*

Cabaret Las Vegas was having technical difficulties, so there was a chance that Yoruba Andabo wouldn't be able to perform. As the clock neared 5 p.m., Rachel[1] was the only white person present, Cuban or non-Cuban, in a public space that became socially Black as Yoruba Andabo's most avid enthusiasts swelled the nightclub. At my suggestion, Rachel and I got there forty-five minutes early to grab a table. Latecomers could expect to stand throughout the whole concert. But then again, once the music started, few people would remain seated. Rachel, a US-American ethnomusicologist doctoral candidate, was studying a neighborhood *cajón* group (drumming ensemble for household *espiritismo* ceremonies) who strove to emulate Yoruba Andabo's *sello* or signature sound. These young Black men from the outskirts of Havana aspired to join the rumba renaissance and build a reputation in their religious networks that would transfer to more widespread appeal.

Rachel told me that after months of hearing "¡*Suena como Yoruba Andabo!*" (Sounds like Yoruba Andabo!) during the *cajón* players' rehearsals, she was eager to see them for herself.

After paying the entrance fee, we settled in the cold metal chairs surrounding the performance area. We had a front seat to Gilberto scurrying back and forth from the sound booth to the stage to the back office, visibly worried. Rather than projecting the latest videoclips of reggaeton and *música popular bailable* (also known as "salsa music" abroad) on the backdrop of the small stage, the venue was dark and silent. Eventually, Yoruba Andabo made it to the stage. They opened with an *espiritismo* prayer song typically played at the beginning of household *misas espirituales* (séances). At the *misas* I had been invited to, these songs were performed among family and close friends in a living room cleared of furniture. In a home setting, the ritual séance opens with this supplication to safely usher in the passage of the spirit guides of all the mediums present. They implore the spirits to come, protect, and guide the living. The living then pass along their messages from the spirit plane.

> *Sea el santísimo . . .*
> *Sea*
> *Sea el santísimo*
> *Sea*
> *Madre mía de la caridad*
> *Ayúdanos*
> *Ampáranos*
> *En el nombre de dios*
> *Ay dios . . .*
>
> Be it sanctified [or holy]
> So be it
> Be it sanctified
> So be it
> My mother of charity
> Help us
> Protect us
> In the name of god
> Oh god . . .

Audience members automatically responded in unison to the familiar chant's calls, collectively affirming a resonant sacred framing for the eagerly awaited performance. But midway through the second number, the audio blew out. Gilberto, exasperated, ran back up to the tech booth. The singers stepped back with seemingly calm resignation. They were professionals, after all. This was not the first time, nor would it be the last, that technological barriers plagued their public performances in state-run venues. We slouched in our chairs quietly, waiting. Eventually, Gilberto reemerged on stage to announce that the venue would return everyone's money. The show tonight was canceled, he said, as the performers filed back to the dressing room.

We all gathered our belongings and made our way to the door. Zulema (a dancer) poked her head out of the dressing room and motioned me to her. She told me that her family was having a *tambor* (drummed ceremony) next week in Coco Solo, a working-class Black neighborhood in Marianao, a good forty-five to sixty minutes from Havana's city center, depending on the mode of transportation. As she was explaining the bus routes that would take me closest to her home, Derlis (Yoruba Andabo's stagehand) cracked open the dressing-room door and told Zulema and Regla (a singer) that they were supposed to meet back here at 8 p.m. By that time of night, Cabaret Las Vegas's weekly drag show was slated to begin, so I figured Derlis must have been referring to another performance at a different venue. I looked at my watch; it was 6:30 p.m.

As we exited the nightclub, I apologized to Rachel, who would have to wait for another opportunity to see what all the buzz around Yoruba Andabo was about. She quickly pocketed the CUC $2 returned to her as she stepped outside. Overhearing the way I spoke to Rachel in English, the man at the door paused before giving me my cash back, unsure of what currency I had paid. I waited to see how he would resolve the confusion that commonly ensues when someone like me, who phenotypically passes for a local, is suddenly suspected of being foreign by association. He consulted with the towering Black security guard to confirm if he remembered. Indeed, I had paid in CUC. Their energy deflated, the crowd dissipated into the streets of Centro Habana as the sun set on their backs. When I reached the curb, I saw the other members of the group congregated in the street, milling around, smoking.

As I made my rounds to say goodnight to each performer, Ronald (lead singer) pulled me aside. Ronald had a charismatic presence on stage. He was known for fusing freestyle rap delivery into his solos, which captivated the youth. His cool fashion sense enhanced his aura of celebrity: gold chain, dark glasses, fitted jeans, flashy sneakers, and bedazzled T-shirt that stretched over his round belly. After drawing a slow breath and complimenting my scent, he addressed me with his customary suave geniality. Ever since my individual interview with him, he was keen on fostering my avid interest in his life as a performer. This time he informed me that they were working later that night in the casa-templo of 10 de Octubre. "You know, where they do the Divination of the Year [La Letra del Año]. It's a religious job," he said, "You will be my guest, okay?" I was so struck by the invitation that I momentarily froze. The name of the borough, the household-temple located on that borough's main artery, and the main avenue itself, were all "10 de Octubre." The 10th of October house on 10th of October Avenue in 10th of October borough is a historic landmark for religiosos in Havana. It is where respected priests of Ifá (the Yoruba oracle of divination) convene annually to give a prognosis for the entire religious community in Cuba and the world. I had waited almost a year for an invite to one of Yoruba Andabo's religious gigs, and that night it finally came.

10 de Octubre is a long bus ride away. It doesn't appear on Havana tourist maps. The house was packed with what felt like over a hundred worshippers, spilling out into the street. It was an elaborate affair: three *montadores* (priests hired to be "mounted" by the divinity, referred to formally as "spirit possession," discussed in more depth below) and a *doble tambor de fundamento* (two sets of consecrated *batá* drums, each requiring three male initiated drummers). The event was a drumming for Ochún, the divine mother of a godfather of this *ilé* (house/worshipping family), who passed away, organized by his godchildren. His godchildren inherited an obligation to his divine mother. They clearly spared no expense. Fulfilling this obligatory offering to Ochún was crucial to their family's *desenvolvimiento*. Religious kin and extended family joined in ceremony to ensure a successful tribute. The time-space of the sacred drumming, singing, and dancing expands to attract the orishas' attention by reminding them of their many lives. In exchange, the orisha will bless the community with their presence, sensed through the bodies of their children, and pass along vital information to those in attendance.

At 10 p.m., a mountain of bills—hundreds and hundreds of bills in both CUC and CUP/MN—had accumulated on the floor in a basket in front of the row of six *batá* drums. These bills at the feet of the men playing for their godfather's divine mother were called *derechos*. A derecho is a sum of money to which the musicians, whose labor makes communication with the orisha possible, are entitled. The labor of drumming creates the condition for danced prayer and the potential for a child of orisha to be mounted, cleanse themselves, and share lifesaving information with the community. As expected, the tambor at 10 de Octubre attracted a multitude of religiosos, and so the drummers were guaranteed a lucrative haul for their labor. In these arrangements, the akpwón, a man or a woman lead singer, can pocket the ceremonial fee for the service of drumming with the agreement that the drummers would evenly divide up the additional cash collected in the basket from the godchildren in attendance. Or he or she can agree to divide up the sum total of derechos accrued for the event: the initial hiring fee paid by the ceremony organizer plus the money given by the worshippers in attendance. There is some variation in how singers and musicians handle these financial matters, but they are always negotiated in advance. Regardless, a minimum of three male drummers and one lead singer, male or female, is required to perform an offering of this kind to the divinity. Musicians can expect a bigger payout when they play at large ceremonies where many religiosos participate. This night, the akpwón, the older brother of a Lekiam (Yoruba Andabo percussionist), sorted the bills and divided them between the six drummers right there on the spot before packing up their belongings to leave. This was their last ceremonial gig of the day.

The atmosphere in the house was electric from the ceremony of danced collective prayer. People wiped their brows and stepped outside to steady their breathing during this brief intermission before Yoruba Andabo's turn to play. Buzz about their performance had spread around the neighborhood. Just as he had done before at the Cabaret, Derlis set up the instruments first for the percussionists (five men), and then microphones for the three singers in the chorus (two women and one man), and for the lead singer, Ronald. Rum and beer passed over lips, readied for more singing to come. The rumba was about to begin, and the household-temple opened up to everyone in the community. As the akpwón, it was Ronald's job to lead the chorus and percussionists to move the crowd. In Yoruba Andabo's signature *batarumba* style, he started off their set with a series of popular call-and-response prayers for Ochún. Camera phones came out of pockets and the crowd exploded in danced delight.

After the performance, close to 1 a.m., when Derlis loaded the equipment back onto the bus and the artists filed back on board to get dropped off near their homes, Ronald portioned out a CUC $20 bill to each member. This was a dignified wage for a couple hours work—equivalent to their monthly state salary. The sudden cancelation of Yoruba Andabo's gig at the state-run venue is indicative of the expected failure of the formal market to guarantee adequate remuneration for their labor. Alternately, previously scheduling a performance at a religious household that same night is also indicative of how rumberos maximize their economic agency through informal, community-based religious networks.

The late-night performance at/on/in 10 de Octubre exemplifies what rumberos colloquially referred to as *trabajo religioso* (religious work). *Trabajo religioso* summoned the mutual aid of spiritual kin. Derechos accrued from *trabajo religioso* ensure that they are paid what they are owed, what they have a "right" (derecho) to receive, as children of orisha, for doing vital spiritual labor that the community needs. *Desenvolvimiento* was another related term I heard commonly among religiosos. I gleaned that it was a state of material and spiritual well-being that they prayed the divinities would help them achieve, as well as what they prayed for others, which religious work helped them all reach. This encompassed unofficial transactions in both currencies for goods, services, and expertise within and across religious kin that fulfilled divine obligations and secured monetary compensation.

In my interviews, I sensed a level of discretion in going "on record" about conducting what the government could see as illegal business, "selling their labor off the books."[2] As a result, Yoruba Andabo members emphasized that the religious work they performed was done as individual "believers" (*creyentes*) or "religious people" (religiosos). Working in the name of god, so to speak, was their birthright. It was also the state's understanding of religious practice as a "private matter," afforded by modernity's investment in secularism, that was critical for sanctioning these kinds of earnings collected by state employees, beyond government oversight. Deborah Thomas's theorization of inheritances, inscribed in and on the body, helps us to think through how rumberos carve out a space for themselves in a ritual economy outside of but in relationship to the state's development guidelines.[3]

When receiving monetary payment to play together in ceremony, they insisted that they were exercising their individual constitutional rights as Cuban citizens to religious freedom. Being reborn Lucumí meant not having to report income from derechos to the state. To make clear the legal jurisdiction of this form of paid labor, I follow their discursive compartmentalization, distinguishing between secular and sacred, though I don't intend to reify the sturdiness of these categories as modern constructions (Asad 1993). Instead, I underscore how rumberos confound normative terms and conceptions of the relationship between the sacred arts and "secular" commercial exchange by making use of secularist juridical legibility to participate in inherited systems for survival and subsistence.

The increased reliance on *trabajo religioso* to make ends meet can reveal the analytical limits of the revolutionary street-to-stage uplift narrative.

According to state discourses, it would seem that only through the state-managed entertainment industry did rumberos, ostensibly immersed in a quaint lifeworld tethered to the past, gain a foothold in the kind of socio-economic advancement that all Cubans are ostensibly now free to seize. Instead we see the limitations of existing metrics for understanding Cuba's dual economy more broadly. Writ large, these conventional frames produce analytical blind spots that tend to reify Black people as inherently less fit for national development, somehow set apart from economic relations, and/or in need of more inclusion within it.

Tracking derechos around rumba performance allows me to analyze how this community of practice goes about the daily work of providing for their families during Cuba's economic reforms. Rumberos' futile struggles to earn a living wage from their labor through formal markets of economic exchange, public or private, are indicative of why Black subjects have reason to be wary of the viability of the national *plan de desarrollo* (development plan) as a means to pursue their well-being. The canceled performance at the Cabaret Las Vegas, where entrance fees were charged in the dual currencies, is an example of the precarity of Yoruba Andabo's performances when commodified to further national development. That night, and others I describe throughout the book, were indicative that, for rumberos, the state's plan for development left much to be desired. I propose that sacred notions of desenvolvimiento, fair compensation (derecho), and mutual aid (*yo te salvo a ti, tú me salvas a mí*; I save you, you save me) anchored within networks of spiritual kinship help these members of Cuba's Black poor fulfill life projects in important ways. Akin to Ana-Maurine Lara's formulation of Black spiritual practices in the Dominican Republic, desenvolvimiento here is not a state of arrival through a teleological progression. Instead, it is a kind of survival that entails its own kind of sovereignty, one that is "co-terminous, palimpsestic, woefully interdependent across multiple registers of temporal-corporeality" (Lara 2020, 124). Yet, these sacred notions of well-being and collective self-determination are pursued in unequal ways, dictated by powerful anatomical metaphors and gendered ideologies, that make rumberas and rumberos exercise economic agency differently.

As Hope Bastian (2018) rightly argues, "the household," not the individual, is the more useful unit of analysis here (91). She builds on the work of scholars in urban planning and economic anthropology to support her case that, in practice, Cubans live in multigenerational households of multiple wage earners, and thus operate within and rely on family networks to make a living (H. L. Taylor 2009; Padrón Hernández 2012). Yet for religiosos, "the household" entails bonds of kinship that are not just prescribed by blood relations. Rather, one's casa-templo or *ilé* (not a physical place, but a lineage of worshipping kin) includes networks of filial relation tied by copresences, African diaspora divinities, rituals, rights, and obligations that necessarily entail the trades of all kinds of goods and services for money. Working in these literal and figurative households allows rumba performers to negotiate with and beyond the state-managed folklore industry and formal private market alike, at once leveraging and limited by gender ideologies. This spiritually guided plan for saving each other, desenvolvimiento, provides a way around the national *plan de desarrollo*, rather than vying for more inclusion within it.

Folklore's Feminized Labor

While waiting my turn in Odalis's living room, a traveling CD/DVD salesman walked up to the open front door. Odalis, who lived just a few blocks down from the Callejón de Hamel, was one of the many Black women *cuentapropistas* who operated a nail salon out of her home. *Manicuri* (manicure) stands had been sprouting up in the inner-city landscape since it became a licensed small private-business category. Manicurist was one of the more common forms of legal entrepreneurship that Black peso-poor women could take advantage of. The initial investment in nail polish was relatively low and, in a city where sandals were a staple in every woman's wardrobe, they had easy access to potential clientele. No matter how dire one's financial situation, at the very least, social norms dictated, a woman should keep her nails done. At 10/15 CUP/MN per manicure or pedicure (approx. USD $0.50), this line of work did not support dreams of wealth accumulation. Only those whose businesses catered to a foreign clientele could reasonably project large returns on their investment. But Odalis could hope that her neighborhood social networks would save her from the boredom and rigidity of a state job and, at best, help her family get by from day to day.

The white salesman leaned against the doorframe holding a laminated cardstock listing the names of the artists in his inventory. He started with those whose songs were the mainstays of the 2013 summer soundscape in this and many other inner-city Havana neighborhoods: "I have Marc Anthony, I have Yoruba Andabo, I have the new Chacal . . ." These were the artists blasting from speakers in homes, cafeterias, bodegas, and tricked-out bicitaxis—salsa, rumba, and reggaeton—the soundtrack of daily errands and recesses. One of the women in the living room, seated by the fan and with cotton balls wedged between her freshly painted toes, motioned the salesman inside so she could look through his laminated catalog. As he patiently waited for her to make a selection, I asked which recording of Yoruba Andabo he carried. He replied that he had their DVD. The woman next to me interjected, "*Rumba en la Habana* it's called." "And I have it in four languages: Spanish, English, French, and Italian," he added to sweeten my interest as he passed me a copy. The DVD came in a thin plastic sleeve that crinkled at the touch. The cheap encasing, no doubt procured in bulk from a connection abroad, guaranteed that selling the disc at CUC $1 would yield a profit. The low-resolution image on the printed sleeve pronounced in bold, italicized, and contoured red letters, "*Rumba en la Habana con . . . Yoruba Andabo ¡Concierto, Tambores Batá, Los Orishas y mucho más . . . DVD-compilación selecta*" (Rumba in Havana with . . . Yoruba Andabo. Concert, Batá drums, the Orishas and much more! . . . Select DVD Compilation). I jokingly asked him if he stood by the quality of the translations. He chuckled, "Well, I can see they are on there, but I can't tell you what the heck they say." In actuality, the DVD only had written segments in three languages (Spanish, English, and French), but his embellishment made no difference to the sale. As I fumbled through my wallet, the other women in the living room-turned-salon began to recall their best-loved scenes from the DVD, a favorite in their households: the "woman dancing with the live snake!" . . . "and the other woman dancing Yemayá!" One woman flapped her wrist in the popular gesture that made her index and middle-finger smack for punctuation.

The first scene they referenced is set in a sugar mill: "*En el tiempo de la colonia . . . tiempo de los negros congos*" (in colonial times . . . time of the Black Kongo people), so begin the lyrics.[4] The dancers wear costumes that signal the colonial epoch. The women dancers wear brightly colored handkerchiefs on their heads, covering their hair from the sun, simple white tops with wide sleeves, and long skirts revealing bare feet. The men are barechested with red and black pants, and red sashes around their foreheads absorb their sweat. Moist brows and bare chests glisten in the sun as the dancers theatrically summon all their might to push the gear of a sugar mill around and around. Dust from the packed dirt clouds around their feet. With a change in percussive tempo, Zulema makes her grand entrance onto the scene, emerging from a dwelling with a huge, thick snake resting across her shoulders. As she spins, the heavy reptile is carried by the air with the regal flair of a weighted velvet cape. Zulema puts the serpent's head fully inside her mouth, demonstrating her mastery over the venomous creature, simultaneously asserting her dominion over the sugar mill itself.

Kristina Wirtz has theorized the performative effect of these kinds of folkloric performances featuring distinctive figurations of Black characters—"Africans, slaves, maroons (escaped slaves), and Black witches" (7) as racializing performances of Blackness that allow for present-day engagement with the significance of Cuba's colonial past as a slave society (Wirtz 2014, 7). The video's editing supports this dialogue between spatio-temporalities, as do the dancers themselves. The video cuts from the scene in the sugar mill to a reenactment of the exact same choreography on a proscenium stage. There, Zulema, as "Black witch," shouts proclamations in Palo Kikongo, a prestige speech spoken between those who practice Palo, based on Kikongo and Spanish (Ochoa 2010). Like *bozal*, also the term used for African-born enslaved people in Cuba, this register of speech projects the continuing presence of the enslaved for their descendants (Wirtz 2007). While pulsing her shoulders back and back in sync with the percussion, Zulema sucks a fat cigar and slowly blows thick smoke in the faces of the other dancing *congos*. Her gestures appear continuous, seamlessly moving from one time-space to the other.

"*Soy una Madre Nkisi de verdad*" (I'm a real Mother Nkisi), Zulema shared with me in an interview, to tell me that her stage play drew from her off-stage role as a high priestess in the Kongo-inspired Palo religion, a practice of praise for the dead (Ochoa 2010). The snake, she said as we sipped coffee at her kitchen table, was her true possession. She pointed her pursed lips toward the winding staircase leading to where the snake lay caged and waiting. Her command of serpent, smoke, and congo spirit is not just an act for the stage and screen. Ownership and care for the snake is a sign of the role she inherited from copresences through her ancestral line, to which she dedicates herself in her daily life. Viewers of the DVD who watch with amazement her choreography on screen will rightfully associate this prowess with her real-life, present-day consecrated control over the *nganga*: a sacred cauldron of repurposed implements of slavery, death, and earth that *paleros* (Palo practitioners) use to exert influence on the life of others upon dispatch (Ochoa 2010). As the wielder of smoke and snake, Zulema's performance indeed makes the DVD a memorable sight to behold.

According to the women in the salon, Jenny's danced solo representing the oceanic Lucumí divinity, Yemayá, was the other most memorable match to Zulema's serpentine solo. Lasting eight minutes, Jenny's solo is also the longest on the entire DVD by far, establishing her performance as the production's focal center. The camera catches her in slow motion just as she rises out of the ocean, wide-mouthed, with a curtain of water pouring down her face like a sea creature emerging from mysterious depths. The wonder she evokes in her captivating opening builds over the course of the solo's duration. She is both internally focused and expansive at the same time. She has the singer, the drummer, the audience, and her tiered cobalt blue skirt all in the palms of her hands as she orchestrates a choreographic journey through the divinity's oceanic dynamism. Her complex footwork and expert skirt-handling aid her in representing salt water's range in movement and impact: from the calm foam that cascades on the horizon to the deadly typhoon with the power to destroy everyone and everything in its path.

Chitchatting after one of our private dance lessons about her frustration with the group's administration, Jenny boasted about how her interpretation of Yemayá earned Yoruba Andabo much of its current following. It was evident from conversations I had with a group administrator that, although there was no doubting Jenny's technical skill as a dancer, there was some doubt about her decision-making ability as dance director due to what they perceived as a lack of choreographic innovation. She, in turn, felt frustrated by how her creativity went unrecognized. Jenny stood up from her seat to give proper emphasis, "And *I* was the one who had the idea of getting in the water. No one told me to do it. *I* had that inspiration!" She claimed that no other dancer had dared to attempt such a dangerous full-body submersion in the ocean and that her record had yet to be challenged, proudly attesting to how she goes to any length to artistically portray the divinity in her fullest bodily capacity.[5] In that conversation, she underscored her bitterness with the way the group's administration often scrutinized and stifled her decision-making capacity. Among other points of disagreement, she noted the lack of weight afforded to her opinion regarding the group's state-subsidized status, which she argued they no longer needed to maintain to have successful careers. To her, state employment was more of a hindrance than a help. Echoed in the impromptu discussion that ensued over nail polish and acetone, the dancers not only propelled the narrative progression of the DVD, but, at least for their women fans, they made important contributions to the reputation that members of Yoruba Andabo had in their communities.

Although Jenny's forceful effect on the viewer did not yield the decision-making power offstage that she wanted, and Zulema's choreography of serpentine command projected the authority and influence she wielded offscreen, neither women benefited from DVD sales. That profit went to *cuentapropistas* (self-employed entrepreneurs) far beyond their scope of influence. In the *merolicos'* (street vendors) offerings, authorized under the newly legalized profession of *comprador/vendedor de discos* (disc buyer/seller), one could find Yoruba Andabo's CDs and DVD alongside the latest pop music hits and pirated international movie releases dubbed in Spanish. Those with the at-home technological equipment to copy and sell DVDs were one node within a booming transnational economy from which rumberos themselves were largely excluded (Cearns 2021).

Before the reforms, the term *merolico* had been reserved for sellers of black-market goods. Now these technologically savvy businessmen, positioned favorably by transnational family networks, could sell pirated goods and media legally as *cuentapropistas*. *Cuentapropistas* made it so the average working-class family, without access to a computer, could enjoy the sights and sounds of their favorite artists, both within Cuba and abroad, from the comfort of their own living room. Instead of smuggling merchandise bought abroad, Cubans were permitted to bring in goods and merchandise by saving their receipts and paying an import tax at the airport (Cearns 2020). Small business licenses had long been reserved for those selling goods produced within one's family unit. Private-sector expansion enabled those with the means to travel (dual citizenship, money, connections) to comfortably sustain the middle-class lifestyle that the reforms had ostensibly opened for everyone (Bastian 2018, 145–50). When the tacit prerequisites for success in "updating" Cuba are transnational networks and technological infrastructure, being a *merolico* is largely a white family business.

Since rumba, and Black popular culture more broadly, is understood as national patrimony, any licensed Cuban entrepreneurs with a CD/DVD burner and laser jet printer can feel entitled to profit from digitized, nationalized Blackness. Barring the unwritten rule that "no politics and no pornography" can be included in their content, *merolicos*, like the DVD seller who made rounds in Centro Habana, can remain largely indifferent about the content of the Black music products they (re)sell outside of the fact of their appeal to consumers (Levine 2021). Even though Yoruba Andabo's dance performances are directly responsible for creating the popular demand for the DVD, the right to subsistence from their embodied labor, which Zulema and Jenny defended in terms of their right as kin to African divinities and descendants of the enslaved, had no currency within *desarrollo*'s logics of trade.

Luckily for Zulema and Jenny, dancing with them at one of Yoruba Andabo's live performances had a value for fellow *religiosos* worth more than

4.1 Jennyselt Galata dancing Yemayá. Photo by Dashiel Rodriguez Alfonso.

what a DVD costing CUC $1 could render. In an interview with Tailyn, the same young rumbera from Centro Habana introduced before, Jenny's ahijada and a self-proclaimed avid follower of Yoruba Andabo since the DVD's official release in 2005, she attested, "I went to my first show of Yoruba Andabo to see Jennyselt dance. I had heard that she was the best Yemayá dancer, and so went to see if it was true." All the excitement via word of mouth surrounding Jenny's standout performance in the DVD motivated Tailyn, a singer in Rumba Morena when we spoke in 2013, to save up and pay the entrance fee. Tailyn was not alone. Yoruba Andabo had managed to expand the audience at their live performances at state-managed public venues by becoming a household name, thanks in part to their dancers' showstopping performances. As in the DVD, during their live shows, Jenny's solo was a main event.

The prominence of the dancers' choreographic virtuosity in the DVD, and the way their solos drew audience members to live performances, is belied by the fact that those same women have the least decision-making power over the group's course of action. Although each artistic component of the ensemble (singers, percussionists, dancers) has its own internal leadership, the role of the artistic director, who negotiates directly with the state agencies on behalf of the group, is categorically held by either a male drummer or lead singer, often a man. As performing ensembles that emerged from a community context where ritual drummers and the akpwón hold vital specialized roles in ceremony, once those groups "crossed over" into the secular entertainment industry, men have historically held leadership positions (Hagedorn 2001). Dancing, on the other hand, is regarded as a layperson's craft that comfortably falls within the purview of the entire community (although executed with unequal talent). In rituals of embodied worship, everyone is responsible for collectively dancing to the drums. These repetitive motions, what looked like monotony to the colonial gaze, are crucial for developing personal intimacy with the divine. While dancers can be any gender, the Western feminization of dance as a less prestigious artistic profession follows with the consolidation of decision-making power among men as the privileged cultural brokers with the state.

Regardless, it was evident that the dancers played a central, rather than peripheral, role for the audience, and they found other ways to secure compensation for their expertise. Dancers charged upward of CUC $20 an hour for private lessons to foreigners (like me), and they were often incorporated into tourist packages for large groups. Moreover, thanks to the overwhelming devoutness of rumba enthusiasts, Yoruba Andabo's professional dancers could reap substantial dividends during the staged performance of Yoruba divinities in between rumba sets. Incorporating a wide repertoire of elements from African-inspired religious practices into cabaret shows gained precedence in the 1930s and 1940s when the "Rumba craze," as I discussed earlier, cultivated an expectation for "Afro-Cuban expressions" to satisfy the middle-class imagination of the racial Other in their construction of cubanidad. However, in this case, for a predominantly Black religioso audience, allusions to the divine in secular settings served other ends for the patrons and dancers alike.

In the *ciclo Yoruba*, the segment when the group performed a limited sampling of praise music for the orishas, the dancers made their entrance one by one, each dressed as a different divinity from the Lucumí pantheon. At Cabaret Las Vegas, the dressing room was adjacent to the general seating, so the dancers had to literally dance through the audience to reach the front. As the dancers slowly made their way closer to the drums, audience members eagerly took their proximity as an opportunity to tuck a bill into their costume, either underneath the rim of the dancer's headpiece or inside the neck collar. Rather than carrying a sexual or flirtatious connotation, this practice is known in West Africa as *dashing* or *spraying*, when audience members place money on the foreheads of exceptional dancers as they perform. In Cuba, these direct cash offerings were public demonstrations of personal devotion to the divinity represented by the dancer. In exchange, the person and the dancer would enact a ritual salute that looked like a two-part hug. This is a ritual greeting done between worshippers during ceremony—touching opposite shoulder to shoulder—in recognition of their sacred relation. Both men and women dancers engage in this intimate exchange of money-for-embrace with audience members throughout the duration of the segment; however, Zulema's and Jenny's celebrity from the DVD no doubt attracted special gratification. The audience's frequent interruptions of each dance solo elongated their duration, thus making the segment (ostensibly a mere interlude) that much more pronounced relative to the duration of the rumba concert as a whole. The performance quality that Jenny and others referred to as *ángel* (which I return to below) was integral for transforming the state-managed venue into one of sacred presence and potentiality conjured, notably, by the interaction between the dancer skilled in divine mimicry and the *demasiado religioso* audience.

Inasmuch as the line between the orisha and the dancer is porous and the artists abide by norms of worship, dancers garnered measurable financial rewards. From the vantage point of an audience member, as Tailyn explained it, "For example, Yemayá is my [patron] orisha, so I am going to give money to her. But apart from that, I'm also giving it to Jennyselt because I think she is an excellent dancer and I grow [spiritually] by seeing her dance. So, I give her money for both things: for being [representing] Yemayá and for being a divine and beautiful being [person] that is very important to me. I enjoy watching her dance and I show it by giving her money." For religiosos, the sacred aura of the divine and the artistic virtuosity of the dancer spill over into one another, blurring personhood.[6] In Tailyn's case, Jenny was also her *madrina* (godmother), making the blurring that much more pronounced. As godparent and godchild, they were spiritually bonded through the filial structure of their *ilé*.

Tailyn further explained that after you undergo initiation (*coronación*) into priesthood, referred to colloquially as *making saint* (*hacerse santo*), when you encounter a representation of that divine energy in the world, you give it money to express your faith. Even if it is a staged performance deemed secular, the offering can generate the reciprocation of the divinity in granting health, prosperity, favor, love, and desenvolvimiento. This ritual logic of reciprocity with the divinity via the body of a human conduit extended into the nightclubs where rumberos performed.

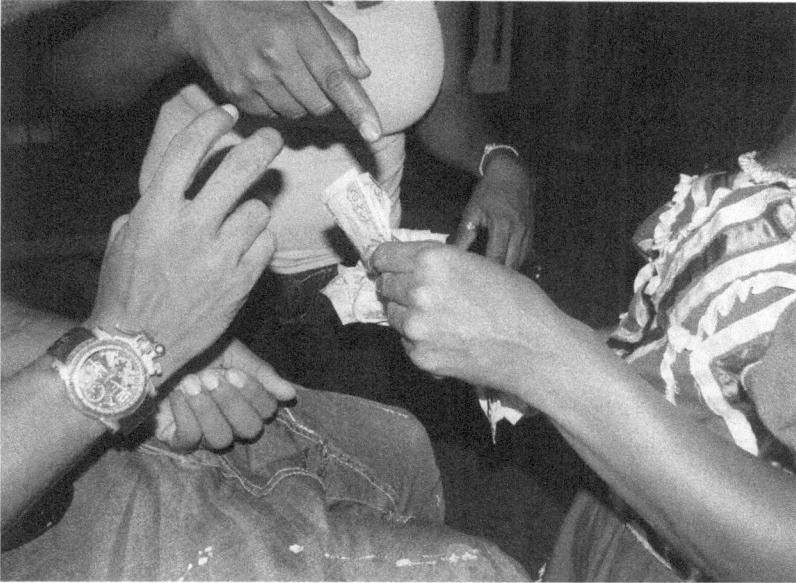

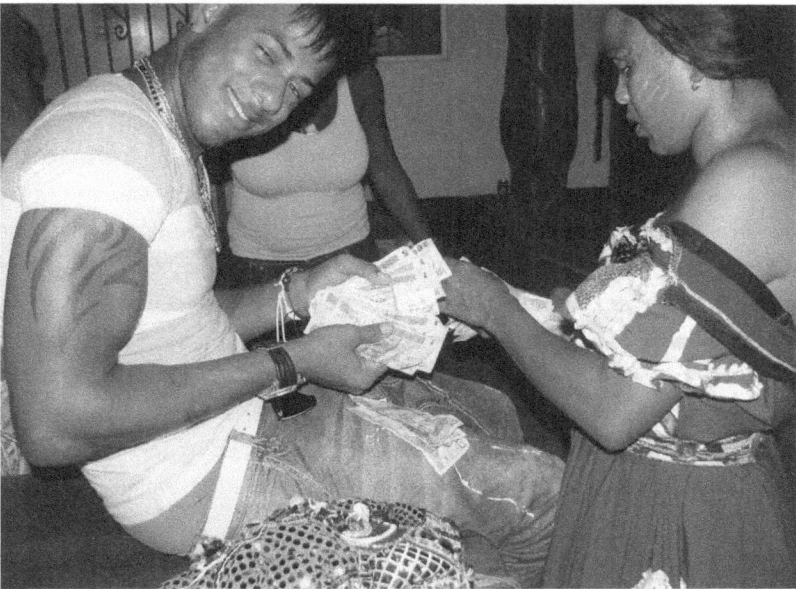

4.2–4.3 Counting and separating bills by currency after performance. Photos by author.

Being connected to these spiritual webs of economic reciprocity was motivating to the dancers. As we spoke in her home in Coco Solo, Zulema, who typically performs Ochún and Elegguá, explained that she was accustomed to what she interpreted as public displays of religious piety during her solos, and even came to expect this as part of how she measured the quality of her artistry. "I like it. When they don't salute me, I feel like I'm doing things poorly or that the audience no longer likes me." When I asked if the interruptions of her solos by the audience ever posed a problem for the other members of the ensemble, she explained, "We are religious. So when that part comes, the singer knows they have to repeat the song to give people the time to salute and dance with you." Zulema continued, "We don't see it as an interruption. . . . It doesn't bother us. For us, it enriches us." Her word choice, *to enrich*, perhaps alluded to the multiple registers of value that only faith could provide. Every dancer had fans and family (of stone), and it was common for them to overlap. Derechos accrued during solos easily amounted to upward of CUC $50 per show, which the dancers justifiably pocketed for themselves. Even if the dancers' authority over the group's direction offstage was relatively low, on stage those same dancers' right to extend the durations of their solos for the purpose of receiving derechos was not contested.

In contrast to other Black women working as manicurists in their neighborhoods, whose constrained entry into the expanding private market reaped meager dividends, the communal, interactive nature of rumba performances facilitated a feedback loop of admiration and piety that, put simply, paid. Whereas the dancers earned direct compensation for their labor in a broader system of reciprocal exchange between worshippers and their patron saints, musicians relied on delayed financial gratification from their secular gigs. Defending these informal exchanges between kin for desenvolvimiento entailed running against state-driven commercial interests. For this, the group's administrators stepped up to protect these fair trades from national development's (*desarrollo*) incursions.

Against Inclusion in *Desarrollo*

I garnered a better appreciation for the way rumba ensemble administrators facilitated the collection of derechos at shows after speaking with Gilberto William Ramos, who manages Yoruba Andabo's gigs contracted through the government Agency of Popular Music. I was living only a block away from Gilberto in Centro Habana at the time. We regularly bumped into each other coming and going on our daily errands. Gilberto allowed me to interview him one sweltering hot morning at his neighbor's place in the *solar* where he used a spare room as an office, across the street from his modest one-bedroom apartment. The office, on the building's second floor, had a window facing the internal courtyard below. He and I sat at a small table with a fan pointing directly on us, surrounded by pictures of Yoruba Andabo. Upon entering the room, you couldn't miss the group's framed award of recognition for their 2006 Latin Grammy nomination in the Best Folk Album category for their album and DVD *Rumba en la Habana con . . . Yoruba Andabo*, also nominated in the Best Audiovisual category that year. They also contributed to the Latin Grammy Award–winning compilation album *La Rumba Soy Yo* in 2001. The foreign exposure this gave them sent them abroad to Europe, South America, and North America, benefiting from the international market for "folkloric music" in cities like Moscow, New York, Toronto, and Caracas. These achievements made their performances in Cuba prime targets for domestic price inflation, which threatened to price out the religious audience they held dear.

In the name of "perfecting" Cuban Socialism, state-run nightclub establishments have incrementally raised their entrance fees, especially for groups with international recognition. In our conversation about their local bookings, Gilberto explained the exclusionary pricing phenomenon using the salsa band Juan Formell y Los Van Van as an example: "You can't set a high price for people who don't have zilch. They'd have to wait a while until Yoruba Andabo plays at an open-air event to see their favorite group, like Los Van Van. At Casa de la Música [to see Los Van Van] it's CUC $20. And you say, 'I can't go because my salary doesn't permit me.'" Ironically, tourists come to Cuba seeking full immersion in a popular pastime with locals, when those very locals are more frequently priced out of live music venues because their favorite groups attract hard currency via tourism.

There is consensus among scholars of social inequality in Cuba that these kinds of profit-driven policies have led to de facto racial resegregation on the island, called "tourist apartheid" (Roland 2011). Those who can afford to spend CUC $20 (a month's state salary) or more on entertainment do not represent Yoruba Andabo's most loyal domestic patrons. In the words of one singer, Yerilú, "Our audience is 99, if not 100, percent religious," meaning that they are almost entirely practitioners of African diasporic religions. While the state sought to capitalize on its world-renowned artists to attract the expendable income of foreigners and middle- and upper-class Cubans, on the part of rumberos, their target audience, and to whom they ascribed much pride, seemed to be local religiosos.

Only a short ten-minute walk from Gilberto's office, Geovani further elaborated on his rationale, as artistic director, for contesting these top-down financial decisions. Geovani lived on the ground floor of a *solar* in Centro Habana's Chinatown district. I had to use the acoustics of the *solar*'s enclosed architecture to get the attention of his wife, who would come scurrying across the courtyard to open the front gate. If my first few attempts were unsuccessful, a fellow resident would peek out their window and yell on my behalf, knowing just how to throw their voice to pick up an echo. Once seated in his living room, Geovani chose his words carefully: "I'm not interested in raising the prices. Because what I want is for everyone to have access . . . all types of audiences. . . . If you raise the price a lot, then only a certain audience comes. He who has more is he who can go; he who has less can't go. Understand? And I've always wanted the public to go. So that everyone has access to see us. Besides, we are subsidized, so ultimately . . ." Geovani's voice trailed off leaving a suspensive ellipsis to fill in the weighted silence, punctuated by a slight tilt of his forehead. Geovani's silence allowed him to discreetly draw attention to how the group's state-subsidized status capped the artists' salaries. No matter how much was charged at the door, state-subsidized artists' financial payoff for shows in state-managed venues had a firm plateau. Framing the tension around the issue of "access" aligns with the Revolution's original rationale for reforming Cuba's cultural policy to create state-subsidized artists and state-managed performance venues in the first place. This was instated based on the principle that culture should be a public good, a right rather than a commodity (Moore 2006). However, Yoruba Andabo's salary ceiling meant that their strategic collusion with the restrictive terms of state-managed folkloric labor had its limits.

Thanks to Yoruba Andabo's reliable following, in no small part due to the draw of live interaction with its dancers, Geovani was able to fend off the government's push toward price inflation. With the help of reliable intermediaries like Gilberto, entrance fees stayed affordable for their religious community. Gilberto recounted one such negotiation: "There have been times when the locale has tried to raise the cover price. And I've sat with the director and told him, 'Look, they want to raise the cover.' And the director says, 'No, it stays the same.' And I go back there and I say, 'It stays or we walk.' 'NO! don't go!' [they say]. 'Okay, so it stays then.'" The male bravado he exuded in his reenactment of their power play was not lost on me. Gilberto heightened the pitch of his voice when impersonating the state bureaucrats, accentuating the contrast with his own lower-pitch declarations in the fast-paced exchange. Aware of the venue's bottom line, Geovani leveraged the value of their fan base's alcohol consumption to negotiate their contracts. While the state would ultimately profit from the alcohol consumed, the members of Yoruba Andabo had more to gain from the derechos that were sure to follow.

Although good for *desarrollo*, Geovani determined that it was not in the group's best interest to buy in wholesale to the terms of folkloric labor for the state. Geovani has made this critique quite explicit in interviews with the Cuban press about why he doesn't follow the trend of pandering to tourists and giving preferential treatment to foreigners at shows.

> The problem is unfortunately tourism, and we forget about the Cuban. And we give priority to tourism in the Casas de la Música, and we do a festival and we give more importance to the tourist that comes over than the Cuban who comes to participate. . . . I play for Cubans. If a foreigner comes and pays the entrance fee, I don't give priority to him. I don't give him a seat and you [a Cuban stand] behind. The person who comes first gets seated in front and so you have to get there early, because I won't make any Cuban stand so that a foreigner can sit. (Martínez y Carmen Souto 2009)

Geovani's statement against catering to foreigners, although it also satisfied a patriotic trope, should not be attributed to nationalism alone. To do so would be to deny the dynamism of the sacred economy in which rumba circulates. In fact, the vibrant life of rumberos beyond staged folklore incentivizes artists to ensure that venues did not price out the kinfolk upon whose faith rumberos rely offstage. To be sure, since the "crossover" of rumberos into the Cuban mainstream, Black men have been disproportionately positioned to act as cultural brokers and negotiate with state actors over Black women. Exercising the gendered agency his role as cultural broker afforded to determine the extent to which their labor could be exploited for the development of the nation, Geovani stood firm against prohibitive cover fees.

These business accords have certainly influenced the demographic of the audience at Yoruba Andabo's domestic shows. At their regular weekly showcases in state-run nightclubs during my fieldwork period, whether in venues like Cabaret Las Vegas, Las Palmeras, or Palacio de la Rumba, the audience was either exclusively or predominantly *gente de color*, meaning Black and mulato Cubans.[7] A historian friend of mine from the United States once remarked, after I took her to her first Yoruba Andabo show in 2013, that she was struck by the continued existence of these unmistakably Black social spaces she associated with the racially segregated pre-1959 era.

Rather than vying for more inclusion within *desarrollo* and adopting its labor logics as their own, rumbero administrators defended rumba against super exploitation and foreign buying power. They seized public venues as spaces for religiosos to gather, which then resulted in future ceremonial hires in casa-templos for higher sums off the books. These sums would not lead to capital accumulation for the purpose of social mobility, but instead were bound for recirculation among kin to fulfill religious duties of reciprocal care for desenvolvimiento. Laboring *across* different regimes of prestige cast as secular or sacred—*between* private lessons, diplomatic gigs, state-run venues, and religious work—enabled Yoruba Andabo to carve out a space of economic agency beyond "nationalized Blackness."

Religious Work for Desenvolvimiento

> There are *religiosos* who have the need to host a religious party in their house, like a *tambor* or a *rumba*, etc. . . . and they are going to find the best group [to play]: Yoruba Andabo. Because we are linked with the religion directly. . . . The person that contracts us has a religious drive and looks to Yoruba Andabo to enhance their devotion. [And they can brag], "You know who is going to play at the religious party of so and so? You know who is going to play for me? Yoruba Andabo, the best group around!"
> —"CHAN" CÁRDENAS (lead vocalist and founder), 2013

The Revolution's "upliftment" narrative—lauding rumba's ascendance from the streets to the national stage—mirroring that of proletarian triumph due to the 1959 Revolution, obscures how rumberos' ability to sustain their families now largely relies on their "descent" back into the very places that the Revolution ostensibly "uplifted" them from. Put simply, although officially employed by the state, all members of Yoruba Andabo were, directly or indirectly, sustained materially by the labor demands of desenvolvimiento. This religious labor market—where religiosos were paid derechos in exchange for "religious work"—is underwritten by the way in which material reciprocity ("I save you, you save me") is stitched into the social bonds of spiritual kinship between divinities, godparents, and godchildren in *familias de piedra* (families of stone). This is not to say that Yoruba Andabo's religious popularity supersedes the economic importance of, for example, private lessons for foreigners and international tours. Nor does it minimize the social currency of being recognized by foreign/international institutions like the Latin Grammys or UNESCO as one of the best representatives of Cuban heritage—a cachet that, in turn, affords the hard-currency-strapped island its cultural distinction in a global market. However, it does unsettle the commonsense understanding of the national stage as rumberos' aspired final destination. This reconceptualization of rumba as labor points us toward the materiality of the Black corporeal undercommons.

Practitioners used the verb *salvar* (to save) to describe the work they did in their communities. In the words of Vladimir (a dancer) speaking in 2013, "Thanks to many artists, we the religiosos have done tambores to save a people." The ability to affect human life through the strategic curation of fleeting spectacle speaks to the Pan-Yoruba belief in what art and performance theorists Henry John Drewal and Margaret Drewal (1990) call "the creative capacity to shape the world" through ritual (xvi). Although the Drewals' study of Yoruba people in Nigeria cannot be transposed directly onto the Cuban context wholesale, taking the central belief undergirding ritual performance seriously is necessary for understanding the important social role of performing artists for desenvolvimiento in the faith communities that rumberos constitute and serve.

In the multiple African diasporic religions practiced in Cuba, practices consolidated during slavery in cabildos de nación and reinvented as casatemplos in the twentieth century, drummed ceremonies are dense sensorial occasions that rehearse the capacity for collective synchrony with the divine. These moments pronounce copresence with the dead and aliveness in the body against social death. Ritual performances are the nuclei that bring together *familia de piedra* and "blood" kin across generations, residing literally or figuratively in an *ilé* or casa-templo. The fashioning of family through rites of initiation has strong historical meaning for a people stripped of personhood and kinship relations during the transatlantic slave trade and through chattel slavery. The ritual confluence of drumming, song, and dance induces an extended network of people to come together as a filial community in recognition of their mutual interdependence with spirit and each other. This interdependence is at once spiritual and material.

Afro-Atlantic religious historian Rachel E. Harding stresses the importance of the body within the religious systems of the enslaved. Expert synchrony of complex artistic elements was necessary for developing "intimacy with the divine" in and through the body in movement (Harding 2003, 154). The agentive physical repurposing of their bodies (in dance, work stoppage, escape, gesture, ritual) fashioned a space she calls "a refuge in thunder" (2003). Although her study focuses on the history of Candomblé in Brazil, she extends the argument more broadly to assert that the numerous systems of knowledge the enslaved developed in the wake of the transatlantic slave trade sustained an imperative "alternative orientation" to the world and each other within a fundamentally dehumanizing and oppressive system of terror (Harding 2003, 104–46). These are religions grounded in addressing the lived conditions of the here and now, rather than oriented around the promise of better days in an afterlife. Religiosos wield the rhythms, songs, and movements that represent and please different personified spirits and divinities in hopes of achieving a state of intimacy, accompaniment, mutuality, exchange, shared responsibility, and balance with nature and the dead.

This condition of balance through interdependence is understood to be beneficial for the living and is represented through direct payments in cash, called *derechos*. While *derecho* might be translated semantically into English as "fee," I find the literal translation, "right," most evocative. It speaks to a popular practice of "laying claim to an unfulfilled promise" elaborated alongside and within capitalist modernity (Thomas 2004, 8). Through ritual, kinfolk asserted their right to survival. In contrast to the forms of unpaid and dehumanizing labor to which the enslaved and their descendants have been subjected, ritual work that saves comes with derechos/rights.

During my fieldwork, I most often heard of religiosos holding drummed ceremonies in celebration and gratitude or homage, but it was not uncommon to hear of drummed ceremonies to resolve urgent issues such as family-related crises, health problems, or money troubles. Jorge Luis Hernández told me about the distinct sense of responsibility he felt when serving as akpwón in a religious ceremony: "If you are performing in a religious house the people hosting the religious party are doing it with a lot of faith to resolve the issue at hand. In the religious field, you have to treat a religious person for X motive. . . . [The artist] has to be very clear because you are playing with that person's life." The weight of the stakes involved in performing religious work far surpassed the symbolic labor of "national representation." Even if singing the same call-and-response chants performed on stage, the intention was distinct. In ceremony, Jorge Luis sang with the awareness that his talents were being entrusted to engender a potentially lifesaving effect. This shared spiritual epistemology shaped their theory of social change, which designated which interlocking skills and services were required to successfully shape fate. This lifesaving service deserved compensation.

Santeros mark the day of their initiation into priesthood, thought of as a rebirth, with special rituals. Blood and stone family are expected to partake in the anniversary celebration, called the *cumpleaños de santo* (saint birthday), with food and prayers. Practitioners with the motivation and means to do so hire live musicians to play for the occasion. This is how I ended up outside an apartment just one short block from the *malecón* (boardwalk) on that Saturday afternoon in April 2014. The edge of Centro Habana that jutted up against the Bay of Havana was just a short twenty-minute walk from where I was living. I left with plenty of time to enjoy the stroll toward the ocean. When I arrived at the address Ronald gave me, I took one last look at the waves and called his cell phone. After a few rings, he came out to the balcony and indicated which buzzer to press downstairs at the front entrance of the building.

Knowing that the members of Yoruba Andabo had been hired to play at the *cumpleaños de santo* for a Cuban priest that afternoon, I was somewhat surprised to see the prominent blue symbol next to the specified buzzer. This symbol indicated that it was a licensed rental business operating in cuc. When I began traveling to Cuba in 2004, the blue symbol delineated rental properties exclusively for foreigners. They had amenities deemed mandatory for foreign clientele (running water, hot water, air conditioning, room service, etc.). Conversely, housing that lacked such amenities, marked with a red symbol, were exclusively for Cuban nationals who paid in MN/CUP. Although considered lower in quality, red-symbol rentals were attractive to Cubans from distant provinces who lived off a state salary and who otherwise would not have an affordable place to stay in Havana. Foreigners are still not legally permitted to rent in red rentals, a rule intended to control the distribution of occupancies in a country with a limited housing inventory. Near the beginning of my doctoral fieldwork in 2012, the state approved celebrated reforms to the migratory laws to facilitate the return of Cubans living abroad, creating new norms for who rented cuc-operated homes. In previous eras of the Revolution, Cubans who permanently left the island were written out of the beloved community as traitors or deserters and labeled "anti-Cuban." After Raúl Castro's reforms, the buying potential of Cuban expatriates, and their remittance-receiving relatives in Cuba, became an important economic engine that was to be incentivized.

Indeed, the client sponsoring the ceremony, a deep-brown-skinned man, was a *santero* born in Cuba who lived abroad. This made his social designation within their community not only a consecrated "son" of Ochún, but also, in terms of the size of the derecho the musicians would receive, he was a *cubano criollo* (Cuban creole). *Cubanos criollos* paid for ritual services at rates somewhere in between Cubans living in Cuba and foreigners without any "Cuban origin."[8] The term *criollo* (creole) has historically been used since the colonial era to distinguish between foreign-born subjects (from Africa or Europe) and their American-born (*criollo*) descendants. The repurposing of this important social designation among religiosos reflects the utmost salience of one's geopolitical coordinates within a global market in which the Cuban state and everyday Cubans alike struggled for a fair trade. Although this son of Ochún lived abroad, with the majority of his consecrated items and his religious family still residing in Havana, he returned annually to celebrate the anniversary of his *coronación* (crowning).[9] Using his family connections—a cousin who lived around the corner from Ronald—he was able to hire Yoruba Andabo to play a rumba for the special occasion. The rumba was an offering to the man's divine mother, constituting both a public sign of thanks for all the blessings that the divinity had given him that year, and a supplication that she continue to show him favor and desenvolvimiento on his life path. Having members of Yoruba Andabo perform a rumba for his divine mother, like the CUC rental property where the ceremony took place, was a social-status symbol.

When I arrived upstairs, Ronald greeted me in his typical fashion. "Coconut oil, right? I love it," he remembered my scent with a smile. I had grown accustomed to these flirtatious advances and greatly appreciated that he never pushed for them to progress in exchange for increased access to this private realm of labor. Ronald had asked the *Cubano criollo*'s permission for me to attend the ceremony and observe the musicians' work in the altar room, which was off limits to all but the *Cubano criollo*'s closest blood and stone family members.

The first thing I noticed was the apartment's emptiness. The beige walls looked freshly painted, without any wall hangings. Shiny white and black tiled floors created a sleek backdrop that stood out to me as stark and rare. I had grown accustomed to attending these celebrations in the homes of Valentín's close-knit family members, full of the warmth and wear of intergenerational living. Here, the entryway and living room were spotless, cleared of any furniture except for a long banquet table stocked with an assortment of hard-currency alcoholic beverages and soft drinks. The sparsity and openness of the common rooms, where most of the attendees gathered, contrasted with the smaller adjacent room where the altar was set up. This altar room was bursting from floor to ceiling with colorful, draped fabric representing the colors of the divinities. Bouquets of flowers, fruit, and pastries were carefully arranged across the floor at the base of lavishly dressed ceramic pots. The setup was pretty standard, but there were notable high-ticket CUC items in the display, like high-end canned beer. The installation signaled that Ochún's son was doing well for himself abroad and that he was grateful for and worthy of continued blessings. The money you give to orisha comes back to you threefold, the saying goes.

Jorge Luis stood to the left of the altar facing out to the three drummers, leading the prayer songs. Ronald stepped in as the middle drummer this time. Regla, the only woman from Yoruba Andabo present, stood beside them singing the prescribed responses to Jorge Luis's calls. The *Cubano criollo* and his sister stood directly behind the hired musicians facing the altar to witness their work and partake in the musical offering. Although only a limited number of us were inside the room, the entire family sung along just outside the threshold. Their prayers echoed off the bare, beige walls and were carried outside by the salty breeze.

Then they all poured into the spacious living room. It was the family's duty to dance together. As soon as Ronald sang his first note, the client made a cross with a CUC $20 bill and placed it on a plate at the foot of the drums. His entire family joined in unison doing a basic side-to-side step, alternating legs, and sang each response. A baby was passed from arm to arm as each relative's carriage was weakened by holding its weight during constant movement. At one point, the client, having sweated through his purple satin button-down shirt, removed it and handed it off to someone without missing a step. An elderly woman wearing a freshly pressed dress that swallowed her small frame miraculously stayed afoot, dancing in front of the drums the entire time. Her frail body seemed to move not out of physical strength, but out of purpose. After the dancing portion of the ceremony concluded, the members of Yoruba Andabo were offered food—the nourishment was another gesture of reciprocation. But they couldn't stay for long, Ronald explained. They packed up and rushed off to their next ceremony of the afternoon across town.

Yoruba Andabo members were hired privately as liturgical experts to perform at *tambor de fundamento*, *güiros*, *Abakuá* plantes, and spiritual *cajones* throughout the vast span of the city and its outskirts. Rumba music in particular was most often solicited for *veladas de santo* (saint celebration parties) and *cumpleaños de santo*. Generally speaking, three to four drummers and one akpwón was the bare-minimum requirement, which allowed them to fulfill the high demand for this religious labor. The worshipping community itself was expected to know the liturgy, sing the chorus to all the songs, and dance to each song with the appropriate choreography of prayer. When the performing arts play such a vital part in enhancing life chances, enlisting "Yoruba Andabo, the best group around," as Chan put it, was worth financial sacrifice. How those derechos circulated were deeply entwined with ideologies of gender.

Ritual Division of Labor's Logics

Drummed ceremonies are at once an obligation to copresences that must be fulfilled by spiritual kin and the means through which the work of copresences for their kin is accomplished. The specialized labor required to make manifest this blessed exchange entails differential possibilities for earning potential among rumberas and rumberos. Gendered norms of ritual labor division and divine guidance determine the specific artistic functions that differently gendered devotees can serve, and the sources of earnings rumberas and rumberos can expect by extension. Yoruba Andabo was able to satisfy the diverse musical needs of numerous casa-templos in the city by splintering their sixteen-member ensemble into smaller units of four to seven. All the drummers were ordained to play all the necessary ceremonial instruments, and they could sing the liturgy too. As the director of percussion explained to me, "Here at Yoruba Andabo, no one has a fixed instrument. Everyone rotates. So if someone is missing, anyone can always fill in." But "anyone" didn't mean everyone, or rather, anybody.

Ritual drumming was a role exclusive to cisgendered men, those without wombs. Katherine Hagedorn notes that although exclusionary gender norms in drumming have changed over time, there maintains a strict taboo against people with wombs playing *consecrated* drums in ceremony (2001, 89–97). The phenomenal life-force attributed to wombs is both magnificent and, at times, feared. It is believed that if a menstruating person plays a consecrated drum, the drum can harm their reproductive capacities. Possibly worse for the community at large, feminine power transmitted through touch could run amok, ruining the drum's ability to "speak" to the divinity and thus undermining the ceremony's efficacy. Much scholarship has been dedicated to parsing the theological, sociopolitical, and historical basis of gender ideologies in African diasporic religious practice as linked to sex and biological reproduction over time.[10] Suffice to say, where "anatomical features are metaphors for spiritual powers," and thus determine how behavior is interpreted, Lucumí ritual logics are not categorically resistant nor reducible to patriarchal social norms (Drewal 1992 [1989], 179). Indeed, the Santería religion has even been described as "female normative" in that many religious roles and ritual labor are described through feminine metaphors, thereby troubling a clear-cut characterization of the religious realm as patriarchal per se (Clark 2005). It is also the case that the structures of hierarchy within casa-templos lend themselves to women holding seniority over men. However, I am limiting my discussion to the artistic labor needs of tambores that Yoruba Andabo members filled in order to highlight the gendered implications of the group's organizational dexterity and how that impacts each member's earning capacity. The nimble reassignment of drumming and singing roles among the members disproportionately benefited the men in the group.

The masculinization of the act of drumming, restricting payment for this labor to some over others according to a binary ideology of gender, can be situated in relation to the social construction of *spirit possession* or being *mounted* as an effeminate (Beliso-De Jesús 2013), if not genderqueer act (Escalante 2019). This intimate act is often described in equestrian terms—*a horse* (devotee) being mounted by the divine. The most highly respected *montadores* (mounts or mountees) are capable of transmitting verbal messages from the divine to the community. These sacred messages can range from general wisdom to highly specific instructions, powerful affirmations, and potentially lifesaving guidance.[11] For some scholars of African diasporic religion, "the experience of accompaniment, of 'self co-constitution with God,' agitates at the center of the meaning of possession in New World African-based religion" (Harding 2003, 156). For others, its naming bears the very trace of colonial dispossession in the making of a particular kind of modern rational political subject against which "the savage" was defined (Johnson 2011). Nomenclature aside, the dire need for divine accompaniment and guidance amid uniquely American conditions of terror and abjection influenced the increased frequency and greater intensity of these occurrences in the New World relative to their continental African counterparts (K. M. Brown 2001).[12] Carrying the gods across the Atlantic "corporeally—in and as the bodies of the enslaved" (Escalante 2019, 388) was essential labor that destabilizes strict classifications of the self and of gender. Regardless of the social meaning ascribed to the devotee's anatomy, the essential labor of spirit possession both rehearses gender and performs its instability. For the duration of the mounting, the child's assigned gender is dimmed by that of the divinity without negating its simultaneous presence, thus offering a genderqueer way of understanding the relationship between the human and the more-than-human (Escalante 2019). Hence, drumming and spirit possession are densely gendered roles and gendering acts that co-constitute one's subjectivity.[13]

My interest is in how forms of gendered/gendering ritual labor factored into the economic agency of Yoruba Andabo members. While those assigned women at birth are categorically excluded from the labor and derechos allocated to drumming, the relative openness of the essential labor of spirit possession did not necessarily correlate to more economic opportunities for its dancers. In other words, unlike drumming, high technical proficiency in the specialized choreographies of the orishas did not translate to religious license to be hired for that service in ceremony. Even without being subject to taboos related to anatomy, rumberas faced an additional barrier to remuneration for this specialized form of essential labor. For to be danced through by the divine was the result of divine will. Eligibility to be mounted lay beyond personal volition. In other words, an individual cannot self-elect to become possessed; they are claimed. They must be chosen by the more-than-human to serve the community in this capacity. Human agency and skill enter in terms of learning how to make one's body more hospitable for the divine to dwell in. With practice one can become a clearer vessel through which to deliver divine messages to others, regulating the entrance and exit of spirit to ensure one's physical safety; of paramount importance, the moment of mounting must coincide with liturgically appropriate occasions that will benefit the worshipping community (a point I return to in chapter 5). Preselection for this sacred occupation is revealed to devotees through divination, while others inherit this grace through their ancestral line: "It's in the blood." If chosen by the divine, the community endorses this choice by hiring them to play this role, interchangeably called *montador* (mount or mountee), *bailador/a* (dancer), or *elegun*.

The high premium on spirit possession in Cuba has enabled a subset of its practitioners to be compensated for this form of specialized labor over time, but ultimately it was a labor that was supposed to be shouldered by an entire community. During the time of my fieldwork, the services of a reliable *bailador/a* cost roughly cuc $35–50 per ceremony and was considered an exceptional, not mandatory, financial sacrifice. Thus it occurred with less relative frequency than the drummings themselves. Similar to how, in the formal market for professional rumba, dancers were considered ornamentation to the required musical component, ritual *bailadores* were considered nice to have at tambores but not always necessary. More common was for casa-templos to invest in paying for highly skilled musicians capable of inciting those with this latent gift among the congregation to be mounted free of charge. The unique relationship between this feminized form of labor, personal agency, and demand structured dancers' constrained ability to capitalize on their folkloric prestige in the casa-templos relative to drummers.[14]

While their reputations as folkloric dancers in Yoruba Andabo preceded them, neither of the women dancers in Yoruba Andabo was at liberty to dance in ceremony for pay.[15] Zulema was crowned Ochún and had decades of professional experience representing that divinity in a folkloric context, but her divine mother had yet to possess her body in ceremony. Zulema suspected that her current employment as a state-subsidized folkloric dancer was the reason. Her profession demanded that she regularly dance on occasions that would be inappropriate for Ochún to come, thus exposing her to undue professional risk and potential risk to her physical safety. She speculated that perhaps when she eventually retires as a folkloric dancer, the time will come. She foresaw that being mounted for pay was part of her retirement plan, so to speak. In this way, religious labor would one day supplement her meager state pension. Zulema spoke with reverence about continuing her mother's legacy as a respected *bailadora* in her community one day. She became speechless at the thought of what it must feel like. "I can't tell you because it has never happened to me, but I know it must feel different. Beyond compare," she exhaled, "Imagine! There are things that you have to feel to know."

Conversely, Jenny knew this divinely given sensation firsthand. Eleggúa did on occasion choose to mount Jenny, but never when she danced outside her own casa-templo. Furthermore, Eleggúa forbade her from ever doing that kind of labor for pay. Instead, he vowed to always help her in her professional career in exchange for her continued devotion as a child of orisha who respects her elders and as a madrina (godmother) who "gives birth to" and nurtures ahijados (godchildren). It would seem that both Zulema and Jenny's folkloric duties inhibited or limited their financial yield as dancers in their religious communities. Unlike the drummers or singers in the group, these world-renowned dancers were compensated financially as any other religiosa in the less than glamorous day-to-day work of giving birth to and raising ahijados and caring for their families of stone.

Paramount, then, were the derechos they received from audience members, as discussed earlier, during their formal shows. That is when their superior skill of uncanny mimesis, which the director and rest of the ensemble facilitated, paid off. Jenny encouraged me to go to *el foco* (the focal point), meaning a drummed ceremony, to watch the divinities materialize through their children's bodies. That is how the best folkloric dancers learned about the "true" characteristics and expressions of the divinity, how they *manifiesta* (manifest) on earth. It is this capacity for uncanny mimesis, appearing at once completely grounded in one's physicality and beyond one's own agency, that gives great folkloric dancers the mesmerizing, awe-inspiring performance quality called *ángel*. This was what drew audience members to shower Yoruba Andabo's dancers with derechos while performing in state-managed venues. "Zulema, *she* has *ángel*," Jenny emphasized to describe what I still lacked and could never achieve simply with technical dance proficiency taught in class. *Ángel* could not be taught, it had to be experienced and sensed through embodied prayer, shoulder to shoulder, dancing with family.

While the masculine gendering of ritual drumming is nimble yet restrictive and feminized or genderqueer mounting holds no guarantees, the role of akpwón stands out as a gender-neutral service that also offers equal financial opportunity across gender expression. Eligibility to lead the congregation in song is not restricted by anatomical metaphor. The preference for one lead singer over another is often attributed to their level of mastery of the vast liturgical repertoire as well as their keen ability to sense the affective dynamism of a dancing congregation and respond accordingly. In tambores de fundamento, for example, the akpwón must recognize when an orisha may be "close," and know which lyrics to sing to goad the orisha down into the body of their horse. This requires the ability to recognize "the tells" that a person's body may exhibit when they are experiencing the first sensations of divine initiative. When possession is not the goal, as in the celebratory rumba of 10 de Octubre or by the malecón described earlier, the akpwón must similarly be able to gauge what songs will animate the crowd and carefully curate a sequence to suit the energetic progression necessary for the party to fulfill the offering. Akpwónes distinguish themselves as much for their memorization of the liturgy, people skills, and intuition—characteristics that were not associated with any particular sex or gender role. Yet, with only one akpwón for every three drummers in a single ceremony, the chances of a woman getting hired are doubtless much lower.

Ideologies of gender within religious labor shape differential possibilities for earning potential among spiritual kin. Since drumming services are habitually required, males experienced higher demand for their services in casa-templos. Thus, the prestige Didier and Lekiam garnered on folkloric stages most easily translated into higher wages for similar work in casa-templos. In contrast, fame on folkloric stages impeded Zulema's and Jenny's capacity to earn additional income through ceremony. Rather, and more often than not, dancers cashed in on devotees' piety at folkloric performances in state-managed venues. Relatively less employable for their artistic skill in the sacred market, they are more likely to seek out secular employment teaching folkloric dance to foreigners like me. The converging logics that position rumberas and rumberos differently within these various labor markets troubles conventional assumptions about how state endorsement of professional status correlates to earnings. Rumberas and rumberos pursued desenvolvimiento by laboring for and alongside family, and even if it was inegalitarian in terms of the financial return, unlike labor contracts made with the state, it was easier for them to accept as fair.

Market Crossings and the Struggle for a Fair Trade

Despite the various restrictions entailed in religious work, another element that made it feel fairer was its accessibility. The ability for anyone to initiate labor contracts within the Black corporeal undercommons contrasted with the cumbersome chain of command of intermediaries dictated by state bureaucracy. Whereas state protocol requires business deals with performance ensembles be made between the agency, the venue, and the artistic director via the manager, religiosos bargained directly with each other to arrive at the sum of money they were entitled to for their labor. For instance, if wanting Yoruba Andabo to perform religious work in one's casa-templo, whoever had the closest personal connection to a member of Yoruba Andabo would initiate the negotiation. Like the cousin-connection with Ronald described above, or the link between brothers at 10 de Octubre, potential religious clients leveraged family (blood or stone) ties to hire people to whom they already had a proximate relationship. They often lived and grew up together in the same marginalized Black communities, living and doing religious work together, shoulder to shoulder, for generations. The geographic concentrations of blood and stone families were compounded by patterns of intergenerational cohabitation constructed by persistent housing shortages that have disproportionately impacted Black families, even after decades of revolutionary urban reforms. These webs of shared experiences, conditions, and locations formed the basis of social proximity that made embarking on these informal labor contracts feel less risky. Moreover, one's embeddedness in these webs of spiritual-spatial intimacy increased one's chances of being hired to do religious work for others, in turn.

As different performers and clientele explained to me, in a typical hiring process for a drummed ceremony, a client contacts an akpwón or drummer whom they know and trust. The artist negotiates the terms of the derecho for the ceremony's specific musical needs in a verbal contract. The standard amount for each kind of ceremonial service is calculated according to the citizenship status of the client: Cuban, *cubano criollo*, or foreigner.[16] Under this decentralized system, the fee for service is discussed and agreed upon verbally. Performing artists of higher prestige charge inflated rates across all three pricing tiers. Based on anecdotal reports, derechos for Yoruba Andabo members were almost a third more (and in CUC) to conduct the same ceremonial labor as any other neighborhood drumming ensemble. As if there were a correlation between celebrity and ritual efficacy, they were entitled to more money for the same ritual labor. In addition to monetary compensation, providing a meal and drinks for the artists is expected but always confirmed.

Once the derecho amount for service was secured, the first point of contact in Yoruba Andabo would invite other artists to join them on an individual basis, and they would discuss how it would be divided. It was common for Yoruba Andabo members to contract fellow groupmates to play at ceremonies in their own religious households. Payment was given to the first point of contact up front upon arrival. That point person would then be responsible for administering the distribution of money at the time of completion. Unlike in state-mediated secular gigs, members participated in religious work on a voluntary basis, were paid immediately and directly, and didn't need to report or relinquish any percentage of their earnings to a central governing body. Derechos gave rumberos and their families access to an informal source of income that granted them more opportunities to meet their basic needs and put aside money for when (not if) they had to sponsor a ceremony to fulfill their own religious obligations.

It might be fruitful to think about the economics of the Black corporeal undercommons in relation to Georges Bataille's conception of an "unproductive sharing of wealth," wherein value is produced to be recirculated rather than accumulated according to the logics of capital ([1991] 2017). Each religious practitioner trains in (sometimes multiple) niche specializations, studying under an elder within a hierarchal system of religious seniority before they can pocket their pay. However, once they earn their right to compensation, the money would soon enough be put back into circulation. Desenvolvimiento entails a constant striving to be in alignment and balance with the divine, which requires hiring other hands in the community to perform more religious work. A strong religious reputation and a deep network of relationships positioned families to please copresences, put food on the table, complete repairs on their house, participate in some conspicuous consumption, or at least enjoy a live rumba performance with friends in a cool air-conditioned venue. Once there, they could maybe buy a round of hard-currency beers and offer some cash to the dancer representing their mother or father orisha—remembering that the money one gives to orisha comes back threefold.

One could argue that rumberos preferred religious work over state-managed folkloric or diplomatic work for the same reason that others were drawn to *cuentapropismo* (self-employment), for the sense of autonomy from the state it offered. However, this desire to distance themselves from state jurisdiction should not be mistaken for an ascription to the myth of rugged individualism promoted by neoliberalism. Instead, I saw an investment in religious labor agreements similar to those once privileged by the revolutionary project to begin with—motivated by a sense of accountability to one other through a shared sense of higher purpose to satisfy a collective need beyond the individual. In the Black corporeal undercommons, there was no centralized entity to control prices and monitor price inflation, nor to ensure even partition of work among all the skilled practitioners available. Nevertheless, shared accountability to copresences motivated religious kin to engage in these informal exchanges. In this informal realm of economic interdependence, where money is intended for recirculation, accountability—reliably fulfilling one's duty to kin and the more-than-human—not equality or competition, was the glue that kept the economy in motion. From this vantage, the logic of both rugged individualism and egalitarianism seemed bankrupt. When calculating derechos for the many hands needed to do the labor required, in the balance was not profit or the "social good" but the appraisal of their spiritual integrity and their ancestral line by association. Wherein desenvolvimiento requires economic interdependence, rumberos impel us to recognize the non-sovereign nature of social relationships—political, intimate, and affective—all of which require brokered and negotiated forms of interdependency and relinquishing of autonomy (Bonilla 2017). In other words, they impel us to reckon with *cuentapropismo*, counting on one's self, as a myth, and an undesirable one at that, rather than an ideal. They traced this spiritually guided practice of mutual aid, saving each other and endeavoring to protect the community's material interests, to a shared cabildo heritage.

This sacred inheritance offered an accessible and less risky means of economic participation and protection. Perhaps this greater transparency and decision-making capacity over their labor, and the protections that come with sacred accountability, account for the greater sense of intimacy that performers described having with their *demasiado religioso* audience. Yoruba Andabo members all spoke about the affinity they shared with religiosos that they didn't share with the Cuban mainstream or tourist audiences. This explains the sense of loss, disappointment, and even bitterness that followed when, as members of a prestigious state-subsidized group, they were routinely obligated to cancel potentially lifesaving religious work to perform on short notice for state functions in the name of a more abstract notion of *el pueblo* (the people) or "folklore," when hailed as the cultural property of the nation (chapter 1).

Nonetheless, Yoruba Andabo's artistic director was adamant about clearing up the dangerous "confusion" that religious bookings could cause. He was wary of jeopardizing their state-subsidized status, which he and the other founders, especially, valued. Even if all the members of Yoruba Andabo were performing together in a household, Geovani insisted that they were not working *as* "Yoruba Andabo," but as religious individuals. Frequently, he argued, only the point person would be a member of Yoruba Andabo and the rest of the hired artists would be *aficionados* (amateur, per the state's accreditation system), or they might be affiliated with different professional rumba groups. Most commonly, the musicians would be some mix of Yoruba Andabo members and *aficionado* religious artists linked to the primary contact through consanguinity or religious kinship. It was, in fact, very rare that the entire sixteen-member group would conduct religious work all together at once. Yet, from the perspective of the religious community, a single member could be enough to signify the presence of the whole and warrant the higher derecho.

Boastful commentary by religiosos enhanced this confusion, according to Valentín:

> [W]hen everyone sees Jorge Luis [at a tambor], they say "Yoruba Andabo." But if Ronald comes, they say "Yoruba Andabo." If Chan were to be there, like when I went . . . to the birthday of Chan's Ochún. Who was singing? Jorge Luis. But Ronald is playing in el Cerro with another group of Yoruba Andabo. Maybe he has to supplement with someone but, [it is still]

Yoruba Andabo. And everyone says, "Yoruba Andabo, Yoruba Andabo, Yoruba Andabo." . . . So Jorge Luis is in el Cerro, Ronald is in Cayo Hueso, and Lekiam is in Pogolotti . . . and Yerilú is in San Migel del Padrón. But when they see Yerilú there, they say "Yoruba Andabo." So Yoruba Andabo is many places and a single thing.

Valentín referenced the artists' nimble ability to conduct religious work simultaneously in multiple locales, freed from capitalist logics that rely on a singular corporate identity that the state entertainment industry depends on. Within a spiritual epistemology that recognizes personhood as abundant and divinely multiplied, Yoruba Andabo could, for all intents and purposes, be many places at once.

On the one hand, this multiplicitous recognition allowed group members to charge inflated "Yoruba Andabo" rates for service that could then be recirculated into more hands. On the other hand, the single corporate identity the artistic director insisted on had important legal repercussions, as folkloric groups are vetted by the state and, by definition, not supposed to serve a sacred function. Careful to protect themselves while "crossing" between labor regimes that rely on different conceptions of personhood, Geovani insisted that the precept of religious freedom gave them an inalienable right to engage in this kind of economic trade at their own discretion, without calling into question their entitlement to a subsidy from the state. After all, religious practice in a secular state is a private matter.

During my time living in Havana, I learned to see, hear, and smell the material traces of the Black corporeal undercommons, beyond state jurisdiction and private market exclusion. It was a place where fair trade seemed possible, a space where you were given what you were spiritually entitled. Spiritually motivated economic transactions were ubiquitous and built into the landscape and daily rhythm of the city. In Centro Habana, where I mostly lived, religious ceremonies were commonplace. In the middle of the night, what sounded like a baby's shrill cry was actually a kid goat (600 MN/CUP or CUC $25) purchased from a specialized animal breeder in the countryside. In the days leading up to the ceremony, choice livestock were held safely in custom-built pens inside households or on the rooftops of apartment buildings. These animals were destined to be offerings to the orisha. In the morning, the fresh smell of animal remains placed carefully on the curbs at busy intersections, in garbage dumpsters, near cemeteries, or close to bodies of water displayed the sacrifices officiated by skilled experts who were paid the night before.

In the afternoon, the sounds of hired musicians drumming (1,000–1,200 MN/CUP) reverberated down the narrow streets. Opened front doors revealed a crowded room of people singing and dancing for hours in unison. If it was a very special occasion, a hired *bailador/a* (CUC $35–50) danced in front of the drums. In a backroom, simple or elaborate altar installations with colorful fabrics draped from ceiling to floor (CUC $2–8 per meter) were constructed the day before by specialized throne makers (CUC $5–10). These temporary homages to the divinities, dressed in cloth and dramatically adorned, were an expected part of household interior design. On celebratory days of the year, they provided a sacred portal to approach, formally greet, salute, communicate and make offerings to the divinities, and display the grandeur of the divinity and the well-being of their child (D. H. Brown 1993).

At dusk, it was common to see people dressed head-to-toe in all white, scurrying home under white parasols, meaning they had undertaken a weeklong ritual to be "crowned" as a "son" or "daughter" of a divinity (costing CUC $1,500 or the equivalent in CUP/MN or more). The considerable material sacrifices of initiation, sometimes a life's savings, had been presented to their godparent's altar. Their godparent used the derecho to purchase the goat heard crying the night before, along with other live animals, ritual labor, and fabric, and the many other materials entailed when "birthing" a child of orisha. And then there was the derecho for the musicians to play when that new life is presented to the larger worshipping community and to the drums. A person who had already undergone the same initiation ceremony could sell their labor (50 CUP/MN to CUC $50) to *trabajar un santo* (work a sainthood initiation) at the ceremonies of their ever-expanding household of stone kin that (hopefully) reached beyond national borders to warrant a higher rate of compensation.

Sacred epistemologies instilled a different orientation to trade. The commercialized chain of reciprocity within one's intergenerational network was propelled by the understanding that they were mutually interconnected, kin by spiritual attachment, and shared a fate. Although ensuring meaningful returns for one's time and energy, desenvolvimiento did not traffic in the old revolutionary discourse of equality or the nascent neoliberal discourse of upward mobility. *Trabajo religioso* certainly did not radically shift one's class position. Instead, well-being was ensured through reciprocal exchanges with the earth, the living, the dead, and the divine. Religious work gave Black peso-poor people the potential to earn more in a few hours or days than they would working for a month for the state or selling their labor to a *cuentapropista*. Neither boasting a claim to a guaranteed salary, as in the public sector, nor promising surplus gains, as in the "emergent" small-business realm, the Black corporeal undercommons sustained the ability of people with common faith to "save themselves" on their own terms.

In short, desenvolvimiento was labor-intensive, required family, and deemed fair. As Cuba opened to greater foreign investment, Black peso-poor families of stone created the opportunities for a more dignified sustenance than *desarrollo* seemed to provide. In this way, the collective pursuit of desenvolvimiento proclaims a politics of pragmatism as much as a politics of adequacy (Garth 2020). It was about how to work with the resources within one's networks to feasibly meet a collective standard for a good, dignified, decent life, which is deeply entangled with an ideal for living with the human and more-than-human. This ideal exceeds what the state may consider "basic needs" and does not limit itself to the formal means of constructing a "respectable life." Despite the exclusions and inflations also involved, with faith they could be rationalized as just, which is more than whatever national development could offer. The Black corporeal undercommons is an affirmation that those accountable to copresences can wield their creative capacity to, if not entirely shape their world, at least create a refuge to weather the economic storm.

Many members of the Black peso-poor were increasingly driven to work "full-time" in *la religión* instead of keeping a state job or trying their luck in the formal private sector. Sponsoring religious work required considerable savings accumulated through financial strain, sacrifice, and transactions that were off the books. The assurance that the funds that faith afforded would recirculate was, for many, more promising than the logics of exploitation, exclusion, and competition that ostensibly facilitated class mobility. Thus, the everyday buzz of their labor registered as idleness under government employment statistics tracking unemployment relative to state vacancies and *cuentapropia* licensures. Moving away from formal labor and toward religious labor, unavoidably, positioned them in closer relation to deviance, a social stigma that younger generations born since the Special Period were less invested in keeping at bay. Reciprocity, not respectability, was of greater consequence to their well-being.

Reciprocal exchange—"*Yo te salvo a ti, y tú me salvas a mí*" (I save you, you save me)—was both a refrain and a social contract inherited (and underwritten) by one's ancestors to be accountable to one another's survival. It has been theorized that the concept of a "spiritual contract" countered the violent extraction of forced labor from their bodies in the Americas. Stephan Palmié (2002) asserts that the monetization of sacred services in Afro-Cuban religions is an adaptive response to the modern push of market forces on a crumbling socialist regime. Similarly, in her study of the economic mobilizations of Afro-Cuban religions, Jalane Schmidt (2016) attests that the sale and consumption of hard-currency religious products has occurred in relationship to market pressures that affect and are affected by cultural change since the economic crisis of the 1990s. By producing state-manufactured religious merchandise to garner the attention of Cuban consumers and international visitors alike, the Cuban tourism industry has encouraged the monetization of Santería, in particular, called *santurismo* (Schmidt 2016). It is no wonder, then, that practitioners report that the orishas themselves prefer offerings purchased in hard currency (Palmié 2002, 166–67). It would follow that public displays of piety become yet another medium through which racialized subjects signal their economic inclusion in an exclusionary system of competition (Hernández-Reguant 2010).

If indeed the ethic of reciprocal exchange is inseparable from macro-historical-economic pressures, one can expect the norms of reciprocity in the Black corporeal undercommons to reinforce the idea that in Cuba's increasingly stratified society, interdependence with spiritual kin saves lives. Yet, I contend, less appreciated is the way the sacred announces a vision for an alternate conception of development that rumberos privilege and defend against incursion, one they choose to call fair, or perhaps even more sacred, call their own.

Para Salvar a Tu Familia (To Save Your Family)

While beading an *eleke* (initiation necklace) for a godchild at his dining room table, El Gordo spoke to me about how he balances his obligations as a state-subsidized folkloric drummer and religious work. His calloused hands did not in any way hamper his ability to carefully pick up each bead with a small needle and fashion a repeating alternating pattern of red and white. During our conversation, he would get up every thirty minutes or so to zap the plate of food sitting in the microwave for another thirty seconds. The electricity could go out in the neighborhood at any moment, he explained, so when his daughter came home from school for lunch, even if the electricity had gone out, she would have a warm plate of food to eat. That June in 2013, blackouts were happening almost daily in different pockets

4.4 Julio "El Gordo" César Lemoine. Photo by author.

of the city. El Gordo lived in Vedado, not far from the US Interest Section, but his building was not spared. As was typical for buildings that specifically served foreigners, the US Interest Section had a private generator that did not extend to the surrounding neighbors' homes. The smell of seasoned pork that his wife, who was currently at work, had cooked the night before reminded me of yet another realm of (unremunerated) work that keeps rumberos' lives afloat. He bragged that he had no problem cleaning, washing dishes, and doing the laundry, but cooking was his wife's domain. "But, I do a little bit of everything. With the stomach that I have, you have to know how to cook for yourself," he laughed.

As a child in the 1980s, El Gordo lived near a community center in Old Havana where someone offered free music lessons to children. The community center was not far from the ward of Old Havana called Belén, home to some of the most famous rumberos. There was an audition for kids to get into the class and he was selected. That is when he learned that he had rhythm. As a young boy, he thought he was going to be a painter, but with his family's encouragement, he finished school and became a mechanical engineer. For a while he maintained a dual life, going to school during the day and to rumbas at night. "*Folklórica nocturna*," he called it. That was when he started playing *batá*, bongos, and *timbales*, absorbing lessons from the great rumbero, Pancho Quinto (born in Belén), one of the founders of Yoruba Andabo. He would wake up early on a Sunday and go to where Pancho was playing, *pegado al linea del fuego* (stuck in the line of fire), to learn all he could. "That's how it was back then. You had to be there when the elders were playing and pay attention. When they said, 'come, play,' you had to be able to jump in on the spot." For about ten years, he straddled both lives, working as a mechanical engineer during the day and playing rumba as an *aficionado* at tambores, *guïros*, and so on, at night and on weekends.

At that time, he did not yet have the extra pounds that would later earn him his nickname. He was still Julio César, an engineer from a white family, but with a newfound appreciation for a cultural practice that revolutionary institutions made accessible to all. Then around 1990, another respected Yoruba Andabo percussionist, El Chori, died, and the director asked Julio César to be his replacement. It was a big deal for a young white man to be given that vote of confidence to carry on the tradition. Giving him a place within the group also placed him within their lineage. Immersion into the world of rumba entailed increasing Afro-religious involvement, including initiation. In his case, that also meant disconnection from his blood family. "They never understood and never got involved," he said. "*Me convertí a una persona religiosa*" (I converted into a religious person). He became El Gordo, the rumbero, a son of Changó, and eventually a beloved godfather to other rumberos. His family of stone, along with his wife, were Black. His filial relation to Changó, in many ways, was indebted to the ancestors of Pancho Quinto as much as to the state's institutionalization of the form as national folklore.

Telling me the story while looking down at his hands, he suddenly noticed that he was speaking of the orisha that he was beading a necklace for at that moment: Changó. "See? Look at that." After all these years, he remained in the line of fire. Changó, in addition to being the divinity of fire made manifest in the energetic force of justice and strategy, is considered the owner of the drum. El Gordo's patient answers to my questions synchronized with the meditative accuracy of his beadwork and his methodical breaks to get up and zap the food for yet another thirty seconds. Our interview that morning was perhaps a metaphor for this keen ability to keep in sync multiple demands on his time—caring for his daughter, an interview with an anthropologist, and preparations for an upcoming religious ceremony. El Gordo insisted that the discipline in being a son of Changó and later becoming a *babalawo* (priest of Ifá: the system of divination) trained him to manage life's challenges strategically and at the right tempo.

Faith kept him always moving forward in his life, *pa'lante*, on the right path with *ire* (blessings). Priests of Ifá, like himself, helped people navigate the path of desenvolvimiento. "Us *babalawos*, being priests of Ifá . . . all that we give to people is advice, to know which way to go. . . . We use Ifá in order to save humanity, to save yourself, to save your children, to save your family." Without denying the difficulties and sacrifices that living with the divine often entailed, for him it was entirely possible to realize your fullest potential if you kept your focus on religious work, *el foco*.

When I asked why he continued to play at state-brokered gigs at all, if he ultimately made more money per gig doing religious work, he replied, "Because private [religious] work pays more but it's not always there. For example, in one month you could have four, five, or six [religious] gigs, but then you will go three months without anything. It depends on how the *pataki* [parable] goes." *Pataki* is the word for the corpus of religious parables conveyed in the system of divination. The parables create interpretive frameworks for practitioners to determine how to best navigate and manage the challenging life situations they encounter. He continued, "Private work is when you can, but Yoruba [Andabo] is constant. But apart from that, Yoruba Andabo [as a state-subsidized group] gives you an institution. It's like rice and beans. Rice and beans you have every month."

These few sentences pointed to a complex analysis of the shifting economic terrain rumberos navigated. "Rice and beans" was an allusion to the basic foodstuffs included in the monthly government rations. The guaranteed universal distribution of these staples of the Cuban diet had long been a barometer for the strength of the government safety net (like education and health care) and commitment to food as a universal human right. Like Yoruba Andabo's meager state salary, it was common knowledge that the government rations were never enough to feed an entire household throughout even half the month. And after the fall of the Soviet Union and the tightening of the US embargo, even less so. More and more items were reduced or removed from the ration card or were insufficiently stocked. Likewise, the state stopped giving new rumba ensembles subsidized status. However, for those who depended on a guaranteed state salary, the ration card (*la libreta*) symbolized the revolutionary principle that all Cubans who work for the good of the national project should be entitled to consistent, basic welfare.

By contrast, "private work," that to which you are spiritually entitled through religious work, paid more but made no claim to constancy or universal allotment. "It depends on the *pataki*," he explained. These parables teach that each human challenge correlates to allegorical precedents in the lives of divine avatars who, like their children, have also undergone innumerable hardships. Only by following the wisdom embedded in the story can the person find the most constructive and beneficial course of action for their given circumstance. Just as only intentional, strategic movements while fulfilling divine obligations meant that his daughter could count on a hot lunch to eat, even if the lights went out and the ration ran out.

Building on Garth, El Gordo's pursuit of a "decent meal" for his daughter was "deeply entangled with desire to live in idealized ways in the face of change" (2020, 7). It was beyond the metrics of "basic needs" afforded by the state, but nonetheless considered vital to his sense of dignified well-being. El Gordo contrasted the inherent unpredictability of the private market, with the predetermined guarantee of state insufficiency (rice and beans). This positioned religious labor as the key to not only making up the difference, but also asserting an entitlement to a more holistic kind of nourishment anchored in divine purpose, accompaniment, and interdependency, which he found in Black belonging.

During my fieldwork, even the guarantee of rice and beans began to seem uncertain. Local economists heavily debated the need for rations as they reevaluated the "inefficiencies," "unnecessary subsidies," and "burdens" of the "old ways" that insisted on a kind of egalitarianism that was not only untenable but perhaps misguided. Public debate arose about whether universal rations of basic foodstuffs were wise for Cuba's strapped economy, considering that it largely relied on foreign imports (70–80 percent, according to the World Food Program), or even if it was still necessary given that Cubans were now "free" to earn higher salaries in the private market.[17] Cubans with more purchasing power stopped claiming their rations, instead opting to pay for products in the hard-currency stores that promised better quality. Proposals to discontinue rations altogether and instead sell everything according to supply and demand, or to streamline the system and only distribute rations to families who "qualify," were characteristic of the changing perspectives on the value of universal social welfare.[18] Buzz about these changes were heard over manicures, when women would boast about trying the new scented rice imported from Brazil for sale at the *chopin* (hard-currency store), in contrast with the tedious task of sifting through stones in the rationed rice from the bodega imported from Vietnam or China.

In the earlier years of the Cuban Revolution, the symbolic capital given to Black popular cultural forms was intended as an aesthetic representation of Cuba's anti-colonial remaking. The Revolution's call for the anti-colonial "aesthetic nourishment" of its citizenry also afforded the performers of those cultural forms—deemed folkloric—a specialized role to play in the revolutionary struggle to come, teaching their artistic skills to a wider audience. At first, in exchange for a government wage, their enduring faith had to be hidden (Ayorinde 2004; Berry 2010). Only then could the narrative of this cultural form, excavated from "the streets" to the "national stage," represent a revolutionary teleology that mirrored the ascension of the proletariat, stripped of its atavistic maladaptation to capitalism, to his rightful place of dignity within the modern nation. At the same time, orishas seized that period of national exposure and institutional backing as an opening to give birth to new life. In turn, new lines of spiritual kinship were born by hands otherwise kept apart by the social distances that the Revolution closed. However, recent attempts by the PCC to steer the political economy toward an embrace of formerly stigmatized market logics has led rumberos and their families to critically reevaluate the extent to which their labor contract with the state still serves them.

A Higher Power

Quoting Raúl Castro at the last session of parliament in 2016, "Capitalism is a social fact that can no longer be feared." As the state recalibrated its guidelines for what all citizens should dread or be entitled to, rumberos defended their own definition of "basic needs." In updating Cuba, their sense of adequacy was inextricable from the demands of copresences and the right to fair compensation for their labor.

Rather than relying on the state's designs for development (*desarrollo*), rumberos strive for desenvolvimiento. The salvation that comes from being in good standing with the divine was not an event reached in the afterlife, but a collective practice in the here and now, embodied through interdependence between kin. Exchanges mediated by copresences held the power to mitigate the undervaluation of Black people's labor and the potential to account for cost inflation in a society characterized by a weakened state social safety net and an increasingly neoliberalized labor market. Where embodied acts of devotion are vectors for a kind of right to sustenance, an entitlement to resources, uniquely accessible through a power higher than state authority, the Black corporeal undercommons be.

While transnational since its inception through slave trade and alongside Cuban migratory waves ever since, after African diasporic religious affiliation ceased to be criminalized by the state, these family networks extended throughout the city and suburbs, and expanded exponentially abroad (Beliso-De Jesús 2015). My own membership as a distant relative in the faith is evidence of the religion's reach and also allowed me to earn their trust to honor the meanings they assigned to the dynamic ways they labored on and off stage. I hoped that by only showing up at ceremonies when explicitly invited by someone with the authorization to grant my access past its threshold, I could show my respect for the rules of entrance that my godmother in Brooklyn, NY, taught me money could never buy. But should I ever want to enlist their services to fulfill divine obligations of my own, I would be sure to pay the derecho that my citizenship status warranted to constitute what they felt was a fair trade. Such exchanges with extended kin, whose travel in and out of Cuba was made easier by reforms under Raúl, saved families. In this sense, the religion's expanded reach made it possible for rumberos to leave but also feel hopeful about staying in place.

Attending to how everyday Black popular practices of reciprocation for well-being embody economic change requires a reconsideration of conventional understandings of the relationship between the sacred and commercialism. In contrast to the idea that the monetization of the Black sacred arts is somehow a "deformation" of the form's integrity or distortion of the form's "purity," I join those that have attributed Santería's resiliency and relevance to its adaptations (Menéndez 2002). In the context of a faltering welfare state, African diasporic religious epistemologies and practices partly maintained their social relevance within Black peso-poor communities in Havana precisely because they delivered entitlements that made up for the gap where the state not only fell short but could never fill. Rather than being seen as a sacrilege or profane, they defended cabildo principles of collective self-organization and reciprocation through their bodies. Meeting the immediate material needs of the membership was not only central to the cabildos during slavery, but also sacred; religious labor protected this sacred entitlement to material adequacy from development's incursion.

Just as the government allotments of food could no longer sustain a family, the emergent private sector came with its own form of undernourishment for Black families. Where rationed rice and beans represented both constancy and insufficiency, and *cuentapropismo* meant exclusion and exploitation, divine guidance gave needed tools to devise a path for kin to find their way with dignity. The dances of the cabildos—and the attendant infrastructure of self-organization and mutual aid they embody—afforded vital and accessible means through the tough times of inevitable hardship and scarcity month to month. In the words of Tailyn, Yemayá's faithful daughter, both literally and figuratively, "Rumba is my food; it fills me up." Here, religious labor is not oriented toward a future accumulation of capital, but accrues value through its recirculation. Inasmuch as one invests in fulfilling divine obligations, the money you put toward the religious labor of others will return—threefold—to save you too.

Although the distinction between secular and sacred can seem moot in this postmodern age of cultural criticism, taking it seriously allowed me to appreciate the artistry in how rumberas and rumberos made a living through religious labor while negotiating the risk of breaching their labor contract with the state. Ironically, the legitimacy ascribed to folklore and "religious freedom" is, to a large extent, what granted me access to do the study, and also made inviting me to see rumba from this other vantage point harmless. However, given the new state sanctioning of more forms of property and labor contracts once deemed immoral, younger generations had less reason to worry themselves with managing state optics. In the changing economy, appearing to limit one's embodied labor to folkloric stages offered less in return. Instead, Black youth looked up to Yoruba Andabo precisely for their ability to move across markets thought of as separate. They accrued added value precisely from their movement between realms, blurring the boundaries between the folkloric stages (at the international and national scale) and altar rooms in the neighborhoods where they grew up. Whether at state-run nightclubs or household temples, all these sites of rumba performance represent important nodes of exchange that are valuable to Black peso-poor families for how they converge. It might be more useful to reconsider the "(secular) stage" not as a final or even real destination rumberos aspire to, and instead to position state-subsidized folkloric performance as one strategic node within a broader life project to fulfill divine obligation and acquire inheritances.

For a community that increasingly depended on their faith to meet their material needs, folkloric dance's state-endorsed symbolic currency indeed afforded situational advantages and more choices, if not more obligations. If nothing else, it was a prime platform to display sacred registers of expertise to a wider religious audience. This folkloric prestige gave Yoruba Andabo social capital that was leveraged to protect the added wages from derechos and legitimize charging more for ritual labor offstage. It was a means to reap the benefits of international travel without feeling the need to defect. That is to say, it enabled both travel abroad and permanence in place.

Jenny, for one, proudly vowed never to leave Cuba, but she would eventually leave Yoruba Andabo. After a dance directorship with Osain del

Monte also went sour, she dreamed of one day founding her own rumba ensemble for youth. Similar to Geovani and Lekiam, she voiced concern about the next generation and wanted to do her part to actively draw them into the profession. Hers would be an ensemble geared toward mentorship and professional development with a focus on young girls. Unlike the other ensembles she danced for, this one she would lead on her own terms. In the meantime, she was always accompanied and aided by guiding spirits who helped her navigate the intersecting economic milieus where men predominate as privileged brokers and agents of trade. Like Zulema, she trusted the ways copresences guided her steps, and she made the most of the labor they positioned her to do, when they positioned her to do it, and the wages they ensured she had a right to claim.

To be sure, within the coordinates of the Black corporeal undercommons, not everybody has equal capacity to exercise the kind or scale of agency that members of Yoruba Andabo disparately seize. Religiosas and religiosos self-consciously labored for divine reciprocity on unequal footing. A Black feminist lens helps us appreciate how gendered meanings legitimize how labor is apportioned and remunerated unequally among kin. The logics of anatomical metaphors and divine agency create different paths and pressures. But then again, egalitarianism was never promised nor the goal. Even if it is accompanied by its own gendered limitations, it is telling that the Black corporeal undercommons represents a realm of trade that still feels more fair and hopeful than the one offered by the formal economy.

5   UNDERWORLD ASSEMBLY

Some might analyze orisha movements in rumba as the secularization of highly powerful religious dancing. Others may see it as sanctification, the process of making rumba special or holy by means of expressive behavior from a religious context. The mixture may, however, confirm that the original purpose of rumba was liberation and protest through music/dance (Martinez-Furé in Chao Carbonero and Lamerán, 1982: 114). It may demonstrate religious persistence within a contemporary social order that is basically atheistic and generally antireligious. It may be a minuscule but public display of faith from a spiritual world view. All possibilities depend on the answers to questions that are most avoided in Cuba at this time.

YVONNE DANIEL, *Rumba*

One September day in 2013, at Yoruba Andabo's weekly Wednesday showcase at Cabaret Las Vegas, Gilberto took the microphone on several occasions to announce their upcoming performance at the Teatro Avenida (Avenida Theater). He made a point to highlight the nominal cost of the tickets in *moneda nacional* and asked the audience to spread the word so all their family and friends would come out and could enjoy. While this was hardly the first time they had performed at a large theater in the city, when it did occur, it was considered a special occasion.

The Teatro Avenida was a soon-to-be relic on 41st Avenue. As part of the many socialist reforms instated in 1959, the Cuban revolutionary government seized movie theaters that had once catered to the elite's taste for the imported Hollywood glamour of the era. When the state made culture accessible to the masses as a public good rather than a commodity, the council that would become the Cuban Ministry of Culture assigned the cinemas to theater troupes and dance companies where they could rehearse for free and put on shows that all citizens could easily attend at subsidized rates. However, small rumba ensembles, due to their historical association with the streets, were deemed not to need this type of theatrical accommodation. As we have seen, professional rumba ensembles most frequently circulated between gigs in the street (i.e., Callejón de Hamel), open-air patios (i.e., El Palenque, UNEAC), and eventually, a limited circuit of small-scale state-managed nightclubs catering to local patrons (i.e., Cabaret Las Vegas, El Palacio de la Rumba), not to mention domestic spaces (i.e., Casa de 10 de Octubre). While the proscenium structure impeded the kind of participation that the audience enjoyed in those other spaces, a night at the theater meant that patrons would pay a fraction of the cost of entry in CUP/MN currency for the comfort of air conditioning, a guaranteed seat, and a clear view.

Located on the avenue that connects Miramar (arguably the most affluent neighborhood in Havana) and Marianao (one of Havana's poorest), the Teatro Avenida occupied the figurative juncture of an ideological clash between what the Revolution once aspired to be and its updated becoming. Around the theater, you could see new private businesses serving predominantly white consumers with CUC purchasing power. The economic changes under Raúl Castro facilitated an increasingly visible return to pre-revolutionary racialized segregation of social spaces. The flight of middle- and upper-class Cubans from shared public spaces to the comforts of exclusive, private-business establishments left the largely Black lower classes to make use of under-resourced public institutions, services, and social milieus (Bastian 2018, 150). If indeed Havana's public spaces have been left in the dust of a kind of "white flight," on this night at the theater, rumberos collectively rehearsed ways to reclaim public space on their own terms.

This one night of cultural performance allows me to expand my analytical frame to consider a wider scope of the everyday Black people who form Rumba events and whom rumba forms, including those who move at the ostensible edges of its virtuosic display. They are Black folk round da way whose choreographies push us collectively beyond what statist designs of national progress can offer. The norms of cultural display at proscenium theaters had shaped my expectations of what might transpire that night in September. I anticipated that both the artists and the audience would mostly adhere to the institutionalized norms of spectatorship for concert dance. Perhaps for that reason, the night is seared in my memory, ever present in my kinesthetic recall. Its durability is a forceful demonstration of the way rumba harnesses the collective potential to transform one's sense of time and place. I was pushed, and so I push the reader, to reckon with what movements for Black life, more broadly, can look like. This chapter meditates on where that coordinated motion critically pushes us to go.

Even as a regular at rumbas across the city, whether outdoors in courtyards or in living rooms with the furniture pushed back or in cramped nightclubs tucked away from the tourist gaze, for me this night may have crystalized the imperative for a concerted meditation on the Black corporeal undercommons as mode of popular assembly. This imperative energizes my reclamation of what Fernando Ortiz termed the *Afro-Cuban underworld* with disdain, signaling the traces of a choreo/geography he knew unsettled the nation. To go there, I linger on coordinated movements that are not-not the divine. As choreographies of fugitivity, they not only run up against the norms of folkloric cultural display, but fundamentally unsettle how personhood, agency, and therefore resistance are defined and taken up in specific historical moments and in diasporic relation. More pointedly, I consider spirit possession's call to assembly, the force of argument it drives, the spatial claim it propels, and the possibilities it brings forth for Black lives.

Outside the Theater

The show was supposed to start at 9 p.m. We got to the theater early, at about 8 p.m., to be sure to get a ticket. The rundown cinema-turned-performing arts theater did not attract crowds of tourists, or even many people from the immediate surrounding neighborhood any longer, but it was a special occasion for peso-poor rumberos. That night I brought Rachel and Malcolm,[1] a US African American medical student living in Cuba, along with me. This was my second attempt to make good on Rachel's request to see Yoruba Andabo perform, after my first attempt was foiled by technical difficulties at Cabaret Las Vegas (chapter 4). By contrast, Malcolm was just looking for a night of release before the stress of another school year set in. Malcolm's studies at Cuba's prestigious international medical school prevented him from getting out much and experiencing Havana's robust nightlife. Unlike the more popular performance venues in the area, such as the upscale Miramar *Casa de la Música* (House of Music) and the historic Tropicana Club, the Teatro Avenida had no inflated price for foreigners

5.1 Teatro Avenida. Photo by Michael Eastman.

and did not sell refreshments in CUC. It did not sell refreshments at all. Few patrons with CUC purchasing power were expected to make it out to this rundown location, a dusty shadow of its pre-revolutionary form. As 9 p.m. approached, more and more rumberos from Havana's inner-city Black enclaves assembled around the theater.

8:15 p.m. They reached the vestibule in front of the main doors of the converted cinema in waves. Each public bus deposited another group of proto-audience members dressed in their carefully color-coordinated ensembles: electric greens, blues, pinks, and of course, the epitome of elegance, all white. After spilling out from the compressed bellies of vehicles traveling from neighborhoods far away, people blotted foreheads with handkerchiefs and started to flap fans fervently to regain coolness in the night air. The majority, women and men alike, wore *ide* around their wrists, a public marker of the divinity who claimed them as kin. These colors popped against the many shades of their Black skin. The crowd exchanged greetings in a steady cacophony of cheek-to-cheek kisses. Malcolm, Rachel, and I joined them as they made their way to the box office to retrieve our thin paper tickets.

8:30 p.m. Groupings of friends, families, and lovers were laughing and drinking beverages purchased at the gas station down the street. To get to the gas station they had to pass residents dining in a newly opened, upscale restaurant modeled after restaurants in Miami's metropolis. While the people inside purchased their meals using hard currency acquired via remittances from family members abroad or from their own entrepreneurial ventures, those waiting on the sidewalk to enter the theater had been saving up all week, maybe even all month, for this special Friday night outing.

Word of mouth had spread quickly about Yoruba Andabo's show at Teatro Avenida, tipping off two women who made their way down the avenue pushing improvised carts that held huge garbage bags carrying individually wrapped snacks (*chuchería*) bought on the black market. They could bet that the audience would want something cheap and convenient to hold them over. The cart women, also Black and struggling to make a living, made it their business to find out about all the most popular concerts in the city. Yanilda, also a *chuchería* vendor, lived around the corner from the bodega back in Centro Habana, where I stayed. She did odd jobs during the day and then perused the cultural newspaper listings to see what events might be worth bringing her cart to that night. She did mental calculations about which events to cover, depending on the route from her house, the expected size of the audience, and how many other sellers might be there. Depending on those variables she figured the likelihood of police presence, which would make it riskier for women like her without a license to conduct business. Their goods were lightweight and sold in Cuban pesos. Both elements, light and cheap, were vital. They hoped to make sales in their clientele's most easily accessible currency before the police officers came to bust their operation. The cart made vending and fleeing more possible. These *chuchería* vendors could trust the crowd to quickly part the way, when the time came, for them to make their escape on foot down the sidewalk and into the dark night.

8:50 p.m. The theater had yet to begin seating. Aware that the show was supposed to commence at 9 p.m., people tightly swarmed the entrance. With no explanation for the delay, the crowd grew suspicious and turned impatient.

9:00 p.m. The show was supposed to begin any moment, but the ushers had yet to remove the chain and collect tickets. The crowd's frustration mounted, growing in anxiety as if they would miss what they came from so far to see. None was a stranger to waiting on lines, a daily rite of passage that characterized dealings in the public sector. *Colera* (a woman who waits on lines) was another unlicensed occupation overrepresented by Black women. She sold the service of standing for hours or selling her place in long lines to purchase items that people with cuc desired and could afford to not be inconvenienced for.[2] In any case, if you were poor you had no choice but to grow accustomed to waiting your turn in public, knowing that others paid to make turns expendable. But somehow, this wait on that night felt particularly offensive.

Holding their flimsy papers high to legitimate their right of entry proved unsuccessful. Some tried to verbally negotiate with the theater staff from different angles: "Hey! I've been here since 8 p.m.!" "Look, here is my ticket!" "Hey *papi*, would you do me a little favor and let me in, my feet hurt in these high heels." "I really need to pee. You won't make me pee on myself out here will you? Have a little humanity, no?" "*Compaaadre*, this isn't the way to treat people. What's going on??" "Let's go, what's the hold up?!"

9:15 p.m. Still no explanation from the theater staff. It was not uncommon in Havana for conditions to suddenly change. In the private sector, seemingly arbitrary exclusionary rules would be enforced without notice and without explanation. Security guards at upscale business establishments were well known for racial profiling in the name of "safety for patrons" (who, if you are Black, probably aren't you) or in the name of arbitrary "rules of the establishment" that don't feel so arbitrary. This was especially the case if you were Black and labeled an *ambiental*, a person whose presumed habitus was delinquency, or as Ortiz once called it, *la mala vida*, the space-time of poverty and crime ostensibly tied to rumba. As elaborated in chapter 3, practices of racial profiling in the private sector mirrored the racialized application of the penal code for *social dangerousness* disproportionately applied to Black people based on negative stereotypes about unruly gender since the Special Period. As a Black woman who "passed" for a local, and who was therefore often presumed to be a *jinetera*, I had also grown accustomed to being denied entry to places around the city, places that Black Cubans collectively learned they did not belong in. These experiences made me particularly sensitive to the frustrations that had been mounting at that time, shared in passing conversation as well as in forums and independent publications by anti-racist scholar-activists. Maybe even on the long bus ride to the theater, still the cheapest form of transportation in the city, the proto-audience members would have discussed how difficult it was to pay for a collective cab, or hail a cab (even if they had the fare), because drivers had become more selective about who they would serve.

One woman's desperation (or drive) transformed the scene. Suddenly, she emerged from the crowd and imposed her body upon the state of regulation.[3]

She had spotted an opportunity during a split-second when the security guards were distracted, leaving the entryway wide open. Unfazed by her carefully bleached and ironed white outfit, she knelt to the concrete and dashed underneath the slack chain. There was a commotion. From where I stood, I could not see if she made it through safely or not. But those standing behind the barrier seized the moment of audacity that the Black woman in white modeled and leveraged their collective weight in solidarity. The crowd aimed to barge their way into the theater by force. A wall of guards formed behind the now-taut chain.

My friends and I—compressed near the middle of the crowd—were thrown off our center of balance by a tidal wave of force from behind. Falling onto those in front of us, the weight of our bodies added to the collective offensive maneuver. We made eye contact. Their eyes asked what I thought we should do. Without words, I decided that the only way to go was all in with the crowd. My body changed from feeling awkwardly pushed to *pushing* with the singular determination to leverage our collective might. *There were more of us than them. We had to win.* We joined those around us already pressing forward relentlessly, yet seemingly gaining only inches in proximity to the goal. The security guards responded in kind with more intransigence, sweat dripping down their foreheads from sustaining a counterweight to our mass. The guards were tall with bulging muscles, physically primed for the challenge. The longer the security guards delayed entrance, the harder we pushed, and vice versa. It was a rising flood against a dam—bound flow.

The theater manager, a short white man in a polo shirt and a black blazer, descended on the scene barking orders to staff while devising an ad hoc strategy to de-escalate the situation. He demanded sternly for *"order and discipline* or else no one will get in!" Either his words were not heard or the crowd consciously objected to those terms. Or maybe they objected to his state-endowed authority as manager of this public space in which they had assembled. The tension between the us pushing in and the security guards pushing out created an ominous yet exhilarating sensation in my body, as if at any moment a match would light and the whole theater would go up in flames, into beautiful disorder.

Protesting voices from the mass yelling "We have tickets!!! Let us in!!!" were now less a plea to authority than an appeal to each other. This was not so much panic as the deep-seated intensity of claiming what they deserve: a right to enter, a right to occupy the space. In describing the London Riots of 2011, Harney and Moten discuss the response that is already there before the call goes out to riot, Jack Halberstam points out (Halberstam 2013, 7). These rumberos had already been in an ongoing conversation. Their collective coordination of clenched musculature outside the theater was the response before the bodily call demanded its physical enunciation. It was already too late to surrender. They had already claimed space. They were already in motion, in refusal of the social contract to wait their turn for selective possible denial of entrance.

The fact was that everyone had a ticket. The seats were assigned. Yet a seat number on a thin square of paper was flimsy in counterweight to the distrust that accompanied the accumulative effect of uncertain entry into certain spaces in the city's "updating" landscape. As skin pressed against sweaty skin—similar to the smushed contents of a public bus in Havana during rush hour—I drifted into silent meditation on being packed tight in the hold of a slave ship moving with others. This might have been what Harney and Moten describe as the hapticality of the undercommons, "this other kind of feeling (for) each other," that became common in Blackness through the transatlantic slave trade (2013, 98). My weight was suspended by our sweaty Black mass in active struggle going somewhere we could not be sure, but sure we would get there together.

This mode of moving—in a Black mass openly and publicly pushing against a statist conception of authority—was a rarity in the revolutionary Cuban political landscape. After 1959, any collective direct action not mandated by the state was deemed counterrevolutionary and was lumped together with the many ploys funded by "the enemy" to divide "the people" and undermine the revolutionary government. Therefore, non-state-sanctioned public protest was written out as a viable tactic of civil disobedience for Communist Party members, those who identified as socialist, or even simply those who wanted to live in peace on the island. As discussed at length in chapter 1, Black-standpoint politics or Black advocacy groups had long been pegged as counterrevolutionary on principle, as race-based organizations were criminalized after official desegregation. In the eyes of PCC leadership, Black Cubans have largely been looked upon paternalistically as *owing* the Revolution for the free access to education, health care, and so on, that the government afforded. Because of their presumed loyalty as grateful subjects, they have been commonly regarded as Castro's "secret weapon" (de la Fuente 2001b, 66). As far as Fidel Castro was concerned, which he made clear in a legendary encounter with a Black participant in the 1961 Bay of Pigs invasion, Black Cubans should have no good reason to go against the hand that fed them (Benson 2016, 224–26).

The people beside me in struggle that night did not see themselves in those limited terms at all. They were pushing against accumulated racialized indignities: rapid starkening of class stratification limiting their life choices and chances, systematically denied employment in jobs with higher remuneration, without adequate housing to rent out in hard currency, without inherited monetary wealth and convertible resources to start businesses, without family abroad to subsidize the rise in costs of living, and without connections to *dirigentes* (political leaders) or foreign investors to make national development work for them. On this night, the mass of rumberos seemed to push back against the physical manifestation of the many barriers blocking their paths in updating Cuba. Sustaining the pressure, body to body, defended another source of power that entitled them to a kind of dignity that only they could provide to each other. The space created from this collective coordination of physical force was an embodied counterbalance to the rhetoric of socialist perfectibility and progress since 2010 that explained away or overlooked the starkly racialized lived realities and their gendered implications.

A similar frustration with the state's tolerance of tiered citizenship came to a head in 1994, when a protest broke out in Centro Havana, not far from where the Palacio de la Rumba would later be erected. Then and there residents crashed the windows of a dollar store (meaning a store that was stocked with highly coveted products that could only be bought in US dollars). An angry, malnourished crowd of neighbors surrounded the store and asserted their entitlement to its goods to feed their families. Scholars argue that the patterns of suffering that led to the "riot" were a result of institutionalized inequality that caused distinctly differential life chances according to race (de la Fuente and Glasco 1997; Sawyer 2005). The US embargo was certainly designed to economically starve the Cuban people into the kind of misery that would incite a government overthrow. Predictably, the Cuban armed police swept in to quash the melee. Since that event in the 1990s, to my knowledge at that time, there had not been anything that could be considered an organic mass uprising with a distinctly racialized undertone. Thus, I heard the screams outside the Teatro Avenida—"Have a little humanity" and "This isn't the way to treat people"—as part of a larger chorus singing back to a longer history of disappointments, dismissals, and deferrals.

It warrants reflection that this reminiscent kind of exertion of collective Black physical counterforce erupted around a rumba performance. Although not written on picket signs, this collective choreography of unruliness might be gesturing toward a Black politics of deviance that Black popular culture makes possible (Cohen 2004). As political scientist Cathy Cohen implores of Black study, we must look more closely at what is happening in spaces that are ostensibly peripheral to anything that looks like political behavior. Or rather than assuming the label of deviance, thereby centering the state as the arbiter of social order, perhaps the Black woman in white's site-specific improvisation reminded those present of their collective power to transform the terms of their admission, which is the terms of their belonging in that place. In the hold outside the public theater, "another kind of feeling had become common" (Harney and Moten 2013, 98).

9:30 p.m. Exasperated, the manager eventually surrendered to the movement and gave the order to allow entrance. The ushers ripped tickets at a dizzying pace, nervously trying to keep up with the rate of people spilling in. As rumberos flooded the large theater, the energy did not dissipate. Instead, it was channeled through the aisles and up the stairs to the mezzanine level where we found our seats.

Inside but Not of the Theater

9:50 p.m. A tumultuous sea of black and bright colors pulsed above the bolted seats. From my assigned seat in the mezzanine, I could see almost the entire audience and the stage below as if from a bird's-eye view. The audience transformed the rigid, decaying theater setting to one of vibrancy and movement. The show had yet to begin, but the heightened focus usually created by marked-off moments of virtuosic display (a.k.a., cultural performance) was already established. Even with an empty stage, the sight was breathtaking. Any moment now, surely, the show would begin . . .

Finally, someone walked on stage and approached the microphone. It was the manager of the theater again. He made an announcement saying that the performance could not start until *"everyone sits down!"* He took the paternalistic tone of a principal at an assembly on the last day of high school. The official tried to once again bring order and discipline to a people who had already just rehearsed what it felt like to collectively refuse the choices given.

At nearly 10 p.m., roughly one hour after the advertised start time, the musicians finally took the stage. Yoruba Andabo's shows at Cabaret Las Vegas typically began with an *espiritismo* chant and then a rumba classic. However, this time, without any verbal preambles, the musicians began drumming *batá*. I recognized the specific rhythm: *elubanche* for Elegguá, the divinity who opens and closes all paths. I sensed the sharp collective pivot among the audience most readily in the aural register: shifting almost instantly from a cacophony of chatter drowning out the manager's commands to collectively creating a silent space for the talking of the drums. Perhaps they heard it as the sacred call to assembly that it was. In ceremony, *elubanche*, Elegguá's signature prayer, marked the beginning of a conversation with the divine. The rhythm clears an opening in space and time for kin to gather with copresences.

When Yerilú, as akpwón, began signing the chant, and no dancer immediately appeared, a different sense of excitement took over. Elegguá was also known to be the ultimate trickster and so the audience was on high alert. Rather than exhibiting free flow with ambient focus, people began to deliberately search in anticipation of Elegguá's appearance, aiming to outsmart the orisha who catches you by surprise. Those seated stood up to get a better vantage point. Those of us in the balcony sent someone to rush to the front edge to peek and see if indeed there was a dancer advancing from the doors at orchestra level. There was an electric anticipation, or rather, recognition, that Elegguá was imminent. Although Elegguá never arrived that night in the form of a professional dancer, the energy of limitless possibility was incarnate in the audience then, like before. Collectively, anything was possible. *There were more of us than them.*

The *batá* rhythm changed to *ñongo*. Then Lázaro entered from the back at orchestra level. His shoulders were broad and commanding even in the large amphitheater. His chest and arm muscles flexed. He was wearing the signature *mariwo* (raffia palm frond) skirt of Oggun, the warrior orisha of iron and labor, and carried a machete that looked heavy. His eyes were closed, and he was smoking and chomping compulsively on a lighted cigar. Even without vision, he took confident, steady strides down the aisle. He was led by the whispers of Valentín to guide him. Thick smoke from his cigar left a pungent trail in the air, tracing his path.

Valentín and Lázaro choreographed this specific entrance to engage sight, smell, and faith in spiritual agency. During an interview in his tiny studio attic apartment in Belén, Valentín would later elaborate on their choreographic decisions. They wanted to reenact how the divinity comes down to earth in ceremony, mimicking the process of total surrender to spiritual agency that happens to a mount. Their interaction drew from the labor of care that is required of kin in the moment when divinity *se manifiesta* (manifests itself) through the body of their child in spirit possession, and the personhood of a religioso becomes an assemblage with the more-than-human.

"They usually come with their eyes closed. Then they must be opened to see in the human plane," he told me. Always at the optimal moment of anticipation, Valentín positioned himself directly in front of Lázaro and placed his thumbs over the dancer's eyelids. He wiped them slowly for a few long moments before more whispers. Then Valentín slapped Lázaro's shoulders with a brusque whack. With that, his eyes burst open. It was the audience's own embodied experience of performing or witnessing those same gestures in ceremony, which sensitized them to an embodied awareness of the codes being referenced. The strength of that sense-memory created the choreography's performative power.

This particular rendition of Oggun had become a *sello* (signature stamp) of Yoruba Andabo's audacious take on folkloric dance. Depending on the audience's threshold of belief in the kind of personhood possible in that given place and time—a distinction that defines the particular "competence" of a religioso audience—it would be witnessed as either a solo, a duet, or a trio, and thus a call for collective action (Hagedorn 2001, 57–58; Johnson 2011). Yoruba Andabo and their audience together produced a "chronotope of spiritual immanence," making tangible the copresence of the living and the deified (Wirtz 2016, 355). The flexible arrangements in the smaller nightclub venues where the group typically performed facilitated this sacred spatiotemporality. Lázaro and Valentín relied on an audience that could collectively call upon "restored behavior" to co-create this performative encounter between the "not-not" divinity, the body of their child, and the kin entrusted with their mutual care (Schechner 1985). They relied on audience members who would answer the nonverbal call to push back chairs, tables, or any physical obstacle that could impede Lázaro's not-not Oggun's chosen trajectory. They relied on sons of Oggun in the audience to feel it is their duty to approach not-not Oggun with a derecho in hand. As expected, no matter how packed the venue, rumberos made way for Lázaro's not-not Oggun to proceed according to his/their volition. This is exactly what Cuban cultural bureaucracy has historically tried to stave off, instead enlisting concert dance techniques to produce a "chronotope of nostalgia, as always already obsolescent" (Wirtz 2016, 361).

However, Lázaro had *ángel*. An expert in the mimicry of this most personal intimacy with the divine, his not-not Oggun inspired the audience's embodied awareness of more-than-human agency and thereby earned the degree of credibility collectively lent to the constant possibility of divine copresence wherever they be: in a casa-templo and even at the theater.

His eyes bulged defiantly. Although given the power of sight, Lázaro's not-not Oggun made no eye contact with the packed theater of onlookers.

Instead, he looked past the multitude as if they were not there. He was seemingly in the theater but not of it. Lázaro's not-not Oggun then traveled down the aisle aggressively striking his machete against the floor—Pang! Pang!—clearing thick brush that only he could see. Shreds of the raffia skirt, representing *el monte*, a figurative space of wilderness, flew into the air as collateral damage and testament to the strong effort used to wield the metal instrument. With this labor, he slowly cleared a path to the stage, stopping only to slowly and fiercely slice the machete across his tongue without drawing any blood.

Lázaro's not-not Oggun had captured the attention of everyone in the theater without executing a single step in time with the music. His actions were irreverent to the rules of professionalism for folkloric dancers, to start and stop with the music. Lázaro's not-not Oggun performed a resoluteness, a clarity of purpose, that only augmented the audience's belief that divine copresence had been made manifest. The drummers and akpwón's calls were taken as proposals within a conversation, not commands. They were arguments to be responded to if, and when, they were most compelling. The musicians and the audience members beckoned, but could not demand, his attention. Apparently, the dancer was driven by a higher authority, a different sense of duty.

Finally, he stomped up the short staircase and obliged the akpwón with a few of Oggun's signature *ñóñgo* steps center stage, which she had lyrically called. It was as if he wanted to demonstrate that he was indeed listening and, at the same time, make clear his agentive refusal to be a slave to folkloric expectations: to be predictable and capable of exact repetition, to limit his dancing to the raised platform built for that purpose. Lázaro's not-not Oggun walked past the musicians and directly to the short staircase stage right. Descending from the stage, he abandoned its premise altogether or, at least, blurred its boundaries.[4] Once again at eye-level with the audience, weighted stomps propelled him through the aisle with strong forward-moving force in continuous flow. This exemplified the kind of creative choices within the constraints of concert dance, audaciously pushing at the edges of secular respectability expected of professional folkloric dancers, for which Yoruba Andabo had earned respect among its loyal local following. These choices referenced a longer historical genealogy of careful considerations about on what terms, and to what extent, one would conform to the folkloric trope one was assigned. For Yoruba Andabo, more daring choices were executed when they felt safe enough to do so in the spaces created when family dances shoulder to shoulder.

Suddenly, mid-aisle, Lázaro's not-not Oggun started to break into spasmodic movement. The direct continuous flow of motion we saw before became indirect and erratic. His cheeks puffed rapidly, drawing air in and out at a fast pace. His frenzied shifts of weight caused him to teeter beyond his center of gravity. These signs all accumulated as mnemonic devices, to me and the other religiosos, for what Fred Moten has called "the break" (2003), which is the formal resistance to objectification that is the essence of Black performance and Black radicalism. Even if reaching this state of full-bodied co-constitution is what motivates ceremony, it is not uncommon for individuals to try to maintain composure, temper, or even resist this most awesome expression of corporeal intimacy with the divine. As we saw in chapter 4, regarding the skill sets that ritual artists provide to the community during ceremony, a good akpwón must be able to recognize "tells" of this internal spiritual struggle taking place in the body of practitioners and use their expert knowledge of the liturgy to enhance and facilitate the manifestation of divine will. To fulfill the ceremony's function, the practitioner must learn to fully relinquish self-control, which is their attachment to a sense of individual personhood (and personal agency), and allow the divine to dance through them. This lesson in surrender is a duty that cannot be done alone.[5] That is what family is for: to share in the collective labor of ushering the body through this spiritual threshold for the well-being of the community.

His performance certainly registered a break from the conventions of national folkloric dance, and even pushed at the edges of the planned mimesis he and Valentín previously established. This break looked like surrender to a different sense of subjectivity in relation to time and space; it looked like the public demonstration of personhood situated in a divine continuum felt as Black. What looked like unruly abandon to a modern political project of civil subjecthood was a carefully transmitted and coordinated bodily technique in becoming plural, becoming an assemblage, asserting and bearing witness to one's collective more-than-humanness. This proliferation of being requires repeated rehearsal and is the grace of embodied prayer. Those in the audience who had the kinesthetic memory of what it feels like to pray in this way could remember this flash of the spirit in their bodies.[6] That is how a night at the theater can become a fugitive space of the most intimate process of divine assemblage. That is how public space can become yet another refuge for religiosos to dwell with the kin they created.

A low murmur of whispers dispersed through the audience. The degree of intimacy necessary to register the movements made by Lázaro's body as a familiar sight heightened the social and sensual impact of seeing it take place in a nationalized theater by a state-subsidized professional. Seeing the process of possession makes it easier to imagine and thus easier to embody (Hagedorn 2001, 109). The plausibility of spirit possession at the Teatro Avenida conferred by the audience was a collective vote of confidence in the belief that there are always other forces at play, other authorities beyond the state, felt in and through the body. It was also a vote of confidence in Yoruba Andabo's skill and faith, as ritual artists, to usher them collectively through reconstituting the places they found themselves in. In other words, to recognize a break from folkloric conventions in public space was a recognition of the way they themselves break with secular civic personhood wherever they be with kin.

Without waiting for a bow to mark completion (because unlike at typical folkloric performances, clear demarcations between acts were not the goal), Yerilú immediately began singing a call for Yemayá, the divine oceanic mother, to enter. Only then did the house lights finally lower, directing all focus to Jenny, who was entering from the stage's wing wearing an ornate blue dress with a billowing, multi-tiered skirt. To witness her dance in person, for children of that saltwater divinity around the world, was considered a blessing in and of itself. Despite the chairs bolted down in straight rows and the dimming of the house, taking these obvious cues to be seated felt kinesthetically inappropriate. In the smaller venues where they typically performed, the audiences, as "participant-observing publics" (Daniel 2005), stood and danced in common, as in ceremony. Similarly, on this night, everyone remained afoot.

When the *aro*, Yemayá's signature prayer song, commenced, Jenny went, as regulars at their shows could expect, to ceremoniously "salute" the drums. Yet another break from the folkloric script; this was a ritual gesture of respect and acknowledgment to the divinity within the drum that allows for communication with the divine. Her maxim, "*Hay que llevar la emoción del foco al scenario*" (You have to bring the emotion from the focal point to the stage), was put into action and built upon the social fact of Oggun's plausible presence. The *batá* drums Yoruba Andabo performed with on stage were unconsecrated. However, Jenny executed the ceremonial gesture to signal to the audience that her dance should be put in the same interpretive frame as what they vividly remembered.

Like Lázaro, Jenny took pride in her ability to convince the audience to question the source of her choreographic grace. During some downtime at a Yoruba Andabo tech rehearsal, she quizzed me on the decisions she made during her most recent professional gig, to gauge how closely I was paying attention. She bragged, "Someone thought I was mounted and invited my Yemayá to come dance at a ceremony they had coming up! Ha!" For her, this misrecognition, by another religiosa no less, spoke to the rigor of her study of the choreographic repertoire of spiritual immanence while dancing shoulder to shoulder with family in ceremony. From that rigor came *ángel* and warranted the boldness of the salute gesture's framing of her solo.

On stage, Jenny commenced a careful sequence of controlled improvisation in the form of a whirlpool, depicting the ocean's ability to not only give life to her children but also take it away. She began her play of persuasion with the audience-turned-congregation, expertly prolonging the intensity of Yemayá's prayer to orchestrate the most opportune launch of her climactic moment of signature spinning. Jenny had trained me to see how the percussionists followed her lead, rather than the other way around. Deploying carefully timed shifts of weight with her steps, she directed the singer's cues to the drummers, conducting the ensemble's sonic progression. As Jenny expected of me as her student, I was fully engrossed in her movements, imprinting the sense memory of those same steps in my body.

Suddenly, out of the corner of my eye, I noticed a Black woman steadily advance from the orchestra level. She was barefoot. The woman must have kicked off her shoes, a tell that divinity was settling in. Her torso was pulsing as she moved down the aisle toward the steps leading to the stage. Having obeyed Jenny's command to "go to *el foco!*" I recognized why those in her row had made way for the woman to move past them, enter the aisle, and join the assembly, daring not stop her progression. They, too, were playing their role in the dance. Believing is doing (Mason 1994).

The barefoot woman seemed to be drawn toward the stage, en route to salute the drums. As Jenny had trained me to notice, I couldn't help but see that her feet maintained a firm runner's stance in *muelleo*, giving her a steady and supple base that enabled an incremental forward-moving trajectory, even while her upper torso pulsed profusely. Another wave of whispers traveled throughout the theater. It was also in that moment that I noticed the security guard for the first time at the base of the stairs. I immediately felt nervous, unsure what would happen if she tried to advance past him and attempt ascent. The guard did his professional duty to protect the threshold that separated the audience from the stage, the so-called fourth wall Western practices of spectatorship train you to believe in. But she believed no wall, nowhere, could keep her back. The guard methodically put out his arm to block the approaching woman while maintaining an outward gaze. But the woman's convulsing yet sturdy body was not deterred. The guard then took her by the shoulders with both hands, pushed her back, and released her. But the barefoot woman came right back again, torso now throbbing with more force. Everyone in the theater's focus was enthralled in this contest between professional duty to maintain order and what looked like a divine calling to salute the drums. The guard tried to stop her again and failed, again. I looked to Jenny, who was visibly aware of the situation, keeping her eye on the woman to her stage left. The rest of the ensemble on stage stole short glances in that direction as well.

At this point, I reckoned, Geovani, as director, could have made the call to stop the show. However, Jenny's not-not Yemayá was at the helm. She kept on dancing, and so the drummers were obliged to stay in sync with her. The show went on accompanied by what looked like an abundance of sacred potential, on stage and in the aisle. The already blazing atmosphere fed off the energy of the drums fulfilling their ritual role to make divinity manifest for the family. It felt like copresence had been bodied forth, in more than one body, multiplied. To regard Jenny and the barefoot woman as ensembles (or assemblages) of copresence, dancing in counterpoint—pressed up against each other, once again—blurred the boundaries of the nationalized theater's ostensibly secular constitution, ostensibly nationalized ownership, ostensibly linear temporality.

As the prayer reached its rhythmic climax, the not-not Yemayá down below only increased in persistence. The security guard's inability to gain control of a woman much smaller in physical size but wielding a relentlessly driven force created the conditions for further plausibility that she was governed by a higher power. The helplessness of the theater official recalled saltwater's ability to move large matter, with repetition, over time.

With Jenny leading the musicians to the climax of the prayer, only moments away, Lázaro's not-not Oggun dropped his machete and marched down the aisle to swiftly lift the woman in a solid big hug, raising her body completely up off the floor. Her bare feet dangled in the *mariwo* between his legs. Once the woman was suspended, Jenny's not-not Yemayá began to spin and the drummers let loose in rhythmic climax. The pounding vibrations of the drum were visible in the head, neck, and shoulders of the woman, held captive in Lázaro's not-not Oggun's firm embrace. His arms bulged evidencing the strong effort he was using to keep her in his arms. Meanwhile, Jenny's not-not Yemayá led the akpwón and percussionists to play several musical climaxes, accompanying the maelstrom of her rotations across the stage. Taken by the multimodal density of the moment, the audience erupted in deafening cheer.

Jenny's not-not Yemayá expertly absorbed all that energy into her wide, blue, dual-tiered skirt, then incrementally slowed the rotation of its clockwise spin. The drummers mirrored her deceleration to a tee, and so did the not-not Yemayá in the aisle. Until finally the percussionists, Yerilú, all the Yemayás present, came to a complete halt, in perfect unison.

Jenny walked downstage center to the stage's apron and took a bow to thunderous applause. Down below, the barefoot Black woman lay limp, like a sleeping child, in Lázaro's arms. All were dripping in sweat.

Intermission.

Reclaiming the "Afro-Cuban Underworld"

When the house lights came up, Rachel and Malcolm both turned to me with their jaws dropped in shock. "Does this always happen?!" Rachel asked in disbelief. The truth was, I had not witnessed anything quite like this before. However, the scenario of divine agency reordering the social in public space instantiated an all too familiar choreo/geography of fugitivity. While rumberos were pleased to watch performances of their favorite groups in the comfort of air conditioning on a hot night, they also knew it as a kind of enclosure. State-sponsored stagings of rumba as national heritage afford a kind of inclusion that had its limits. Yoruba Andabo and their audience played at the edges of what the norms of folkloric professionalism and decorum could contain.

What may have been described by white colonial elites as a black cloud over the city when cabildos paraded through the streets could be reclaimed as a recognition of the kind of affective force of argument conveyed at the Teatro Avenida: that another sense of order takes place through divine potential residing with/in the body. Cabildo choreography's power to blur lines between personal choice and spiritual will opens space for underworld assembly. Although she was a different woman than the one in white from before, outside the theater, the intensity of this woman's deep-seated determination to answer a higher call of duty brought the two struggles into uncanny conversation for me. These fugitive assemblies—similarly marked by ñáñigos doing as they pleased or by Black women's dashes and leaps and escapes—are what Ortiz neither could nor dared to fully render in his derisive description of the "Afro-Cuban underworld." Neither words of Black pathology nor national patrimony can fully capture the political imagination of such spirited movements of collaboration and mutual recognition. The resonance of such calls to assembly cannot be walled behind the space-time delineated for what a secularist notion of "religion" calls ceremony or what a nationalist notion of Blackness calls folklore.

Five years later, after interpreting for her class for foreigners, Silvia would insist to me that the foundational postures that characterized rumbera moves should not be seen as isolated from the techniques of embodied prayer. "Each cabildo," Silvia remembered of her childhood, "carried out their divinities on a float accompanied by drummers every year." The women of the casa-templo of Divine Charity, for example, carried Ochún. "Each time they passed a house more families joined the procession." For Sylvia, rumba, even if officially categorized as secular, revolved around and spilled out from these fugitive Black choreo/geographies that resignified Palmares, the town and the people. To physically join the moving assembly in the street when called by the drums put everyday, hidden networks of mutual aid and practices of reciprocity on public display. It pronounced the coordinated collective force of family of stone in that place. From this standpoint of divine relation, rumberas' dashes and leaps and escapes model and beckon creative improvisations within constraint. This same argument is echoed in Yesenia Fernández-Selier's analysis of how "the rumba body" is made: "*Rumba* is ingrained in the repertoire of ritual practices that blossomed in the *cabildos*, organizations that allowed African descendants to unite by their ethnic backgrounds. . . . Through these institutions and oral transmission, dancers and musicians learned the codes of the divine" (2012–2013, 89). These divine codes constituted the grammar for an ongoing corporeal conversation about Black life in divine social relation that rumba forms, and that forms rumberos.

The dances of the cabildos call for an inward meditative focus but also collaboration with family; they call for low arms kept close to the body, feet in parallel and hips'-width apart; they call for a low center of gravity for a firm base of support; they call for a readiness for sudden shifts in weight, sensing when to step aside or push in the moment with others. These quotidian social choreographies embodied the grace of powers higher than state authority that already possessed the formerly enslaved before becoming Cuban, for whom they maintain a duty to claim space and make way.

In the days that followed the performance at Teatro Avenida, I tried to talk with some of the members of Yoruba Andabo about their reflections on that evening's performance. The deflections, incriminations, and evasions that ensued keep me from forgetting the various kinds of constraints that make breaching such boundaries of interpretation risky. A drummer immediately got defensive, denying any responsibility for the spirit possession: "But we were playing normally. We weren't doing anything [wrong]." He was aware that the Ministry of Culture could hold the group accountable for goading a spirit to come down "out of place." "But well, the woman got mounted. Her spirit was lifted. And [the orisha] really wouldn't let her go," he admitted. Either unable or unwilling to reconcile the tension, he looked away from me and shrugged.

Ethnomusicologists have documented how folkloric spectacles in Havana in the early revolutionary period were subject to strict surveillance because of their tacit association with ongoing religious practice and Black identity politics (Moore 2006; Hagedorn 2001). Although the prohibition on religious practice was lifted in the early 1990s, the taboo against defaming the metaphorical border between the sacred and the secular is maintained by the Cuban cultural bureaucracy. Kristina Wirtz's more recent research on folkloric spectacle in Oriente province sheds light on the present-day criteria required for state-subsidized folkloric ensembles with regard to "inappropriate" practices of audience engagement. Wirtz recounts a conversation with a choreographer of a well-known professional folklore ensemble in that region. The choreographer relayed how, in the late 1980s, he created a piece that was so popular for its likeness to a *bembé* ceremony that audience members actually treated it as such, "dancing in the aisles and, in some cases, even succumbing to possession trances" (Wirtz 2014, 225). Wirtz shares that "the government then prohibited further performances of this piece because it promoted religion" (2014, 225–26). The ensemble has never reinstated the work.

Valentín vehemently denied that spirit possession was what happened that night at all: "It's art. It's not sacred. . . . That thing about getting mounted, for me, is ridiculous. . . . The drums were *aberíkula* (unconsecrated)." Valentín referenced the ceremonial protocols that designated specific conditions for where, when, and how the spirit may appear. These protocols not only curate efficacious conditions for the divinity to dwell among kin, but ensure the physical safety of and care for their children who are called to perform this essential embodied labor for the community. Valentín was resolute that the proper ritual conditions were *not* in place for such a thing to happen. To feign otherwise is not only ridiculous but disrespectful to one's orisha. For him, at stake should not be Yoruba Andabo's reputation (which he feared was the case), but the reputation of the casa-templo within which that woman should have been properly raised to cultivate necessary discernment around how to properly channel her divinely given capacity.

Jenny refused to be interviewed about the matter altogether. She avoided me for weeks until she could be assured that my interests in meeting lay in my own dance training rather than commentary on the recent event. I would never know if she would have admitted a sense of pride in facilitating the coordination required to move a theater full of people to such an intimate degree. Or maybe she would have explained the happening in terms that put her at a safer distance from the woman who danced along with her down in the aisle. As a foreign researcher whose academic visa was sponsored under the Ministry of Culture, I respect her right to opacity (Glissant 1997), which is rightfully defended in these moments of "ethnographic refusal" (Simpson 2007).

Religious persecution is a lingering trauma for rumberos, not unlike the collective memory of UMAP camps that scare younger generations from stepping out of line (Bastian 2018, 105). Moments such as these remind me of how quickly Geovani's face changed when I once asked about the unique ways in which the group's religious following engaged with the dancers when they perform the orishas. Specifically, I was referencing how they rushed to salute the dancers in ritualistic fashion. He became very serious and paused. His gaze at me became piercing. Then, as if answering from rote, he stated, "The religious part is the religious part, and the stage part is the stage part. The stage doesn't have anything to do with religious life . . . with the religion I practice." On the one hand, I felt chastised for asking a question that, by his look, I should have known not to expect an answer for. On the other hand, Geovani had openly boasted that their shows attracted a religious audience and expressed pride in his ability to keep tickets affordable so that they could attend. This reputation among religiosos rested in no small part on their uncanny ability to "bring the emotion of el foco to the stage." To engage this contradiction would be to take personal responsibility for what audience members were moved to believe was appropriate in those settings.

These evasive shifts in posture, refusals in their own right, sometimes also accompanied shifts in tense. In an interview with Zulema, when I posed the same question, I was struck by her use of the past tense— "Elegguá was . . ."—as if the orisha were a mythic figure of days gone by, as preferred by the cultural bureaucracy (Wirtz 2016, 361). Later in that same sitting, she invited me to a bembé at a neighbor's house taking place that week, where she and her family would be invoking Elegguá to join them (in the present tense) in celebration. Nimble spatiotemporal repositioning, from nostalgia to immanence, was also part of the repertoire of restored behavior that rumberos enacted in the everyday. These discursive maneuvers teetered at the edge of, without relinquishing, their attachment to folkloric professionalism.

It is difficult to parse how much of the reactions to my inquiries about that night at the Teatro Avenida were motivated by pragmatic rather than ideological or theological matters. As discussed in chapter 4, their state salary, guaranteed although undoubtedly insufficient, relied upon the group's reputation under state rubrics of virtue and professionalism, whereas ritual wages, lifesaving but without guarantees, relied upon being in good standing with the elders and divinities who would be indirectly implicated in a ceremonial breach. Perhaps some combination of both, or none of these concerns, motivated Lázaro to hold the barefoot woman tight and keep her from reaching the drums that night. To be sure, the scramble to explain away culpability, or not provide comment at all, highlights the complex convergence of inherited duties that cocreate "the moments of attention that lock a body into a larger frame of reference that matters" (Masco and Thomas 2023, 22). Needless to say, Yoruba Andabo's creative maneuvers within places of constraint captivated the imagination of an audience poised to gather in a way that mattered to them deeply, and urgently. Ironically, the difficulty of locating agency or intentionality was what both protects their creative license and continues to draw their audiences to form rumba within their fold.

Characteristic of the research process as a whole, silences as much as admissions say volumes about the tensions rumberos hold in their bodies from navigating multiple attachments at once. Silvia would never forget the day she returned from college in Havana one year in her early adulthood to pay respect to her great-grandmother on the anniversary of her death, buried in the cabildo of her hometown. She was the first generation in her family to go to college, which created a path for social mobility that she owes to the Revolution. But a revolutionary education did not replace her sense of duty to her family's dead. She put her hand on her chest, remembering the visceral impact of finding that the cabildo had been bulldozed and replaced with a row of houses for "the people." According to the planners carrying out the Revolution's urban reforms, those buildings were not an efficient use of public space. By the same token, prayer was not a productive use of time. The crack in Silvia's voice when she implored the next generation of rumberas to "defend the essence" indexes the scars left by the ancestral indignities committed alongside upliftment. To "defend the essence" inherited from her ancestors through rumba is also to publicly mourn what gets lost in becoming a revered symbol of revolutionary triumph. Maintaining feet hips'-width apart and the pulse in one's chest was not-not about protecting a sacred refuge they restore in and through their bodies. The affordances of the project of the Cuban Revolution and the aspirations of communities that exceed the nation-state, sometimes overlapping, at other times diverging, are both worth defending.

The sensitivity of this memory signals the riskiness of the interpretive territory we are in. It makes me think carefully about whose interests it really serves to get caught up in the quest to pin down a definitive account of agency (or blame) for the actions that ensue where rumba takes place. I consider the logics that motivate such indictments of personal responsibility and pay attention to its strategic disavowal. Saba Mahmood reminds us to glean agentival capacity "not only in those acts that resist norms but also in multiple ways one *inhabits* norms" (Mahmood 2004, 15). Taking such a stance positions us to recognize the risky dance of defending rumba revolution after revolution, reform after reform. Like in the procession from the Temple of Divine Charity carrying Ochún on top of their heads, and even making way for the women pushing *chuchería* carts in escape from the police, rumberos carried themselves with a dignity conferred in collective motion whenever and wherever they be. Performance frames of analysis offer an opportunity to loosen our own attachment to logocentric regimes of knowing that condition how agency is calibrated and instead permit us to glean consciousness from the kinesthetic on equal footing with the utterances of choice words. The way cabildo choreographies body forth the agency of copresences is best appreciated through this political-sensual-spiritual interpretive posture.[7]

Brujería (witchcraft) was the discourse of atavistic danger once used to mediate white elites' own fear of Black people collectively driven to move in more-than-civil social relation. Much later a rubric of centralization and efficiency justified labeling folkloric excess as waste. I can't help but think back to the perceived monotony of a cabildo dancing and the perceived ease with which Black women especially were thought to, in Ortiz's Afro-Cuban underworld, abandon themselves in dance. The restored behavior the not-not possessed beckon for collective rehearsal looks like excess if one's spatial gauge is centrist and looks like monotony if one's temporal gauge is linear, in the same way cabildo choreographies signal abandonment if one's sense of loyalty is focused on sovereignty as defined by patriarchy, national-ism as defined by the state, and agency as defined by possessive individu-alism, alone. The grace of a torso, maintaining a steady pulse over a lowered center of gravity, barefoot in the aisle, makes boldly apparent what had to become folklore for a particular kind of Cuban polity to be born. At the Teatro Avenida we are invited to remember a choreo/geography of fugitivity. Here, rather than summon the idea of flight or escape, we might consider the kind of assembly that makes such abundant personhood plausible as its own kind of refusal.

Call Her Bruja

What or, rather, where was at risk in letting that Black woman not-not possessed reach the drums? What does a crowd rallied around and rooting for a Black woman not-not possessed risk, and where do they make pos-sible? That is to wonder, what kinds of belonging become imaginable and collective action justified in prayer? That is to want to know, what kinds of rights are being articulated, claimed, and defended in rumba?

Sylvia Wynter attributes the power laden in Black popular music to the displacement of "the techniques of possession" from the plantation cosmos to the aesthetic domain, where it continues to make "the ultimate revolu-tionary demand, the demand for happiness/fulfillment now" (1977, 46). In her talk, "'We Know Where We Are From': The Politics of Black Culture from Myal to Marley," she cites Afro-Caribbean diasporic religions as opening up "the path to a parallel experience of freedom which one *knows* because one *partakes* in it—the aesthetic experience makes known a freedom articulated by a popular tradition, which transcends and goes beyond the telos of the liberation of the productive forces, a telos conceptualized *as* freedom within both the Liberal democratic capitalist and the Marxist-statist paradigms of production" (48). Her poignant words carry a particularly weighted affec-tive charge when thought in relation to the specific conceptualizations of freedom afforded Black life throughout Cuban nation-building. What if that night at the Teatro Avenida was remembered as such a space of know-ing and partaking in that ultimate revolutionary demand?

The Black corporeal undercommons I theorize underscores that Wyn-ter's "where" is mapped in movement. The struggle for words to describe it and agency to account for it is indicative of the frameworks such embod-ied techniques unsettle. As Yolanda Covington-Ward (2015) illustrates so instructively in the Lower Congo, micro-interactions of the body, uttered in the gestures of everyday cultural performance, constitute subjectivity, shape belonging, and are vitally important in framing and staking political claims that address themselves to and beyond state authority (3). Indeed, at the Teatro Avenida, gesture, *the corporeal*, was the register through which the limits of the civil were breached, through which the enclosures of Havana's updates were temporarily suspended. What would it mean to concede that the gestures that make the formerly enslaved most recognizable to each other are what make them accountable to the dead, are what make us crazy, dangerous, *brujos*, out of place? Just like the pushing against the guard outside the theater, the pushing against the guard inside can be felt as the ultimate revolutionary demand that cabildo dances enact.

Rumba calls us to feel, which is to know, which is to partake in the audacity of a collective shift of weight. To do so asserts a freedom that comes when unafraid of scraping one's knees to abscond the chains, which exudes the confidence of knowing the company you are in. In such a way, rumba calls us to move together, in but not of public space, and remember what it feels like to feel (for) each other. Which is to say, rumba emboldens physical resistance against the techniques of management deputized to regulate Black aesthetic experience. However, given that virtuosity in this choreo/geography does not solely belong to the individual as agent, words like *resistance* take me farther from what I believe rumba has to offer, and farthest from what its underworld assembly has the power to defend.

Incidentally, that night at the theater may have equally appeared out of step with the broader movement for Black lives taking place at that time around the globe. In the 2010s, instead of videos clips of street protest coming from Havana, we were more likely to see still images of Black people dancing as if frozen in time, smiling against a backdrop of deteriorating buildings rendered quaint, signaling the simpler joys of long-gone days, feeding tourists' taste for revolutionary nostalgia and hot flesh. One might conclude that Black Cubans either dance to forget their hardship and poverty, or dance because they know no hardship at all.[8] It would seem that Black people in Cuba were caught up in the past or caught up in revolutionary promise and thus immune to the contagion of diasporic rebellion sweeping the hemisphere. The folkloric narratives of the Black *bruja*, the *guapo ñáñigo*, and the mulata rumbera aid in naturalizing these easy-to-think explanations for what it means when Black people dance in the streets, crowding out the sense of/for other assemblages and their attendant reformulations of personhood, space, time, solidarity, and order. They close off rumba from the spirited call one has to partake in to know. It is the kind of formation that defends a set of social relations that the nation, however perfectible, can never make obsolete.

A Black performance studies lens brings forth the barefoot woman in a grounded stance, pulsing from her torso, yet relentlessly forward moving, as a critical intervention to easy-to-think narratives about what moves Black people to dance, where, and when, and how we might partake in forms of fugitive, diasporic relation. Just as at the theater, I invite us to appreciate how the choreographic device of counterpoint—when one or more groups execute different sequenced movements in different places on stage simultaneously, to constitute a single unit in the space-time of the performance—brings into view a third space of diasporic potentiality that we might always already occupy.

This positions us to expand the analytical frame beyond Cuba, so we can apprehend the force of choreo/geographic counterpoint among the bodily techniques of insurgent Black collectivity in places as far and near as Baltimore, Rio de Janeiro, New York, and Cauca (Bowen et al. 2017). While occupying distinct sociohistorical contexts, choreo/geographic counterpoint allows for a conversation that can appreciate the synchrony of movements against Black dehumanization that transcends nation-state boundaries. Looking away from placards and instead attending to the corporeal—the shapes, patterns, techniques, and effort qualities that link the behaviors restored when enacting a contestatory racial politics of space—we are open to consider Havana alongside these other Black social movements in a deeper, hemispheric, political-sensual-spiritual relation. Such relational agentival capacities make themselves felt somewhere around the yearning to embody the swagger of Abakuá gestural speech, as they do in the timely deployment of Ochún's affectation, as they do in the diasporic exaltations of the names of the dead who cannot rest. In collective motion, in synchrony, Black people across the hemisphere asserted accountability to and claimed a legitimacy higher than legality. And in so doing, they rehearsed bodily techniques of collective counterweight against the guards of state power.

During this same period, members of a newly formed anti-racist network in Havana, La Articulación Regional Afrodescendiente de América Latina y el Caribe, Capítulo Cubano (ARAAC Cuba), bet on the benefits of not taking to the streets. Founded in concert with Black civic formations across the Latin American region, ARAAC Cuba debated and ultimately decided against mass public demonstration as a viable strategy to achieve their goal of raising awareness about the impunity of the reform's anti-Black effects.

They thought their cause in Cuba could not withstand the suspicion of counterrevolutionary activity that inevitably overshadows independently organized mass mobilization post-1959.[9] While far from staying silent on the sidelines, unlike the rumberos at the Teatro Avenida, they opted to maintain their physical composure.

But in updating Havana, the organizational capacity it takes to defend the pathway taken by the not-not possessed did not get you labeled the kind of deviant that reads as counterrevolutionary. Perhaps these unruly demonstrations are less easy to gauge because they inhabit a kind of politics that cannot—and should not—be mapped onto the available ideological (pro- or counterrevolutionary) coordinates. Perhaps they will stay protected because they are dancing. That is to say, the Black corporeal undercommons should deepen our curiosity about the relationship between embodied Black vernaculars of political praxis within and beyond the contemporary Cuban context.

Rather than ask what rumberos can tell us about the limits of the cultural politics endorsed by the state, the Black corporeal undercommons brings attention to the unique relationship between the sacred, gender, agency, and the body, productively unsettling conventional masculinist modes of political resistance through which Black activism is typically recognized. Building on the work of Katherine McKittrick (2006), Aisha Finch (2015) contends that masculinist oppositional political cultures lean on the state's valorization of the colonial rubric for what was considered an assault on white power and control. Finch offers a way to rethink slave rebellion in Cuba that speaks to the rereading of Black radical praxis we might need: "A Black feminist reading practice defines Black insurgency, at its core, as a challenge to white patriarchal control of the affective gauge, as much as confrontation against racial violence" (2015, 115). Remembering the improvisations of everyday Black women outside/in the Teatro Avenida as choreo/geography challenges us to look beyond conventional markers of political behavior in the public sphere modeled after roles and postures traditionally assigned to men (Cohen, Jones, and Tronto 1997). A Black feminist reading practice allows dancing in common at the theater, in a courtyard, on the streets, in the club, and in the living room with the furniture pushed back, encircled by the kin we create, to figure as its own mode of Black insurgency, not so much in resistance to the state but deep in prayer.

Admittedly, the Black feminist in me willfully lingers in the kinds of intimacies shared in these assemblies among femmes and through the feminine, what Saidiya Hartman has called "the everyday anarchy of ordinary colored girls," their beautiful embodied experiments (2019, xiv). In studying Black girls' intimate histories of social upheaval at the beginning of the twentieth century, Hartman (2019) turns to the language of improvisation. She defines improvisation as "the aesthetic possibilities that resided in the unforeseen collaboration in the place of enclosure, the secondary rhythms of social life capable of creating an opening where there was none—exceeded the interpretive grid of the state authorities and the journalists" (284). Echoing Cox's hermeneutics of social choreography, these dance vocabularies describe "beautiful experiments" that emerge from "cramped creation." "Not the master's tools, but the ex-slave's fugitive gestures, her traveling shoes" (Hartman 2019, 227). Fugitive gestures on the move—"embodied meaning making, physical storytelling, affective physicality"—take us places (Cox 2015, 28). Rumberas have a way of reminding us that there are always other openings, other focal points to orient our affective gauge and that order our steps. Their gestures provide the signposts for the political space that this book's treatment of rumba seeks to make thinkable. Such gestures may reinforce prevailing notions of Black people as always already unfit for development. At the same time, if Blackness, like socialism, is already cramped by its rendering as pathological under a geopolitical order gauged to whiteness and global capital, we have no choice but to improvise and create openings for movements that exceed the grid. This overturning of the ideological and affective scaffolding of modernity —"a cultural logic that prescribes and regulates national feelings" (Muñoz 2006, 680)— is perhaps the very work that popular dance is best suited to do.

What would it mean if, as Harney and Moten challenge Black study, we started from the premise that "there is *nothing wrong with us* (precisely insofar as there is something wrong, something off, something ungovernably, fugitively living in us that is constantly taken for the pathogen it instantiates)" (2013, 50)? How might that have changed the way that evening could be remembered aloud? What would it mean if we always started from the premise that *there is more of us than them* because *there is always more than us to us*? But then again, if performative acts are political acts of agency "spoken with the whole body" (Merlene Nurbese Philip cited in McKittrick 2006, xxvii), for whose sake would such verbal admissions to an anthropologist serve?

This proposition tempers my regret about never getting a chance to speak with the two Black women who refused the options given, whose dashes, leaps, and escapes beckoned our company that evening. The rumbera in white and the barefoot one who refused to be still: both were moved to quite literally push against the power of state proxies that guard the thresholds of civility. One Black woman dressed in the color of ceremony, the other ritually undressed, both possessed. These are the same lascivious, feverish *brujas* that Ortiz (and Marx, if he had considered the Black female subject) warned us about, whose site-specific improvisations force us to reckon with an underworldly set of relations that won't let go.

In this way, I join Cox's call for greater attunement to radical readings of Black women's movement within constraint, for it "can disrupt and discredit normative reading practices that assess young Black women's bodies as undesirable, dangerous, captive, or out of place" (Cox 2015, 28–29). Rather than look to the macho cultural broker, the elected official in a suit, the beard in a green uniform, the soapbox and bullhorn, this Black feminist attunement to movement calls us to remember the radical imagination formed from a sense of shared fate with the more-than-human. Black women's social choreographies have a way of letting us know when we have arrived (to where they may have always already been under the surface of things). State policing of collective prayers for alternative worlds deemed pathological, profane, deviant, or just excessive reveals the constrained terms of citizenship in which we must improvise daily. When Black women improvise ways to repurpose their bodies, the very site of their subjection, they reveal other choices that we all can choose to follow, or at least defend.

Even as I lift up the fugitivity of the moves called forth by Black women in Havana, techniques of possession teach how virtuosity does not belong to any one individual or gender or place or time. These fugitive choreographies, coordinated around rumba, among everyday Black people dancing, uncannily recall the power and poetics of water. Water's gendering in Yemayá signifies how power relations are never stable, but rather constantly in circulation (Otero and Falola 2013). Yemayá's *aro* prayer mobilizes waves of kin against the current. In this embodied prayer, they are the whirlpool slowly surfacing from the depths. Parting ways for Black women running down the boulevard into the night, wading in lines, diving underneath chains, leveraging collective momentum in waves, pulsing above bolted seats in rhythm, steadily lapping barefoot down an aisle, and standing together, they form other spaces for being in relation. Listening for the call in each other, they remember Yemayá's capacity to take the lives she once gave, demanding her children of the transatlantic, and all those who yearn to feel the power of her intimate and ultimate embrace, to come forward. Her waves relentlessly erode at the contours of occupied lands.

Crowded masses making way for spirited children of stone on the move, if we allow their assembly, pronounce the precarity of the patriarchal state as the supreme and rightful arbiter of social order and the limits of citizenship as the ultimate container for where we are from. These spirited assemblies, I contend, might be akin to Black feminism's shrug to the project of a particular kind of legibility under party politics. At the same time, they teach us that spirited moves in public space are never not not-not political. They compel the collective recognition of a deeply felt belief that the more-than-human bear on the everyday struggles and circumstances of those who became citizens. I imagine these movements as the threshold to a deeper conversation between the spiritual descendants of the fugitive, free, and enslaved, simmering underneath the surface of things, about Black life alongside and beyond the prospects of nation-building. The alternative spaces devised during slavery for knowing how to do this continue to be a problem for state power modeled on white, patriarchal, capitalist domination.

Cabildo choreo/geographies rehearse the coordination required for improvising new kinds of subjectivities in the places we make home in the wake of slavery. Those listening for the call will recognize that such fugitive assemblies position us to refuse the limited options given for collective dignity. Like the dark cloud, the *ambiente* that colonial elites feared, Black women who "knew about different possibilities of social order-ing" not subject to patriarchal authority must always look like *brujas* (I. Perry 2018, 28–29). Hence, they will always need to be jettisoned out of time, culprits of bad timing, out of step with progress. No wonder a rumbera possessed looks like wild abandon. The choreography she embodies is a call to disorder nations.

CONCLUSION

I was scheduled to fly back to the United States early the next morning, so I chose to calmly, yet persistently, wait for a chance to speak with Caridad "Cary" Diez. Diez was the principal musicologist responsible for putting together the file about "Cuban rumba" for its inscription as "intangible cultural heritage" by UNESCO, a title awarded in 2016. It was around midnight on November 11, the last night of the 2018 Rumbazo festival, when I was finally able to get fifteen minutes of her, albeit divided, attention. As the main local organizer and producer of the festival, she was constantly being pulled away in different directions. When she returned to me, each time, I needed to remind her of where we were in the conversation. I could tell that I was being an inconvenience. But she resumed where she left off with poise. If not for Ned Sublette, the US coproducer, putting in a good word for me by praising my stepping in as impromptu interpreter for the other foreign festival participants, I might not have had a chance at all. The constant interruptions to our discussion were almost dizzying, but she spoke calmly and clearly to everyone with respect. Social cues clearly indicated that this was a bad time to talk. But it was my last and only chance to speak with the person who played such a key role in securing rumba's place within the auspices of the state's institutional apparatus.

Diez explained that she saw the UNESCO nomination for rumba as a strategic mechanism to pressure the Cuban state to maintain a degree of responsibility for the welfare of current and future rumberos. Well-established groups, considered *históricos* for their longevity, like Yoruba Andabo, were granted subsidized status in the 1980s and have retained it. Setting aside the debates among the members around whether subsidized status was more a help than a hindrance to making ends meet, the fact was that this status was no longer being extended to newer groups who upheld the tradition in their neighborhoods. The Ministry of Culture was responding to pressure to trim its budget and pursue a more self-sustaining funding

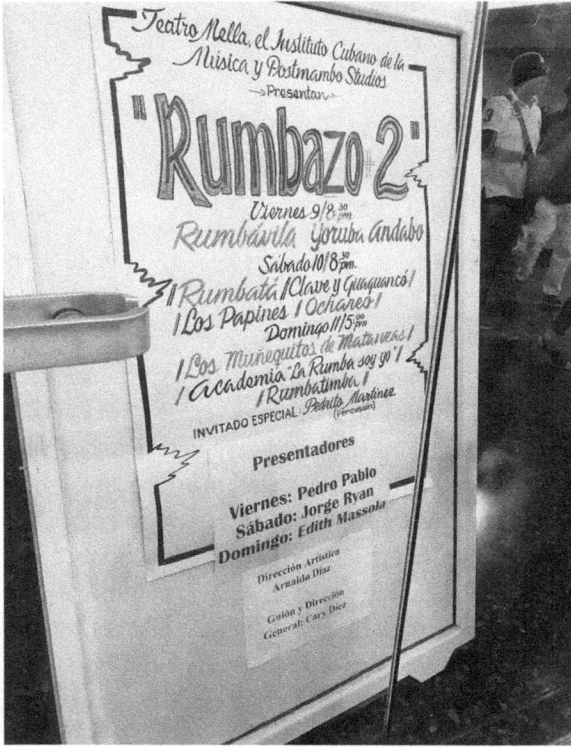

C.1 Poster for Rumbazo #2 performance at Teatro Mella. Photo by author.

model, as were other state institutions more broadly (M. D. Perry 2016). Diez maintained that the state's obligation to subsidize historic groups should never be rescinded and the new groups deserved to be supported by the state as *portadores* (culture carriers), too. International recognition of rumberos for being *portadores* of a valued element of world heritage, Diez believed, could bring needed appreciation that would translate into allocation of material resources to help its practitioners weather the current period of economic change.

Diez had worked tirelessly on the UNESCO file for seven years as the lead expert on the Comisión Nacional de Salvaguardia del Patrimonio Cultural (National Commission of Safeguards of Cultural Heritage). She relied on her strong relationships with rumba networks as a scholar and producer to conduct the research necessary for rumba to meet the stipulated standards of "intangible heritage." It was a community-based effort, she insisted, and required the participation, cooperation, and coordination of many rumba groups. To make the application appeal to the international body, she had to follow specific guidelines that required several layers of translation. This was no easy feat. "Lots of things are lost, others are diluted," she admitted. Beyond the more obvious challenge of conveying the totality of rumba's sensorial content (in terms of dance, music, song, craftsmanship, and popular participation) through the written word, the file could only be submitted in French or English. Everything she wrote had to be translated, edited again to fit the word-count limit, and somehow still capture the meaning.

However, she continued, the most difficult part was "translating all of the spirituality the *portadores* are capable of generating, the history they transmit, and the force of their expression. . . . How do you condense all of that spirituality and the complexity of perspective in a few words, words that will be translated yet again?" I was immediately struck by the way she marked the critical importance of faith in the context of a genre that, historically, the Ministry of Culture had recognized on the basis that the form (and the people) would become secularized, become folklore.

I probed more about the research process itself, particularly how and if it was complicated by the fact that she was an outsider, and a *mestiza* middle-class woman, in a very Black, working-class, male-dominated community. She nodded in agreement with my provocation. She attributed her success in overcoming those barriers to her training as a "disciple" of Argeliers León (introduced in chapter 1), the head musicologist in charge of the ethnographic research that would establish the CFN and a student of Fernando Ortiz. She said that León taught her to always show respect when you arrive in a community, because only through humility will they open up to you, "little by little, earning trust this way." I couldn't help but recall to myself what León did with that trust in the early years of the Revolution. Back when the state officially adopted an atheist position, León advocated using ethnography to carry out "revolutionary indoctrination." Tracing her intellectual lineage proudly to León situated her within a political orientation that believed in an emancipatory vision of state socialism that the 1959 Cuban Revolution still represents for many.

She paused for a moment and studied me intently before adding, "And the fact that I entered into the religious world that the majority of them belong to helped a lot, too. That opened many more doors to my understanding." I was intrigued by her reveal of this other genealogy to which she also traced her orientation to the work, a religious one that during León's time with the CFN would have been terms for exclusion from membership to the Cuban Communist Party. Perhaps she had noticed the *ide* on my left wrist, a marker of my own spiritual affiliation that my godmother had once instructed me to always wear while doing fieldwork. "Because practically everyone who does it is religious. And in it [rumba] is where lots of different kinds of religiosity interlock. This interlocking," she said as she locked the fingers of both hands together, "is the spirituality of rumba."

This late-night exchange touches on at least a few of the points I have raised in this book. First, it brings into focus the external pressures to render rumba legible in particular ways to particular audiences in particular moments. While the institutionalization of Afro-Cuban studies may have overdetermined the terms upon which rumberos can be understood, rumberos have actively seized its platform to create opportunities for themselves at every historic juncture. This makes it hard to pin down an absolute definition of the cultural form because it does not exist in a vacuum. Like the culture concept itself, as Trouillot teaches, rumba is always situated within a history of power and therefore cannot be taken as "disembodied truth" (2003, 99). When advantageous to do so, rumberos readily adopt the terms intelligible within standardized, hegemonic regimes of knowing. While I've argued for a loosened grip on rumba as a national symbol, many rumberos still see good reason to preserve the social pact that comes with state affiliation under socialism. Still, standardized rubrics of ethno-national heritage, historically underwritten by anthropological methods, may have worthy exchange value at the state and international level, but they are limited in their ability to fully represent what the form means to or does for its practitioners.

This connects to a second point that has been foregrounded in the ethnography, the waning of the Cuban state's investment in the livelihood of rumberos as it recalculates how to chart a viable path for Cuban socialism going forward. This reflects a larger process of redirecting state resources away from sectors where poor people's labor has historically been compensated under the logic that they should now compete in the labor market. Thus, foreign backing becomes necessary to make the case for rumba as a national asset worthy of continued prioritization. If we pay close attention to it, the choreo/geography of rumba dances in the gap where the state no longer claims it can or should provide for its citizens post-Fidel. This is a challenge to the facile narratives of post-1959 racial harmony and Black upliftment that rumberos are often called upon to evince. The rumberos in this book represent the organizational capacity of mutual aid among the Black working class articulated in their everyday confrontation with the limits of the "more perfect" version of Cuban Socialism, itself a response to the constraints of elaborating such a vision under the pressures of US imperialism.

Third, it highlights the critical role of sacred filiation for entering the space of social relation that rumberos form. Diez intimated that rumberos inhabited a social world that interlocked members across difference and that was closed off to those who did not ascribe to its sacred epistemology. I have shown that those differences also pertain to gender, generation, and passport privilege. They maintain a threshold, a boundary, that when you get close enough you realize only kin can pass. To be initiated as kin is to be granted a kind of access that comes hand in hand with rights and responsibilities, ties that bind you to webs of care and accountability. The strategic benefit of bringing state institutionality into those webs has its limits and is therefore carefully and constantly renegotiated over time.

Finally, I am called to reflect upon how my own writing will, too, fall short in conveying the complexity of spirituality, history, and politics that can be known through rumba. Most acute to my senses was the embodied motion across concept-metaphors and across markets, through strivings and tensions, and along gendered lines of difference that they proudly rehearse and remake as their own. I have only dared interpret as far and as much as my relationship to others, both human and more-than-human, permit understanding at this time. For every aspect focused on and emphasized in these pages there are others that are lost and diluted. Nevertheless, I share my partial perspective in hopes that my situated knowledge, in the words of Donna Haraway (1988), will appeal to the audience it is intended to address: Cubanists and Caribbeanists, of course; those dedicated to Black popular culture, performance, and embodied practice more broadly, certainly. But especially those across disciplines and sites of colonial geopolitical demarcation who, too, seek to learn from and defend the radical imagination of she who will never be cited in the genealogy of Black radicalism because she never wrote it down in a manifesto, printed it on a placard, or articulated it in an interview, because maybe she was busy dancing. I trust that as long as the clave carries on, others will continue the conversation.

Throughout this book, I demonstrate what is yielded analytically from studying rumba with an embodied Black feminist (political-sensual-spiritual) interpretive posture. This positioned me to look back critically at the official narrative of racial uplift and inclusion that rumba represents on a different footing in order to more clearly situate key unfulfilled desires that rumberas and rumberos sought as the Cuban state updated its socialist model for the twenty-first century. This engagement with rumba as both an embodied practice and an epistemology required me to take a long view of Black political dispossession and imagination in Cuba. In the process, I clarified the enduring stakes of Yvonne Daniel's prior assertion—that rumberos deserve a looser hermeneutical hold than official discourses permit—and even went a step farther to show how it is that rumberas and rumberos themselves have never stopped creating and defending the wiggle room they need to move with dignity. As seen in the moments I've recalled at El Teatro Avenida, El Cabaret Las Vegas, El Palacio de la Rumba, El Callejón de Hamel, in *solares*, dirt clearings, and living rooms, and more, rumba marks other kinds of belongings, other aptitudes of analysis, other rubrics of morality, other designs of development, other forms of public assembly. As such, rumba points the way to a repertoire of constrained improvisations that may "condition other choices and other politics" (Allen 2011, 193).

I insist that the commonly accepted premise upon which the rumba dance-music genre has been granted pride of place throughout the history of Cuban national development politics—that it was never sacred to begin with—reduces the dances of the cabildos to their colonial misrecognition and precludes an appreciation for how and why practitioners continue to form and are formed by rumba. Most urgently, it obscures the difference sacred belonging has made for the life chances and choices of a meaningful sector of the Black poor during Cuba's most recent era of economic change. The significance of these spirited maneuvers sheds light on the state's crisis of legitimacy post-Fidel in terms that are perhaps not as easy or comfortable to think.

Despite Raúl Castro's concerted effort to present the reforms as a continuation of the revolutionary project spearheaded by Fidel, the PCC's vision of twenty-first-century socialism and what I call its New Man 2.0 has left much to be desired by its most marginalized citizenry. The specificity of the neo-imperial context in which the Cuban state has had to elaborate its project for more robust independence cannot be ignored or understated. However, to better understand the kind of subject formed by rumba is to know why the recalibration of the PCC's guidelines toward private market expansion did not necessarily lead this sector of the Black peso-poor to despair. They were never only looking to just the state or the private sector to define the full extent of their possibilities for well-being to begin with. Instead, they took refuge in the rights conferred on them as legitimate heirs to families of stone.

As all Cubans "adjust to the adjustments" (Bastian 2018) in the political economy of the Revolution, this community of practice, organized around casa-templos, unsettles dominant understandings of "the household" (defined as a biological nuclear family unit that pools resources) in studies of the Cuban economy and personhood (defined as autonomous, property-bearing citizen-subject) in the social sciences. Families of stone offered an agentive means for those without the normalized inheritances of whiteness to claim resources they cannot be dispossessed of. In short, *fé* ensured Black families a lifesaving birthright they give to each other. Secularized master narratives of Black popular culture obscure how Africans and people of African descent formed affirming identities and bonds during slavery that have enabled them to create other chances and choices than the ones given. Rumba reminds us that descendants of the enslaved have never stopped negotiating their own belonging to and defense of communities that exceed the bounds of the liberal, statist political project, revolution after revolution, reform after reform. Putting those formed by rumba at the center, and their differently gendered processes of cramped creation, allows us to appreciate the salience of Black sociality and the dimensionality of dignified life that this racialized sector of the peso-poor feel a duty to defend post-Fidel.

As Zulema attested, there are things you have to feel to know. Those who yearn for a call to a more robust and nuanced discussion about Black life and revolution may come closer to knowing an epistemology, a feminist praxis, a mapping device, a means of labor, and a mode of assembly that do not show up on maps that retrace the dominant terms of political debate about Cuba-US relations. Instead, they may glean a contestatory racial politics of space rehearsed in the cabildos during slavery, inspiring my conceptualization of a Black corporeal undercommons. To defend rumba, then, might be better understood as the defense of a Black sense of place, to borrow McKittrick's (2011) phrasing, mapped in movement. This movement draws from a fugitive, urban maroon repertoire for reshaping the figurative and literal enclosures Black people occupy. The kinesthetics of rumba makes knowable the contours of power in Black spatialities that might otherwise remain hidden (Jazeel 2014, 90). It is from this grounding that they collectively assessed and addressed the systemic constraints otherwise called development and otherwise praised as progress or *perfeccionamiento*.

We see that embodied practice is a uniquely expressive and discreet strategy for articulating and challenging particular assessments of the past, solutions for the present, and visions for the future that might otherwise be mistaken for protest if they weren't done in prayer. The affective force, not to mention grassroots organizational capacity, of religious duty has much to do with the challenges confronting Black communities who have reached the limits of prescribed modes of respectable political address determined by party politics. This spirit-based politics should not be mistaken for an indictment of socialism, much less Cuban sovereignty. To do so would be to miss how it speaks to the diminishing gains of secularism in a weakened welfare state, as well as the relevance of the political imaginaries forged in slavery that shrug the logics of perfectibility under coloniality. This ethnography seeks to honor the everyday choreo/geography of collaborative actions Black body-politics in Cuba and beyond make possible and warranted to collectively save themselves.

Other anthropologists of the Caribbean have studied how the popular practices of "the folk" are taken up as tools for political mobilization on a national scale. People take up and repurpose those formulations in their everyday lives to advance their own economic and political ambitions in ways that are neither simply imitative nor oppositional (Thomas 2004, 231). Similar to Thomas's estimation of Jamaican popular culture's move to modern Blackness, the Black corporeal undercommons is born from local negotiations with global processes, and its political meanings are neither univocal nor univalent. It is an embodied conversation rife with internal debate, suspicions, frustrations, and tensions. Nevertheless, it is imbued with the spirited potential to alter working-class Black people's sense of socioeconomic possibilities. Whether or not this collective potential is adequate for delivering practitioners from the dismal effects of economic reform under the hostile conditions of global capitalism, it is significant in that it marks a decline in the public power of institutionalized definitions of Blackness and in the state as the legitimate arbiter of well-being and belonging. That this is the case might engender something other than dismay. Instead, rumberos in Havana insist, it is worth defending.

This is why it is important to, thinking with Trouillot and Bonilla (Bonilla 2013) about Haiti and the Caribbean more broadly, "resist the temptation to traffic in the odd" or the exceptional when imagining the Cuban context. This is not to diminish the historical and political significance of its Revolution for the world, but as a way of relinquishing its purpose in modern thought, which is to fill a kind of "savage slot" (Bonilla 2013, 153), guapo in its defiance. Instead, rumba encourages us to shift our gaze and rethink the state-centered moral geography that may obscure bottom-up understandings of Black life more broadly. Rumberos join with other Caribbean kin to teach us about other models of liberatory imagination that take us outside the frameworks that privilege nationalism and other Western understandings of the human, possessive individualism, and communitarian belonging, produc-

C.2 Zulema Pedroso dancing Ochún, Yoruba Andabo performance at Piano Bar Delirio Habanero. Photo by author.

tively blurring the domains of spirituality, politics, and being (Thomas 2022, 236). To attend to the ruptures of common sense that rumba offers is to appreciate the lens it provides to see a much broader Black political imaginary, one that is much broader than party politics, and poised for diasporic dialogue. If that which is formed through rumba is most acutely felt when moving shoulder to shoulder with family, blood, and stone, then it articulates an ephemeral, performative, and affective space mapped through relationships built across space and time (Thomas 2022, 238). I contend that rumba forms an analytical space to collectively feel and contemplate the full-bodied pursuit of the kinds of aspirations that Black people have not been readily afforded under designs for national development in the Americas. As theorized by Silvia, rumba is an ongoing forum for conversation about Black life in the wake of slavery. For the descendants of the enslaved in the Americas, having this conversation in plain sight has always been a risky dance. Notably, the African diaspora's dead actively guide and keep this conversation in motion.

Defending Rumba in Havana rehearses what a critical Black feminist study of Black popular dance can contribute to social theory and political thought, and not just in Cuba. Each chapter creates a clearing to think with the taken-for-granted gendered dynamics that bind spiritual, economic, and political life. They remind us how people dancing make demands and legitimize actions through the means, the scripts, and the repertoires available to them. Just as others have explained the co-constitutive relationship between race and class, the social meanings of gender are often reproduced through spiritual subjectivities, rights, and obligations. Havana is a unique site from which to observe how collective racial affiliations and recognitions are embodied in gendered ways and why Black collectivities lean in to the historical memory of gendered scripts. However, the way gendered ideologies are taken up as faithful tools to navigate macroeconomic change and racial hierarchy might look familiar for a reason. Clear to me was that a colonial heteronormative gaze structures the field of vision within which rumba's Blackness is produced, and rumberas and rumberos are strategically dancing with it while finding a way to keep dancing together. This ethnography dwells in the complexity of the appeal of gendered affirmations of personhood as a persuasive exercise of power at specific historical junctures and in particular social situations.

Turning a mirror back on the discipline of anthropology, from which Afro-Cuban studies emerged, I've highlighted the politics of maintaining easy-to-think narratives about Black people dancing in the wake of slavery, in the wake of revolution, in the wake of reform. This is why rumba, and Black popular dance more broadly, echoing Haitian-American anthropologist Gina Athena Ulysse (2015), needs new narratives. Much like the rumberas I learned from, Ulysse models how the dignity we yearn for as Black women while navigating our professional paths cannot be given. It is only endowed to us through a practice of attunement with spiritual imperatives. On the stages we are positioned to perform, whether in the academy or in the street, we can't afford to refrain from being accountable to the calls we are poised to answer from our locations as artists, as daughters and granddaughters of the Caribbean, as descendants of the enslaved. May we feel a collective sense of duty to always respond by calling attention to the naturalized circulation of limiting racialized gender scripts and the reproduction of heteropatriarchal hierarchies, both outside and within the spaces we defend. Or perhaps I must admit that I am driven by a desire to move us toward a more dignified place where I, too, would rather live. You can call me a mad Black *bruja*. The spirit won't let me go.

EPILOGUE

It was an old tradition in Jenny's family to hold a *misa*, a séance, at the end of the year. She invited me to come sit *misa* with her because maybe the spirit guides would deliver some information that would help me with what I was trying to achieve in my life. This was certainly what she hoped for herself. It was December 2022, during my first trip back to the island since the onset of the COVID-19 pandemic. Just a month prior, Jenny had moved out of her family home into a small two-bedroom house alone in the Barrio Obrero (Worker's Neighborhood).[1] In the corner of her front entryway, closest to the street, was a doll. The doll was a Congo spirit named Francisca that guarded the threshold. Francisca's piercing eyes stood out against her dark skin. She was dressed in a long cobalt blue dress, representing her connection to Yemayá, with layers of ruffles cascading over the small stool where she sat. At a quick glance, it seemed as if she were floating in the cool air, hazy from the combination of drizzle and humidity. It was the kind of winter chill that seeps into your bones. Jenny came to the door in a thick gray hoodie over a blue and yellow striped skirt trimmed with white lace—the skirts that *santeras* wear when doing religious work. Jenny made coffee and we caught up while waiting for the *espiritistas* (spirit mediums) to arrive so the *misa* could begin.

Her mother, a daughter of Changó, had warned her before her death in February of 2020 that sudden uprootedness was coming. She had directed Jenny to acquire her own home: a place that she could never be dispossessed of. When transcribing this divination, which Jenny had received at her knife ceremony, an important milestone in the life of a religioso, her mother's spiritual attunement allowed her to glean this additional insight. While Jenny was dancing in prayer at a tambor early in the pandemic, Changó reminded her of this divinely inspired cognizance.

As COVID-19 began to spread in 2020, religious ceremonies were closely scrutinized by the Cuban police, who were charged with enforcing the public health mandates to wear a mask and keep social distance. Religiosos cautiously navigated how, or whether, to comply with the state's stringent measures to stop the spread while still fulfilling their obligations to divine kin. They drew from the strategies used in the early years of the Revolution when religious practice was banned, holding clandestine ceremonies. When religious work ran late into the night, Jenny hosted sleepovers for her godfamily to avoid them breaking the national curfew, risking incurring large fines.

On this afternoon, Changó came down to remind her what he had instructed her. Without giving it a second thought, she reassured him, interpreting his words as a general command to her as a child of orisha to humble herself in reverence of the divine. Dancing and singing for sustained periods of time with a mask was hard. After taking a quick break outside, she returned to the drumming. Changó was still down and beelined directly to her. He sternly repeated his command to *remember what he had said*. For the orisha to repeat the same message in that way, there must have been something she had not fully understood the first time.

Jenny's father died early in the pandemic. Disagreements about his care, whether or not to put their last hopes in the overextended public health system after exhausting what could be done through religious work, caused fractures in the family and Jenny was forced to move out. The conflict compelled Jenny to go back to her *itá* book, where she had recorded all the divinations she has received for her life. Each bit of information given in divinations accrues relevance and new meaning for the recipient over time, based on the specific context and situations they find themselves. Removing the notebook from the plastic bag it was wrapped in, she pored over the pages of messages from each orisha received throughout her life as a priestess. They were transcribed on her behalf during the ceremonies in which orishas were born into her care. Her eye was suddenly drawn to a handwritten note by her mother, now a spirit. "There it was . . . so clear, 'My daughter, they are going to kick you out of the house! You need to get your own place!'"

When her mother wrote those words, housing prices were exorbitant in the real estate market, dominated by Cubans buying on behalf of foreigners who could pay in cash (Bastian 2018). But in 2022, prices had plummeted as roughly 313,488 Cubans (roughly 3 percent of Cuba's 2021 population) migrated to the US that year alone, selling their homes for money to make the trip (Albizu-Campos Espiñeira and Díaz-Briquets 2023). In fact, that year witnessed the biggest migration wave in all of Cuban history to date, totaling more than the past five years combined, exceeding the number of migrants in the four years between 1959 and 1962, and almost double the total departures from exoduses in 1980 and 1994 (Center for Democracy in the Americas 2023; see also Albizu-Campos Espiñeira and Díaz-Briquets 2023). People were anxiously selling all their belongings on the black market for USD to pay for coyotes to guide them through the *travesía* (from Central America through the Mexico-US border). Many migrants took advantage of Cuba's 2021 agreement with Nicaragua, which allowed Cuban citizens to enter the country without a visa. After landing in Managua, they'd spend their life savings and risk their lives to make their way up North. Then there were the nearly 10,000 who dared to make the journey across to the US by raft (Albizu-Campos Espiñeira and Díaz-Briquets 2023). There was so much USD currency in circulation on the street that it was informally accepted by practically all business establishments and private vendors.[2] In 2022, even middle-class people who had lived relatively well since Raúl's economic "update" were fleeing in search of the growing number of things—both material and immaterial—that they were convinced were not available in Cuba anymore (Bastian 2020). The loss of faith in the state's ability to foster a decent life on the island spread like the virus.

Rather than wait on agencies like the World Health Organization via COVAX to negotiate with the US, which had stockpiled far more vaccinations than it could reasonably disburse, to close the "vaccine equity gap" for poor countries around the world, the Cuban state put faith in its own biotechnology to save its people. By May of 2021, Cuba's homegrown vaccines had finally passed clinical trials and were ready for national distribution. They named one Abdala, "the name given by Cuba's National hero, José Martí, in his dramatic poem of the same name, to a young Black African who fought and died for the independence of his country," as *Granma* explained it (Ríoseco 2022). The other vaccine was named SOBERANA (Sovereign), underscoring the stakes of this medical mission. The viability of Cuban socialism seemingly hung in the balance of its public health effort.

Although initially successful, the health system's ability to perform routine surgeries or treat everyday maladies and chronic illnesses was overrun by the massive vaccination effort. Cubans could no longer rely on even the limited social safety net they had come to expect—foods like milk and bread, goods like soap, medicines like antibiotics, services like electricity. With the closure of airports in March of 2020 to stop the spread of the virus and Trump's policies to block the influx of remittances, many in Cuba compared the economic conditions of pandemic times with the 1990s Special Period. Moreover, the long-anticipated currency unification in January 2021

brought crippling inflation. A major hurricane and a series of critical oil re-
finery explosions compounded their daily miseries. These series of down-
falls provided ample motivation to fight (*luchar*) or take flight. It was a perfect storm for political unrest.

The historic exodus came in the wake of an equally historic uprising on
July 11, 2021. What quickly became known as *11-J* marked the biggest public
demonstration since the 1959 overthrow of the Batista government by the
infamous 26th of July Movement. At the height of the pandemic in Cuba,
the public health system was failing. People were sending loved ones to the
hospital never to see them again, and the frequency and duration of rolling
blackouts due to systemic electrical-grid failures drove Cubans to a state of
helplessness and desperation at home. Blackouts would be anywhere from
twelve to forty-eight hours long. This meant that the little food one had
fought so hard to acquire, through either waiting in hours-long lines or
paying exorbitantly inflated prices, would spoil. It was a succession of long
blackouts in San Antonio de los Baños, just west of Havana, that was said to
catalyze the first group of people to take to the streets. Videos of protesters
from impoverished and Black neighborhoods and towns, chanting "Patria
y Vida!" (Fatherland and Life!), spread like wildfire across the island.

"Patria y Vida" became the anthem of the *estallido* (uprising). The chant
was inspired by a rap song written by Cuban rap artists living abroad and
those in Cuba, released the February prior (Yotuel, n.d.). Whereas the willingness to die for Cuban sovereignty had been upheld as a measure of one's
revolutionary commitment, encapsulated by the popular slogan "Patria o
Muerte" (Fatherland or Death), in the height of the pandemic, when finding
food was a struggle and people were dying at an exponential rate, protesters
desperately cried for the means to live. The expansion of internet access
since the normalization of US-Cuba relations laid the infrastructure for
first the song, and then the videos and images of protest, to go viral via social
media, inspiring others to take to the streets.

To stop the spread of the viral protest videos, the Cuban government
shut down the internet on the entire island. Then Cuban President Díaz-
Canel did an emergency broadcast, calling for all Cuban revolutionaries to
take to the streets and attack the protesters (Cubadebate 2021). Over the
course of three days, similar protests erupted across cities throughout the
country.[3] Mass arrests and long prison sentences swiftly followed, spurring
doubts about due legal process.

While the protests were mostly peaceful, images of overturned police cars and crowds facing off with uniformed squads in the streets were

alarming for a viewing public that had associated such civil unrest with the United States, the capitalist empire. For a country that had earned an international reputation for being a model of progressive racial politics, redistributive social policy, and peace, it was jarring to see these public spectacles of civil disobedience emerging from the ranks of the paradigmatic "humble masses" whose interests the state ostensibly represented.

The harshness of the Cuban state's response to the protests made even its most ardent defenders question its leadership's legitimacy. "If Fidel were alive, it would have never happened," Jenny said with certainty about the uprising and Díaz-Canel's response. Jenny spoke to a widespread sentiment that Fidel's successors had not earned his same credibility. "Fidel" represented a time when the daily sacrifices citizens were asked to make came in exchange for something that felt worthy in return. For many, that social pact made with Party leadership, to make personal sacrifices for the common good, had been long lost since the unfolding of the reforms, and with it their legitimacy. Even if falling short of his own ideal, people had faith that Fidel earnestly believed in the progressive vision to create a more just society for the working class. That vision, born well before the Revolution, was the impetus for the construction of the neighborhood where Jenny now laid her head.

The US news media framed the events as an anti-government uprising, underscoring the need for total regime change. The Cuban state accused the protesters of being CIA operatives and "enemies of the Revolution," orchestrating a foreign invasion. Others saw it as a desperate cry for the state to fulfill its promise to provide the basic needs for dignified life that the Revolution once ensured. While many agreed that day-to-day life in Cuba was hard to bear, they were equally afraid of the kinds of unwanted changes that the protests might legitimize on the part of the Cuban and US governments alike.

J-11 represented a strong popular sentiment, seen erupting from its most marginalized, poor Black neighborhoods. "If I thought it was going to make a difference, I would have been out there in the streets too," Jenny admitted when thinking back on the uprising that summer. Despite the Abdala being injected in their arms, during the peak of the pandemic's death toll, they refused death as a badge of honor. While ever conscious of the stakes of public displays of discontent for a Revolution besieged by the threat of US invasion, the material returns of Cuban sovereignty had diminished to such an extent that it could no longer quiet their anguish. And after the state's *mano dura* (strong hand or iron fist) approach to squelching the dissenters, for many, the moral righteousness of the fight for Cuban independence wasn't good enough reason to stay put.

Somewhere among the statistics of the historic exodus were rumberos. At the time of my visit, Yoruba Andabo was no longer functioning as an ensemble because most members had defected that fall. Only four returned from a tour abroad in October, including El Gordo, Yamilé, and the new artistic director, Didier.[4] When Didier's wife stayed abroad, most believed that it was only a matter of time before he also left. The members of Rumba Morena, the all-female rumba ensemble who performed at El Callejón de Hamel, also added to the count. That year, Tailyn, Jenny's goddaughter, and her groupmates landed a tour in Mexico, and they were trying to reach the US. Tailyn was the first to make it across the border. After a long period of no sign of life, she finally resurfaced in Las Vegas to say she was working in a kitchen. Departures represent both a loss and a potential blessing for those left behind, expanding the geographic span of their kinship networks abroad.

With loved ones dying and disappearing in the *travesía*, the only place Jenny believed she could realize the divine guidance she had received was in the home-place she created with orisha, her ancestors, and her stone family in Havana. "*Allá*" (there), meaning abroad or the "capitalist world," "*la gente vive de crédito*" (people live on credit), "nothing you own is really yours. If you don't pay what they say, then they can take the roof from over your head. And one day they say 'pay this amount' and the next day its triple the amount and you still have to pay it or else. You can think you own your house but then they say they own the land it's sitting on, and they can kick you off." Jenny had seen enough during her travels teaching and performing in North America, Europe, and Latin America to know that moving abroad permanently would seal her to a fate that diverged from her *itá* and her mother's sacred guidance. "*Nadie me puede hacer el cuento* [No one can sell me a bill of goods] because I've traveled, and I've seen with my own eyes." *Allá*, she could never truly lay claim to a place of belonging, a place of and for her own.

While she talked, a dark-skinned man of small stature, dressed in blue coveralls and a red baseball cap, showed up with a bucket and some tools. She introduced him as "Elegguá Sin Caramelos" (Elegguá Without Candy). He was a child of Elegguá, just like Jenny. Her ancestors had brought him to her path to do repairs on the house. With his help, she planned to make it a place where she would be happy to stay. In the bedroom, he immediately got to work, quietly listening as we talked. With the furniture pushed back against the wall, he proceeded to mix plaster in the middle of the bedroom floor. He then began patching up the holes from the electrical work he had done days before. The people she knew who had left Cuba found themselves squatting, "packed twelve people into a trailer, doing whatever to survive." "Am I right?," turning to Elegguá Sin Caramelos hard at work. He nodded in agreement. "*Allá*, if you are hungry, there is no one to give you some rice and beans off their stove and say, 'here, eat.'" He affirmed. At the same time, Jenny understood the determination to leave and the drive to take to the streets. "*Esto está de pinga de verdad* . . ." (this is fucked fo' real . . .), she said with a somber sternness.

Her remarks evoke an organic and scalding critique of capitalism, articulating a defense of a kind of social relation that she had no faith could be sustained outside of Cuba. But if the last few years were any indication, Cuban Socialism post-Fidel inspired little faith. "Thanks to Olofi and los Eggun we have been able to continue forward." Copresences and spiritual kin could bring down the information she needed to save her life, give her shelter, and maybe some rice and beans when her rations predictably ran out. The kind of place to call home Jenny sought was far from anything sold in the "American Dream," nor did the *Guidelines* bring it any closer. Only religious work with family of stone could help shape her fate in her favor. Shoulder to shoulder with family, she had the means to purchase the place that her mother foresaw, that Changó reminded her of, that Yemayá now guarded, that Elegguá now repaired. The place she inhabited and defended was, like the Black corporeal undercommons more broadly, a place created through mutual obligation, interdependence, and care, embodied in coordinated motion.

The *espiritistas* were running late, so she gave me a tour of the rest of the house. Some parts of the walls were crumbling from slow deterioration and others had been broken for piecemeal repairs. In the site of decay, with the help and protection of spirits, Jenny embarked on a grand renovation. We walked down a narrow alleyway out to the backyard. To the right was a broken-down structure of columns and rubble that once housed animals for ceremonies. "The prior owners were religiosos," she explained. Where I saw concrete rubble, she saw a wealth of potential that would soon be restored to its original ceremonial use, nourishing *soperas* and the many mouths that ritual feeds. Directly across, she'd turn what looked like a shed into a fully functioning kitchen, to cook ceremonial foods. Farther back another shed housed the shrine for her ancestors. To the right, a tall cement wall kept the large trees from falling into a clearance. Here she envisioned a structure to shelter, adorn, and care for all her orishas. Pointing to the overgrown weeds, Jenny saw a built-in pool and a platform for drummers adjacent to the shrine.

Her eyes lit up as she described the emergent surroundings with excitement. In less than two months the first ceremony was scheduled to take place. There was so much to be done in such a short time, I worried. It will be ready by then, she reassured me. As if the beautiful compound she envisioned was already manifest, she trusted that the copresences who populated the grounds were actively working to refashion her surroundings into the place of nascent potential she was meant to call home.

The tour ended back in her kitchen. She washed our empty cups of coffee in the sink. To the right of the faucet there was a single glass of water with a clear, plastic ruler inserted inside. She removed the ruler, rinsed it, refilled the glass with tap water and reinserted the ruler. Noticing my gaze, she explained "*Es para arreglar todo que está en desarreglo*" (It is to fix everything that is in disorder). She smirked, waiting for me to grasp the power of the play on words in Spanish. "It's a simple *obra* [work] but sometimes the most simple are the most effective: a glass of water with a ruler [*regla*] inside for a spirit, Maria de Regla, that is syncretized with Yemayá. . . . She is helping me with all the house renovations."

In a few days' time Jenny would go to a *tambor* for Yemayá at a nearby beach. Dancing shoulder to shoulder with family, the power of their collective prayers would be fortified to move stone into place.

NOTES

Preface

1 This is a basketball analogy that Daniel draws from Sally Ness's (1992) use of the image to describe the possessive relationship between Filipino society and *sinulog* dance.

2 An important exception to this has been the work of Faye Harrison, exemplified in her essay "'Three Women, One Struggle': Anthropology, Performance, and Pedagogy" (1990) which was published in the inaugural issue of *Transforming Anthropology*, the journal of the Association of Black Anthropologists. However, she is arguably least known for this arts-based work, and her background in performance is often ignored for how it informed her praxis of decolonizing anthropology.

Introduction

1 Rumba's Blackness does not preclude the participation of people who may be categorized as non-Black (within Cuba's spectrum of racial classification). The performativity and social construction of Blackness in relation to rumba, space, and spiritual belonging is elaborated in the following section and resurfaces throughout the ethnography.

2 I thank Julie Skurski for highlighting the significance of this scholarly focus within the rumba literature.

3 The currency was later unified in 2021. That pandemic context is addressed in the epilogue. However, during the period of research for this book, the dual currency system still applied.

4 Other scholars of the Caribbean have similarly analyzed popular visions of belonging among the poor as they negotiate the effects of neoliberal capitalist globalization in the context of "post-colonial" nation-building. A prime and useful example is Deborah Thomas's (2004) analysis of the changing relationship between national and popular culture and the political economy of development in Jamaica as a result of intensified globalization (3). She puts forth "modern blackness" as the emergent

framework used by working-class Jamaicans to assess present and future possibilities, which is distinct from the "folk" or "revolutionary" blackness promoted by the institutionalized middle-class models of progress (231). Within that, she identifies artistic representation and the performing arts—namely, popular music, theater, and dance—as key realms through which people experience and mediate their relationships to global processes that constitute particular subjectivities. She posits, and my ethnography emphatically affirms, that this eschewal of prior visions of territorially bound belonging and creole multiracial subjectivity should constitute something other than crisis.

5   See Devyn Spence Benson (2016) for a history of anti-racist activism in the 1960s. A special issue of *Cuban Studies* 48 (2019) compiles the positions and demands of the most prominent members of the contemporary "Afro-Cuban Movement."

6   Excellent studies of the re-stratification of Cuban society under Raúl Castro in "New Cuba," with specific attention to lines of race and class, include Hansing (2017) and Hansing and Hoffmann (2019). See Anasa Hicks (2019) for a gendered labor study of domestic service in "new Cuba."

7   "Stone" here references the stones that are imbued with sacred powers when an orisha is "born."

8   It warrants mention that none of the rumba ensembles in their networks had white women as members. See chapter 2 for a discussion of the politics of race and gender for women dancers.

9   The way I arrived at this nomination performs what it describes, in that agency is not individually conceived; I got there through a push from Thomas F. DeFrantz. Perhaps it was more of a nudge in the direction of Moten and Harney's *The Undercommons: Fugitive Planning and Black Study* (2013), based on a cursory description of a feeling that in it was language for what I was only just beginning to put into words. This book has, in a way, become a response to that call, from that nudge, for that feeling. No doubt, DeFrantz's scholarship and community-building praxis within the study of African diasporic dance has created a generative commons to think seriously through "orisha dancing *and* the sacred praise dance after the night at the club" (DeFrantz 2020).

10 See Deschamps Chapeaux's (1983) study of fugitivity in the city of Havana. Chapter 1 describes how the cabildos de nación figured into the city's sociopolitical and sonic landscape during and after slavery.

11 The jailing of Black historian and Communist Party member Walterio Carbonell and the suppression of his book *Critique: On the Emergence of National Culture* (1961), an inspiration for later generations of Black intellectuals, is an important example (Benson 2016; Fernández Robaina 2022).

12 Given the context, another viable translation could be, "One's own business, not someone else's!" The English-language version of the newspaper, which would have the official translation provided by the PCC, was

not accessible via the *Granma* internet archive at the time of publication. Either way, the exaltation of self-employment over state employment is unmistakable.

1. Black Inclusion, Black Enclosure

1   "The Cuban Five" refers to five Cuban men who were arrested in 1998 in the United States and sentenced for espionage for their involvement in an undercover mission to infiltrate Cuban-American organizations in Miami that have historically targeted the Cuban government since Fidel Castro's legendary 26th of July Movement overthrew the US-backed Cuban president, Fulgencio Batista, in 1959. After the Cuban Revolution, a sector of the Cuban population (primarily the white and upper-/middle classes) fled to the United States as political exiles, the bulk of whom settled in South Florida. They have been the most vocal proponents of anti-Castro and anti-Communist mobilization in that area, becoming an important voting block that has continued to influence the United States' harsh foreign policy toward the island. In Cuba, the Five are revered as martyrs and model patriots who defended the Cuban Revolution from the so-called Cuban-American terrorists. The Cuban campaign for the release of all five prisoners has gained international attention and support from Cuba's allies around the world, and during my fieldwork was a mainstay on Cuban TV. In school, Cuban children learned to list the names of the "Five Heroes" from rote memory: Gerardo, Ramón, Antonio, Fernando, y René. After fourteen years of imprisonment in the United States, Fernando González Llort was the second of the famous Cuban Five to return home, thanks to negotiations that took place after the brief normalization of diplomatic relations between the United States and Cuba under the Obama administration. The concert took place a mere two days after his release and repatriation.

2   I thank Reviewer 1 for helping me to articulate and refine the focus of this chapter accordingly.

3   Here I am drawing on the concept of racial states by David Theo Goldberg (2001).

4   To endeavor to critically examine seminal ethnographic writings about the Spanish-speaking Caribbean within their historical moment of production is not altogether new but rather aligns with critical assessments of the relationship between epistemology and power in anthropology, ethnomusicology, and art history of the African diaspora (Thornton and Ubiera 2019; Garcia 2017; Fabian 1983; Palmié 2013; K. Thompson 2011; Garcia 2013).

5   The performance of secrecy in the construction of group identity is prevalent across the African diaspora. In chapter 3, I delve into the gendered

identity politics within rumba performances of "secretism," as termed by Paul Christopher Johnson (2002, 2022) in reference to candomblé in Brazil.

6　Having sacrificed their lives for the nation-to-be in exchange for citizenship, Black and mulato war veterans sought their rightful share of whatever freedoms the Republic would afford (Helg 1995). In 1908, they formed El Partido Independiente de Color (The Independent People of Color Party, PIC). The first of its kind in the Americas, this group advocated for the interests of Black people who sacrificed their lives for the nation. In 1912, a bloody race massacre of thousands of Black men and women squashed this political initiative and left a powerful imprint on Black consciousness.

7　One such example is the Lucumí Santa Rita de Casia y San Lázaro Society in Havana. Melina Pappademos (2011) references a newspaper article from 1915 suggesting that the activities of that society's *brujo* leaders were tantamount to political mobilization because locals went to them to solve their problems (109).

8　A concerted historical contextualization of the evolution of Ortiz's thinking and writing about race, and its reflection in his political and cultural advocacy, is important but beyond the scope of this book. Many scholars have dedicated themselves to this valuable work and should be consulted (e.g., Coronil 1995; Moore 2018). Some scholars contend that the ways in which his ideologies around race transformed over time shouldn't be overstated given the extent to which his thinking, and the relationships of power that undergirded his work, stayed the same (Moore 1994; Hagedorn 2001). Depending on when importance is placed and why, he stands as a prime example of positivist biological determinism or Caribbean theories of hybridity, of virulent racism or progressive anti-racism. The "Ortiz Perplex" is what Stephan Palmié (1998, 353) names this difficulty in pinning down his remarkable albeit contradictory intellectual legacy. Rather than being regarded in isolation, Ortiz's thinking over the course of his life should be considered the product of the dialogues and exchanges between intellectuals based in Cuba and abroad whose discourses mutually shaped the anthropology of the African diaspora as a field (Yelvington 2001, 2005).

9　Rumba's nationalization was critical for making it an effective signifier for Socialist Cuba's folk heritage after 1959. Although it stood out on the international stage as an audacious affront to the greatest military superpower, the rebel Caribbean island was on trend with the global boom of post-war era, state-sponsored, folk-dance ensembles displaying a proletarian aesthetic (Shay 2002).

10　This contradiction was rationalized on the grounds of successfully undoing de facto racial segregation that had been sedimented during the period of US influence over the Cuban Republic. Black people who professed a political consciousness that challenged the leadership of the white political vanguard were silenced (Benson 2016, 117–19). State propaganda often made strategic comparisons to US Jim Crow–style racism to discredit vocal dissatisfaction with racial discrimination domestically (Benson 2016).

11   Robin Moore gives an illustrative account of the kinds of persecutions devotees of Afro-Cuban religions faced in his book *Music and Revolution: Cultural Change in Socialist Cuba* (2006). State officials publicly attacked rituals as misguided, confused, and backward. Devotees were imprisoned, their homes were raided for religious paraphernalia and ceremonial activity, altars were destroyed, and children were physically torn from private initiation ceremonies. People who declared religious faith were denied membership in the Communist Party, whose affiliation was beneficial in terms of education and career opportunities. Wearing any clothing or adornment associated with religious faith meant relinquishing access to goods and employment. Children were taught by their teachers to deride religious faith, and the Ministry of Education produced reports that singled out Afro-Cuban religions as the primary factor contributing to delinquency. Some studies even went so far as to diagnose devotees as certifiable schizophrenics and to characterize belief in Afro-Cuban religion as a symptom of a psychological pathology (208–11).

12   Payroll budgets at the National Theater of Cuba in 1960 show that modern dancers made six to seven times as much as folkloric dancers (Schwall 2019, 41). This meant that folkloric dancers had to continue working second and third jobs, doing menial labor while maintaining a rigorous rehearsal and performance schedule (Schwall 2019, 42).

13   The Departamento de Lacras Sociales (The Department of Social Ills) at the Ministry of the Interior (MININT) along with members of the Federation of Cuban Women (FMC), the Committees for the Defense of the Revolution (CDRs), and other state organizations oversaw the campaign to "rehabilitate prostitutes," deciding on policies to combat sex work. Although both men and women engaged in sex work at the onset of the Revolution, the campaign to rehabilitate and reeducate sex workers was exclusively aimed at women (Hynson 2015).

14   In 1971, "Fidel placed prostitution in the category of social crimes" and "government leaders identified sex workers as delinquents rather than victims" (Hynson 2015, 152). The rationale behind the failures of the past "therapeutic" measures to fully eradicate prostitution would be traced to an essential difference in Black women's biology. Hynson describes scientific research conducted by various Cuban health agencies between 1959 and 1965 that determined that a sexual compulsion commonly known as *uterine fire* (*fuego uterino*) disproportionately assailed women of mixed Spanish and African descent (Hynson 2015, 147–48).

15 For an etymological explanation of Carabalí in relationship to Calabar, see Miller (2000, 166).

16 This is not to argue that Mambí combatants, guerrilla fighters in Wars for Independence, were not also Abakuá practitioners. The Abakuá presence within the Mambí army, particularly with regard to the protection they offered to the mulato general Antonio Maceo, is a point of pride within contemporary Abakuá circles.

17 The rebellious stance associated with the Abakuá brotherhood is referred to as *guapo* in present-day lexicon. I expand on *guapería* as a choreography of sovereignty tied to sacred Black masculinity in chapter 3. The militant stance of Fidel Castro (a synecdoche for the Cuban Revolution) vis-à-vis the US government is still often described among Cubans as *guapo*, boasting all the insurgent defiance of a leftist Caribbean underdog.

18 For more on the wider practice of Cubans appropriating film to discuss and debate everyday problems during the post-Soviet period, see S. Fernandes (2006).

2. Black Feminist Aptitudes

Portions of chapter 2 were published in "Black Feminist Rumba Pedagogies," *Dance Research Journal* 53, no. 2 (2021): 27–48.

1 This chapter builds on Melissa Blanco Borelli's (2016) pathbreaking theorization of "hip(g)nosis," which troubles the patriarchal characterization of rumbera moves.

2 I started formal dance classes at three years old, which led to conservatory training in ballet in Paris, then the Dance Theater of Harlem, and eventually modern dance at the Ailey School in New York City. I first encountered rumba during a summer dance intensive in Cuba in 2004, run by New York University's Tisch School of the Arts under the auspices of the Ludwig Foundation in Havana. Introductory classes in Black popular dance were given at the headquarters of Danza Contemporanea at the Teatro Nacional de Cuba. Later, undergraduate ethnographic research for my honors thesis was conducted in Miami, where I trained as an apprentice under Neri Torres, artistic director of IFÉ-ILÉ Afro-Cuban Dance and Music Company, and performed with them on several occasions. After completing my undergraduate degree, I performed as a member of Areytos Performance Works, under the artistic directorship of Sita Frederick in NYC. There I learned a great deal from Cuban fellow dancers and collaborators, Yesenia Selier (*ibae*), Carlos Mateu, and Abraham Salazar. I also trained for several years under Xiomara Rodríguez at the Museo del Barrio in Harlem, NYC, and returned to Havana to take private lessons with Siria from Conjunto JJ and Alfredo O'Farril (former soloist from Conjunto Folkorico Nacional), Jennyselt Galata, Zulema Pedroso, and

Yamilé Sardiñas. During my eighteen months of doctoral fieldwork, I took private lessons for sixty to ninety minutes twice a week.

3 Sincere gratitude to Reviewer 2 for bringing this analytical framework to my attention.

4 Black feminists in Cuba have made clear that Black experiences pre- and post-Revolution are distinctly gendered (Rubiera Castillo and Martiatu Terry 2011). They join numerous Black feminist activist-scholars throughout the African diaspora in their call for the urgency in teaching and learning counterhegemonic means of assigning self-worth to Black women's bodies as the site of their subjection (e.g., Collins 2000; Caldwell 2006; Guillard Limonta 2016).

5 Writing of the Special Period, Alejandro de la Fuente asserts that "the migration of people from the eastern provinces to Havana has been frequently interpreted as a black assault on the city" (2001a, 327). De la Fuente reports that in 1997, the government banned migration to the capital, prompted by 92,000 people who attempted to legalize their residency in Havana earlier that year. The internal migration policy imposed fines on both immigrants and their landlords, as well as forced deportations back to their place of origin.

6 Both the rhythm and the wooden sticks on which the rhythm is played are called the clave: rumba's metaphorical "spinal cord" (Jottar 2009a, 4).

7 See "Les chemins de la beauté," accessed April 26, 2024, https://boutique .arte.tv/detail/chemins_beaute_serie.

8 Translation mine from the French original.

9 To underscore the extent to which this performance strategy is not delimited by a biological notion of race, Melissa Blanco Borelli (2009) shows how what she terms "corpo-mulata performance" was adopted by white women cabaret performers cast as rumberas in the 1950s.

10 Adrian Hearn (2008) cites Rogelio Martínez Furé for characterizing this practice of withholding and disguising sacred knowledge as a customary pedagogic technique within African-based religions in Cuba more broadly, and thus not specific to the gender of the student (64). However, the rumberas I spoke with testified to its concerted gendered application.

11 This point about the radicalism and pragmatism of the political visions generated by lower-class Black people has been made elsewhere in the Caribbean, with Jamaica being a prime example (Thomas 2004, 233).

3. Sacred Swagger and Its Social Order

Epigraph: This quote is from note 22 in the article. Daniel indicates to see Fernando Ortiz, *Los negros curros* (1958).

1 El Rumbazo #2 was an immersive rumba event organized and curated by US musicologist Ned Sublette and Cuban musicologist Caridad Diez,

with funding by Sublette's Post Mambo Studies organization and the support of the Cuban Ministry of Culture.

2 Footage from their collaboration with the Rolling Stones can be seen in the documentary *The Rolling Stones Olé Olé Olé! A Trip across Latin America* (2016). Other unconventional appearances by Osain del Monte include TEDxHabana in 2015 and the movie *The Fate of the Furious* in 2017.

3 For a more in-depth discussion of elite perceptions of the Abakuá brotherhood over time, see chapter 1.

4 The clave sets the tempo of the song and indicates the type of rumba that will be played.

5 See Audra Simpson's notion of "nested sovereignty" as a politics of refusal, an alternative to state "recognition," in *Mohawk Interruptus* (2014).

6 In a guest lecture on Abakuá history on December 20, 2012, as part of a larger course on race at the University of Havana, Tato Quiñones, an elder Abakuá, explained how they would identify little boys who might qualify to be Abakuá men when they come of age. At the playground, the child who fights back when another child tries to steal from him or pick on his friend shows promise to become Abakuá. This kind of behavior demonstrates loyalty and a readiness to defend a moral code even to the point of violence, highly valuable principles to the brotherhood.

7 *La diana* in rumba is the lead singer's opening vocal stylings. This establishes the tonal center or key of the song (Bodenheimer 2010).

8 Examples of mass organizations include Central de Trabajadores de Cuba (CTC), Federación de Mujeres Cubanas (FMC), La Unión de Pioneros de José Martí (UPJM), Unión de Jóvenes Comunistas (UJC), Comités de Defensa de la Revolución (CDR), and Federación Estudiantil Universitaria (FEU).

9 The space would be called "La Peña del Ambia" and has been maintained every Wednesday since then, alternating between *trova* and rumba music.

10 Dressing in white from head to toe is associated with elegance, while among religiosos, the color white has added sacred significance and is worn at ceremonies.

11 Many thanks to Jossianna Arroyo for reminding me of this song, which is a chronicle of the discrimination experienced by rumberos when granted access to this premiere cultural institution.

12 Jafari Allen found in his ethnographic research that *el ambiente* denotes a space of extralegality and potential danger also used to index the gay and lesbian scene (2011, 134). I take this to reinforce the broader social anxieties around particular kinds of self-making deemed an assault on white middle-class propriety encompassing "unruly" gender, race, and erotic subjectivities.

13 Hanna Garth (2021) analyzes the local construct of level of culture as a term that indexes, even though it is used to disavow, a transnational logic of anti-Blackness.

14 "Me atrevo decir que el mito que está soportando la realidad que acá denuncia el autor es el 'miedo al negro,' aquel que hace pensar que las personas negras somos 'fajaloteras,' o sea, recurrimos rápidamente a la violencia—dada nuestro poca capacidad de racionamiento, vale acotar—, entonces ahí un hombre negro de 6 pies se convierte un símbolo de fuerza extrema" (Abd'Allah-Álvarez Ramírez 2016).

15 Here I am invoking bell hooks's formulation of "white supremacist capitalist patriarchy" (1984, 51).

16 In March 2016, Fidel Castro stood by this claim in a letter to Obama stating, "The hateful, racist bourgeois custom of hiring strongmen to expel black citizens from recreational centers were swept away by the Cuban Revolution" ("El hermano Obama," *Granma*, March 28, 2016, quoted in Clealand 2017, 2).

17 The hegemonic revolutionary narrative frames the 1868 Grito de Yara as a pivotal anti-racist act representing the benevolence of the white-creole revolutionary vanguard, for which Black people should feel indebted. This narrative has served to squelch anti-racist critiques of revolutionary leadership. Anti-racist activist-scholars, however, have argued that the enslaved were the true protagonists of the anti-slavery movement, which they had waged for more than a century prior (Carbonell 1961). Accordingly, the Grito de Yara is reframed as an act of white self-interest in a historical pattern of exploiting Black men as a brute force in fulfilling nationalist agendas versus centering Black intellectual and political leadership. These debates around the role of Black protagonism, white paternalism, and political debt in the history of Black struggles for equality in Cuba has persisted from colonialism through the 1959 Revolution. See Helg (1995).

18 I thank Juana María Rodríguez for bringing my attention to the transgressive power of public displays of male homosocial intimacy that find refuge and expression in opacity. Celiany Rivera-Velásquez and Beliza Torres Narváez (2016) acknowledge the tacit behaviors of policing and surveillance that sustain these arenas of homosociality as nonhomoerotic.

19 "Abakuá words are supposed to motivate inanimate forces into action" (Miller 2000, 167).

20 Needing to get permission to hold events that entail drumming is not uncommon for other Afro-religious ceremonies post-1990s religious liberalization. However, the systematic stationing of policemen outside the event is reserved for Abakuá functions.

21 To read more about how female power is located within the Abakuá origin story in the figure of Sikán (transformed into the drum) as well as mention of all-female Calabar Nnimm societies that did not survive the Middle Passage, see R. F. Thompson (1984, 236). Daniel briefly notes that, "although they are not generally discussed," women do hold ceremonial roles within Abakuá organizations and constitute separate,

"complementary" formations (2005, 137). For a discussion of the recurring theme of silence in relationship to femininity in Leopard societies in Calabar and Cuba, see "Emblems of Prowess" in Robert Farris Thompson's *Flash of the Spirit* (1984, 225–68).

22 In his guest lecture at the University of Havana, Tato Quiñones adamantly wanted to dispel the notion that Abakuás were *negros curros*, an urban class of free Blacks during the colonial period known for their flamboyant fashion. Written accounts typically reference Fernando Ortiz's *Los Negros curros* ([1958] 1986). Tato said that *negros curros* were ostentatious in their dress, wanting to attract attention to themselves, while Abakuás were deliberately more subdued and secretive, not wanting to attract undue attention to themselves. He said that now people tend to associate the two because the youth have lost the values of Abakuá and have taken to drawing attention to themselves through visible tattoos that pronounce their affiliation, whereas originally, even the closest neighbors of Abakuá men would not know they were members of the brotherhood and would only find out after their death.

23 Black Cuban visual artist Belkis Ayón has been a leading voice in critiquing the paradigms of gender and power within the Abakuá and advancing a renarrativization of their origin story from a Black feminist standpoint. This is seen pointedly through her 1998 works, *Perfidia* (Treachery) and *Resurección* (Resurrection), for instance, where she positions herself as Sikán, a central figure in Abakuá mythology, whose treachery forms the basis of justification for women's exclusion. For a recent study of Belkis Ayón's artistic interventions on this subject, see Noël (2022).

4. Moving Labor across Markets

Portions of chapter 4 originally appeared in "'Salvándose' in Contemporary Havana: Rumba's Paradox for Black Identity Politics," *Black Diaspora Review* 5, no. 2 (2016): 24–54.

1 "Rachel" is a pseudonym.

2 I suspect that the fact that my research was conducted under the auspices of a well-respected cultural research institute under the Cuban Ministry of Culture contributed to their caution. Ironically, they probably wouldn't have agreed to participate in the study at all if the Ministry of Culture hadn't approved it.

3 Much gratitude is owed to this generative conceptual framework Thomas shared at her Morgan Lecture, "Bodies, Knowledge, and Modes of Repair" at University of Rochester, November 1, 2023.

4 These lyrics are an allusion to Benny Moré's song "En el tiempo de la colonia," written by Mario Recio and recorded in August 1954: "En el tiempo de la colonia, tiempo de Sese eribó" (Moré 1982).

5   Many religiosos are warned against, and even forbidden from, immersing themselves fully in the ocean to the point of submerging one's head underwater. They fear that Yemayá, the ocean mother, will take them away to be with her, to their death.

6   I focus in on the politics of this performative blurring in chapter 5.

7   When a foreigner did attend their shows, a male singer might dare to discretely offer to sell them a CD for CUC $5 as a souvenir. These individual sales were done at the risk of drawing the venue administration's attention, as their labor contract with the state-managed venue prohibited them from selling unauthorized merchandise for personal gain.

8   Cuban Americans, descendants of Cubans living in the US, function slightly differently. Their rates were largely influenced by levels of family intimacy and reciprocity with god-families living in Cuba. They could sometimes negotiate exchanging foreign goods (i.e., appliances) for services instead of money.

9   After the immigration reforms, as Bastian argues, more Cubans began to live transnational lives (2018, 149). However, the new social group of "circular migrants" she describes enjoys significantly higher racialized class privilege than the religioso subjects in my account.

10   Debates about gender in Yoruba religion and philosophy more broadly stretch across the Atlantic, are long-standing, and reflect a range of scholarly approaches and positions. For some, see James L. Matory (1994), Oyèrónké Oyěwùmí (1997), Mary Ann Clark (2005), and Aisha Beliso-De Jesús (2015).

11   See the epilogue for such an example.

12   I find Rachel E. Harding's explanation of possession or trance in Brazilian Candomblé to be most helpful here. She describes the spirit possession as "the performance of *reclamation* of the body," wherein the body was the prime site of degradation through its commodification, enslavement, and signification (Harding 2003, 154).

13   As a further example of the dense layering of gendered meanings rumberos inhabit, individual drummers are known as having a masculine (*varón*) or feminine (*hembra*) sound, correlating to the perceived strength or softness of the hits their hands make on the drum's skin.

14   While identified as an economic barrier here, in the following chapter I return to the specificity of the relationship between personal agency, gender, and spirit possession, where their conjuncture opens space for alternative demonstrations of political solidarity among a broader worshipping community across casa-templos.

15   Zulema's mother, on the other hand, was a highly respected *montadora*. She was crowned a daughter of Changó, the fiery force of nature representing male virility, justice, and the art of strategy, and was sought after by casa-templos around the city for tambores de fundamento. Zulema invited me to attend one such ceremony where her mother's

Changó "came down." For this labor she was always paid in advance. Zulema alluded to, without disclosing, the special rituals and psychological preparation that her mother had to undergo whenever she was hired to perform this role. When the time came in the ceremony, Zulema escorted her mother from the back room dressed in a custommade outfit in red and white, the colors of Changó. Everyone cleared a passageway so that she could salute the *batá* drums. The household danced in unison behind her, keeping step with her movements. When her Changó arrived, her small frame seemed to multiply in stature. The sight commanded sheer awe. Although Zulema's mother had no institutionally recognized dance training to speak of, the religious community recognized and revered the ability for Changó, the epitome of masculinity, to have his clearest expression through her body.

16　Even the highest rates charged to foreigners are still cheaper than the cost of enlisting the same religious work in the United States.

17　See "Cuba," World Food Programme, accessed February 25, 2019, https://www1.wfp.org/countries/cuba.

18　For a more extended discussion of the shifting ideologies expressed in state discourses about the Revolution's subsidy program, see Bastian (2018, chap. 1).

5. Underworld Assembly

1　"Malcolm" is a pseudonym.

2　For a study of how stigma against *coleras* was shaped in state media during the pandemic, see Bastian and Berry (2022).

3　See "Blackness and Governance" (Harney and Moten 2013, 47).

4　See Hagedorn's (2001) chapter "Blurring the Boundaries: Merging Sacred and Profane" for an archive of instances where practitioners summoned the sacred during folkloric performances in spaces officially deemed profane, and how they were negotiated and interpreted by choreographers, performers, state bureaucrats, and audience members.

5　I am deeply grateful to Deborah Thomas, who helped me to articulate this lesson and who is developing this idea in a forthcoming book which was the subject of her 2023 Morgan Lecture at the University of Rochester.

6　This concept and phrasing nods to R. F. Thompson (1984). As Paul C. Johnson writes in his Atlantic genealogy of *spirit possession*, the term carries the political threat of nonhuman agency from a time when colonial authorities were deeply concerned with consolidating their own ownership over people as things. The language used to interpret this set of identifiable bodily practices cannot be extricated from a particular modern political project that is both troubled by the idea of an occupied

Black body, yet also finds that body necessary for the production of the rational individual and the modern civil subject (Johnson 2011, 396).

7   Here, I am dancing shoulder to shoulder with Lyndon K. Gill (2018), quoted in the book's introduction.

8   This discourse is prominently reproduced in travel writing about Cuba by US visitors. I've copied a particularly emblematic example here, published in *UCLA Magazine* (April 1, 2006), about a photo exhibit aptly titled "Dancing to Forget": "The first time photographer Gil Garcetti . . . went to Cuba, he followed a percussive beat to a narrow avenue in Havana Vieja. Coming toward him were a dozen or more dancers, men and women in matching polka-dot outfits, gyrating to an Afro-Cuban rhythm, their faces lit up with joy. . . . Garcetti's goal with his Cuba images was to capture the ubiquity and passion of dance among people whose lives are mired in hardship and poverty. Said Garcetti: 'Viengsay Valdes, Cuba's prima ballerina, told me, "Every day is a struggle. But we dance and we forget about all that." '"

9   See Berry (2019) for a more detailed analysis of ARAAC-Cuba's formation in 2012, operation, and eventual dissolution.

Epilogue

1   When it was inaugurated as a public housing project in 1947, Jesse Horst (2014) writes, the Barrio Obrero was still incomplete for lack of state funding. Only a few hundred homes were available for the more than 26,000 workers from Havana and Guanabacoa who entered their name in the raffle. While politicians continuously sought to claim public housing as a success of their administrations, for most it represented the ongoing inadequacy of the government's responses. Fidel Castro wanted to carry forward the progressive vision of these political predecessors and fulfill the unfinished duty of the Cuban state to make housing a citizenship right rather than a luxury. Ensuring adequate housing for every citizen remains a key social aspiration that the Revolution has been unable to fully achieve.

2   A popular Cuban blog, *ElToque.com*, published the daily black market exchange rate from USD. That December it was roughly 176 CUP/MN to 1 USD.

3   For a map of the reported protests with links to photographs and videos, see https://proyectoinventario.org/mapa-manifestaciones-cuba-11j/.

4   There had already been a lot of turnover in the group after the 2016 death of the founding artistic director, Geovani del Pino. The reins of musical directorship had been passed down to the youngest member, ushering in the leadership of the next generation, and not without tension.

REFERENCES

Abd'Allah-Álvarez Ramírez, Sandra. 2016. "Negrón de discoteca: ¿Nuevas formas de racismo en Cuba?" *Negra cubana tenía que ser*, August 30, 2016. https://negracubanateniaqueser.com/2016/08/30/negron-de-discoteca-nuevas-formas-de-racismo-en-cuba/.

Acosta, Leonardo. 1991. "The Rumba, the Guaguancó, and Tío Tom." In *Essays on Cuban Music: North American and Cuban Perspectives*, edited by Peter Manuel, 51–73. Lanham, MD: University Press of America.

Albizu-Campos Espiñeira, Juan Carlos, and Sergio Díaz-Briquets. 2023. "Cuba and Its Emigration: Exit as Voice." *Horizonte Cubano /Cuban Horizon*, Columbia Law School, March 10, 2023. https://horizontecubano.law.columbia.edu/news/cuba-and-its-emigration-exit-voice.

Alexander, M. Jacqui. 2005. *Pedagogies of Crossing: Meditations on Feminism, Sexual Politics, Memory, and the Sacred*. Durham, NC: Duke University Press.

Allen, Jafari S. 2011. *¡Venceremos? The Erotics of Black Self-Making in Cuba*. Durham, NC: Duke University Press.

Allen, Jafari S., and Ryan Cecil Jobson. 2016. "The Decolonizing Generation: (Race and) Theory in Anthropology since the Eighties." *Current Anthropology* 57 (2): 129–48.

Álvarez Ramírez, Sandra. 2008. "Esclavitud y cuerpos al desnudo: La sexualidad y la belleza de la mujer negra." *Revista Sexología y Sociedad* 14 (37): 36–39.

Álvarez Ramírez, Sandra. 2011. "Habana Noir." *Cuban Studies* 42:172–75.

Anderson, Mark. 2019. *From Boas to Black Power: Racism, Liberalism, and American Anthropology*. Redwood City, CA: Stanford University Press.

Andrews, George Reid. 2004. *Afro-Latin America, 1800–2000*. Oxford: Oxford University Press.

Argyriadis, Kali. 2008. "Speculators and Santuristas: The Development of Afro-Cuban Cultural Tourism and the Accusation of Religious Commercialism." *Tourist Studies* 8 (2): 249–65.

Arnedo, Miguel. 1997. "The Portrayal of the Afro-Cuban Female Dancer in Cuban Negrista Poetry." *Afro-Hispanic Review* 16 (2): 26–33.

Arroyo, Jossianna. 2003. *Travestismos culturales: Literatura y etnografía en Cuba y Brasil*. Pittsburgh: Instituto Internacional de Literatura Iberoamericana.

Arroyo, Jossianna. 2013. *Writing Secrecy in Caribbean Freemasonry*. New York: Palgrave Macmillan.

Asad, Talal. 1993. *Genealogies of Religion: Discipline and Reasons of Power in Christianity and Islam*. Baltimore, MD: Johns Hopkins University Press.

Ayorinde, Christine. 2004. *Afro-Cuban Religiosity, Revolution, and National Identity*. Gainesville: University Press of Florida.

Barcia Zequeira, María del Carmen. 2003. *La otra familia: Parientes, redes y descendencia de los esclavos en Cuba*. Havana: Casa de las Américas.

Barcia Zequeira, María del Carmen, Andrés Rodríguez Reyes, and Milagros Niebla Delgado. 2012. *Del cabildo de "nación" a la casa de santo*. Havana: Fundación Fernando Ortiz.

Barnet, Miguel. 1979. "Nieves Fresneda: Los pies en la tierra." *Cuba en el Ballet* 10 (3): 34–35.

Bastian, Hope. 2018. *Everyday Adjustments in Havana: Economic Reforms, Mobility, and Emerging Inequalities*. Lanham, MD: Lexington Books.

Bastian, Hope. 2020. "COVID-19 and Inequalities in Havana." *ReVista: Harvard Review of Latin America*, August 5, 2020. https://revista.drclas.harvard.edu/covid-19-and-inequalities-in-havana/.

Bastian, Hope, and Maya J. Berry. 2022. "Moral Panics, Viral Subjects: Black Women's Bodies on the Line during Cuba's 2020 Pandemic Lockdowns." *Journal of Latin American and Caribbean Anthropology* 27 (1–2): 16–36.

Bataille, Georges. (1991) 2017. *The Accursed Share: An Essay on General Economy*. Translated by Robert Hurley. Vols. 2 and 3. New York: Zone Books.

Beliso-De Jesús, Aisha. 2013. "Yemayá's Duck: Irony, Ambivalence, and the Effeminate Male Subject in Cuban Santería." In *Yemoja: Gender, Sexuality, and Creativity in the Latina/o and Afro-Atlantic Diasporas*, edited by Solimar Otero and Toyin Falola, 43–84. Albany: State University of New York Press.

Beliso-De Jesús, Aisha. 2014. "Santería Copresence and the Making of African Diaspora Bodies." *Cultural Anthropology* 29 (3): 503–26.

Beliso-De Jesús, Aisha M. 2015. *Electric Santería: Racial and Sexual Assemblages of Transnational Religion*. New York: Columbia University Press.

Benson, Devyn Spence. 2016. *Antiracism in Cuba: The Unfinished Revolution*. Chapel Hill: University of North Carolina Press.

Berry, Maya J. 2010. "From 'Ritual' to 'Repertory': Dancing to the Time of the Nation." *Afro-Hispanic Review* 29 (1): 55–76.

Berry, Maya J. 2016. "'Salvándose' in Contemporary Havana: Rumba's Paradox for Black Identity Politics." *Black Diaspora Review* 5 (2): 24–54. https://scholarworks.iu.edu/journals/index.php/bdr/article/view/21032.

Berry, Maya J. 2019. "La movilización del tema afrodescendiente en la Habana, 2012–2014: Un estudio de las posibilidades del performance." *Cuban Studies Journal* 48 (June): 276–302.

Berry, Maya J. 2021. "Black Feminist Rumba Pedagogies." *Dance Research Journal* 53 (2): 27–48.

Berry, Maya J., Claudia Chávez Argüelles, Shanya Cordis, Sarah Ihmoud, and Elizabeth Velásquez Estrada. 2017. "Toward a Fugitive Anthropology:

Gender, Race, and Violence in the Field." *Cultural Anthropology* 32 (4): 537–65.

Blanco Borelli, Melissa. 2009. "'¿Y ahora qué vas a hacer, mulata?': Hip Choreographies in the Mexican *Cabaretera* Film *Mulata* (1954)." *Women and Performance: A Journal of Feminist Theory* 18 (3): 215–33.

Blanco Borelli, Melissa. 2016. *She Is Cuba: A Genealogy of the Mulata Body*. Oxford: Oxford University Press.

Bledsoe, Adam, and Willie Jamaal Wright. 2019. "The Pluralities of Black Geographies." *Antipode* 51 (2): 419–37.

Blue, Sarah A. 2007. "The Erosion of Racial Equality in the Context of Cuba's Dual Economy." *Latin American Politics and Society* 49 (3): 35–68.

Bodenheimer, Rebecca M. 2010. "Localizing Hybridity: The Politics of Place in Contemporary Cuban Rumba Performance." PhD diss., University of California, Berkeley.

Bodenheimer, Rebecca M. 2013. "National Symbol or 'a Black Thing'? Rumba and Racial Politics in Cuba in the Era of Cultural Tourism." *Black Music Research Journal* 33 (2): 177–205.

Bonilla, Yarimar. 2013. "Ordinary Sovereignty." *Small Axe* 42 (November): 152–65.

Bonilla, Yarimar. 2017. "Unsettling Sovereignty." *Cultural Anthropology* 32 (3): 330–39.

Booth, David. 1976. "Cuba, Color and the Revolution." *Science and Society* 40 (2): 129–72.

Bowen, Larnies A., Ayanna Legros, Tianna S. Paschel, Geísa Mattos, Kleaver Cruz, and Juliet Hooker. 2017. "A Hemispheric Approach to Contemporary Black Activism." *NACLA Report on the Americas* 49 (1): 23–35.

Brathwaite, Edward Kamau. 1975. "Caribbean Man in Space and Time." *Caribbean Studies* 11 (September).

Brock, Lisa, and Digna Castañeda Fuertes, eds. 1998. *Between Race and Empire: African-Americans and Cubans before the Cuban Revolution*. Philadelphia: Temple University.

Bronfman, Alejandra. 2004. *Measures of Equality: Social Science, Citizenship, and Race in Cuba, 1902–1940*. Chapel Hill: University of North Carolina Press.

Brooks, Daphne. 2006. *Bodies in Dissent: Spectacular Performances of Race and Freedom, 1850–1910*. Durham, NC: Duke University Press.

Brown, David H. 1993. "Thrones of the Orichas: Afro-Cuban Altars in New Jersey, New York, and Havana." *African Arts* 26 (4): 44–87.

Brown, David H. 2003. *The Light Inside: Abakuá Society Arts and Cuban Cultural History*. Washington, DC: Smithsonian Institution.

Brown, Karen McCarthy. 2001. *Mama Lola*. Oakland: University of California Press.

Bustamante, Michael. 2018. "Cuba after the Castros." *Washington Post*, April 18, 2018. https://www.washingtonpost.com/news/made-by-history/wp/2018/04/18/cuba-after-the-castros/.

Butler, Judith. 1990. *Gender Trouble: Feminism and the Subversion of Identity*. New York: Routledge.

Cabezas, Amalia L. 2009. *Economies of Desire: Sex and Tourism in Cuba and the Dominican Republic*. Philadelphia: Temple University Press.

Cabrera, Lydia. 1940. *Cuentos negros de Cuba*. Havana: Imprenta La Veronica.

Cabrera, Lydia. 1948. *Por qué: Cuentos negros de Cuba*. Havana: Ediciones C. R.

Cabrera, Lydia. 1954. *El monte: Igbo-Finda; Ewe Orisha, Vititi Nfinda (Notas sobre las religiones, la magia, las supersictiones y el folklore de los negros criollos y el pueblo de Cuba)*. Havana: Ediciones C. R.

Cabrera, Lydia. 1957. *Anagó: vocabulario lucumí*. Havana: Ediciones C. R.

Caldwell, Kia Lilly. 2006. *Negras in Brazil: Re-envisioning Black Women, Citizenship, and the Politics of Identity*. New Brunswick, NJ: Rutgers University Press.

Campt, Tina. 2017. *Listening to Images*. Durham, NC: Duke University Press.

Carbonell, Walterio. 1961. *Crítica: Cómo surgió la cultural nacional*. Havana: Ediciones Yaka.

Carpentier, Alejo. 1946. *La Musica en Cuba*. Mexico: Fondo de Cultura Economia.

Carrazana Fuentes, Lázara Y., Rodrigo Espina Prieto, Ana Julia García Dally, Estrella González Noriega, Niurka Núñez González, María Magdalena Pérez Álvarez, Pablo Rodríguez Ruiz, Hernán Tirado Toirac, and Odalys Buscarón Ochoa. 2011. *Las relaciones raciales en Cuba: Estudios contemporáneos*. Havana: Fundación Fernando Ortiz.

Castor, N. Fadeke. 2017. *Spiritual Citizenship: Transnational Pathways from Black Power to Ifá in Trinidad*. Durham, NC: Duke University Press.

Castro Ricalde, Maricruz. 2020. "Rumberas, pero decentes: Intérpretes cubanas en el cine mexicano de la edad dorada." *Hispanic Research Journal* 21 (1): 70–89.

Castro Ruz, Raúl. 2016. "El desarrollo de la economía nacional, junto a la lucha por la paz y la firmeza ideológica, constituyen las principales misiones del Partido." In *Informe Central al 7mo Congreso del Partido Comunista de Cuba*. Havana: El Granma.

Cearns, Jennifer. 2020. "The 'Mula Ring': Material Networks of Circulation through the Cuban World." *Journal of Latin American and Caribbean Anthropology* 24 (4): 864–90. https://doi-org.libproxy.lib.unc.edu/10.1111/jlca.12439.

Cearns, Jennifer. 2021. "Introduction to el Paquete." *Cuban Studies*, no. 50, 99–110.

Center for Democracy in the Americas. 2023. "US-Cuba News Brief," no. 738, February 14, 2023.

Chevannes, Barry. 2002. *Learning to Be a Man: Culture, Socialization and Gender Identity in Five Caribbean Communities*. Mona, Jamaica: University Press of the West Indies.

Childs, Matt D. 2006. *The 1812 Aponte Rebellion in Cuba and the Struggle against Atlantic Slavery*. Chapel Hill: University of North Carolina Press.

Clark, Mary Ann. 2005. *Where Men Are Wives and Mothers Rule: Santería Ritual Practices and Their Gender Implications*. Gainesville: University Press of Florida.

Clark Hine, Darlene. 1989. "Rape and the Inner Lives of Black Women in the Middle West." *Signs* 14 (4): 912–20.

Clealand, Danielle Pilar. 2017. *The Power of Race in Cuba: Racial Ideology and Black Consciousness during the Revolution*. Oxford: Oxford University Press.

Cohen, Cathy J. 2004. "Deviance as Resistance: A New Research Agenda for the Study of Black Politics." *Du Bois Review* 1 (1): 27–45.

Cohen, Cathy J., Kathleen B. Jones, and Joan C. Tronto. 1997. "Introduction: Women Transforming U.S. Politics: Sites of Power/Resistance." In *Women Transforming Politics: An Alternative Reader*, edited by Cathy J. Cohen, Kathleen B. Jones, and Joan C. Tronto, 1–12. New York: New York University Press.

Collins, Patricia Hill. 2000. *Black Feminist Thought: Knowledge, Consciousness, and the Politics of Empowerment*. New York: Routledge.

Concha-Holmes, Amanda D. 2013. "Cuban Cabildos, Cultural Politics, and Cultivating a Transnational Yoruba Citizenry." *Cultural Anthropology* 28 (3): 490–503.

Coronil, Fernando. 1995. "Introduction." In *Cuban Counterpoint: Tobacco and Sugar*, ix–lvi. Durham, NC: Duke University Press.

Corvalán, Eric, dir. 2008. *Raza*. Havana: Cuban Higher Institute of Art, Martin Luther King Memorial Center, and DelFin Producciones.

Covington-Ward, Yolanda. 2015. *Gesture and Power: Religion, Nationalism, and Everyday Performance in Congo*. Durham, NC: Duke University Press.

Cox, Aimee Meredith. 2015. *Shapeshifters: Black Girls and the Choreography of Citizenship*. Durham, NC: Duke University Press.

Cubadebate. 2021. "Díaz-Canel al pueblo de Cuba: 'La orden de combate está dada, a la calle los revolucionarios.'" *CubaDebate.cu*, July 11, 2021. http://www .cubadebate.cu/noticias/2021/07/11/miguel-diaz-canel-comparecera-en -cadena-de-radio-television-a-las-400-pm/.

Daniel, Yvonne. 1990. "In the Company of Women in Cuba." *African Commentary* 2 (7): 16–19.

Daniel, Yvonne. 1991. "Changing Values in Cuban Rumba, a Lower Class Black Dance Appropriated by the Cuban Revolution." *Dance Research Journal* 23 (2): 1–10.

Daniel, Yvonne. 1994. "Race, Gender, and Class Embodied in Cuban Dance." *Contributions in Black Studies* 12 (1): 70–87.

Daniel, Yvonne. 1995. *Rumba: Dance and Social Change in Contemporary Cuba*. Bloomington: Indiana University Folklore Institute.

Daniel, Yvonne. 2005. *Dancing Wisdom: Embodied Knowledge in Haitian Vodou, Cuban Yoruba, and Bahian Candomblé*. Urbana: University of Illinois Press.

Daniel, Yvonne. 2009. "Rumba Then and Now: Quindembo." In *Ballroom, Boogie, Shimmy Sham, Shake: A Social and Popular Dance Reader*, edited by Julie Malnig, 146–64. Urbana: University of Illinois Press.

Daniel, Yvonne. 2010. "The Economic Vitamins of Cuba: Sacred and Other Dance Performance." In *Rhythms of the Afro-Atlantic World*, edited by Ifeoma C. K. Nwankwo and Mamadou Diouf, 19–40. Ann Arbor: University of Michigan Press.

Daniel, Yvonne. 2011. *Caribbean and Atlantic Diaspora Dance: Igniting Citizenship*. Urbana: University of Illinois Press.

Davis, Adrienne. 2002. "'Don't Let Nobody Bother Yo' Principle': The Sexual Economy of American Slavery." In *Sister Circle: Black Women and Work*, edited by

Sharon Harley and the Black Women and Work Collective, 103–27. New Brunswick, NJ: Rutgers University Press.

DeFrantz, Thomas F. 2020. Opening remarks. Collegium for African Diasporic Dance (CADD) Conference, "Fluid Black::Dance Back," Duke University, Durham, NC, February 21, 2020.

de la Fuente, Alejandro. 1995. "Race and Inequality in Cuba, 1899–1981." *Journal of Contemporary History* 30 (1): 131–68.

de la Fuente, Alejandro. 1996. "Negros y electores: Desigualdad y políticas raciales en Cuba, 1900–1930." In *La nación soñada: Cuba, Puerto Rico y Filipinas ante el 98*, edited by Consuelo Naranjo, Miguel A. Puig-Samper, and Luis Miguel García Mora. Spain: Aranjuez.

de la Fuente, Alejandro. 2001a. *A Nation for All: Race, Inequality, and Politics in Twentieth-Century Cuba*. Chapel Hill: University of North Carolina Press.

de la Fuente, Alejandro. 2001b. "Recreating Racism: Race and Discrimination in Cuba's 'Special Period.'" *Socialism and Democracy* 15 (1): 65–91.

de la Fuente, Alejandro. 2008. "The New Afro-Cuban Cultural Movement and the Debate on Race in Contemporary Cuba." *Journal of Latin American Studies* 40 (4): 697–720.

de la Fuente, Alejandro. 2019. "Cuba's Struggle between Racism and Inclusion." *New York Times*, May 28, 2019.

de la Fuente, Alejandro, and Stanley R. Bailey. 2021. "The Puzzle of Racial Inequality in Cuba, 1980s–2010s." *Du Bois Review: Social Science Research on Race* 18 (1): 73–96.

de la Fuente, Alejandro, and Laurence Glasco. 1997. "Are Blacks 'Getting Out of Control'? Racial Attitudes, Revolution, and Political Transition in Cuba." In *Toward a New Cuba? Legacies of a Revolution*, edited by Miguel A. Centeno and Mauricio Font, 53–71. Boulder, CO: Lynn Rienner.

de la Hoz, Pedro. 2014. "El canto de la Patria es nuestro canto: Desde la escalinata con los cinco." *Granma*, March 3, 2014.

Deschamps Chapeaux, Pedro. 1983. *Los cimarrones urbanos*. Havana: Editorial de Ciencias Sociales.

Drewal, Margaret Thompson. (1989) 1992. *Yoruba Ritual: Performers, Play, Agency*. Bloomington: Indiana University Press.

Drewal, Margaret Thompson, and Henry John Drewal. 1990. *Gelede: Art and Female Power among the Yoruba*. Bloomington: Indiana University Press.

Dubois, Laurent. 2006. "An Enslaved Enlightenment: Rethinking the Intellectual History of the French Atlantic." *Social History* 31 (1): 1–14.

Dubois, Laurent, and Richard Lee Turits. 2019. "U.S. Occupations in the Independent Caribbean." In *Freedom Roots: Histories from the Caribbean*, edited by Laurent Dubois and Richard Lee Turits, 139–87. Chapel Hill: University of North Carolina Press.

Economist Intelligence Unit. 1991. "Cuba." In *Cuba, Dominican Republic, Haiti, and Puerto Rico: Country Reports, International Tourism Reports*, 19–31. London: Economist Intelligence Unit.

Escalante, Alejandro Stephano. 2019. "Trans* Atlantic Religion: Spirit Possession and Gender Ideology in Cuban Santería." *TSQ* 6 (3): 386–99.

Escuela, Mauricio. 2019. "Cuba Denounces War on Our People." *Granma*, May 22, 2019. http://en.granma.cu/cuba/2019-05-22/cuba-denounces-war-on-our -people.

Espina Prieto, Mayra, Lilia Núñez Moreno, Lucy Martín Posada, Lartiza Vega Quintana, Adrián Chailloux Rodríguez, and Gisela Ángel Sierra. 2004. *Heterogenización y desigualdades en la ciudad: Diagnóstico y perspectivas*. Havana: Centro de Investigaciones Psicológicas y Sociológicas (CIPS).

Fabian, Johannes. 1983. *Time and the Other: How Anthropology Makes Its Object*. New York: Columbia University Press.

Farber, Samuel. 2011. "Racism against Black Cubans: An Oppression That Dared Not Speak Its Name." In *Cuba since the Revolution of 1959: A Critical Assessment*. Chicago: Haymarket Books.

Farber, Samuel. 2013. "Raúl's Cuba: Don't Expect Real Reform." *Boston Review* 38 (5): 34–39.

Fernandes, Deepa. 2017. "Havana's Small Business Boom Exposes a Stark Racial Divide." *The World*, PRI, April 3, 2017. https://theworld.org/stories/2017/04 /03/havanas-new-economy-exposes-stark-racial-divide.

Fernandes, Sujatha. 2006. *Cuba Represent! Cuban Arts, State Power, and the Making of New Revolutionary Cultures*. Durham, NC: Duke University Press.

Fernandez, Nadine. 1999. "Back to the Future? Women, Race, and Tourism in Cuba." In *Sun, Sex, and Gold: Tourism and Sex Work in the Caribbean*, edited by Kamala Kempadoo, 81–92. Lanham, MD: Rowman and Littlefield.

Fernández Robaina, Tomás. 1994. *El negro en cuba: 1902–1958*. Havana: Editorial de Ciencias Sociales.

Fernández Robaina, Tomás. 2022. "For My Teacher, Walterio Carbonell." *Zanj: The Journal of Critical Global South Studies* 4 (1): 21–26. DOI:10.13169 /zanjglobsoutstud.4.1.0003.

Fernández-Selier, Yesenia. 2012–13. "The Making of the *Rumba* Body: René Rivero and the *Rumba* Craze." *Sargasso: A Journal of Caribbean Literature, Language, and Culture* 40 (1–2): 85–100. https://dloc.com/UF00096005/00040/images.

Ferrer, Ada. 1999. *Insurgent Cuba: Race, Nation, and Revolution, 1868–1898*. Chapel Hill: University of North Carolina Press.

Ferrer, Ada. 2014. *Freedom's Mirror: Cuba and Haiti in the Age of Revolution*. Cambridge: Cambridge University Press.

Finch, Aisha K. 2015. *Rethinking Slave Rebellion in Cuba: La Escalera and the Insurgencies of 1841–1844*. Chapel Hill: University of North Carolina Press.

Fleetwood, Nicole R. 2011. *Troubling Vision: Performance, Visuality, and Blackness*. Chicago: University of Chicago Press.

Frank, Marc. 2010. "Cubans Brace for 'Reorganization' of Labour Force." *Reuters*, July 20, 2010.

Freeman, Carla. 2014. *Entrepreneurial Selves: Neoliberal Respectability and the Making of a Caribbean Middle Class*. Durham, NC: Duke University Press.

Freyre, Gilberto. 1946. *The Masters and the Slaves*. New York: Alfred A. Knopf.

Fusco, Coco. 1998. "Hustling for Dollars: *Jineterismo* in Cuba." In *Global Sex Workers: Rights, Resistance, and Redefinition*, edited by Kamala Kempadoo and Jo Doezema, 151–61. London: Routledge.

Gagliardi, Susan Elizabeth. 2018. "Seeing the Unseeing Audience: Women and West African Power Association Masquerades." *Africa: Journal of the International African Institute* 88 (4): 744–67.

Garcia, David F. 2013. "Contesting Anthropology's and Ethnomusicology's Will to Power in the Field: William R. Bascom's and Richard A. Waterman's Fieldwork in Cuba, 1948." *MUSICultures* 40 (2): 1–33.

Garcia, David F. 2017. *Listening for Africa: Freedom, Modernity, and the Logic of Black Music's African Origins*. Durham, NC: Duke University Press.

García Velasco, Miguel Ángel, dir. 2016. *Asere crúcoro (Saludo a los que están, a los presentes)*. Cuba: AfroKuba. https://vimeo.com/162614161.

Garth, Hanna. 2020. *Food in Cuba: The Pursuit of a Decent Meal*. Redwood City, CA: Stanford University Press.

Garth, Hanna. 2021. "'There Is No Race in Cuba': Level of Culture and the Logics of Transnational Anti-Blackness." *Anthropological Quarterly* 94 (3): 385–410.

Gates, Henry Louis, Jr. 1988. *The Signifying Monkey: A Theory of African-American Literary Criticism*. Oxford: Oxford University Press.

Gill, Lyndon K. 2018. *Erotic Islands: Art and Activism in the Queer Caribbean*. Durham, NC: Duke University Press.

Gingerfilm Latin. 2011. "Rumba Guaguancó—'El Solar de los 6'—Casa de Amado—La Habana 2011." YouTube. Video. 03:10. https://www.youtube.com/watch?v=gJVT_5swkhA.

Glissant, Édouard. 1997. "For Opacity." In *Poetics of Relation*, translated by Betsy Wing, 189–94. Ann Arbor: University of Michigan Press.

Godreau, Isar P. 2006. "Folkloric 'Others': *Blanqueamiento* and the Celebration of Blackness as an Exception in Puerto Rico." In *Globalization and Race: Transformations in the Cultural Production of Blackness*, edited by Kamari Maxine Clarke and Deborah A. Thomas, 171–87. Durham, NC: Duke University Press.

Goldberg, David Theo. 2001. *The Racial State*. Oxford: Wiley-Blackwell.

Gordon, Edmund T. 1997. "Cultural Politics of Black Masculinity." *Transforming Anthropology* 6 (1–2): 36–53.

Gordon, Edmund T., et al. 2007. "The Austin School Manifesto: An Approach to the Black or African Diaspora." *Cultural Dynamics* 19 (1): 93–97.

Gordon, Edmund T., and Mark Anderson. 1999. "The African Diaspora: Toward an Ethnography of Diasporic Identification." *Journal of American Folklore* 112 (445): 282–96.

Guerra, Lillian. 2005. *The Myths of José Martí: Conflicting Nationalisms in Early Twentieth-Century Cuba*. Chapel Hill: University of North Carolina Press.

Guerra, Lillian. 2014. *Visions of Power in Cuba: Revolution, Redemption, and Resistance, 1959–1971*. Chapel Hill: University of North Carolina Press.

Guevara, Ernesto Che. (1965) 1967. "Man and Socialism in Cuba." Guevara Internet Archive, 1999. Accessed June 26, 2024. https://www.marxists.org/archive /guevara/1965/03/man-socialism-alt.htm.

Guillard Limonta, Norma R. 2016. "To Be a Black Woman, a Lesbian, and an Afro-Feminist in Cuba Today." *Black Diaspora Review* 5 (2): 81–97.

Guridy, Frank. 2010. *Forging Diaspora: Afro-Cubans and African Americans in a World of Empire and Jim Crow*. Chapel Hill: University of North Carolina Press.

Guss, David. 2000. *The Festive State: Race, Ethnicity, and Nationalism as Cultural Performance*. Oakland: University of California Press.

Gutiérrez, Laura G. 2010. "*Fue en un cabaret*: Nation, Melodrama, Gender, and Sexuality in Contemporary Mexican Performance." In *Performing Mexicanidad: Vendidas y Cabareteras on the Transnational Stage*, 101–31. Austin: University of Texas Press.

Hagedorn, Katherine J. 2001. *Divine Utterances: The Performance of Afro-Cuban Santeria*. Washington, DC: Smithsonian Institution Press.

Halberstam, Jack. 2013. "The Wild Beyond: With and for the Undercommons." Introduction to *The Undercommons: Fugitive Planning and Black Study*, by Stefano Harney and Fred Moten, 2–12. New York: Minor Compositions.

Hall, Stuart, Chas Critcher, Tony Jefferson, and John N. Clarke. 1978. *Policing the Crisis: Mugging, the State, and Law and Order*. London: Macmillan International Higher Education.

Hanchard, Michael. 2006. *Party/Politics: Horizons in Black Political Thought*. Oxford: Oxford University Press.

Hansing, Katrin. 2017. "Race and Inequality in the New Cuba: Reasons, Dynamics, and Manifestations." *Social Research: An International Quarterly* 84 (2): 331–49.

Hansing, Katrin, and Bert Hoffmann. 2019. "Cuba's New Social Structure: Assessing the Re-stratification of Cuban Society 60 Years after Revolution." Working Papers GIGA Research Programme: Accountability and Participation. Hamburg, Germany.

Haraway, Donna. 1988. "Situated Knowledges: The Science Question in Feminism and the Privilege of Partial Perspective." *Feminist Studies* 14 (3): 575–99.

Harding, Rachel. 2003. *A Refuge in Thunder: Candomblé and Alternative Spaces of Blackness*. Bloomington: Indiana University Press.

Harney, Stefano, and Fred Moten. 2013. *The Undercommons: Fugitive Planning and Black Study*. New York: Minor Compositions.

Harrison, Faye V. 1990. "'Three Women, One Struggle': Anthropology, Performance, and Pedagogy." *Transforming Anthropology* 1 (1): 1–9.

Harrison, Faye V., ed. 1991. *Decolonizing Anthropology: Moving Further toward an Anthropology for Liberation*. Washington, DC: American Anthropological Association.

Hartman, Saidiya. 2008. "Venus in Two Acts." *Small Axe* 26 (June): 1–14.

Hartman, Saidiya. 2019. *Wayward Lives, Beautiful Experiments: Intimate Histories of Social Upheaval*. New York: Norton.

Hearn, Adrian H. 2008. *Cuba: Religion, Social Capital, and Development*. Durham, NC: Duke University Press.

Helg, Aline. 1995. *Our Rightful Share: The Afro-Cuban Struggle for Equality, 1886–1912*. Chapel Hill: University of North Carolina Press.

Henry, Matthew. 2004. "He Is a 'Bad Mother*$%@!#": 'Shaft' and Contemporary Black Masculinity." *African American Review* 38 (1): 119–26.

Hernández-Reguant, Ariana. 2002. "Radio Taino and the Globalization of the Cuban Culture Industries." PhD diss., University of Chicago.

Hernández-Reguant, Ariana. 2006. "Havana's *Timba*: A Macho Sound for Black Sex." In *Globalization and Race*, edited by Kamari Maxine Clarke and Deborah A. Thomas, 249–78. Durham, NC: Duke University Press.

Hernández-Reguant, Ariana, ed. 2010. *Cuba in the Special Period: Culture and Ideology in the 1990s*. New York: Palgrave Macmillan.

Hicks, Anasa. 2019. "Domestic Service in a New Cuba." NACLA *Report on the Americas* 51 (3): 262–67.

Higginbotham, Evelyn Brooks. 1993. "The Politics of Respectability." In *Righteous Discontent: The Women's Movement in the Black Baptist Church, 1880–1920*, 185–229. Cambridge, MA: Harvard University Press.

Holland, Sharon Patricia. 2012. *The Erotic Life of Racism*. Durham, NC: Duke University Press.

hooks, bell. 1984. *Feminist Theory: From Margin to Center*. Boston: South End.

hooks, bell. 2014. *Black Looks: Race and Representation*. New York: Routledge.

Horst, Jesse. 2014. "Shantytown Revolution: Slum Clearance, Rent Control, and the Cuban State, 1937–1955." *Journal of Urban History* 40 (4): 699–718.

Howard, Philip A. 1998. *Changing History: Afro-Cuban Cabildos and Societies of Color in the Nineteenth Century*. Baton Rouge: Louisiana State University Press.

Hurston, Zora Neale. (1935) 2008. *Mules and Men*. New York: Harper Perennial.

Hynson, Rachel. 2015. "'Count, Capture, and Reeducate': The Campaign to Rehabilitate Cuba's Female Sex Workers, 1959–1966." *Journal of the History of Sexuality* 24 (1): 125–53.

Hynson, Rachel. 2020. *Laboring for the State: Women, Family, and Work in Revolutionary Cuba, 1959–1971*. Cambridge: Cambridge University Press.

Israel, Esteban. 2009. "Spain Issues Cuba's First 'Grandchildren' Passport." *Reuters*, February 5, 2009. https://www.reuters.com/article/us-cuba -spain-citizenship/spain-issues-cubas-first-grandchildren-passport -idUSTRE51502U20090206.

Jazeel, Tariq. 2014. "Subaltern Geographies: Geographical Knowledge and Postcolonial Strategy." *Singapore Journal of Tropical Geography* 35 (1): 88–103.

Johnson, Paul Christopher. 2002. *Secrets, Gossip, and Gods: The Transformation of Brazilian Candomblé*. New York: Oxford University Press.

Johnson, Paul Christopher. 2011. "An Atlantic Genealogy of 'Spirit Possession.'" *Comparative Studies in Society and History* 53 (2): 393–425.

Johnson, Paul Christopher. 2022. "Architectures of Secrecy." In *The Routledge Handbook of Religion and Secrecy*, edited by Hugh B. Urban and Paul Christopher Johnson, 71–84. New York: Routledge.

Jottar, Berta. 2009a. "The Acoustic Body: Rumba Guarapachanguera and Abakuá Sociality in Central Park." *Latin American Music Review* 30 (1): 1–24.

Jottar, Berta. 2009b. "Zero Tolerance and Central Park Rumba Cabildo Politics." *Liminalities: A Journal of Performance Studies* 5 (4): 1–24.

Jottar, Berta. 2013. "Rumberas." Paper presented at Columbia College, Chicago, IL.

Kelley, Robin D. G. 1994. *Race Rebels: Culture, Politics, and the Black Working Class.* New York: Free Press.

Kempadoo, Kamala. 2004. *Sexing the Caribbean: Gender, Race, and Sexual Labor.* New York: Routledge.

Kivland, Chelsey L. 2020. *Street Sovereigns: Young Men and the Makeshift State in Urban Haiti.* Ithaca, NY: Cornell University Press.

Knauer, Lisa Maya. 2009. "Audiovisual Remittances and Transnational Subjectivities." In *Cuba in the Special Period: Culture and Ideology in the 1990s*, edited by Ariana Hernández-Reguant, 159–77. New York: Palgrave MacMillan.

Kutzinski, Vera M. 1993. *Sugar's Secrets: Race and the Erotics of Cuban Nationalism.* Charlottesville: University of Virginia Press.

Lainé, Daniel, and Pierre Combroux, dir. 2013. "Cuba, la saveur des Caraïbes." In *Les Chemins de la Beauté.* France.

Lane, Jill. 2005. *Blackface Cuba, 1840–1895.* Philadelphia: University of Pennsylvania Press.

Lara, Ana-Maurine. 2020. *Queer Freedom: Black Sovereignty.* Albany: State University of New York Press.

Levine, Mike. 2021. "Sounding *El Paquete*: The Local and Transnational Routes of an Afro-Cuban *Repartero*." *Cuban Studies*, no. 50, 139–60.

Lewis, Jovan. 2020. *Scammer's Yard: The Crime of Black Repair in Jamaica.* Minneapolis: University of Minnesota Press.

Lorde, Audre. (1978) 1984. "The Uses of the Erotic: The Erotic as Power." In *Sister Outsider: Essays and Speeches*, 53–59. Trumansburg, NY: Crossing Press.

Madison, D. Soyini. 2010. *Acts of Activism: Human Rights as Radical Performance.* Cambridge: Cambridge University Press.

Madison, D. Soyini. 2014. "Foreword." In *Black Performance Theory*, edited by Thomas F. DeFrantz and Anita Gonzalez, vii–ix. Durham, NC: Duke University Press.

Maguire, Emily. 2011. *Racial Experiments in Cuban Literature and Ethnography.* Gainesville: University Press of Florida.

Mahmood, Saba. 2004. *Politics of Piety: The Islamic Revival and the Feminist Subject.* Princeton, NJ: Princeton University Press.

Martí, José. 1963. *Obras completas.* Vol. 1. Havana: Editorial Nacional de Cuba.

Martínez Furé, Rogelio. 2001. "Cubanía." *Bohemia*, no. 10, 10–12.

Martínez Rodríguez, Raúl. 1995. "La rumba en la provincia de Matanzas." In *Panorama de la música popular cubana*, edited by William Álvarez Ramírez, 139–47. Cali, Colombia: Editorial Facultad de Humanidades y Editorial Letras Cubanas.

Martínez y Carmen Souto, Yanira. 2009. "¿Y la rumba que? Entrevista a Geovani del Pino, director de Yoruba Andabo." *La Calle del Medio*, 12–13.

Martín Posada, Lucy, and Lilia Núñez Moreno. 2013. "Geografía y Hábitat: Dimensiones de equidad y movilidad social en Cuba." In *Desarrollo económico y social en Cuba: Reformas emprendidas y desafíos en el siglo XXI*, edited by Jorge I. Domínguez, Omar Everleny Pérez Villanueva, Mayra Espina Prieto, and Lorena Barberia. Mexico: Fondo de Cultura Económica.

Masco, Joseph, and Deborah A. Thomas. 2023. "Introduction: Feeling Unhinged." In *Sovereignty Unhinged: An Illustrated Primer for the Study of the Present Intensities, Disavowals, and Temporal Derangements*, edited by Deborah A. Thomas and Joseph Masco, 1–23. Durham, NC: Duke University Press.

Mason, Michael Atwood. 1994. "'I Bow My Head to the Ground': The Creation of Bodily Experience in a Cuban American *Santería* Initiation." *Journal of American Folklore* 107 (423): 23–39.

Matory, James Lorand. 1994. *Sex and the Empire That Is No More: Gender and the Politics of Metaphor in Oyo Yoruba Religion*. Minneapolis: University of Minnesota Press.

McKittrick, Katherine. 2006. *Demonic Grounds: Black Women and the Cartographies of Struggle*. Minneapolis: University of Minnesota Press.

McKittrick, Katherine. 2011. "On Plantations, Prisons, and a Black Sense of Place." *Social and Cultural Geography* 12 (8): 947–63.

Menéndez, Lázara. 2002. *Rodar el coco: Procesos de cambio en la Santería*. Havana, Cuba: Fundación Fernando Ortiz-Editorial de Ciencias Sociales.

Meza, Ramón. 1891. "Día de Reyes." *La Habana Elegante*, January 11, 1891.

Miller, Ivor L. 2000. "A Secret Society Goes Public: The Relationship between Abakuá and Cuban Popular Culture." *African Studies Review* 43 (1): 161–88.

Miller, Ivor L. 2004. "The Formation of African Identities in the Americas: Spiritual 'Ethnicity.'" *Contours* 2 (2): 193–222.

Miller, Ivor L. 2009. *Voice of the Leopard: African Secret Societies and Cuba*. Jackson: University Press of Mississippi.

Moore, Robin D. 1994. "Representations of Afrocuban Expressive Culture in the Writings of Fernando Ortiz." *Latin American Music Review* 15 (1): 32–54.

Moore, Robin D. 1997. *Nationalizing Blackness: Afrocubanismo and Artistic Revolution in Havana, 1920–1940*. Pittsburgh: University of Pittsburgh Press.

Moore, Robin D. 2006. *Music and Revolution: Cultural Change in Socialist Cuba*. Oakland: University of California Press.

Moore, Robin D., ed. 2018. *Fernando Ortiz on Music: Selected Writing on Afro-Cuban Culture*. Philadelphia: Temple University Press.

Moré, Beny. 1982. "En el tiempo de la colonia." *Sonero mayor*, vol. 4. EGREM, LD-3708.

Moten, Fred. 2003. *In the Break: The Aesthetics of the Black Radical Tradition*. Minneapolis: University of Minnesota Press.

Muñoz, José Esteban. 2006. "Feeling Brown, Feeling Down: Latina Affect, the Performativity of Race, and the Depressive Position." *Signs* 31 (3): 675–88.

Negrón-Muntaner, Frances. 2015. "The Look of Sovereignty: Style and Politics in the Young Lords." CENTRO *Journal* 27 (1): 4–33.

Negrón-Muntaner, Frances, and Raquel Z. Rivera. 2009. "Nación Reggaetón." *Nueva Sociedad*, no. 223, 29–38.

Ness, Sally. 1992. *Body, Movement, and Culture: Kinesthetic and Visual Symbolism in a Philippine Community*. Philadelphia: University of Pennsylvania Press.

Noël, Samantha A. 2022. "Disrupting Subaltern Geographies: The Artistic Intersections of Belkis Ayón." In *Transnational Belonging and Female Agency in the Arts*, edited by Basia Sliwinska and Catherine Dormor, 161–78. London: Bloomsbury Visual Arts.

Obsesión. 2011. "Tú con tu ballet." No. 2, *El Disco Negro*, Magia López Cabrera and Alexey Rodriguez Mola, January 30, 2011.

Ochoa, Todd Ramón. 2010. *Society of the Dead: Quita Manaquita and Palo Praise in Cuba*. Oakland: University of California Press.

Ong, Aihwa. 1999. *Flexible Citizenship: The Cultural Logics of Transnationality*. Durham, NC: Duke University Press.

Ortiz, Fernando. (1906) 1973. *Hampa Afrocubana: Los negros brujos: Apuntes para un estudio de etnologia criminal*. Miami: Ediciones Universal.

Ortiz, Fernando. 1916. *Hampa afrocubana: Los negros esclavos: Estudio sociológico y de derecho publico*. Havana: Revista bimestre cubana.

Ortiz, Fernando. (1920) 2001. "The Afro-Cuban Festival 'Day of the Kings.'" In *Cuban Festivals: A Century of Afro-Cuban Culture*, edited by Judith Bettelheim, 1–40. Princeton, NJ: Markus Reiner.

Ortiz, Fernando. (1924) 1991. *Glosario de afronegrismos*. Havana: Editorial de Ciencias Sociales.

Ortiz, Fernando. 1940. "Los factores humanos de la cubanidad." *Revista Bimestre Cubana*, no. 45, 161–86.

Ortiz, Fernando. 1950. "La 'tragedia' de los ñáñigos." *Cuadernos Americanos* 9 (4): 79–101.

Ortiz, Fernando. (1958) 1986. *Los Negros curros*. Edited by Diana Iznaga. Havana: Editorial de Ciencias Sociales.

Ortiz, Fernando. 2018. "The Religious Music of Black Cuban Yorubas." In *Fernando Ortiz on Music: Selected Writing on Afro-Cuban Culture*, edited by Robin D. Moore, 186–211. Philadelphia: Temple University Press. Originally published as "La música religiosa de los yorubas entre los negros cubanos," *Estudios afrocubanos* 5 (1945–46): 19–60.

Otero, Solimar, and Toyin Falola. 2013. "Introduction: Introducing Yemoja." In *Yemoja: Gender, Sexuality, and Creativity in the Latino/a and Afro-Atlantic Diasporas*, edited by Solimar Otero and Toyin Falola, xvii–xxxii. Albany: State University of New York Press.

Oyěwùmí, Oyèrónké. 1997. *The Invention of Women: Making an African Sense of Western Gender Discourses*. Minneapolis: University of Minnesota Press.

Padrón Hernández, Maria. 2012. "Beans and Roses: Everyday Economies and Morality in Contemporary Havana, Cuba." PhD diss., University of Gothenburg.

Palmié, Stephan. 1998. "Fernando Ortiz and the Cooking of History." *Iberoamerikanisches Archiv* 24 (3/4): 353–73.

Palmié, Stephan. 2002. *Wizards and Scientists: Explorations in Afro-Cuban Modernity and Tradition*. Durham, NC: Duke University Press.

Palmié, Stephan. 2013. *The Cooking of History: How Not to Study Afro-Cuban Religion*. Chicago: University of Chicago Press.

Pañellas Álvarez, Daybel. 2015. "Impactos subjetivos de las reformas económicas: Grupos e identidades sociales en la estructura social cubana." In *Cuba: los correlatos socioculturales del cambio económico*, edited by Mayra Paula Espina and Dayma Echevarría, 164–82. Havana: Ruth Casa Editorial.

Pappademos, Melina. 2011. *Black Political Activism and the Cuban Republic*. Chapel Hill: University of North Carolina Press.

Partido Comunista de Cuba. 2011. "Resolución sobre los lineamientos de la política económica y social del partido y la revolución." VI Congreso del Partido Comunista de Cuba, Havana.

Perry, Imani. 2018. *Vexy Thing: On Gender and Liberation*. Durham, NC: Duke University Press.

Perry, Imani. 2020. "Racism Is Terrible. Blackness Is Not." *Atlantic*, June 15, 2020.

Perry, Marc D. 2016. *Negro Soy Yo: Hip Hop and Raced Citizenship in Neoliberal Cuba*. Durham, NC: Duke University Press.

Price, Charles. 2009. *Becoming Rasta: Origins of Rastafari Identity in Jamaica*. New York: New York University Press.

Quijano, Anibal. 2000. "Coloniality of Power, Eurocentrism and Latin America." *Nepantla: Views from the South* 1 (3): 533–80.

Quinto, Pancho. 1997. "Lenguasá." *En el Solar de la Cueva del Humo*. Round World Records.

Ribeiro, Gustavo Lins. 2019. "Cuba: Anthropological Imaginaries, Flows, and Comparisons." *American Anthropologist* 121 (3): 764–66.

Ríoseco, Pedro. 2022. "José Martí Foresaw His Own Life in the Dramatic Poem Abdala." *Granma*, January 28, 2022. https://en.granma.cu/cuba/2022–01–28/jose-marti-foresaw-his-own-life-in-the-dramatic-poem-abdala.

Rivera-Velásquez, Celiany, and Beliza Torres Narváez. 2016. "Homosociality and Its Discontents: Puerto Rican Masculinities in Javier Cardona's *Ah mén*." In *Blacktino Queer Performance*, edited by E. Patrick Johnson and Ramón Rivera-Servera, 264–74. Durham, NC: Duke University Press.

Roche y Monteagudo, Rafael. 1908. *La policia y sus misterios en Cuba: Adicionada con la policia judicial, procedemientos, formularios, ordenes, disposiciones y cuanto concierne a los cuerpos de seguridad publica*. Havana: Imprenta "La Prueba."

Rodríguez López, Yusimí. 2011. "La revolución hizo a los negros personas." In *Afrocubanas: Historia, pensamiento y prácticas culturales*, edited by Daisy Rubiera

Castillo and Inés María Martiatu Terry, 200–204. Havana: Editorial de Ciencias Sociales.

Rodríguez López, Yusimí. 2015. "From Italy to Centro Habana: The Story of Salchi-Pizza." *Havana Times*, April 24, 2015. https://www.havanatimes.org/?p=110850.

Roland, L. Kaifa. 2011. *Cuban Color in Tourism and* La Lucha: *An Ethnography of Racial Meanings*. Oxford: Oxford University Press.

Roland, L. Kaifa. 2013. "T/racing Belonging through Cuban Tourism." *Cultural Anthropology* 28 (3): 396–419.

Routon, Kenneth. 2005. "Unimaginable Homelands? 'Africa' and the Abakuá Historical Imagination." *Journal of Latin American Anthropology* 10 (2): 370–400.

Rubiera Castillo, Daisy, and Inés María Martiatu Terry. 2011. *Afrocubanas: Historia, pensamiento, y practicas culturales*. Edited by Daisy Rubiera Castillo and Inés María Martiatu Terry. Havana: Ciencias Sociales.

Ruiz, Irene Esther. 2007. "Para Verte Mejor: Un estudio a cerca de la presencia de la mujer negra en la televisión cubana." http://negracuabana.nireblog.com.

Sawyer, Mark Q. 2005. *Racial Politics in Post-revolutionary Cuba*. Cambridge: Cambridge University Press.

Schechner, Richard. 1985. "Restoration of Behavior." In *Between Theater and Anthropology*, 35–116. Philadelphia: University of Pennsylvania Press.

Schmidt, Jalane D. 2016. "The Antidote to Wall Street? Cultural and Economic Mobilizations of Afro-Cuban Religions." *Latin American Perspectives* 43 (208): 163–85.

Schwall, Elizabeth. 2017. "'Cultures in the Body': Dance and Anthropology in Revolutionary Cuba." *History of Anthropology Newsletter* 41. http://histanthro.org/notes/cultures-in-the-body/.

Schwall, Elizabeth. 2019. "The Footsteps of Nieves Fresneda: Cuban Folkloric Dance and Cultural Policy, 1959–1979. *Cuban Studies*, no. 47, 35–56.

Schwall, Elizabeth. 2021. *Dancing with the Revolution: Power, Politics, and Privilege in Cuba*. Chapel Hill: University of North Carolina Press.

Scott, Julius S., III. 2018. *The Common Wind: Afro-American Currents in the Age of the Haitian Revolution*. New York: Verso Books.

Shay, Anthony. 2002. *Choreographic Politics: State Folk Dance Companies, Representation, and Power*. Middletown, CT: Wesleyan University Press.

Simpson, Audra. 2007. "On Ethnographic Refusal: Indigeneity, 'Voice' and Colonial Citizenship." *Junctures* 9 (December): 67–80.

Simpson, Audra. 2014. *Mohawk Interruptus: Political Life across the Borders of Settler States*. Durham, NC: Duke University Press.

Sojoyner, Damien M. 2017. "Another Life Is Possible: Black Fugitivity and Enclosed Places." *Cultural Anthropology* 32 (4): 514–36.

Spetalnick, Matt. 2019. "In Major Shift, Trump to Allow Lawsuits against Foreign Firms in Cuba." *Reuters*, April 16, 2019.

Spillers, Hortense J. 1987. "Mama's Baby, Papa's Maybe: An American Grammar Book." *diacritics* 17 (2): 65–81.

Spivak, Gayatri. 1988. "Subaltern Studies: Deconstructing Historiography." In *In Other Worlds*, 197–221. New York: Routledge.

Stoler, Ann Laura. 2002. "Colonial Archives and the Arts of Governance." *Archival Science* 2 (1–2): 87–109.

Stout, Noelle. 2014. *After Love: Queer Intimacy and Erotic Economies in Post-Soviet Cuba.* Durham, NC: Duke University Press.

Sublette, Ned. 2004. *Cuba and Its Music: From the First Drums to the Mambo.* Chicago: Chicago Review Press.

Taylor, Diana. 2003. *The Archive and the Repertoire: Performing Cultural Memory in the Americas.* Durham, NC: Duke University Press.

Taylor, Henry Louis. 2009. *Inside El Barrio: A Bottom-Up View of Neighborhood Life in Castro's Cuba.* Sterling, VA: Kumarian Press.

Thomas, Deborah A. 2004. *Modern Blackness: Nationalism, Globalization, and the Politics of Culture in Jamaica.* Durham, NC: Duke University Press.

Thomas, Deborah A. 2019. *Political Life in the Wake of the Plantation: Sovereignty, Witnessing, Repair.* Durham, NC: Duke University Press.

Thomas, Deborah A. 2022. "What the Caribbean Teaches Us: The Afterlives and New Lives of Coloniality." *Journal of Latin American and Caribbean Anthropology* 27 (3): 235–54.

Thomas, Deborah A. 2023. "Bodies, Knowledge, and Modes of Repair." Lewis Henry Morgan Lecture, University of Rochester, November 1, 2023.

Thompson, Krista. 2011. "A Sidelong Glance: The Practice of African Diaspora Art History in the United States." *Art Journal* (Fall): 6–31.

Thompson, Robert Farris. 1984. *Flash of the Spirit: African and Afro-American Art and Philosophy.* New York: Vintage Books.

Thornton, Brendan Jamal, and Diago I. Ubiera. 2019. "Caribbean Exceptions: The Problem of Race and Nation in Dominican Studies." *Latin American Research Review* 54 (2): 413–28.

Trouillot, Michel-Rolph. 2003. *Global Transformations: Anthropology and the Modern World.* New York: Palgrave Macmillan.

Trouillot, Michel-Rolph. 2015. *Silencing the Past: Power and the Production of History.* Boston: Beacon.

Ulysse, Gina Athena. 2015. *Why Haiti Needs New Narratives: A Post-quake Chronicle.* Middletown, CT: Wesleyan University Press.

Urfé, Odilio. 1982. "La música folklórica, popular y del teatro bufo." In *La cultura en Cuba socialista*, 151–73. Havana: Editorial Letras Cubanas.

Valerio, Miguel A. 2022. *Sovereign Joy: Afro-Mexican Kings and Queens, 1539–1640.* Cambridge: Cambridge University Press.

Vaughan, Umi. 2012. *Rebel Dance, Renegade Stance: Timba Music and Black Identity in Cuba.* Ann Arbor: University of Michigan Press.

Wade, Peter. 1995. "The Cultural Politics of Blackness in Colombia." *American Ethnologist* 22 (2): 341–57.

Wade, Peter. 1997. "Blacks and Indians in Latin America." In *Race and Ethnicity in Latin America*, 25–39. London: Pluto.

Weinreb, Amelia Rosenberg. 2009. *Cuba in the Shadow of Change: Daily Life in the Twilight of the Revolution*. Gainesville: University Press of Florida.

Wenger, Etienne. 1998. *Communities of Practice: Learning, Meaning, and Identity*. Cambridge: Cambridge University Press.

West, Cornel. 1988. "On Afro-American Popular Music: From Bebop to Rap." In *Prophetic Fragments: Illuminations of the Crisis in American Religion and Culture*, 177–87. Grand Rapids, MI: William B. Eerdmans.

Williams, Brackette F., ed. 1996. *Women Out of Place: The Gender of Agency and the Race of Nationality*. New York: Routledge.

Wirtz, Kristina. 2007. "Enregistered Memory and Afro-Cuban Historicity in Santería's Ritual Speech." *Language and Communication* 27 (3): 245–57.

Wirtz, Kristina. 2014. *Performing Afro-Cuba: Image, Voice, Spectacle in the Making of Race and History*. Chicago: University of Chicago Press.

Wirtz, Kristina. 2016. "The Living, the Dead, and the Immanent: Dialogue across Chronotopes." *HAU: Journal of Ethnographic Theory* 6 (1): 343–69.

Wirtz, Kristina. 2017. "Mobilizations of Race, Place, and History in Santiago de Cuba's Carnivalesque." *American Anthropologist* 119 (1): 58–72.

Wynter, Sylvia. 1977. "'We Know Where We Are From': The Politics of Black Culture from Myal to Marley." Houston Conference, November 1977.

Yelvington, Kevin A. 2001. "The Anthropology of Afro-Latin American and the Caribbean: Diasporic Dimensions." *Annual Review of Anthropology* 30:227–60.

Yelvington, Kevin A. 2005. "The Invention of Africa in Latin America and the Caribbean: Political Discourse and Anthropological Praxis, 1920–1940." In *Afro-Atlantic Dialogues: Anthropology in the Diaspora*, edited by Kevin Yelvington, 35–82. Santa Fe: School of American Research Press.

Yotuel. n.d. "Patria y Vida—Yotuel, Gente De Zona, Descemer Bueno, Maykel Osorbo, El Funky." YouTube, Video. 04:03. https://youtu.be/pP9Bto5lOEQ.

Zorina, Z. A., and T. A. Obozova. 2011. "New Data on the Brain and Cognitive Abilities of Birds." *Zoologichesky Zhurnal* 90 (7): 784–802.

Zurbano, Roberto. 2011. "Cuba: Doce dificultades para enfrentar al (neo-)racismo o doce razones para abrir el (otro) debate." *La Jiribilla*, no. 529.

Zurbano, Roberto. 2013. "For Blacks in Cuba, the Revolution Hasn't Begun." *New York Times*, March 24, 2013.

Zurbano, Roberto. 2014. "ARAAC: 24 meses después: Una propuesta de trabajo, un momento de revisión, una reflexión compartida." *Afromodernidades*, October 6, 2014.

INDEX

Abakuá, 116, 165; Africanist communities, 141; agency, 143; antisocial element, 78; Antonio Maceo and, 272n16; audience and, 139–40; belonging, 162, 164; Black consciousness, 137; Black corporeal undercommons and, 75; Black male youth, 45, 134; Black popular classes and, 62; *brujería* and, 77; cabildos and, 27, 59, 75, 131; Calabar imaginary (*see* Calabar); Carabalí, 75, 76; Cardenas, 75; ceremonial repertoire, 152; choreography, 131, 132, 134; class and, 95; *columbia rumba* and, 22, 73; commerce and, 77; constitution, 159; criminality and, 76, 77, 145; cross-racial initiatory relationships, 77; Cuban socialism and, 78; dancing, 76; *diablitos* (little devils), 75–76, 77; *dialecto*, 153, 154, 155; *ecobios* (brothers by initiation), 77, 145; Efik-speaking, 75; Ékue, 132; female power and, 275n21; feminist origin story, 276n23; Fidel Castro and, 159, 160; freedom and, 77; Freemasonry and, 78; folklore and, 79, 77; gender and, 135; Guanabacoa neighborhood, 95; *guapería*, 138–40, 145; in Havana, 75; heritage, 133, 140, 164, 165; heteropatriarchy and, 168; heterosexuality, 136; ideal manhood, 136; individual capital accrual, 150; Ireme, 130–31; jailing of, 78; jobs and, 77; knowledge, 159; labor organizing, 78; lands (*tierras*), 76, 134; language, 155, 163; Leopard societies, 75; Mambí army and, 272n16; *marchas*, 153; in Matanzas, 75; the medical student insurgents and, 136–37; membership, 136, 164; memorial ceremonies, 136, 137; Ministry of Interior and, 79; moral code, 132, 274n6; Moruá, 137, 155; murder of, 136; *ñáñigos*, 76; national history and, 138; nationalist rhetoric and, 78, 79; *negros curros* and, 276n22; non-initiated and, 156; order and, 76, 161; origins, 154; Osain del Monte and, 130; outlawed, 76; overrepresentation, 76; *plante*, 158; policemen and, 275n20; port workers and, 77, 78, 139, 143; powers (*potencias*), 76; racial integration and, 143; religion and, 59, 79; rhythm, 135; rumba and, 21, 45, 77, 78, 130–32, 134, 140, 156, 165–67; rumberos and Sikán, 275n21; sacred fraternities, 45; self-governance, 76, 131; slavery, 75; societies, 75; songs, 146, 153; sovereignty and, 76, 132, 135; space and, 135, 139, 148; Spanish crown and, 76; "Tato" Quiñones and, 136; territory, 157, 159, 162; transmission, 164; urban landscape and, 76; violence and, 76; white men and, 76–77; women and, 162; words, 275n19; world, 132; Yoruba Andabo and, 140, 144–47, 150, 153–57. *See also* Calabar Protest ("Protesta Carabalí"); Ireme

Abdala (vaccine), 261, 262

Abd'Allah-Álvarez Ramírez, Sandra: *Negra Cubana tenía que ser* blog, 148

aberíkula (*batá*) drums, 238. See also *batá*: unconsecrated

Acosta, Didier, 83, 84, 85, 203; on Abakuá, 146; Yoruba Andabo and, 264

activism, Black, 245

aficionado (amateur), 206; Julio Cesar "El Gordo" as, 212

Africanist community, 136, 141, 157

Africanist societies, 63, 79

Africanization, 59

Afrocubanismo, 66, 67; miscegenation and, 96; mulata and, 68; rumberas representation and, 96; white artists and, 69. See also *Afrocubanistas*

Afrocubanistas, 67, 75; cultural production, 69

Afro-Cuban religions, 210

agency, 91, 117, 246; Abakuá, 143; Black and, 27; Black corporeal undercommons and, 245; blackened, 10; choreographies of fugitivity and, 221; citizenship and, 12; copresences, 241; creative practices, 12; dancers and, 202;

and, 221; post-Fidel Castro, 4; realm of trade, 218; reciprocity and, 210; "respectable life" and, 209; revolutionary vanguard and, 85; right to sustenance, 216; rumba and, 9, 46, 60, 80; sacred choreo/geography, 44; shifting economy and, 172; as signifier, 59; sociality, 57; trade, 207; wealth and, 204; white political rule and, 66

Black *cuentapropistas*, 179

Black divine continuum, 232

blackface theater, 67

Black feminism, 90, 123; Black Cuban feminists, 17, 273n4, 276n23; Black feminist consciousness, 92; choreographic aptitude and, 91; spirited assemblies and, 248

Black geographies, 133

Black identity and religious practice, 238

Black life: and divine codes, 237; and freedom, 242

Black Lives movement, 243

Black masculinity, 7, 45, 123, 141, 277n15

Black *ñáñigo* narratives, 243

Blackness, 68–70; Abakuá and, 77; affirming understanding of, 116, 117; alternative spaces of, 57; ancestry, xii; anti-, 4, 60, 74, 83, 165, 274n13; Black corporeal undercommons and, 256; citizenship and, 60; class and, 23, 48; colonial imaginary and, 104; commodification, 114, 115; Cuban elitism and, 146; *cubanidad* and, 140; digitized, 183; eroticized market for, 114; feeling and, 226; folklore and, 43, 237; force and, 149; modernity and, 86; nationalized, 69, 183, 192; as natural resource, 86; non-Black and, 267n1; order and, 246; performance of, 181; power and, 21; promiscuity and, 113; revolutionary, 268n4; revolutionary cultural nationalism and, 73; rumba and, 258, 267n1; rumberos and, 26; as a sign, 32; social problem, 64; transatlantic slave trade and, 226; tropes, 116–17. *See also* labor

Black people: aspirations, 257; dancing, 258; enclosures, 255; and Grito de Yara, 275n27; laboring bodies of, 60; and legality, 244; peso-poor, 169, 179, 209, 216, 254

Black performance, 232; Black performance studies lens, 244; Black performers, 67

Black physical counterforce, 227

Black poetry, 67

Black political consciousness, 271n10

Black political dispossession, 16, 165, 166, 254

Black political imaginary, 132, 133, 257

Black popular culture, 254; dance, 5, 79, 91, 272n2; music, 242; and symbolic capital, 214–15

Black pride, 18

Black public assembly, 18

Black radicalism, 232, 253

Black refusal politics, 136

Black self-determination, 146

Black sense of place, 255

Black sociality, 255

Black social movements, 244

Black solidarity, 168

Black sovereignty, 131, 133, 148, 157, 165

Black women, 241, 247; and sexuality, 113; and uterine fire, 271n14

Black writers, 67

Blanco Borelli, Melissa: "corpo-mulata performance," 273n9

blood, 178, 200; Abakua and, 160; criminal aggression and, 147; Jenny, 125; Lázaro's not-not Oggun, 231; networks, 64; *religiosos* and, 178; right of, 30; rumba and, 3, 117

blood family, 10, 14, 41, 103, 193, 195, 196, 203, 212, 257. *See also* stone family

Boas, Franz, 23

Bolívar, Natalia, and Román Orozco, 78

botao, 22, 90, 119, 120; clave and, 126

bozal, 181

brujas, 248; improvisation and, 247; narratives, 243; Ortiz and, 247

brujería (witchcraft), 241

cabildo, 20, 21, 39, 42, 53–55, 63, 128, 158, 268n10; Abakuá, 62, 79; Black women and, 241; Carabalí, 52, 54, 58, 75; choreo/geographies, 248; choreography, 236; coartación, 56; comparsas, 69, 161; Congo, 54; copresences agency and, 241; dances, 57, 58, 243; de nación, 54, 62; divinities and, 237; geographies, 241; heritage, 171, 206; Iremes, 159; Lucumí, 54; material needs and, 216; membership, 56, 57, 77; networks, 58; order and divine potential, 236; power, 236; principles, 216; processions, 56, 57; rebellion and, 57, 58; religion and, 59; Revolution's urban reforms and, 240; sovereignty and, 79, 142; women and, 58, 59, 116

Cabrera, Lydia, 41

Cabrera, Silvia Martiza, 108–9, 111–14, 116–18, 121–22, 124, 128; cabildos and, 237, 240, 257; "*racismo profesional*," 149; rumba and, 237, 240–41

cajón, 173

and, 141; *Negrón* and, 148–50; rumba and, 139–41; sacred swagger, 150; sovereignty and, 167; territory and, 150; Yoruba Andabo and, 140–41

guapo, 129, 146, 272n17; Abakuá heritage and, 140; *ambiente* and, 145; folkloric consumption and, 141; narratives, 243. *See also* Abakuá; *guapería*; rumba

Guidelines, The (2011), 30, 35

Guillén, Nicholas, 67

Guridy, Frank, 62

Guss, David, 145

Hagedorn, Katherine, 278n4

Halberstam, Jack, 225–26

Hamel Alleyway. *See* Callejón de Hamel

Hampa Afro-cubana (Ortíz), 12, 22, 64–65, 221, 236; Abakuá and, 147; racial casting, 149

Haraway, Donna, 253

Harding, Rachel, 16, 172; on spirit possession, 277n12

Harney, Stefano, and Fred Moten, 12, 225–26, 232, 246, 268n9

Harrison, Faye, 267n2

Hartman, Saidiya, 245

Hearn, Adrian, 273n10

heritage: Abakuá, 45, 133, 166; Black pride and, 18; Black self-determination, 151; cabildo, 171, 206; Cuban, 71, 193; mixed cultural, 67; rumba as intangible cultural, 5; rumba's religious Abakuá, 140; world, 250; Yoruba Andabo and, 140, 193

Hernández, Jorge Luis, 207; as akpwón, 194

heteropatriarchy, 16; American social order and, 79; anti-Black, 97; colonial gaze and, 92; Cuban ethno-nationalism and, 44; Cuban femininity and, 112; economic opportunities, 112; *guapería* and, 168; as lingua franca, 77; order and, 168; rumba and, 21; rumberas and, 112

hip-hop, 5, 114, 130

horse (devotee), 199

Hoz, Pedro de la, 47

Hurston, Zora Neale, x, xiv

Ide, 108, 252; as public marker, 222

Ifá, priest of (*babalawos*), 213. *See also* Orula

Ilé, 175, 179, 186, 193. See also *casa-templo* (*ilé*)

immigration reform, 61, 277n9

improvisation, 45, 127, 254; "aesthetic possibilities," 246; Black feminist refusal and, 119; collective power and, 228; intention and, 89; Jenny and, 234; meaning, 97; phrasing and,

121; power relations and, 91, 92; relational, 121; rumbera repertoire of, 119; sacred force, 118; vaccination and, 120, 121

Independent People of Color Party (Partido Independiente de Color), 62; Black and mulato war veterans and, 270n6

informants, 80; CFN, 72; colonial division of labor and, 70–71; Fernando Ortiz and, 86; Geovani del Pino, 84; Nieves Fresneda, 74

internet, 268n12; *estadillo* protest and, 262; *jinetera* and, 96

Ire, 213

Ireme, 76, 139, 161, 162, 164; audience and, 135; authority, 166–67; ceremonial, 159; dance, 154–55; gestural speech, 130–31, 157; gestures, 162; homosocial order and authority, 168; Leopard Societies and, 154; medical student insurgents and, 136–37; mimicry, 157; sacred landscape, 155; sacred legitimacy, 138; white masculinity and, 166; Yoruba Andabo, 146, 152, 153–55, 157, 160. *See also* Abakuá; *diablitos*; *ñáñigo*

Itá, 260; Jenny and, 264

jazz craze, 66

jinetera (hustler or prostitute), 32, 96; denied entry, 224

Jottar, Berta, 113

July 11, 2021 (11-J uprising), 262–64. *See also* internet

kinesthetic memory, 232

Kings Day (Día de Los Reyes), 52–55, 57, 76, 164; Abakuá procession, 164; *marchas* and, 153

Knauer, Lisa Maya, 10

La Articulación Regional Afrodescendiente de América Latina y el Caribe, Capítulo Cubano (ARAAC Cuba), 244–45

labor, 45, 80, 134, 255; and Abakuá, 77–78; (Black) feminist consciousness and, 91; Black people, 60; Black performance theory, xiv; buttocks, 122; camp, 74; capital accumulation and, 132, 133, 148, 216; ceremonial, 158; CFN (Conjunto Folklorico Nacional) and, 72; classifications and, 199; colonial, 70; colonial access and, 115; communication and, 175; community, 232, 238; compensation, 42–43, 91, 128, 188, 215; competition, 252; conceptions of personhood and, 207; contracts, 203, 215; *cuentapropista*, 209; dancers, 188, 271n12; *derechos* and, 204, 208; *desenvolvimiento*, 8; dignity and, 91;

Moore, Robin, D., 52, 66; on Afrocubanista creations, 69; on Afro-Cuban religions, 271n11; on Fernando Ortiz's work, 23; on nationalizing Blackness, 69

Mora, Pancho (Quinto): UNEAC and, 145; Yoruba Andabo and, 212

Moré, Beny: "En el tiempo de la colonia, tiempo de Sese eribó," 276n4

mounting: genderqueer, 202; feminized, 202

Moya, Diego Miguel de, 55

muelleo, 88, 120, 234

mulata, 68, 74, 106, 108; agency, 115, 124; Black femininity, 68; Cuban femininity and, 92, 104; culture, 96; embodying the, 128; eroticism, 68; ethno-nationalism, 94; folkloric narratives, 243; hip(g)nosis, 115; identity, 115; Jenny as, 106; nation and, 66, 86; Ochún, 103; rumba and, 66; rumbera, 68, 90, 112, 114, 119, 128, 243; as sexually available, 74; *teatro bufo* and, 67; trope, 90, 97, 112, 115. *See also* mulato; mulataje (mixedness); rumbera: mulata

mulataje, 106

mulato, 67, 73, 94, 129; Antonio Maceo, 272n16; audience, 192; cabildo dance functions and, 56; government discourses of, 73; informants, 71; Liberation Army and, 60; *régimen de castas* and, 21; war veterans, 270n6

Museo del Barrio, 272n2

ñáñigo, 54, 76, 77, 78; dance in the street, 243; fugitive assemblies and, 236; narratives, 243; personhood and, 168; tourism and, 79

nationalism, 6, 59, 157, 191, 256; Abakuá and, 79; as camouflage, 78; cultural, 48, 66, 69, 73, 130, 156, 168; defined by the state, 242; ethno-, 5, 67, 80, 94; raceless, 5; revolutionary, 80; tropes, 50

National Union of Cuban Artists and Writers (UNEAC), 144; Abakuá and, 144, 146; Eloy Machado "El Ambia," 144; La Peña del Ambia, 274n9; rumba ensembles, 220; Yoruba Andabo and, 144–46

National Women's Federation (Federación de Mujeres Cubanas), 74

Negrón: *ñáñigos* and, 150, 168; New Men 2.0 and, 149; racialized and gendered figure, 149; rule over territory, 168

negros curros, 129

neighborhoods: 10 de Octubre, 175; Atarés, 73; Barrio Obrero (Worker's Neighborhood), 259, 279n1; Belén, 64, 211, 212, 229; Cayo Hueso, 2, 86, 92; Colón, 64, 73; El Cerro, 73; Guanabacoa,

95; Jesús María, 39; La Victoria, 73; Pogolotti, 41, 42, 146; Regla, 174; San Miguel del Padrón, 93; Vedado, 71, 144, 145, 146, 169, 211. *See also* Centro Habana

neo-racism, 38, 167; Roberto Zurbano, 37

New Man, 33–35, 45; color-blind, 131; neo-liberal white masculinity, 131; New Man 2.0, 34, 35, 112, 149, 254

Obama, Barack (US president), 36–37, 269n1

Obini Batá, 110

Obsesión, 5–6

Ochún (orisha), 105, 119, 158, 175, 196, 257; altar, 196–97; *casa-templo* and, 237; folkloric context, 201; staging of, 102–5; Temple of the Divine Charity and, 241

O'Farril, Alfredo, 272n2

Oggun (orisha), 230; Lazaro and, 230–33, 235; *mariwo*, 229, 235; *ñongo* steps, 231; Yoruba Andabo and, 230–33

Old Havana: Belén, 64, 211; Jesús María, 63

Olofi, 265

orishas, 80, 229; akpwón and, 202; ceremony, 175, 200; child of, 208; community and, 175; dance, 89; danced prayer, 175; dancers, 186; *derecho*, 175; hard currency and, 210; Lucumí divinities, 1; money and, 197, 205; movement, 219; mythic figure, 239; offerings, 207; rumba and, 80, 81, 89, 219; specialized choreographies, 200; stone, 268n7; *tambores* and, 103; Yoruba Andabo and *ciclo Yoruba*, 185, 239. *See also* individual orishas

Ortíz, Fernando, 53–55, 64, 68, 69; anthropology and, 22; Argeliers León and, 251; *batá* drumming and, 69; Black sociality and, 12; Black women and, 241; Cuban intelligentsia, 66; fugitive assemblies and, 236; ideologies, 270n8; Society of Cuban Folklore and, 67. *See also* individual works

Orula (orisha), 108

Osain del Monte, 120, 129, 130, 139; and Abakuá, 146, 274n2

Oya (orisha), 116

Palacio de la Rumba, 97, 98, 99, 122, 254; audience, 191–92; rumba ensembles, 220

Palés Matos, Luis, 67

palenques, 21

Palo: Kikongo, 181; Monte, 59

Panter Calderón, Adonis, 129. *See also* Osain del Monte

and, 237; economy, 191; embodied practice, 254; ensembles and white women, 268n8; essence, 117, 241; faith and, 251; feminist meaning, 118; folkloric, 80, 171; *folklórica nocturna*, 211; fugitive choreographies, 247; gendered relation, 127; genre, 87; *guaguancó*, 67, 88; *guapería* and, 139–41; heritage, 145; immersion into, 212; improvisations, 254; inclusion and, 148, 253; kinesthetics, 255; labor and, 171–72, 175–79, 193; logics of reciprocity, 171; market, 115; maroon music and, 22; meaning, 156; mutual aid capacity, 252; as national cultural patrimony, 5, 86; as national heritage, 166, 236; nationalization, 270n9; official narrative, 144; old-school style, 120; orishas and, 80; patriarchy and, 121, 122; performers, 178; *plan de desarrollo*, 179; power and, 252; racial democracy and, 50; religion and, 80, 81, 171; religious heritage, 140; as repertoire of signs, 117; reputation, 24; rights and, 242; sacred entitlement, 151, 172; sensorial content, 251; social dance, 90; socialism and, 252–53; sovereignty and, 134; spirituality of, 252; state-sponsored stagings of, 236; tourists and, 97, 134; as UNESCO's intangible cultural heritage, 5, 249; Yambú, 21, 22

Rumba Morena: exodus and, 264; Tailyn Duperey and, 36, 264

rumberas: affective gauge, 246; agency, 124; archetype, 119; Black feminist consciousness and, 123; Black feminist vision, 124; choreography, 113, 118, 124, 248; Cuban femininity, 92, 101; Cuba's unique mulata culture, 96; dancing, 89, 110; *derechos* and, 204; discourse, 97; discrimination, 112; drumming, 110; economic opportunities, 112; employment, 91; female liberation, 92; heteropatriarchy and, 112; improvisations, 125; interpretative frameworks, 124; job opportunities, 109; labor, 128; miscegenation fantasies, 96, 101; mulata, 68, 92, 96, 97, 112, 115, 119, 128; as national symbol, 124; as objects, 96–97; popular cultural imaginary and, 89; portrayal, 88; professional status and, 203; racialized gender, 112; role, 89, 110; theorizations, 124; trope, 74, 90, 97, 108, 112, 115, 126, 128; value, 92; white women and, 273n9

rumberos, 3; citizen-subject and, 167; copresences demands, 215; *cuentapropismo* and, 205; *derechos* and, 204; dignity, 241; economic agency, 178; exodus, 264; faith communities, 193; gendered meanings, 277n13; labor, 80, 133, 215; multiple attachments, 240; national stage,

193; political economy and, 215; as *portadores*, 250; PPC peso-poor, 221; professional status and, 203; public space and, 220; religious norms and, 171; religious persecution, 239; restored behavior and, 240; sacred filiation, 253; subsidized status, 249; transnational economy and, 183

Salazar, Abraham, 272n2

San Antonio de los Baños, 262

San Lázaro Society in Havana, *brujo* leaders, 270n7

San Miguel del Padrón borough, 93

Santería, 27, 59, 80; Cuban tourism and, 210; as female normative, 199; resiliency and, 216; ritual labor, 199. See also *santeros*; *santurismo*

santeros, 259; rituals and, 195

santurismo, 82; monetization of Santería, 210

Sardiñas Yamilé, 119, 124; class, 120–22; *muelleo*, 120; old-school style, 120; role-playing, 122; Yoruba Andabo and, 264

Schmidt, Jalane, 78; folkloric performance and, 145; religious products and, 210

Schwall, Elizabeth: Black dance, 87

secularism, 11, 13, 217; binary categories of, 16; Black popular culture and, 143–44, 255; Black working-class Cubans and, 81; cabildos and, 79; citizenship and, 58; constitutional reform of 1991, 82; Cuban Constitution of 1991 and, 25; Cuban economy and, 172; dance and, 70, 94, 235; discourse, 26; drumming and, 84; earnings and, 177; entertaining industry, 185; Euro-Western categorization, 65; festivals and, 65; folkloric consumption and, 141; Jenny dancing and, 235; juridical legibility and, 177; liberal personhood, 51; liberal subjecthood, 13–14, 18; modern conceptions of, 7; mulato ethno-nationalism and, 94; musicians and, 188; politics and, 52; professional folkloric dancers and, 231; regimes of prestige, 192; religion and, 237, 238; religious practice and state, 207; rumba and, 52–53, 60, 80, 81, 237, 250–51; rumberos and, 44; the sacred and, 27, 52; self-paid manumission, 20, 56; *sociedades de color* and, 62; stage performance and, 186, 217; state institutions and, 94; state-mediated gigs and, 204; teaching employment and, 203; welfare state and, 256; white civility, 140; Yoruba Andabo and, 233

Sevilla, Ninón, 68. *See also* rumberas

Shapeshifters: Black Girls and the Choreography of Citizenship (Cox, 2015), 12

pansion, 4; Raúl Castro, 4–6, 30, 87, 261; as regression, 31; revolution and, 220; rumba and, 18, 148; rumberas and, 112; rumberos and, 150, 165, 215, 227; socialist model, 253; social landscape of, 46; success in Cuba's, 183; trappings, 42; Yoruba Andabo and, 171. See also *perfeccionamiento* (perfecting)

US Interest Section, 211

vaccinating, 88. See also *guaguancó* (rumba); *vacunaos* (vaccinations)

vacunaos (vaccinations), 21, 89, 90; male gaze and, 123

Valerio, Miguel, 165

Vedado: *ambientales* and, 145; emerging economy, 169; Yoruba Andabo and, 144

ventriloquism, 68, 74

whitening, 61

William Ramos, Gilberto, 173, 188–90

Wirtz, Kristina: Carabalí songs, 153; folkloric performances, 181

World Health Organization, 261

Wynter, Sylvia, 242

Ximeno y Cruz, Dolores María, 53, 59

yambú (rumba), 21, 22

Yemayá (orisha), 233–36, 277n5; *aro*, 233, 247; faith in, 186; Jennyselt Galata and, 181–86, 233–36, 265; power and, 247; reciprocity and, 186; Tailyn Duperey and, 216; women and, 247

Yoruba: belief, 193; *ciclo*, 185; religion, 58

Yoruba Andabo, 5, 14, 40, 43, 50, 126, 132; Abakuá and, 140–47, 156, 197; agency, 192, 200, 218, 240; audience, 140, 170, 184, 189, 190–91, 202, 206, 230, 240; *batá* druming, 228; Black enclosure and, 52, 75; Black peso-poor families and, 216; *casa-templos*' needs and, 198; *ciclo Yoruba*, 185; Cuban Five, 85–86; *cumpleaños de santo* and, 195, 197; dancers, 185–86; *derechos*, 188, 191, 206–7; drummers, 198; El Gordo and, 213; *espiritismo* chant, 228; exodus and, 264; folkloric professionalism, 236; founders, 140; freedom, 207; gendered dexterity and, 199; Geovani del Pino, 10, 26, 27, 48; Grupo Marítimo Portuario, 143–44; *guapería*, 140–41; *güiros*, 197; Ireme, 152, 155, 157, 160; labor, 200; "La Gozadera," 38; *La Rumba Soy Yo*, 189; Latin Grammy nomination, 189; Lázaro and, 230–33; Ministry of Culture and, 120, 238; nodes of exchange, 216; Oggun and, 230; orisha and, 238; Pancho Quinto and, 144, 212; price inflation and, 190; primetime television, 86; professionalism, 236; "Protesta Carabalí," 146, 151–53, 155–57; *pueblo* and, 206; religion and, 83–85, 192; religious following, 239; religious heritage, 140; religious work, 79, 192, 206; repertoires, 82; reputation, 238; *Rumba en la Habana*, 180–82, 189; salary, 190; in state-managed public venues, 184; status, 170, 196, 206, 249; *tambor de fundamento*, 197; Teatro Avenida and, 219–20, 223, 237; UNEAC patio, 144; Valentin, 229–30; *veladas de santo*, 197

Zurbano, Roberto: (neo-)racism, 37

www.ingramcontent.com/pod-product-compliance
Lightning Source LLC
Chambersburg PA
CBHW032343280326
41935CB00008B/430